So many circumstances have combined to influence and change the eating habits of the world that national and even regional traditional standards and styles of food are tending to become blurred and to merge into a form of universal international fare.

This is a change to be deplored. Countries which have prided themselves on the traditional quality and sophistication of their food have so much to lose from the internationalisation of their menus.

Pre-conceived ideas exist on national food e.g. the assumption that almost everyone in Spain lives on paella, and Italians eat little else but pasta. Perhaps the Scots are seen to exist on haggis and whisky. Nothing could be further from the truth.

In his book 'In Search of Scotland' H V Morton wrote "Scotland is the best place in the world to take an appetite". And indeed it is.

The climate of the country is relatively stable and it produces bountiful harvests of excellence from the land and from the sea.

In the not too distant past first class produce was often mistreated by unsophisticated kitchen staff. Not so now.

Scotland's chefs are amongst the best in the world, and prove this by competing with distinction against their leading opposite numbers from other countries - invariably returning home with more medals to add to their collections.

It is in the kitchen that the greatest changes have taken place in the last 12

...lable and ..., creative and ...to meals of such ... you start off without an ...iscover you have one.

...Scotland are as magnificent as the g... ...other nations and set outstanding exa... ...and standards. Alongside them there is an equally impressive network of speciality restaurants, lovely country house hotels, small guest houses, farmhouses and inns, renowned for their genuine warmth of welcome and the excellence of their cuisine.

The best of them have been chosen to be listed in this Guide. The price range varies enormously but so do personal incomes, and at whatever price level you select you should receive good value for money.

Food is such an important element of leisure and of travel that it pays to ensure that you give yourself the opportunity to experience the best.

"Scotland is the best place in the world to take an appetite".

Jack MacMillan

Contents

Taste of Scotland
current members are identified by
the 1993 Certificate of Membership
which should be on display.

The Taste of Scotland Scheme Ltd is sponsored by:

Scottish Tourist Board
Scottish Enterprise
Highlands & Islands Enterprise
Scotch Quality Beef & Lamb Association
Scottish Salmon Board

THE TASTE OF
SCOTLAND
1993

This is to certify that

_____

has been selected for membership of

The Taste of Scotland Scheme

in recognition of its commitment to the pursuit
of excellence in food preparation and service

How to use this Guide

Aberdeen

MAP 5 ◄ Map Reference

Address & Tel. No. etc ▶

ARDOE HOUSE HOTEL
Blairs, South Deeside Road
Aberdeen AB1 5YP
Tel: 0224 867355 • Telex: 739413
Fax: 0224 861283

Description ▶

B9077, 3 miles west of Aberdeen. ◄ How to find it

A very impressive-looking granite mansion with lofty turrets and inscriptions of heraldry and now a high class country house hotel, which is constantly being upgraded and improved. It stands in its own grounds and wooded parkland on the south Deeside road, just five minutes out of Aberdeen. The public rooms are particularly impressive with beautiful carved wood panelling and magnificent fireplaces, and the staircase with its stained glass windows at landing level is especially grand. There is a modern function room with superb views across the Dee. Food in the dining room lives up to the quality image of the hotel: it is imaginative in concept and is presented with the same care and attention that is given to its preparation. There is also the delightful Garden Room in which breakfast is served.

Any seasonal limitations ▶

Open all year
Rooms: 71 with private facilities ◄ Accommodation
Bar Lunch 12 – 2.30 pm (a)
Dining Room/Restaurant Lunch 12 – ◄ Meal times & prices
2.30 pm (a)
Bar Supper 6.30 – 10.30 pm (a)
Dinner 6.30 – 9.30 pm (d)
No dogs

Specimen inclusive terms quoted on per person per night basis ▶

Bed & breakfast £34 – £58.50
Dinner B & B £42.50 – £83.25
Room Rate £46 – £120
Fresh fish from the market daily. Local ◄ Specimen food specialities
seasonal game.

STB ratings ▶

STB Commended 5 Crowns
Credit cards: 1, 2, 3, 5 ◄ Credit cards accepted

Entries

Establishments selected by Taste of Scotland are listed in this Guide in alphabetical order under the nearest town or village.

Island entries are shown alphabetically by island or island group, e.g. Skye, Orkney.

A full list of hotels, restaurants etc is given in alphabetical order in the Index at the end of the Guide.

Special diets or requirements

Although vegetarian meals are more readily available nowadays, we would advise that you mention this requirement when making your booking.

Other special needs, such as diet or facilities for disabled guests, should also be arranged in advance.

Wines and spirits

Except where otherwise stated, all hotels and restaurants are licensed for the service of wines, spirits, beers etc.

Most unlicensed establishments - which tend to be small guest houses or farmhouses - will welcome your taking your own wine, but again please enquire in advance.

Where an establishment is shown to have a 'restricted licence' it generally means that residents and diners may be served alcoholic beverages, but members of the public may not call in for a drink.

Lunches

Nowadays lunchtime eating has become much less formal except in city centre hotels and restaurants. Bar snacks are more usual in some smaller establishments and rural hotels.

To simplify the choice available, we specify Bar Lunch or Dining Room/Restaurant Lunch in this Guide.

Restrictions on smoking

Within the information on each establishment, we have noted where there is no smoking permitted in the dining room or restaurant.

Where an area is set aside for non-smokers, the entry will show 'No smoking area in dining room/restaurant'.

In addition we have highlighted where no smoking is permitted throughout an establishment or where there are restrictions on smoking in guest bedrooms.

Entries which do not give any such information are taken to have no restriction on smoking.

Pets

Pets are accepted in some hotels by arrangement.

It is wise, however, to confirm this when booking as there may be a small charge and sometimes there is a restriction on the areas within the establishment where pets are permitted.

Restaurants generally do not accept dogs.

Foreign Languages

Where establishments have provided us with information on any foreign languages spoken, this has been incorporated within the descriptive paragraph about the establishment.

Prices

Prices are quoted as a **guideline only** and Guide readers are advised to check prevailing prices when making their reservation.

These estimated prices for 1993 were provided by the establishments, based on a three course meal, excluding drinks.

(a)   under £10
(b)   £10 - £15
(c)   £15 - £20
(d)   £20 - £25
(e)   £25 - £30
(f)   over £30

Specimen inclusive terms are listed, once again as a **guideline**.

Where a price range is given, the **lower price** normally indicates the rate **per person sharing** a double room, and the **higher price** the rate for a **single room** or **higher quality room**.

Where a **room rate** is offered, this information is shown in the entry.

Times of food service are listed to show **first and last orders**, unless otherwise indicated.

Credit/Charge Cards

Where an establishment accepts credit/charge cards, those taken are listed under the following codes:

1   Access/Mastercard/Eurocard
2   American Express
3   Visa
4   Carte Bleu
5   Diners Club
6   Mastercharge

How to avoid disappointment

Make an **advance reservation** whenever possible.

Mention you are using the **Taste of Scotland Guide.**

Remember! Many food items are seasonal and that the specialities listed have been selected as examples of the style of food that may be available, but there is no guarantee of availability on any particular day.

Check if any **price changes** have taken place since the publication of this Guide.

Confirm that **credit cards** are accepted.

Comments

Taste of Scotland welcomes comments - both good and bad.

However, **if you have an unsatisfactory meal**, we would always advise that you **speak to the restaurant or hotel manager or proprietor _at the time_**.

It gives an immediate opportunity for the situation to be rectified or explained.

If this fails to solve the problem, do write to the Taste of Scotland Scheme about your experience. While we do not have operational control of any establishment listed, we will pass on your comments for investigation.

But do let us hear of your good experiences too!

We like to give our members feedback on comments from the public, so we provide a comment slip at the end of this Guide for your use.

STB *Grading and Classification Scheme*

Since 1985, the Scottish Tourist Board has been systematically inspecting hotels, bed and breakfasts, and self catering accommodation, defining the standards that visitors expect and helping owners and operators meet those standards.

In a two-tier scheme, accommodation all over the country - from the simplest to the most sophisticated - is GRADED for quality and CLASSIFIED for its facilities.

Every establishment which is a member of the STB Grading and Classification Scheme - and there are over 4,000 - is visited each year. Grading and classification covers both serviced accommodation (hotels, guest houses, bed and breakfast) and self catering accommodation.

Members display blue oval plaques, to tell you whether they are approved, commended, highly commended or deluxe.

The centre panel of the plaque tells you whether the establishment is –

APPROVED (offering an acceptable standard)

COMMENDED (offering a good standard)

HIGHLY COMMENDED (offering a very good standard)

or

DELUXE (offering an excellent standard)

These GRADINGS are awarded by the STB inspectors once they have checked all the important factors that contribute to quality in an establishment. Just as you would, they look for clean, attractive surroundings, well furnished and heated. They sample meals, sleep in the beds, and talk to the staff. Like you, they appreciate atmosphere and a friendly smile of welcome.

Each type of establishment is assessed on its own merits, so that any type of accommodation can achieve the highest grading - and many do, in all categories.

The second section of the plaque displays the CROWN CLASSIFICATION, denoting the range of facilities on offer - things such as private bathrooms, lounges, meal provision and so on. From a basic LISTED classification up to FIVE CROWNS can be added. So more crowns on the plaque mean more facilities.

THE BUTTERY

Rosettes, noisettes & a true taste of Scotland

The Buttery has long been renowned as an excellent eating experience. Which is no doubt the reason we've been awarded AA Rosettes for quality over the last few years.

The Buttery is the place to sample a real taste of Scotland. Venison, Tay Salmon, Oban mussels and a whole host of other good things are there for the tasting.

You can also dine more modestly, but no less grandly in our Oyster Bar.

The Buttery: you could say it's the toast of Glasgow.

Open for lunch & dinner every weekday
& dinner on Saturday (closed on Sunday)

THE BUTTERY
652 ARGYLL STREET, GLASGOW
RESERVATIONS 041-221 8188

see entry page 82
see entry page 58

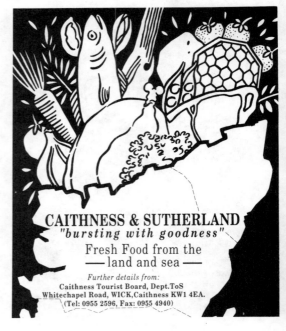

CAITHNESS & SUTHERLAND
"bursting with goodness"
Fresh Food from the
—— land and sea ——

Further details from:
Caithness Tourist Board, Dept.ToS
Whitechapel Road, WICK, Caithness KW1 4EA.
(Tel: 0955 2596, Fax: 0955 4940)

see entry page 103

Carradale Hotel

Our brochure is only a phone call away!

Standing in its own gardens high above the quaint fishing harbour our family-owned hotel offers you a unique combination of personal friendly service, great dining experiences & a host of modern hotel amenities. Visit us in 1993 & be enchanted by Carradale's beautiful hills, glens & beaches!

If sport is your forte, indoors & outdoors there's always lots to do at Carradale – the hotel even boasts its own indoor leisure centre, featuring two international standard glass-backed squash courts, sauna, solarium & table tennis. Outdoors, the scenic & challenging 9-hole golf course has its first tee right alongside the hotel & we can arrange river & sea fishing, pony trekking & dinghy sailing at a moment's notice to name but a few!

Children are especially welcome here at Carradale Hotel, & of course there is no accommodation charge for them when sharing a family room or suite with their parents.

Finally watch out for some great value packages in 1993 – details available in our brochure!

Carradale, Argyll PA28 6RY
Tel (Carradale) 05833-223

Sample Menu.
❧❧
Smoked Mackerel & Whisky Pate
served with toasted oatcakes.
Mushrooms Braemar
rich haggis, whisky & sour cream sauce.
Pheasant & Chive Terrine
crusty bread, hot mustard sauce.
❧❧
Fillet of Aberdeen Angus Steak Bears Heid
topped with pate, red wine & cummin sauce.
Escalopes of Veal Hunters Choice
breaded, sauted in basil & garlic Butter.
Fillets of Lemon Sole Lorna Doone
wrapped with Loch Fyne smoked salmon & tarragon leaf, shellfish sauce with grapes.
❧❧
MacCallums Shortbread Pudding.
Local Strawberries & Clotted Cream.
Homemade Peach Cheesecake.

Clachan Cottage Hotel
Lochside, Lochearnhead, Perthshire FK19 8PU
Tel (Lochearnhead) 0567-830247

The Scottish Highlands and Islands
~ where all the signs point to peace and contentment

Starting with Argyll and the Isles...

From the Mull of Kintyre to Oban and beyond, Argyll stretches serenely across mountains, forests, glens and lochs. Like a necklace around it lie the Isles: Mull, Coll, Tiree, Iona, Colonsay, Jura, Islay, Gigha, Arran, Cumbrae and Bute.

Here you can visit some of Britain's most beautiful gardens: all kinds of flowers flourish in the gentle Gulf Stream climate. You can play golf amid some of the finest scenery in Europe; visit prehistoric standing stones; go cruising in waters Saints and Vikings have sailed; walk wooded mountain trails; and enjoy unrivalled hospitality.

... moving into the centre of the Highlands

embraces Mallaig, Fort William, Inverness, Nairn and the Spey Valley. It's a region of superlatives: Britain's highest mountain, Ben Nevis; Britain's deepest loch, Loch Morar; Britain's oldest monster, Nessie (she may also be the shyest but could well pop out to see you); and Britain's biggest inland waterway, the Caledonian Canal. Here, naturally, you'll have a superlative holiday, whether you're visiting castles, beaches, wildlife centres or the sites of ancient battlefields.

... and then to the Northern Highlands and Islands

Within the broad scope of the Northern Highlands and Islands you'll find far-flung islands; Skye and the Inner and Outer Hebrides. On the mainland you'll discover the dramatically varied scenery of Ross and Cromarty, Caithness and Sutherland.

This is a land of remarkable contrasts. In the course of a day you can come across towering mountains, gentle moors, quiet beaches, stone-age remains and magnificent castles. You can enjoy boat trips, visit bird sanctuaries, go hill-walking or fish for record-breaking skate and halibut. And at the end of the day, you can frequently enjoy a Ceilidh, where the music and dancing continue into the wee small hours.

...and finally to Orkney and Shetland

Just about where ancient mariners thought the world ended, the Orkneys start. And beyond the Orkneys, only 200 miles from the coast of Norway, lie the Shetland Isles. The nearness of Scandinavia has influenced life in these islands down the centuries. Listen carefully to the locals: you'll find their accents owe more to the Viking than the Pict.

Explore the countryside, the ragged cliffs and sandy beaches: you'll see the work of the wild Atlantic and the North Sea everywhere. (You'll also find the work of early man in the ancient forts and burial mounds that dot the landscape.)

Above all be ready to make new friends. If you were expecting to find these islands peopled by inward-looking folk, wrapped in splendid isolation, you'd be wrong. Orcadians and Shetlanders have been welcoming visitors from over the seas since time immemorial. Make this the year they welcome you.

How do you get there?

Easily - by road, rail or air. Excellent roads bring you into the Highlands, some leading you to drive-on, drive-off ferries which connect you to the main islands. For train-lovers, the Inter-City service goes to Inverness, and the tracks in the Highlands lead you along some of the most beautiful rail journeys in the world.

Information and Bookings

For a brochure on the Scottish Highlands and Islands contact Highland Direct on 0800 838 166.

Caithness

Visit our Factory and Visitor Centre

* Marvel at the skills of the paperweight makers from the spacious viewing gallery
* Paperweight Collectors Gallery/ Museum
* Extensively stocked Factory Shop
* Restaurant for good food in comfortable surroundings
* Disabled access to all areas
* Cash Dispenser   * Toilets
* Public Phone
* Tourist Information Centre (May - Oct)
* Factory visits are **FREE**
* **VISITOR CENTRE OPEN ALL YEAR**
  Monday - Saturday 0900 - 1700
  Sunday 1100 - 1700
  (Sundays 1300 - 1700
  October to March)
* **GLASSMAKING**
  Monday - Friday 0900 - 1630
  all year

Where to find Us

ASSOCIATION OF
SCOTTISH
VISITOR
ATTRACTIONS
APPROVED

Situated on the northern edge of Perth on the A9 Western Bypass at the Inveralmond roundabout.

Caithness Glass Visitor Centre, Inveralmond, Perth PH1 3TZ Tel: 0738 37373

PERTH FACTORY AND VISITOR CENTRE

Caithness Glass/Taste of Scotland Prestige Awards

In 1988, Caithness Glass plc, one of Scotland's foremost glass manufacturers and designers, launched the Caithness Glass/Taste of Scotland Prestige Award scheme.

- The object is to give recognition to existing high standards in the hotel and catering trade in Scotland and by so doing, encourage others to emulate the winners.

- The awards are restricted to establishments which are members of the Taste of Scotland Scheme and thus already identified as leaders in their particular category.

- The public is invited to help the judging panel by nominating hotels and restaurants in which they have experienced particularly good standards of food and service.

- Taste of Scotland is pleased to record and congratulate the 1992 award winners in each category:

Hotel of the Year	*Moat House International, Glasgow*
Restaurant of the Year	*Pompadour Restaurant, Caledonian Hotel, Edinburgh*
Country House Hotel of the Year	*Greywalls, Gullane*
Newcomer of the Year	*Harding's Restaurant, North Berwick*
Special Merit	*Three Chimneys Restaurant, Skye*
Overall Excellence	*The Gean House, Alloa*

- These winners' entries have been highlighted in the listings for ease of identification.

- **As we enter the sixth year of the Prestige Awards again we invite our Guide readers to help us select the 1993 winners.**

- The judges will be considering nominations under the same first three categories as 1992, the remaining three trophies will be awarded to establishments identified by the Judging Panel as worthy of special merit.

- In the light of your experience in Taste of Scotland establishments, we would welcome your nomination under any of the above categories.

- You can send us your nominations using the coupons on pages 177 and 179 of this Guide, nomination cards available at Taste of Scotland establishments, or by letter or postcard.

Closing date for entries: 15 September 1993

Roll of Honour

1991

Cameron House Hotel, Loch Lomond
Arisaig House, by Arisaig
The Anchorage, Tarbert, Loch Fyne
Crinan Hotel, Crinan, Argyll
Balbirnie House Hotel, Markinch, by Glenrothes
Summer Isles Hotel, Achiltibuie

1990

The Turnberry Hotel, Turnberry
Knockie Lodge, Whitebridge
The Triangle, Glasgow
Ardanaiseig Hotel, Kilchrenan
The Gleneagles Hotel, Auchterarder
Shieldhill Country House, nr Biggar

1989

Cromlix House, Dunblane
North West Castle Hotel, Stranraer
The Cross, Kingussie
Ostlers Close, Cupar
Smugglers Restaurant, Crieff
Auchterarder House, Auchterarder

1988

Caledonian Hotel, Edinburgh
Murrayshall Country House Hotel, nr Perth
Tiroran House, Isle of Mull
Taste of Speyside, Dufftown
Martins Restaurant, Edinburgh
Broughton's Restaurant, Blair Drummond

Local Tourist Information

For specific information on a particular part of Scotland contact the following:

Angus Tourist Board
Tel: Arbroath (0241) 72609/76680

Aviemore & Spey Valley Tourist
Board
Tel: Aviemore (0479) 810363

Ayrshire Tourist Board
Tel: Ayr (0292) 79000

Banff & Buchan Tourist Board
Tel: Banff (0261) 812419

Caithness Tourist Board
Tel: Wick (0955) 2596

City of Aberdeen Tourist Board
Tel: Aberdeen (0224) 632727

City of Dundee Tourist Board
Tel: Dundee (0382) 27723

Clyde Valley Tourist Board
Tel: Lanark (0555) 2544

Dumfries & Galloway Tourist
Board
Tel: Dumfries (0387) 50434

Dunoon & Cowal Tourist Board
Tel: Dunoon (0369) 3785

East Lothian Tourist Board
Tel: Dunbar (0368) 63353

Edinburgh Marketing
Tel: Edinburgh (031) 557 1700

Fort William & Lochaber Tourist
Board
Tel: Fort William (0397) 70 3781

Forth Valley Tourist Board
Tel: Linlithgow (0506) 84 4600

Gordon District Tourist Board
Tel: Aberdeen (0224) 276276

Greater Glasgow Tourist Board
Tel: Glasgow (041) 204 4400

Inverness, Loch Ness & Nairn
Tourist Board
Tel: Inverness (0463) 234353

Isle of Arran Tourist Board
Tel: Brodick (0770) 2140

Isle of Bute Tourist Board
Tel: Rothesay (0700) 50 2151

Isle of Skye & South West Ross
Tourist Board
Tel: Portree (0478) 2137

Kincardine & Deeside Tourist
Board
Tel: Banchory (033 02) 2066

Kirkcaldy District Council
Tel: Leven (0333) 429464

Loch Lomond, Stirling &
Trossachs Tourist Board
Tel: Stirling (0786) 75019

Midlothian Tourism Association
Tel: (031) 440 2210 (Roslin)

Moray Tourist Board
Tel: Elgin (0343) 543388

Orkney Tourist Board
Tel: Kirkwall (0856) 872856

Perthshire Tourist Board
Tel: Perth (0738) 27958

Ross & Cromarty Tourist Board
Tel: Kessock (0463 73) 505

St Andrews & North East Fife
Tourist Board
Tel: St Andrews (0334) 72021

Scottish Borders Tourist Board
Tel: Jedburgh (0835) 63435/63688

Shetland Islands Tourism
Tel: Lerwick (0595) 3434

Sutherland Tourist Board
Tel: Dornoch (0862) 810400

Western Isles Tourist Board
Tel: Stornoway (0851) 70 3088

West Highlands & Islands of Argyll
Tourist Board
Tel: Oban (0631) 63122

Map Areas

ORKNEY AND SHETLAND

Lerwick

Kirkwall

THE HIGHLANDS

THE NORTH EAST

Thurso

Tongue

A836

Wick

A9

Stornoway

A837

ULLAPOOL

A832

A835

A9

Elgin

A96

A98

Peterhead

A890

INVERNESS

A96

Kyle of Lochalsh

A87

A82

ABERDEEN

Mallaig

Aviemore

THE HEBRIDES

A850

A830

FORT WILLIAM

Pitlochry

A9

A92

DUNDEE

Oban

A82

A85

Crianlarich

PERTH

ST ANDREWS

A9

STIRLING

Kirkcaldy

A917

A82

A80

M9

A92

CENTRAL AND EASTERN

GLASGOW

M8

EDINBURGH

A77

M74

A68

A1

Berwick-upon-Tweed

Galashiels

Jedburgh

A702

AYR

A77

A76

Moffat

A7

A74

Stranraer

DUMFRIES

A75

Carlisle

THE CLYDE

THE BORDERS

THE SOUTH WEST

A83

•

13

Map 1 - The South West

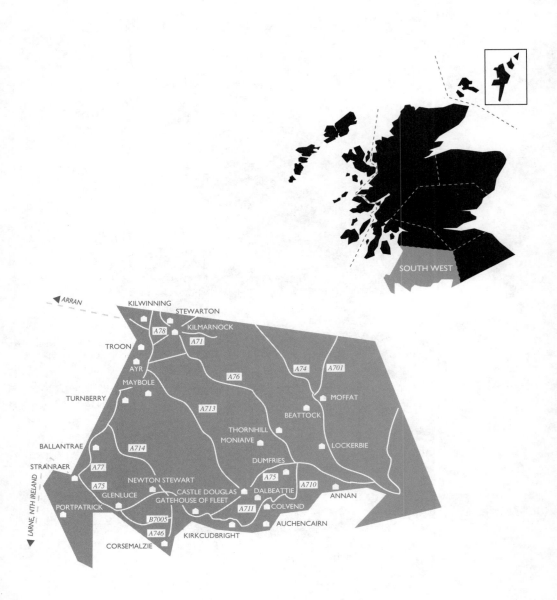

SOUTH WEST

ARRAN

KILWINNING
STEWARTON
KILMARNOCK
A78
A71
TROON
AYR
MAYBOLE
A76
A74
A701
TURNBERRY
A713
MOFFAT
BEATTOCK
THORNHILL
MONIAIVE
BALLANTRAE
A714
LOCKERBIE
STRANRAER
A77
DUMFRIES
A75
NEWTON STEWART
A75
A710
GLENLUCE
CASTLE DOUGLAS
DALBEATTIE
ANNAN
GATEHOUSE OF FLEET
A711
PORTPATRICK
COLVEND
B7005
AUCHENCAIRN
A746
KIRKCUDBRIGHT
CORSEMALZIE

LARNE, NTH IRELAND

Map 2 - The Borders

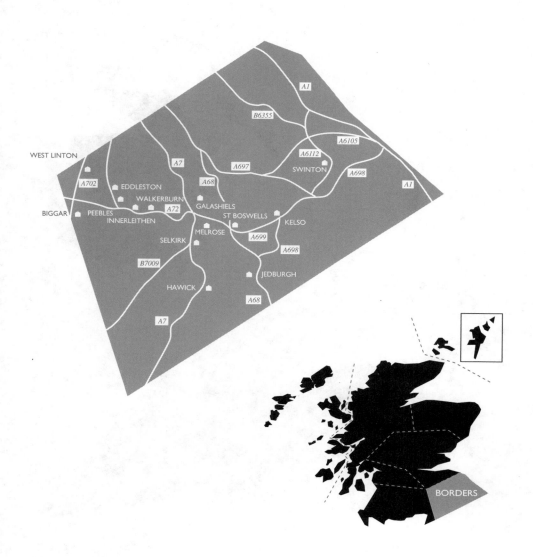

WEST LINTON

A702

BIGGAR

A7

A702

EDDLESTON

WALKERBURN

PEEBLES

INNERLEITHEN

A72

A68

A697

SELKIRK

GALASHIELS

MELROSE

ST BOSWELLS

A699

B7009

HAWICK

A7

A68

JEDBURGH

A698

KELSO

SWINTON

A6112

A697

B6355

A1

A6105

A698

A1

BORDERS

Map 3 - The Clyde

CLYDE

CAIRNDOW
A886
STRACHUR
A815
STRATHLACHLAN
ARDENTINNY
KILFINAN
B836
A880
A8003
KILMUN
DUNOON

LOCH LOMOND
A82
DRYMEN
A811

KIRKINTILLOCH
A80

LANGBANK
M8
GLASGOW
A8
M73
M8

BUTE
A737

LARGS
A736
M74
A73

A78
A735
A77
BOTHWELL
A71

STEWARTON

A735
B778
A71
A74
A721
NEWBIGGING
A702

ARRAN
BRODICK
ARDROSSAN
LAMLASH

Map 4 - Central and Eastern

Map 5 - The North East

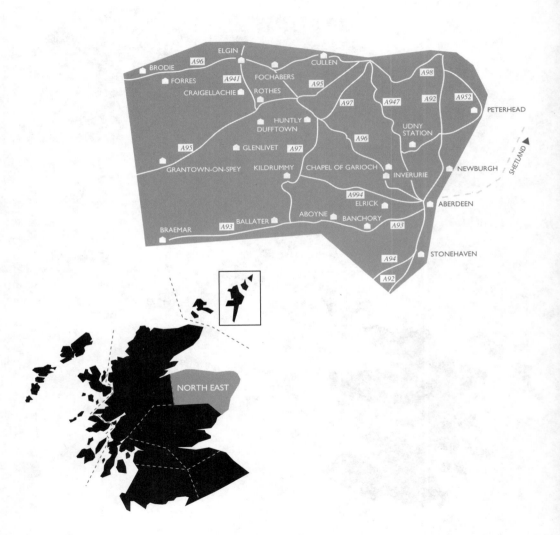

Map 6 - The Highlands

Map 7
- The Hebrides, Orkney and Shetland

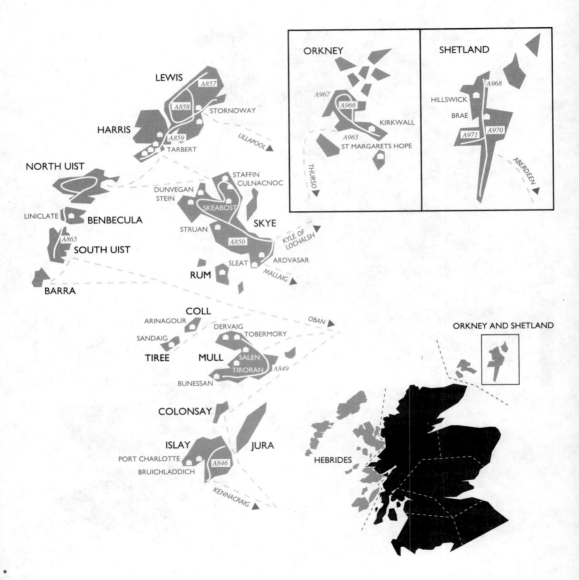

LEWIS

A857

A858

STORNOWAY

HARRIS

A859

TARBERT

ULLAPOOL

NORTH UIST

LINICLATE

BENBECULA

A865

SOUTH UIST

BARRA

DUNVEGAN
STEIN

STAFFIN
CULNACNOC

SKEABOST

STRUAN

SKYE

A850

SLEAT

KYLE OF
LOCHALSH

ARDVASAR

MALLAIG

RUM

COLL

ARINAGOUR

SANDAIG

TIREE

DERVAIG

TOBERMORY

OBAN

SALEN

MULL

TIRORAN

A849

BUNESSAN

COLONSAY

ISLAY

PORT CHARLOTTE

A846

BRUICHLADDICH

JURA

KENNACRAIG

ORKNEY

A967

A966

KIRKWALL

A965

ST MARGARETS HOPE

THURSO

SHETLAND

A968

HILLSWICK

BRAE

A971

A970

ABERDEEN

ORKNEY AND SHETLAND

HEBRIDES

Scotch Whisky
Spirit of Scotland

Scotch whisky is the national drink of Scotland. It is also the natural drink of Scotland, made only from the purest natural ingredients - golden barley, clear water and cool Scottish air.

Scotch whisky can only be called Scotch if it is distilled and matured in Scotland - by law it must be left to mature for a minimum of three years, but in practice most Scotch whisky is left to mature for much longer.

Few would venture to assert the precise moment at which Scotch whisky was first distilled. What is certain is that the ancient Celts practised the art, and had an expressive name for the fiery liquid they produced - 'uisge beatha' - the water of life.

For generations the Scots kept their whisky to themselves, distilling it in homes and farmhouses throughout the Highlands, Islands and glens alike. Then came the Government determined to tax it.

For more than 150 years, the wily Scots continued to distil their whisky, smuggling it down to the towns and cities, and outwitting the hated excise officers and revenue men, who are today the stuff of legend.

However, by the mid 19th century, most distilleries had legalised their businesses, and the foundations of today's Scotch whisky industry were laid.

There are four main stages in the pot still process - malting, mashing, fermentation and distilling. First the barley is steeped in water and then allowed to germinate, before being dried in a peat-fired kiln, the smoke of which contributes to the flavour and aroma of the final product.

Next, hot water is added to the ground malted barley in a mash tun to convert the starch into sugar. Then the mixture is transferred to a fermenting vat where yeast is added and fermentation converts the sugar into alcohol.

Finally, in the distinctively shaped swan-necked copper pot stills, distillation of the new spirit takes place. Most malt whisky is distilled twice, and only when the spirit reaches a high enough standard is it filled into oak casks and stored in cool dark warehouses where the long process of maturation takes place.

Unlike grain whiskies, malt whiskies vary enormously from one distillery to the next and one geographical region to another. The flavour of a malt depends on the water used, the distillation technique unique to that distillery, the size and type of cask, and the atmospheric temperature and humidity during maturation.

The distilleries are divided geographically into Highland, Lowland, Islay and Campbeltown malts.

Highland malts are often subdivided into five further categories: the most famous whisky producing area is Speyside where some of the best known Highland malts are produced - Glenfiddich, Macallan, Cardhu, Glen Grant, Tamdhu and The Glenlivet to name but a few.

The four other types of Highland malt are Eastern, Northern (of which Glenmorangie is probably the best known), Perthshire (e.g. Glenturret) and the Islands, which include Highland Park on Orkney and Talisker on Skye.

Islay malts range from the lighter peated Bunnahabhain and Bruichladdich, through to the more heavily peated Laphroaig and Bowmore. Although close to Islay, on mainland Kintyre, the two remaining Campbeltown malts - Springbank and Glenscotia - have a distinctive style of their own, while Lowland Scotland is more associated with grain whisky production. However there are ten malt whisky distilleries in that region, which extends as far south as Bladnoch in Wigtown.

THE *GAELIC* WHISKY

WHISKY FIT FOR HIGHLANDERS · FIOR UISGE BEATHA NAN GAIDHEAL

TE BHEAG-Blended for the Hebrides. POIT DHUBH-Traditional malt vatted for connoisseurs. POIT DHUBH *Green Label*-Vatted malt unfiltered and unchilled for old fashioned looks and flavour. Three special whiskies from the world's only gaelic whisky company.

Praban na Linne Limited,
Eilean Iarmain,
An t-Eilean Sgiathanach,
IV43 8QR. Tel: 047 13 266

see entry page 125

ISLE ORNSAY HOTEL
Tigh-Osda Eilean Iarmain

The Gaelic Inn on the Sea

*The Taste of Skye
- mostly landed at our own
wharf. Oysters and mussels,
herrings and halibut.
Relish our seafood and relax
in a seaview room. Open all
year. Centrally heated.
Full menus and information
available from:*

Effie Kennedy, Isle Ornsay Hotel, Sleibhte, Skye, IV43 8QR.
Telephone: 04713 332 Fax: 04713 275

23

Cheeses from Scotland

Scotland is well known as a producer of excellent quality cheddar cheeses and recent years have also seen the introduction of a considerable and welcome diversity of cheeses, both old cheeses rediscovered and Scottish variants of established speciality cheeses.

The particular richness of Scottish milk has long been recognised in the quality of Scottish cheeses. The output of Scottish cheddar still dominates and the main creameries are located in the milk producing areas at a further distance from the centres of population - Galloway, Lockerbie, Campbeltown, and on the islands of Bute, Arran, Islay and Orkney.

Speciality cheeses are produced on a small scale throughout Scotland. The cheeses are characterised by a high degree of individuality and often the owner or cheese-maker is available to explain the cheese and its making to visitors.

The varieties and some of the names and places where they are made include:

Traditional Farmhouse (cheddar):

>   Tobermory (Isle of Mull)
>
>   Swannay (Orkney)
>
>   Dunloppe (Galloway)

Semi-soft:

>   Howgate Langskaill and
>
>   Ettrick (Dundee)

Soft-white moulded:

>   Bonchester (Borders)
>
>   Howgate Brie, Camembert,
>
>   Pentland and others (Dundee)

Soft-blue veined:

>   Arran Blue (Arran)
>
>   Dunsyre Blue (Lanarkshire)

Soft-fresh and cream cheeses:

>   Caboc, Gruth Dhu and Gallic
>
>   (Tain)
>
>   St Finan (Aberdeenshire)
>
>   Howgate (Dundee)
>
>   Lochaber Smoked (Glenuig)

Goatsmilk:

>   Sanday Island (Orkney)
>
>   Island Goats (Arran)

Ewes Milk:

>   Brodick Blue (Arran)
>
>   Lanark Blue (Lanarkshire)

In addition, there are several varieties of smoked cheeses produced at Perth, Orkney, Glenuig and Arran.

Wherever you visit, do ask about the local cheeses.

HOWGATE

Scottish *Cheeses* *of Distinction*

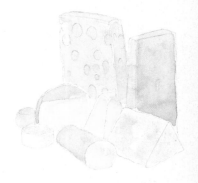

Shetland Islands

Shetland Islands

Urquhart Castle, Loch Ness

Loch Garry

Glenfinnan Monument

Ben Nevis

Tobermory, Mull

Gigha

Pittenween Harbour, Fife

River Falloch, Glen Falloch

SCOTTISH SALMON

Look for the tartan mark when ordering salmon.

Only Scottish Salmon that meets the stringent quality standards of the Scottish Salmon Quality Assurance Scheme, enforced by Food From Britain's independent inspectors, can carry the distinctive tartan quality mark.

It is your guarantee of premium quality salmon which is truly Scottish.

Scottish Salmon

Scottish salmon, well worthy of its title 'King of Fish' is part of the Scottish culinary tradition.

Once, Scottish rivers held such abundant stocks of wild salmon that rich and poor alike could feast on them at will. Poached in vast copper kettles, they graced the Laird's table. The sea captain dined on salmon - pickled, smoked and salted - during his long voyages under sail. So common was it, that historical sources note a clause in Perth apprentices' indentures, limiting the number of salmon meals to not more than three per week!

Wild Scottish salmon have always been a seasonal delicacy, but several factors have caused the numbers landed to decline over the years. With fewer numbers available, the price of Scottish salmon increased. Some 20 years ago, the concept of salmon farming became a reality, offering the potential for salmon to become once more accessible to all.

Scottish salmon, reared in the security of the clear, unpolluted inshore waters of the Scottish lochs, is now available all year round. It is a luxury food at an affordable price and of consistently high quality - a quality now guaranteed by the Scottish salmon tartan Brand Quality Mark.

The Quality Mark was launched in March 1991, making it easier to identify premium quality salmon of a true Scottish nature. These assurances come from the fact that all producers supplying salmon carrying the mark must act in accordance with a comprehensive set of quality standards, and their continued adherence to these is regularly checked by independent inspectors.

Consumers and chefs alike can therefore be confident that every time they buy salmon carrying the tartan mark, they are getting a consistently high quality product.

The nutritional value of salmon is undisputed. A 4 oz portion contains under 200 calories (steamed or poached). It contains protein, calcium and iron, vitamins A and D, riboflavin, and thiamin. Its natural oil includes two fatty acids similar to polyunsaturated vegetable oils. Current medical opinion suggests that these may help reduce the risk of heart disease by altering the blood clotting mechanism, reducing the likelihood of arterial blockage.

Scottish salmon is a truly fine example of the taste of Scotland. It is available all year round and is one of life's affordable luxuries. Scottish salmon is delivered fresh with minimal handling, to fishmongers, market stalls, stores and supermarkets, around the world.

Easy and quick to prepare, Scottish salmon can be served for a family supper or as part of a special celebration meal. It is available fresh or smoked, as whole fish, steaks, fillets or joints, adding variety, quality and flavour to a healthy diet.

In many of the hotels and restaurants recommended in this Taste of Scotland Guide, you will find Scottish salmon featuring as a highlight of the menu. Enjoy Scotland, enjoy Scottish salmon.

The Taste of Scotland

Selects the best in food & accommodation in Scotland

Aberdeen

MAP 5

ARDOE HOUSE HOTEL
Blairs, South Deeside Road
Aberdeen AB1 5YP
Tel: 0224 867355 • Telex: 739413
Fax: 0224 861283

B9077, 3 miles west of Aberdeen.
A very impressive-looking granite mansion with lofty turrets and inscriptions of heraldry and now a high class country house hotel, which is constantly being upgraded and improved. It stands in its own grounds and wooded parkland on the south Deeside road, just five minutes out of Aberdeen. The public rooms are particularly impressive with beautiful carved wood panelling and magnificent fireplaces, and the staircase with its stained glass windows at landing level is especially grand. There is a modern function room with superb views across the Dee. Food in the dining room lives up to the quality image of the hotel: it is imaginative in concept and is presented with the same care and attention that is given to its preparation. There is also the delightful Garden Room in which breakfast is served.
Open all year
Rooms: 71 with private facilities
Bar Lunch 12 – 2.30 pm (a)
Dining Room/Restaurant Lunch 12 – 2.30 pm (a)
Bar Supper 6.30 – 10.30 pm (a)
Dinner 6.30 – 9.30 pm (d)
No dogs
Bed & breakfast £34 – £58.50
Dinner B & B £42.50 – £83.25
Room Rate £46 – £120
Fresh fish from the market daily. Local seasonal game.
STB Commended 5 Crowns
Credit cards: 1, 2, 3, 5

CALEDONIAN THISTLE HOTEL
Union Terrace
Aberdeen AB9 1HE
Tel: 0224 640233 • Telex: 73758
Fax: 0224 641627

City centre.
This large traditional city centre hotel is right in the heart of Aberdeen, overlooking Union Terrace Gardens and just a hundred yards or so from Union Street, the main shopping street of the Granite City. The restaurant and adjacent cocktail bar are well furnished and dignified and offer good standards of food and service. Less formal is Elrond's Cafe, a spacious bar and restaurant with an interesting range of light meals representing excellent value for money.
Open all year
Rooms: 80 with private facilities
Bar Lunch 12 – 2.30 pm (a)
Dining Room/Restaurant Lunch 12.30 – 2 pm except Sat (b-c)
Dinner 6.30 – 10 pm (d)
Bed & breakfast £38 – £98
Dinner B & B £58 – £118
Prawn tails in a Drambuie cream sauce. Layers of salmon, leeks and filo pastry served on a watercress sauce. Loin of lamb roasted pink, glazed with rosemary meringue, set on a pickled walnut sauce.
STB Commended 5 Crowns
Credit cards: 1, 2, 3, 5, 6 + Trumpcard

CRAIGHAAR HOTEL
Waterton Road, Bucksburn
Aberdeen AB2 9HS
Tel: 0224 712275

Turn off A96 at Greenburn Drive. Follow to end then turn left up Waterton Road. Near airport.
A great deal has been done during recent refurbishments to upgrade and improve this fine privately run hotel which has a good reputation with both the business community and local residents. It is not the easiest place to find if you are a visitor to Aberdeen, but persist; it is a good oasis. Food is imaginative with strong emphasis on fresh local produce and is pleasingly presented.
Open all year
Rooms: 55 with private facilities
Bar Lunch 12 – 2 pm except Sun (a)
Dining Room/Restaurant Lunch 12 – 2 pm Sun only (carvery) (a-b)
Bar Supper 6 – 10 pm (a-b)
Dinner 7 – 10 pm except Sun (b-d)
No dogs
Bed & breakfast £51.50 – £85
Tartare of fresh and smoked salmon served on a cucumber salad with a dill dressing. Best end of lamb roasted with a Dijon mustard and herb crust served with a red wine and wild mushroom sauce. Marinated venison sautéd with shallots, fresh herbs and juniper, flambéd in gin and served with a redcurrant jelly sauce.
STB Commended 3 Crowns
Credit cards: 1, 2, 3, 5, 6

CRAIGLYNN HOTEL
36 Fonthill Road
Aberdeen AB1 2UJ
Tel: 0224 584050
Fax: 0224 584050

On corner of Fonthill Road and Bon Accord Street, midway between Union Street and King George IV Bridge. Car park access from Bon Accord Street.
Craiglynn is an impressive granite building, formerly owned by an Aberdeen merchant. The dining room was originally the billiard room of this fine house and features rosewood panelling. The hotel is run in a relaxed yet efficient manner – the theme being "Victorian elegance with modern comforts". The bedrooms are tastefully furnished and decorated, all having direct dial telephones and colour TVs. No smoking in the bedrooms or dining room. There are two elegant lounges to relax in, one of which has an open fire burning during the Winter evenings. Dinner menus are decided upon daily and offer an interesting choice of dishes carefully cooked.
Open all year except Christmas Day + 1 Jan
Rooms: 9 , 7 with private facilities
Dinner at 7 pm (b)
Reservations required for non-residents
No smoking in dining room + bedrooms
Restricted licence
No dogs
Bed & breakfast £29.50 – £49
Dinner B & B £44 – £63.50
Scotch broth. Sole with prawn and whisky cream sauce. Toffee topped peaches . . . just a sample of the choice of dishes offered.
STB Commended 3 Crowns
Credit cards: 1, 2, 3, 5
Proprietors: Chris & Hazel Mann

Credit Card Code		*Meal Price Code*	
1.	Access/Mastercard/Eurocard	(a)	under £10
2.	American Express	(b)	£10 – £15
3.	Visa	(c)	£15 – £20
4.	Carte Bleu	(d)	£20 – £25
5.	Diners Club	(e)	£25 – £30
6.	Mastercharge	(f)	over £30

FARADAY'S RESTAURANT
2 Kirk Brae, Cults
Aberdeen AB1 9SQ
Tel: 0224 869666

4 miles from city centre on north Deeside road. On reaching Cults, turn right at traffic lights – Faraday's 100 yards on right.

This restaurant takes its name from a Victorian engineer, Michael Faraday who is now considered to be the father of electrical engineering. The building, which has been carefully restored, used to be an electric pump station for the area of Cults. A minstrel's gallery overlooks the wood-panelled restaurant, which is decorated in dusky pink and grape colours. The cuisine is prepared by John Inches and his food reflects his background of traditional Scottish cooking, combined with extensive travel through France.

Open all year except Boxing Day, 1 Jan + first 2 wks Jan
Dining Room/Restaurant Lunch 12 – 1.15 pm except Sun Mon (a)
Dinner 7.30 – 9.30 pm except Sun (c-d)
Closed Sun
Facilities for the disabled
Oven baked salmon with parsley butter, grapefruit and lemon sauce. Rock salt roasted Barbary duck breast with a savoury chestnut and prune barquette and served with a Scottish bramble sauce. Tender Spring lamb casserole of red lentils, cream, garlic and fresh herbs, with a mushroom rice pilaff. Meringue syllabub of rhubarb with orange.
Credit cards: 1, 3
Proprietor: John Inches

NEW MARCLIFFE HOTEL
51-53 Queens Road
Aberdeen AB9 2PE
Tel: 0224 321371

Direct access north and south from A92. West end of Aberdeen.

Relaxing and comfortable accommodation with a sophisticated surrounding. Elegant table settings and a quietly efficient service. West end rendezvous for the business community and visitors to the city. Carvery lunches and à la carte dinner. The "in season" produce of Scotland's fields, moors, rivers and seas is cooked with flair in traditional and innovative ways.

Open all year
Rooms: 27 with private facilities
Bar Lunch 12.30 – 2.15 pm (b)

Dining Room/Restaurant Lunch 12.30 – 2.15 pm except Sun (c)
Bar Supper 6.30 – 9.30 pm (b)
Dinner 7 – 9.30 pm except Sun (c)
No dogs
Bed & breakfast £45 – £80
Dinner B & B £65 – £105
Medallions of venison with bramble and port sauce, collops of monkfish with spring onion and ginger sauce, roulade of pork fillet with smoked goose, asparagus and pine kernels. Seasonal fruit pavlova.
STB Commended 4 Crowns
Credit cards: 1, 2, 3, 5, 6
Proprietors: Stewart & Sheila Spence

Aberdour

MAP 4

HAWKCRAIG HOUSE
Hawkcraig Point, Aberdour
Fife KY3 0TZ
Tel: 0383 860335

From centre of Aberdour, take Hawkcraig road, through large car park, then down very steep access to Hawkcraig Point.

Elma Barrie has earned a fine reputation for the high standard of food, hospitality and comfort she offers in her whitewashed old ferryman's house. Situated at the water's edge, next to the harbour, the views across Aberdour bay to the golf course and Inchcolm's 12th century abbey are superb. Seals and seabirds abound, yet the village is only 30 minutes from Edinburgh by road or rail (best by train to avoid the city's traffic and parking problems). The East Neuk of Fife, Gleneagles and St Andrews are all within a pleasant hour's drive and there is much to see and enjoy on the way. Children over eight years welcome.

Open Feb to Nov
Rooms: 2 with private facilities
Dinner 7 – 8.30 pm (c)
Open to non-residents – booked meals only
Unlicensed – guests welcome to take own wine
No smoking throughout
No dogs
Bed & breakfast £18 – £25
Dinner B & B £34 – £42
Home cooking par excellence, using prime Scottish produce.
STB Highly Commended 2 Crowns
No credit cards
Proprietor: Elma Barrie

Aberfeldy

MAP 4

FARLEYER HOUSE HOTEL
Aberfeldy, Perthshire PH15 2JE
Tel: 0887 20332
Fax: 0887 29430

On B846, 2 miles west of Aberfeldy.
Farleyer House has its foundations in the 16th century and stands discreetly secluded by mature trees in 70 acres of grounds in the geographical centre of Scotland. Frances and Gerald Atkins have furnished it with consummate care so that everything about it looks and feels right. But it is for the food that the ultimate acclamation is reserved. Adventurous, imaginative, exciting, superb – Atkins Restaurant at Farleyer is all these things and more. The rich natural larder on their doorstep gives Frances Atkins even more opportunity to demonstrate her skills. More recently the addition of a bistro for light eating has extended the range of food.

Open all year
Rooms: 11 with private facilities
Bistro 10 am – 10 pm (a-b)
Dining Room/Restaurant Lunch 12.30 – 1.30 pm – by special arrangement
Dinner 7 – 9 pm (f)
No smoking in restaurant
Room Rate £50 – £90 (including breakfast)
Terrine of sea trout and langoustine, local woodland chanterelle soup. Salmon with a sauce of broad beans, samphire and garden herbs. Stuffed breast of Guinea fowl with raspberry and peppercorn sauce.
Credit cards: 1, 2, 3
Proprietors: Gerald & Frances Atkins

GUINACH HOUSE
by The Birks, Aberfeldy
Perthshire PH15 2ET
Tel: 0887 20251

On A826, south-west outskirts of Aberfeldy, on road to 'The Birks', Guinach is signposted from Urlar Road.
Guinach House is situated in its own secluded garden grounds, with magnificent views of the Perthshire Highlands. The Mackays are attentive hosts, helping create a relaxed friendly atmosphere for their guests. Interesting and imaginative four course dinner menu served in the small elegant dining room.

Open all year
Rooms: 7 with private facilities
Dining Room/Restaurant Lunch 12.30
– 1.30 pm (a)
Dinner 7 – 9.30 pm (c)
No smoking in dining room
Bed & breakfast from £35
Dinner B & B from £53.50
Fresh Tay salmon, haunch of Atholl
venison, medallions of Scotch lamb,
prime beef. Full Scottish breakfast.
STB Highly Commended 3 Crowns
Credit cards: 1, 3
Proprietor: Albert Mackay

Aberlady

MAP 4

KILSPINDIE HOUSE HOTEL
Main Street, Aberlady
East Lothian, EH32 0RE
Tel: 087 57 682

On A198 in centre of Aberlady village.
The Binnie family has run Kilspindie for
over 25 years. A family and golfing hotel,
set back from the main street of this
small conservation village on the coast, it
is a good base from which to visit the
nature reserve and other attractions of
East Lothian, yet only 20 minutes drive
east of Edinburgh.
Open all year
Rooms: 26 with private facilities
Bar Lunch 12 – 2.15 pm (a)
Dining Room/Restaurant Lunch 12.30
– 2 pm Sun only (b)
Bar Supper 5 – 9 pm (b)
Dinner 7.30 – 8.30 pm (b)
Bed & breakfast £32 – £44
Dinner B & B £44 – £55
Accent on local produce. Trout Rob Roy,
Steak Balmoral, Scampi Maison.
STB Commended 4 Crowns
Credit cards: 1, 3
Proprietor: Raymond Binnie

Aboyne

MAP 5

BALNACOIL HOTEL
Rhu-na-Haven Road, Aboyne
Aberdeenshire AB34 5JD
Tel: 03398 86806
Fax: 03398 87050

Off A93 between Ballater and Banchory.
Set on the banks of the River Dee, this
old baronial building is now a highly

individual and distinctive country house
hotel with first class standards of comfort
and cuisine. The en suite bedrooms are
equipped with all the thoughtful little
extras that contribute to a comfortable
stay. The Hunters Restaurant is
becoming renowned for its imaginative
menus and excellent standards of
presentation, and there is an impressive
wine list. Jean and Roger Leigh have put
a lot of effort into making Balnacoil a
delightful haven of relaxation.
Open all year
Rooms: 12 with private facilities
Bar Lunch 12.30 – 2.30 pm (a)
Dining Room/Restaurant Lunch 12.30
– 2 pm (b)
Bar Supper 6 – 10 pm (c)
Dinner 7 – 10 pm (d-e)
No dogs
Facilities for the disabled
Bed & breakfast from £51 – £60
Dinner B & B £70 – £82
Spinach and smoked salmon roulade.
Baked fillets of cod stuffed with lemon
and lime, wrapped in filo pastry.
Mignons of Aberdeen Angus pan-fried
with strips of smoked salmon.
STB Commended 4 Crowns
Credit cards: 1, 2, 3, 5, 6
Proprietors: Jean & Roger Leigh

HAZLEHURST LODGE
Ballater Road, Aboyne
Aberdeenshire AB34 5HY
Tel: 03398 86921

On A93 on western side of Aboyne.
Imaginative, highly regarded cooking by
Chef Anne Strachan in the intimate
atmosphere of this attractive rose granite
former coachman's lodge to Aboyne
Castle. Wines are personally selected
from top growers and the prices are
friendly. The accommodation in three
individually designed bedrooms, all with
full private facilities, is of a high standard
reflecting the owners' artistic
background. The specially commissioned
furniture exemplifies the best of Scottish
craft design. Hazlehurst has made an ideal
base for a relaxing stay on beautiful
unspoilt Royal Deeside.
Open Feb to Dec
Rooms: 3 with private facilities
Dining Room Lunch available for special
bookings
Dinner 7.30 – 9.30 pm (d)
No smoking in dining room + bedrooms
Bed & breakfast from £25
Fish and seafood straight from the sea,
wild river salmon, game from the ancient

Caledonian forests, home-cured meats.
Creative use of herbs and fresh vegetables
bringing traditional cooking to today's
table.
STB Commended 2 Crowns
Credit cards: 1, 2, 3
Proprietors: Anne & Eddie Strachan

Achiltibuie

MAP 6

SUMMER ISLES HOTEL
Achiltibuie
Ross-shire IV26 2YG
Tel: 085 482 282
Fax: 085 482 251

Prestige Award Winner 1991

Ten miles north of Ullapool turn west off
A835 and continue for 15 miles along
single track road.
Leaving the main road is like leaving one
world and moving into another, and the
terrain to Achiltibuie is primitive,
enchanting and hauntingly beautiful.
The village itself is a haphazard layout of
cottages, but its pièce de resistance is the
Summer Isles Hotel, a haven of civilised
comfort and culinary standards of
astonishingly high level. Mark and
Geraldine Irvine are utterly charming
hosts, bent on ensuring that in this
remote corner of Ross-shire you will want
for nothing – and indeed you won't.
There is everything here, and overlying it
is the sheer tranquillity and beauty of the
place. You will feed on the finest harvest
of seafish, shellfish and the freshest of
fresh locally grown vegetables, fruit and
farm produce all prepared with skill and
presented with flair. Like everyone else
who has been there, you will leave
reluctantly, determined to return.
Open Easter to mid Oct
Rooms: 11 with private facilities
Dinner at 8 pm (e)
Note: Lunch is not served in the hotel,
but is available in the adjoining
Achiltibuie Cafe
No smoking in restaurant
Bed & breakfast £30 – £60
Dinner B & B £60 – £90
Local shellfish – lobster, scallops,
langoustine etc.
No credit cards
Proprietors: Mark & Geraldine Irvine

Airth

MAP 4

AIRTH CASTLE HOTEL

Airth, by Falkirk
Stirlingshire FK2 8JF
Tel: 0324 831411 • Telex: 777975
Fax: 0324 831419

*Junction 7 of M9/A905 from Kincardine
Bridge.*

Airth Castle stands on a small hill and
looks out over the lush grazing of the
Forth Valley. It has been part of
Scotland's history since the 14th century.
The public rooms are spacious and
elegant enjoying fine views over the
surrounding countryside and designed
for guests to make themselves at home
in. There is a splendid air of permanence
about this building which has several
interesting features both externally and
internally and has earned a good
reputation for its food and service. There
is also a leisure club. The hotel has been
further extended and improved during
the past year.

Open all year
Rooms: 75 with private facilities
Bar Lunch 12 – 2 pm (a)
Dining Room/Restaurant Lunch 12.30
– 2 pm (b)
Bar Supper 6 – 8 pm (a)
Dinner 7 – 9.45 pm (c)
No dogs
Facilities for the disabled
Bed & breakfast from £70
Dinner B & B from £85
Credit cards: 1, 2, 3, 5, 6

Alloa

MAP 4

Overall Excellence Award 1992

THE GEAN HOUSE

Gean Park, Tullibody Road
Alloa, Clackmannanshire
FK10 2HS
Tel: 0259 219275
Fax: 0259 213827

*A907 from Kincardine Bridge or
Stirling. Park entrance on B9096
Tullibody, less than 5 minutes from
Alloa Town Hall roundabout.*

A luxurious country house hotel of
the very highest standard. The Gean
House was built in 1912 by a leading
industrialist, Alexander Forrester
Paton, as a wedding present for his
son. Standing in its own grounds with
parks, woodland lawns and a rose
garden, Gean House has been
restored and furnished with elegance
and consummate good taste. There
are many delightful architectural
features, including a minstrel gallery
and inglenook fireplace in the oak-
panelled reception hall. The
bedrooms are superb and beautifully
furnished, with elegant modern
fabrics, big lamps and comfortable
bathrooms. The resident directors,
John Taylor and Antony Mifsud, are
acclaimed restaurateurs and interior
designers – and it shows. Everything
about this magnificent house is
outstanding, and the food reaches
the same pinnacle of excellence and
perfection so evident throughout.

Open all year
Rooms: 7 with private facilities
(3 additional suites pending)
Dining Room/Restaurant Lunch 12 –
2 pm (b)
Dinner 7 – 9.30 pm (e)
No dogs
Facilities for the disabled
No smoking in dining room
Bed & breakfast £69.50 – £79.50
Dinner B & B £97 – £107
Room Rate £60 – £70
*Baked monkfish tails with baby leeks
and mustard sauce. Poached poussin
filled with bacon and pork forcemeat,
dressed with vegetables poached in
same pot. Peach gratin with pawpaw
sorbet and champagne sabayon.*
STB Highly Commended 4 Crowns
Credit cards: 1, 2, 3, 5, 6
Proprietor: John Taylor

Altnaharra

by Lairg

MAP 6

ALTNAHARRA HOTEL

Altnaharra
Sutherland IV27 4UE
Tel: 054 981 222
Fax: 054 981 222

A836, 21 miles north of Lairg.

One of Scotland's famous fishing hotels
situated in the heart of beautiful
Sutherland. The Altnaharra specialises in
all requirements for the angler and the
outdoor enthusiast, with an emphasis on
comfort and cuisine. Also open to non-
residents and non-sporting guests.

Open Apr to mid Oct
Rooms: 20 with private facilities
Bar Lunch 12 – 2.15 pm (b)
Bar Supper 6 – 7.30 pm (a)
Dinner 7.30 – 8.30 pm (c)
No smoking in dining room
Bed & breakfast £30 – £39
Dinner B & B £46 – £55
*Scottish beef, lamb, fresh salmon (subject
to availability), home-made soups and
desserts.*
Credit cards: 1, 3

Annan

MAP 1

NORTHFIELD HOUSE

Eaglesfield Road, Annan
Dumfriesshire DG12 5LL
Tel: 0461 202851

*Situated 1 mile east of Annan on B722
Eaglesfield Road.*

The best places are usually found off the
beaten track and the charming home of
James and Mary Airey proves the point.
They are hosts par excellence and their
warm welcome and thoughtful attention
to every aspect of a guest's comfort is a
joy to experience. The fact that this small
establishment is given a deluxe grading
by the Scottish Tourist Board speaks for
itself. The food is quite delicious with
carefully balanced menus and nothing
routine or run of the mill in content or
presentation. This is a place to seek out
and savour.

Open all year
Rooms: 3 with private facilities
Dinner at 7.30 pm (c)

Non-residents – by prior arrangement
Unlicensed
No children
No dogs
Facilities for the disabled
No smoking in dining room
Bed & breakfast £30 – £40
Dinner B & B £50 – £60
Poached Solway sea-trout served on a bed of spinach with a wine and cream sauce. Breast of pigeon served with a juniper-flavoured sauce. Fillet of prime Scotch beef.
STB Deluxe 3 Crowns
No credit cards
Proprietors: James & Mary Airey

Anstruther

MAP 4

THE CELLAR RESTAURANT
24 East Green, Anstruther
Fife KY10 3AA
Tel: 0333 310378

The county of Fife is blessed with an abundant variety of good eating places, from country inns of character to elegant restaurants with fine cuisine. The atmosphere of both is somehow combined with great success at this former cooperage. It is situated just off the harbour front and approached through a walled courtyard to an interior of stone walls, beamed ceilings and open fires. Chef/Proprietor Peter Jukes' reputation extends far beyond Fife. His treatment of seafood is both simple and masterly. To complement the food there is an enthusiastic wine list bettered by few in Scotland. You should not miss an opportunity to eat at the Cellar, but be sure to reserve a table – there are only eight!
Open all year except 1 wk Christmas/ New Year + 1 wk May
Dining Room/Restaurant Lunch 12.30 – 1.30 pm Fri Sat only (b)
Dinner 7 – 9.30 pm except Sun (d) 4 course menu
Closed Sun: also closed Mon in Winter
Facilities for the disabled
No smoking in restaurant
Fish soups, langoustine, scallops, crab, lobster, turbot, monkfish, etc. Rosettes of lamb with rosemary. Fillet of Scotch beef.
Credit cards: 1, 2, 3
Proprietors: Peter & Vivien Jukes

Appin

MAP 6

INVERCRERAN COUNTRY HOUSE HOTEL
Glen Creran, Appin
Argyll PA38 4BJ
Tel: 063 173 414/456
Fax: 063 173 532

Just off A828 Oban–Fort William at head of Loch Creran, 14 miles north of Connel Bridge.
Superlatives are often over-used. But not here. This is a gem of a place, strikingly different. A uniquely styled modern mansion house luxuriously appointed and with truly magnificent views of the hills and glens. Marie and John Kersley with their family have created a haven of total relaxation and enjoyment. Children over five years welcome.
Open 1 Mar to mid Nov
Rooms: 9 with private facilities
Dining Room/Restaurant Lunch 12 – 2 pm (c)
Dinner 7 – 8 pm (e)
No dogs
No smoking in restaurant
Bed & breakfast £36 – £49
Dinner B & B £65 – £80
Filo pastry of scallops, prawns and mussels in chive and champagne sauce. Salmon set on spinach with tarragon butter cream sauce. Collops of Highland venison with cranberry, mushroom and Port sauce.
STB Highly Commended 4 Crowns
Credit cards: 1, 3
Proprietor: John Kersley

THE STEWART HOTEL
Glen Duror, Appin
Argyll PA38 4BW
Tel: 063 174 268/220
Fax: 063 174 328

A828 – Fort William 17 miles; Glencoe 10 miles; Oban 30 miles.
In a delightful setting of five acres of tranquil landscaped gardens overlooking Loch Linnhe and a mere ten miles from Glencoe, The Stewart Hotel makes a very good base for touring this spectacular area of the country. The original building goes back over a century and was designed as a hunting lodge with the generous internal proportions associated with the period. The restaurant, bar and public rooms are in this part while the modern well equipped bedrooms are in a newer wing. With ready access to plentiful supplies of delicious fish and shellfish for which the west coast is renowned, the chefs create well balanced menus which change daily and are presented with finesse.
Open Apr to Oct
Rooms: 19 with private facilities
Bar Lunch 12 – 1.45 pm (a)
Bar Supper 6 – 6.45 pm (a)
Dinner 7 – 9 pm (c)
No smoking in restaurant
Bed & breakfast £40 – £50
Dinner B & B from £65
Highland venison pan-fried and served with a sauce of red wine and chanterelle mushrooms. Fillet of Scotch salmon wrapped in puff pastry oven-baked and served on a red pepper coulis.
STB Commended 4 Crowns
Credit cards: 1, 2, 3, 5, 6
Proprietors: The Lacy Family

Ardelve

MAP 6

LOCH DUICH HOTEL
Ardelve
by Kyle of Lochalsh IV40 8DY
Tel: 059 985 213
Fax: 059 985 214

Off A87 from Fort William and Inverness (via Loch Ness), 7 miles from Kyle of Lochalsh/Skye ferry.
A superb location for a country hotel at the junction of three sea lochs and looking out over what is probably Scotland's most photographed ancient monument – Eilean Donan Castle. There are also fine views of the mountains of Kintail and Skye. This long established old hotel has recently changed hands and is gradually being upgraded by the new owners. The menus feature carefully prepared and presented food, taking advantage of the abundance of fresh fish and shellfish for which the west coast is famous.
Open all year
Rooms: 18, 5 with private facilities
Bar Lunch 12.30 – 2 pm (a)
Dinner 7 – 9 pm (c)
No smoking in dining room
Bed & breakfast from £22
Dinner B & B from £37
Smoked haddock loaf, queenie scallop crumble, oysters and mussels, wild salmon, local langoustines, lobster, crab. Wild duck, pigeon, venison, heather lamb.
Credit cards: 1, 3
Proprietors: Iain Fraser & Sonia Moore

Ardentinny

MAP 3

ARDENTINNY HOTEL
Ardentinny
Loch Long, nr Dunoon
Argyll PA23 8TR
Tel: 036 981 209
Fax: 036 981 345

*M8 to Gourock, ferry to Dunoon, A815
then A880 – or drive round Loch
Lomond.*
Enchanting old coaching inn circa 1720,
fully modernised but retaining many old
features, with lovely gardens to the sea,
and lying in the mountainous Argyll Forest
Park. The hotel dining room and buttery
are very popular with yachtsmen,
fishermen and walkers. All bedrooms
with private facilities and good views of
the loch or mountains.
Open 15 Mar to 1 Nov
Rooms: 11 with private facilities
Sunday Brunch 12 – 3 pm
Bar Lunch 12 – 2.30 pm (a)
Bar Supper 6 – 9.30 pm (b)
Dinner 7.30 – 8.30 pm (c)
No smoking in dining room
Bed & breakfast £20 – £40
Dinner B & B £45 – £67
*Steaks, lobster salads, prawn soup,
venison casserole, Loch Long
langoustine, Argyll lamb with heather
honey; sweets prepared daily, speciality
coffees with Ardentinny mints.*
STB Commended 3 Crowns
Credit cards: 1, 2, 3, 5
*Proprietors: John & Thyrza Horn,
Hazel Hall*

Arduaine

MAP 6

LOCH MELFORT HOTEL
Arduaine, by Oban
Argyll PA34 4XG
Tel: 08522 233
Fax: 08522 214

On A816, 19 miles south of Oban.
This is an interesting old house, former
home of the Campbells of Arduaine and
extended in such a way as to make the
most of its spectacular position looking
out to the islands across Asknish Bay.
There are glorious uninterrupted
outlooks. The dining room was
refurbished and extended in 1992 to
take advantage of the the view across the

bay to the islands. The menu, rightly, is
not over long and the food is of high
standard. As one would expect in this
part of the west coast there is excellent
shellfish. Presentation is good and service is
discreet and attentive. Informal bar
lunches and suppers are also available.
By 1993 the majority of the bedrooms in
the Cedar Wing will have been
refurbished. The National Trust for
Scotland recently acquired Arduaine
Gardens which are adjacent, with access
through the hotel grounds.
Open 1 Mar to 4 Jan
Rooms: 26 with private facilities
Bar Lunch 12 – 2 pm (a-b)
*Dining Room/Restaurant Lunch (a-b) –
by appointment*
Bar Supper 6.30 – 9 pm (a-b)
Dinner 7.30 – 9 pm (c-d)
Facilities for the disabled
Bed & breakfast £27.50 – £49
Dinner B & B £39.50 – £62.50
*In season: oysters, lobsters, prawns,
mussels, scallops, salmon. Home-made
soups, jams, marmalade, bread, ice-
cream. Fresh local produce, and organic
vegetables.*
STB Commended 4 Crowns
Credit cards: 1, 3
Proprietors: Philip & Rosalind Lewis

Arisaig

MAP 6

THE ARISAIG HOTEL
Arisaig
Inverness-shire PH39 4NH
Tel: 06875 210
Fax: 06875 310

*At edge of Arisaig village on A830 Fort
William-Mallaig, 10 miles before Mallaig
on Loch Nan Ceall.*
This splendid old coaching inn, now a
comfortable country hotel, has its roots
in the early 18th century and has been
added to through Victorian times and
recently. It occupies a splendid site on
the sea shore at the edge of the village
and there are some splendid views, and
some good beaches nearby. It is run by
the Stewart family almost as a large
family home and it is furnished in
keeping with the style of the building.
There are open fires in the public rooms
and comfortably equipped bedrooms.
The food is first class with a heavy
reliance on the excellent seafood and
shellfish so abundant locally. Janice
Stewart who normally presides over the

kitchen shows much flair and
imagination in the presentation of meals.
Open mid Mar to mid Oct
Rooms: 15 , 6 with private facilities
Bar Lunch 12.30 – 2 pm (b)
*Dining Room/Restaurant Lunch (b) – by
arrangement only*
Bar Supper 6.30 – 9 pm (b)
Dinner 7.30 – 8.30 pm (d)
No smoking in main dining room
Bed & breakfast £34.50 – £46.50
Dinner B & B £58 – £70
Room Rate £25.50 – £37
*Local seafood, lobster, prawns, clams,
halibut, turbot etc. Home-made soups
and puddings. Traditional breakfast
with Mallaig kippers.*
STB Commended 3 Crowns
Credit cards: 1, 3
Proprietors: George & Janice Stewart

ARISAIG HOUSE
Beasdale, by Arisaig
Inverness-shire PH39 4NR
Tel: 06875 622
Telex: 777279
Fax: 06875 626

*Just off A830 Fort William-Mallaig, 3
miles east of Arisaig.*
This is a haven of tranquillity and bliss
and you will not want to leave. It is one of
those rare country house hotels with all
the features one hopes to find in such
places. A fine old building on a
commanding site with lovely gardens and
woodland, and magnificent views over
Loch nan Uamh to the islands beyond.
Ruth and John Smither with their son
Andrew have set high standards and this
is apparent throughout the
establishment. The public rooms have
been elegantly furnished as have the
comfortable bedrooms with private
bathrooms. The staff have been trained
to a high degree and polite well
mannered service follows automatically.
The chefs work wonders with the
abundance of delicious local produce
from sea and land, and food is prepared
with care and presented with panache.
An experience to be savoured. Children
over 10 years welcome.
Open early Mar to early Nov
Rooms: 15 with private facilities
Bar Lunch 12.30 – 2 pm (b)
*Dining Room/Restaurant Lunch 12.30
– 2 pm (c)*
Dinner 7.30 – 8.30 pm (f)

Restricted licence
No dogs
Dinner B & B £55 – £110
STB Highly Commended 4 Crowns
Credit cards: 1, 3
Proprietors: Ruth, John &
Andrew Smither

THE OLD LIBRARY LODGE & RESTAURANT

High Street, Arisaig
Inverness-shire PH39 4NH
Tel: 06875 651

In centre of the village.
Overlooking the sea, with views to the
small isles, The Old Library Lodge is a
200 year old stone built stable which has
been tastefully converted into a family
run restaurant with good
accommodation. Making full use of local
shellfish, fish and meat, Alan Broadhurst
has built up a fine reputation with both
locals and visitors. A carefully selected
wine list complements the food which
includes garden produce from the village
and herbs from the Broadhursts' own
herb garden
Open Easter to late Oct
Rooms: 6 with private facilities
Dining Room/Restaurant Lunch
11.30 am – 2.30 pm (a)
Dinner 6.30 – 9.30 pm (c)
Restricted licence
Bed & breakfast from £30
Dinner B & B from £50
Cream of scallop and artichoke soup.
Prawn and lobster tartlet with
Hollandaise sauce. Noisettes of lamb with
Port wine sauce.
STB Commended 3 Crowns
Credit cards: 1, 3
Proprietors: Alan & Angela Broadhurst

Arran
Isle of

MAP 3

AUCHRANNIE COUNTRY HOUSE HOTEL

Auchrannie Road, Brodick
Isle of Arran KA27 8BZ
Tel: 0770 2234
Fax: 0770 2812
One mile north of Brodick Ferry Terminal
and 400 yards from Brodick Golf Club.
Auchrannie is a red sandstone old
Scottish mansion, once the home of the

Dowager Duchess of Hamilton, now a
comfortable elegant hotel with a leisure
centre, indoor swimming pool and a
popular Bistro. However it is the
renowned Garden Restaurant which is
recommended by Taste of Scotland,
where varied menus are presented with
particular emphasis on fresh local
produce including seafood. The hotel
enjoys a unique situation from which to
explore Arran's magnificent scenery – 56
miles of varied coastline and its seven
golf courses. In addition to the
luxuriously appointed bedrooms and
family suites, there are spacious lodges
sleeping up to six persons.
Open all year
Rooms: 28 with private facilities
Dinner 6.30 – 9.30 pm (c)
Taste of Scotland applies to Garden
Restaurant
No dogs, except in lodges
Bed & breakfast £30 – £50
Dinner B & B £42.50 – £62.50
Fresh local dishes with wild salmon,
trout, scallops, lamb, free range fowl etc.
STB Commended 5 Crowns
Credit cards: 1, 3
Proprietor: Iain Johnston

CREELERS SEAFOOD RESTAURANT

The Home Farm, Brodick
Isle of Arran KA27 8DD
Tel: 0770 2810

From Brodick Pier, go north following
coast road towards Brodick Castle and
Corrie for 1 1/2 miles. Restaurant on
right.
Set in the Arran Visitors Centre, the
restaurant, formerly the bothy to the old
home farm of Brodick Castle, has been
established by Tim and Fran James as a
seafood bistro. The decor like the food is
simple, but colourful, the atmosphere
almost continental and the service is
quite charming. Tim, formerly a
trawlerman on the west coast, still creels
for a majority of the shellfish and catches
the wild salmon and sea trout. The
remainder of the fish is bought fresh off
the quays of Kintyre regularly. However
the meat and vegetarian dishes are an
excellent alternative to eating fish. There
is an extensive starter choice to
accompany both the lunch and dinner
menus. The seafood shop attached to the
restaurant enables you to purchase some
of the produce you may have sampled in
the restaurant.
Open 2 wks before Easter to 31 Oct

Dining Room/Restaurant Lunch 12 –
2.30 pm except Mon (b)
Dinner 7 – 10.30 pm except Mon (d)
Closed Mon, except during Jul + Aug
when open for dinner only
Facilities for the disabled
Fresh local fish and shellfish, both simply
and elaborately presented. Seasonal game.
Vegetarian dishes. All home-made.
Credit cards: 1, 3
Proprietors: Tim & Fran James

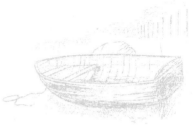

GLEN CLOY FARMHOUSE

Glencloy, Brodick
Isle of Arran KA27 8DA
Tel: 0770 2351

1 1/2 miles from Brodick Pier on road
towards Brodick Castle. Sign at post box
in wall.
Glen Cloy Farmhouse is a beautiful
century old sandstone house, situated in
a peaceful glen just outside Brodick. The
bedrooms are individually furnished and
are cosy and warm. Two of the five
bedrooms have en suite facilities and
there are two other bathrooms. The
chef/proprietor and his wife bake their
own bread, and vegetables and herbs
come from the kitchen garden. The
farmhouse is ideally located to explore
the island's attractions, being close to
golf, castle, and the mountains.
Open 1 Mar to 7 Nov
Rooms: 5 , 2 with private facilities
Dinner 7 – 7.30 pm (b)
Residents only
Unlicensed – guests welcome to take own
wine
No smoking in dining room
Bed & breakfast £18 – £23
Dinner B & B £28 – £35
Home-made mushroom and Arran
mustard soup. Roast Arran lamb with
mint jelly. Fresh chicken with ginger and
lime.
STB Commended 2 Crowns
No credit cards
Proprietors: Mark & Vicki Padfield

GLENISLE HOTEL
Lamlash
Isle of Arran KA27 8LS
Tel: 0770 600 559/258

On main street of Lamlash.
The Glenisle is a white painted country village hotel situated centrally in Lamlash, overlooking the sea. A good selection of Scottish and local produce is offered in the restaurant, the cocktail lounge of which features wooden carvings from the famous Clyde steamer, the Talisman.
Open mid Mar to end Oct
Rooms: 13 with private facilities
Bar Lunch 12 – 2 pm (a)
Dining Room/Restaurant Lunch 12 – 2 pm (a)
Dinner 7 – 9 pm (b)
Bed & breakfast £22.50 – £32.50
Dinner B & B £32 – £42
STB Commended 4 Crowns
Credit card: 1
Proprietor: Alice Toomey

Auchencairn

MAP 1

BALCARY BAY HOTEL
Auchencairn, nr Castle Douglas
Kirkcudbrightshire DG7 1QZ
Tel: 055664 217/311

Off A711 Dalbeattie-Kirkcudbright, along single track road from Auchencairn.
A lovely old country house dating back to 1625 which stands in over three acres of garden in a secluded and enchanting situation on the shores of the bay. In the past it was associated with smugglers. The present day hotel retains much of the old character and charm while providing modern amenities and comforts for guests – full central heating and en suite bedrooms with colour TV, radio, telephone, tea/coffee-making facilities and hairdryer. The cuisine is based on local delicacies such as Galloway beef and lamb, lobster and – of course – Balcary Bay salmon. Excellent hospitality, good food and a superb setting combine to make this an ideal holiday hotel.
Open Mar to mid Nov
Rooms: 17 with private facilities
Bar Lunch 12 – 2 pm (a)
Dining Room/Restaurant Lunch 12 – 2 pm (c) – by prior arrangement
Dinner 7 – 9 pm: 7 – 8.30 pm early/late season (c)

Bed & breakfast £30 – £47
Dinner B & B £40 – £60
Early/late season breaks and 3 or 7 day reductions
Fresh local seafood including Solway salmon and lobster cooked in a variety of ways. Galloway beef and lamb.
STB Commended 4 Crowns
Credit cards: 1, 3
Proprietors: Ronald & Joan Lamb, Graeme A Lamb

Auchterarder

MAP 4

AUCHTERARDER HOUSE
Auchterarder
Perthshire PH3 1DZ
Tel: 0764 63646/7
Fax: 0764 62939

Prestige Award Winner 1989

Off B8062 Auchterarder-Crieff, 1 mile from village.
Country house hotels don't come much better than this. Auchterarder House is superb in every way and Ian and Audrey Brown are constantly striving to raise standards even higher. This fine old red sandstone mansion house is set in 17 $\frac{1}{2}$ acres of beautifully manicured lawns and mature trees. Public rooms are quite exceptional and sumptuously furnished, and the conservatory is a particularly attractive feature. The master bedrooms are so grand in scale that they might have come straight off a Hollywood set which may be one reason why ex-President Ronald Reagan and his wife chose to stay there on a recent visit to Scotland. Food in the elegant dining room is cooked and presented with the

same imagination and flair that is so evident throughout. The Browns are charming and attentive hosts and make everyone feel like a personal guest.
Open all year
Rooms: 15 with private facilities
Dining Room/Restaurant Lunch 12 – 3 pm Sun only (c) – other days by arrangement
Victorian teas in Winter Garden Conservatory 3 – 5 pm
Dinner 7 – 10 pm (f)
Reservations essential
No children
Bed & breakfast £65 – £100
Emphasis on Scottish food and local produce.
Credit cards: 1, 2, 3, 5, 6
Proprietors: Ian & Audrey Brown

DUCHALLY HOUSE HOTEL
Duchally, by Auchterarder
Perthshire PH3 1PN
Tel: 0764 63071
Fax: 0764 62464

Just off A823 Crieff-Dunfermline, 2 miles south of Auchterarder.
A fine old Victorian country manor house set in sweeping lawns and woodland. The proprietors have carried out tasteful and stylish refurbishments. The dining room and drawing room are particularly elegant and there is an attractive bar, a beautifully panelled billiard room and a lovely staircase. There are beautiful views of the Ochil Hills from both restaurants, and open log fires throughout the public areas. Menus are interesting with a clear concentration on fresh local produce, and food is very well presented. A lovely place to stay.
Open all year
Rooms: 15 with private facilities
Bar Lunch 12 – 2.30 pm (a)
Dining Room/Restaurant Lunch 12.15 – 2.30 pm (b)
Bar Supper 6 – 9.30 pm (a)
Dinner 7 – 9.30 pm (c)
Facilities for the disabled
No smoking area in restaurant
Bed & breakfast £40 – £50
Dinner B & B £55 – £65
Wild salmon with mousseline of sole. Poached turbot with a whole grain mustard sauce. Fillet of Scotch beef with a Stilton sauce. Baked duck breast with peach or pink peppercorn sauce.
STB Highly Commended 4 Crowns
Credit cards: 1, 2, 3, 5, 6
Proprietor: Maureen Raeder

THE GLENEAGLES HOTEL
Auchterarder
Perthshire PH3 1NF
Tel: 0764 62231 • Telex: 76105
Fax: 0764 62134

¹/2 mile west of A9, 10 miles north of Dunblane, 1 mile south of Auchterarder.
A magnificent hotel of international reputation and a resort in itself with an exceptional range of leisure and sporting facilities. A spectacular Scottish 'palace' in rolling Perthshire countryside built in grand style in the early part of this century and immaculately restored. Food and accommodation are of the highest standard as would be expected from the only hotel in Scotland to have been awarded the AA's highest accolade of five red stars, and they are richly deserved. In the restaurants, the best of local produce is used to create dishes with a uniquely Scottish flavour, cooked and presented to standards of international excellence. Few will experience Gleneagles without full enjoyment of the occasion and a wish to return as soon as possible. French and German spoken.
Open all year
Rooms: 236 with private facilities
Bar Lunch 12.30 – 2.30 pm (b)
Dining Room/Restaurant Lunch 12.30 – 2.30 pm (d)
Bar Supper 5 – 10 pm (c)
Dinner 7.30 – 10 pm (f)
Country Club Brasserie and Equestrian Centre Restaurant & Bar – residents/members only
No smoking area in restaurants
Bed & breakfast £195 – £260
Credit cards: 1, 2, 3, 5

Auchtermuchty

MAP 4

ARDCHOILLE FARM GUEST HOUSE
Dunshalt
Auchtermuchty KY14 7EY
Tel: 0337 28414

On B936 just outside Dunshalt village, 1¹/2 miles south of Auchtermuchty.
Donald and Isobel Steven welcome you to Ardchoille – a spacious, well appointed modern farmhouse, with superb views of the Lomond hills. Twin-bedrooms have private facilities, colour TV and tea/coffee trays with home-made butter shortbread. Large comfortable lounge. Attractive dining room with elegant china and crystal where delicious freshly prepared meals are presented with flair and imagination. Excellent base for touring, golfing or just relaxing.
Open all year
Rooms: 3 with private facilities
Dinner 7 – 8 pm (c) 4 course set menu + coffee
Dinner for non-residents only by prior arrangement
Unlicensed – guests welcome to take own wine
No dogs
No smoking in dining room
Bed & breakfast £22 – £30
Dinner B & B £37 – £50
Cream of fresh celery soup topped with golden delicious apple. Poached Tay salmon in filo pastry basket with a lemon and parsley sauce. Fillet of Aberdeen Angus beef with creamed Dunshalt mushrooms. Chocolate and almond sponge hearts with pear, crème de menthe and home-made vanilla ice-cream. Scottish cheese board.
STB Commended 3 Crowns
No credit cards
Proprietors: Donald & Isobel Steven

Aultbea

MAP 6

AULTBEA HOTEL & RESTAURANT
Seafront, Aultbea
Ross-shire IV22 2HX
Tel: 0445 731201
Fax: 0445 731214

Off A832, on seafront at Aultbea.
The Aultbea Hotel is situated in an exceptionally beautiful location at the waterside of Loch Ewe and has magnificent views over the Isle of Ewe to the Torridon Mountains. It is believed to have been built for Lord Zetland in the early 1800s. The hotel has been run by Peter and Avril Nieto for the past six years and its reputation for comfort and cuisine has continued to grow. There is a choice of eating styles – the Waterside Bistro which is open all day and where a varied menu from teas and coffees with home-baking to local fish and grills is available; and the more formal Zetland Restaurant, overlooking the loch, where three or four course daily changing table d'hôte menus are offered which feature local seafood, game and a carvery, as well as an à la carte option.
Open all year
Rooms: 8 with private facilities
Food Service 9 am – 9 pm (a-b)
Dinner 7 – 9 pm (c)
Bed & breakfast £25 – £40
Dinner B & B £44 – £60
Local salmon, lobster, prawns and crab. Prime Highland beef and venison. Freshly baked bread.
STB Commended 4 Crowns
Credit cards: 1, 2
Proprietors: Peter & Avril Nieto

Aviemore

MAP 6

THE OLD BRIDGE INN
Dalfaber Road, Aviemore
Inverness-shire PH22 1PU
Tel: 0479 811137
Fax: 0479 810116

200 yards from route to Cairngorms from Aviemore.
A popular and cosy licensed restaurant in a rather quaint building by the river with tables and benches outside, and well patronised by locals and tourists alike. It operates as a conventional bistro and the cooking is good with some innovative touches. The overall atmosphere is pleasing and the whole experience represents value for money. There are Highland evenings every Tuesday and barbecues on good weekends during Summer.
Open all year
Bar Lunch 12 – 2 pm Mon to Sat: 12.30 – 2 pm Sun (a)
Bar Supper 6 – 9 pm (a)
Facilities for the disabled
No smoking area in restaurant
Home-made soups, buidhe and pâtés. Local game and poultry, salmon and seafoods. Superb cheeses – and Ecclefechan Tart!
No credit cards
Proprietor: Nigel Reid

STAKIS AVIEMORE FOUR SEASONS HOTEL

Aviemore
Inverness-shire PH22 1PF
Tel: 0479 810681 • Telex: 75213
Fax: 0479 810862

Country location adjacent to Aviemore Centre.

This large modern hotel provides the ideal base for a visit to Aviemore – the popular Highland leisure resort – and the scenic Spey Valley. The comfortable bedrooms are tastefully decorated and well equipped, and the public rooms are spacious and elegant. The cocktail bar is a focal point in which guests gather for a pre-prandial drink and discuss their day's activities before adjourning to the Four Seasons Restaurant to enjoy some of the Chef's specialities. The hotel's leisure centre houses a heated indoor pool, spa, sauna, sunbeds and gymnasium.

Open all year
Rooms: 89 with private facilities
Bar Lunch 12 – 2 pm (a)
Dining Room/Restaurant Lunch 12.30 – 2 pm Sun only (a)
Dinner 7 – 9.30 pm (c)
Dinner B & B £37 (min 2 nights stay)
Highland game platter, smoked salmon roulade. Salmon and dill butter. Scottish venison, fillet of Angus beef.
STB Commended 5 Crowns
Credit cards: 1, 2, 3, 5, 6

Ayr

MAP 1

BURNS MONUMENT HOTEL

Alloway
Ayr KA7 4PQ
Tel: 0292 42466

In Alloway village on B7024, 2 miles south of Ayr town centre.

An elegant and charming historic hotel located in the famous Alloway village. Splendidly situated in its own grounds with landscaped gardens along the banks of the River Doon with the backdrop of Burns Monument and Auld Brig of Doon. Locally renowned restaurant using only the best of fresh local produce. French and German spoken.

Open all year
Rooms: 9, 8 with private facilities
Bar Lunch 12 – 2.15 pm (a)
Dining Room/Restaurant Lunch 12 – 2.15 pm (b)
Bar Supper 5 – 9.45 pm (a)

Dinner 5 – 9.45 pm (c)
No smoking area in restaurant
Bed & breakfast £35 – £45
Dinner B & B £51 – £61
Room Rate £30 – £40
Imaginative cuisine featuring locally caught seafood, with meat, game and poultry from the hotel's farm; poached fresh local salmon, medallions of Aberdeen Angus fillet steak. Home-made sweets and cheeses.
STB Commended 4 Crowns
Credit cards: 1, 2, 3, 5, 6
Proprietor: Robert Gilmour

FOUTERS BISTRO RESTAURANT

2A Academy Street, Ayr
Ayrshire KA7 1HS
Tel: 0292 261391

Town centre, opposite Town Hall and Tourist Information Centre.

Fouters goes from strength to strength each year, enhancing its reputation for quality, interest and value. It is centrally situated in the vaults of an old bank and Laurie and Fran Black have made full use of the architecture of the place to create a warm, intimate and friendly atmosphere. The menu is interesting and is remarkable value for money. It draws heavily on good local seafood and the abundance of game and poultry from Ayrshire's rich agricultural land. This is a place with a genuine welcome and superb food tastefully presented. Interestingly different and much in demand. Do book in advance.

Open all year except Christmas + Boxing Days, 1 + 2 Jan
Dining Room/Restaurant Lunch 12 – 2 pm except Sun Mon (b)
Dinner 6.30 – 10.30 pm except Mon (d)
Closed Mon
Ayrshire pheasant with game sauce. Red deer with orange and Glayva butter sauce. Local Guinea fowl with redcurrant and green peppercorn sauce. Smoked chicken and venison. Seafood a speciality.
Credit cards: 1, 2, 3, 5, 6
Proprietors: Laurie & Fran Black

THE HUNNY POT

37 Beresford Terrace
Ayr KA7 2EU
Tel: 0292 263239

In the town centre of Ayr, close to Burns' Statue Square.

This small but popular and attractive coffee shop and health food restaurant is run personally by Felicity Thomson. Pine furniture and teddy bear theme give the place character.

Open all year except Christmas + Boxing Days, 1 + 2 Jan
Meals served all day from 10 am – 10 pm (a)
Traditional afternoon teas served 2 – 5.30 pm Sun
Unlicensed
No smoking area in restaurant
All home-made soups, scones, brown sugar meringues, cakes and dish of the day. Puddings include seasonal fruit crumbles, hazelnut meringue cake. Scottish cheeses with oatcakes.
No credit cards
Proprietor: Felicity Thomson

LA NAUTIQUE

28 New Bridge Street, Ayr
Ayrshire KA7 1SX
Tel: 0292 269573

In the centre of Ayr opposite Town Hall.

As the name 'La Nautique' implies, this restaurant has a strong nautical theme throughout the interior with ships' figureheads and naval memorabilia conveying an 'on board' ambience. Lunchtime meals and snacks are available. In the evening a supper menu is offered in the Below Decks Bistro and a more extensive à la carte menu featuring a wide range of dishes is served in the Captain's Gallery. There is a light French touch to good quality local Scottish products.

Open all year
Bar Lunch 12 – 2.15 pm except Sun (a)
Bar Supper 6 – 9.45 pm except Sun (a)
Dinner 7 – 9.45 pm except Sun (b)
Closed Sun
Evening à la carte intermingles French haute cuisine with traditional Scottish fare using top quality local produce.
Credit cards: 1, 2, 3
Proprietor: Andrew Kinniburgh

PICKWICK HOTEL
19 Racecourse Road
Ayr KA7 2TD
Tel: 0292 260111
Fax: 0292 285348

On A719 Ayr-Dunure Road, 1/2 mile from Ayr town centre and a few minutes walk from the seafront.
A magnificent period character building set in its own extensive landscaped gardens and featuring a traditional Dickensian theme characteristic of its name. The hotel is family run and features 15 excellent bedrooms, all with full private facilities. In addition to the hotel dining room, there is the Ocean Room restaurant which has its own separate entrance. Within the sumptuous surroundings of this restaurant has been created the atmosphere of the old ocean-going liners. There is an interesting seafood menu complemented by a wine list for connoisseurs. French and German spoken.
Open all year
Rooms: 15 with private facilities
Bar Lunch 12 – 2.15 pm (a)
Dining Room/Restaurant Lunch 12 – 2.15 pm (a)
Bar Supper 5 – 10 pm (a)
Dinner 5 – 10 pm (c)
Dogs accepted by prior arrangement
No smoking area in restaurant
Bed & breakfast £45 – £55
Dinner B & B £60 – £77
Poached local salmon and prawns, locally caught sole fillet stuffed with prawns, suprême of chicken lined with smoked salmon and goats milk cheese, fillets of prime Aberdeen Angus steak stuffed with haggis.
STB Commended 4 Crowns
Credit cards: 1, 2, 3, 5
Proprietor: Robert S Gilmour

THE STABLES RESTAURANT & COFFEE HOUSE
Queen's Court, Sandgate
Ayr KA7 1BD
Tel: 0292 283704

Immediately behind the Tourist Information Centre in the Sandgate.
In the centre of Ayr is a tiny Georgian courtyard which is a haven of little shops with a tea garden. The Stables were built of local stone probably in the late 1760s. The dinner menu (evenings only) could best be described as ethnic Scottish. The Coffee House offers lighter fare made on the premises. Children are welcome. In the evenings menus available in French,

German, Italian and Spanish.
Open all year except Christmas + Boxing Days, 1 + 2 Jan
Coffee House open 10 am – 10 pm (a) except Sun
Dinner 6.30 – 10 pm except Sun Mon (b)
Closed Sun
No smoking room – daytime only
Smoking discouraged
Mussels in syboe butter, roasted lamb carved at table, venison and juniper pie, cranachan and local cheeses. Wines from Moniack Castle and English vineyards. Family owned smokehouse (Craigrossie) provides smoked fish and meats.
Credit cards: 1, 2, 3
Proprietor: Ed Baines

Ballachulish

MAP 6

THE BALLACHULISH HOTEL
Ballachulish
Argyll PA39 4JY
Tel: 08552 606• Fax: 08552 629

On A828 at the Ballachulish Bridge.
The Ballachulish Hotel commands an inspiring panorama over Loch Linnhe to the peaks of Morvern and Ardgour. In this friendly family owned hotel, careful restoration and refurbishment have ensured a skilful blend of traditional style with modern, international standards. Gracious baronial lounges lead to the welcoming Cocktail Bar and the Loch View Restaurant. Guests enjoy complimentary membership of 'The Isles' pool and leisure centre at the Ballachulish's sister hotel nearby. French and German spoken.
Open all year
Rooms: 30 with private facilities
Bar Lunch 12 – 2.30 pm (a)
Dining Room/Restaurant Lunch 12 – 2.30 pm (a)
Bar Supper 6 – 10 pm (a)
Dinner 7 – 10 pm (c)
Note: during High Season meals served all day 12 – 10 pm
Bed & breakfast £29.50 – £52
Dinner B & B £49 – £71.50
Smoked Highland goose breast in lemon and lime essence, roast saddle of venison with juniper berry and Scottish wine sauce. Pheasant Glenarthur filled with asparagus forcemeat. Highlander's toffee pudding with whisky butterscotch sauce.
STB Commended 4 Crowns
Credit cards: 1, 3
Proprietors: The Young Family

Ballantrae

MAP 1

BALKISSOCK LODGE
Ballantrae
Ayrshire KA26 0LP
Tel: 046 583 537

Take first inland road off A77, south of River Stinchar at Ballantrae (signed to Laggan caravans) and follow for 3 1/2 miles. Turn right at T-junction and continue along single track 'no through road' to its end.
Leaving the A77 immediately south of Ballantrae takes you at once into another world of gentle rolling hills, total peace and quiet and wonderful panoramic views. It also takes you to Balkissock which has recently been refurbished and takes full advantage of its location to provide a thoroughly relaxing atmosphere. Janet and Adrian Beale are thoughtful hosts and Janet's skill in the kitchen is evident in her imaginative menus and the degree to which she makes use of the fine supply of local produce for which Ayrshire is famous. Occasional speciality and gourmet events are held for serious lovers of good food. Vegetarians and vegans can make their requirements known in advance and be well looked after. There is a wealth of sporting and recreational activities in the locality.
Open all year
Rooms: 3 with private facilities
Dinner 7 – 9 pm (c)
Non-residents – by prior arrangement
Unlicensed – guests welcome to take own wine
No dogs
No smoking in dining room
Bed & breakfast £22.50 – £40
Dinner B & B £32 – £50
Home-baked herb or granary rolls. Interesting soups. Venison with blueberries. Local salmon with dill and champagne. Duckling with cloves, honey and lemon. Ballantrae Bay lobster. Carrot roulade with lemon and fresh ginger. Brandy snap baskets with home-made ice-cream. Cranachan. Pavlova. Scottish cheeseboard.
STB Commended 3 Crowns
Credit cards: 1, 3
Proprietors: Adrian & Janet Beale

COSSES

Ballantrae
Ayrshire KA26 0LR
Tel: 046 583 363 • Fax: 046 583 598

From A77 at southern end of Ballantrae, take inland road signed to Laggan. Cosses is c. 2 miles on right.

Cosses is one of those special places that one loves to discover – converted farm buildings tucked away in a remote and secluded valley of lovely garden and woodlands. It is only a couple of miles from the well travelled A77 but it is in a different world. The accommodation is limited – two double bedrooms each with private bathroom – but the larger, in an out-building, is really a delightful little suite of sitting room, large bedroom and large bathroom. The sitting room can be converted into another bedroom if required, making a compact family unit. Robin and Susan Crosthwaite are charming hosts and invite you into their own sitting room for a complimentary aperitif before dinner. Susan is an accomplished Cordon Bleu cook and her meals are exquisite testimony to the fact. Though she may only be cooking for two or four people she goes to much trouble to prepare an inviting and well balanced menu and to make you feel like her own personal dinner guests. Seasonal vegetables, herbs and fruit are from the kitchen garden. In this lovely part of south west Scotland this is a place you would not want to miss. Book early!

Open all year
Rooms: 2 with private facilities
Dinner 7 – 9.30 pm (c)
Residents only
Unlicensed – guests welcome to take own wine
Bed & breakfast £26 – £40
Dinner B & B £44 – £60
McLellan cheddar cheese souffle. Local prawns rolled in smoked Scottish salmon. Crailoch pheasant with whisky, cream and thyme. Ballantrae lobster. Home-made shortbread layered with cream and raspberries from the garden. Selection of Scottish cheese.
STB Highly Commended 3 Crowns
No credit cards
Proprietors: Susan & Robin Crosthwaite

Ballater

MAP 5

BALGONIE COUNTRY HOUSE

Braemar Place
Ballater AB35 5RQ
Tel: 03397 55482
Fax: 03397 55482

Off A93 at western edge of Ballater.

Built in 1899 in the heart of Royal Deeside, Balgonie is now a small country house hotel set in tranquil mature gardens overlooking the golf course towards the hills of Glenmuick. There is much to appeal to the visitor to this area, ranging from hill-walking, golf and fishing, touring castles and distilleries, or simply relaxing in peaceful surroundings. Balgonie makes an ideal home from which to explore the many facets of the area. The menu is well balanced and interesting, reflecting the wealth of local produce such as game, salmon, beef and lamb with seafood fresh from the coast, and herbs and soft fruits from Balgonie's own garden. French and German spoken.

Open all year
Rooms: 9 with private facilities
Dining Room/Restaurant Lunch 12.30 – 2 pm (b)
Dinner 7 – 9 pm (d-e)
Facilities for the disabled
No smoking in dining room
Bed & breakfast £40 – £50
Dinner B & B £65 – £75
Terrine of venison. Trellis of salmon and turbot with watercress sauce. Rich butterscotch flan topped with dark chocolate mousse.
STB Deluxe 4 Crowns
Credit cards: 1, 2, 3
Proprietors: John & Priscilla Finnie

THE COACH HOUSE HOTEL

Netherley Place, Ballater
Aberdeenshire AB35 5QE
Tel: 03397 55462
Fax: 03397 55462

Beside church green in centre of Ballater.

The Coach House is conveniently situated in central Ballater beside the village green. Ballater is probably the heart of Royal Deeside and an ideal base from which to explore the many castles, stately homes and whisky distilleries so plentiful in the area. There is a cosy lounge bar where locals and visitors alike assemble to chat and the restaurant offers good seasonal produce, carefully presented and served with courtesy.

Open all year
Rooms: 6 with private facilities
Bar Lunch 12 – 2.15 pm (b)
Dining Room/Restaurant Lunch 12 – 2.15 pm (b)
Bar Supper 5 – 9 pm (b)
Dinner 7 – 9 pm (c)
Bed & breakfast £24 – £30
Dinner B & B £40 – £46
Deeside smoked salmon with dill mustard. Guinea fowl in white wine, mushroom and shallot cream sauce. Venison Macduff. Trio of lamb cutlets in a ginger sauce. Aberdeen Angus steaks.
STB Commended 3 Crowns
Credit cards: 1, 2, 3, 5
Proprietors: Jim & Gena Campbell

CRAIGENDARROCH HOTEL & COUNTRY CLUB

Braemar Road, Ballater
Royal Deeside AB35 5XA
Tel: 03397 55858 • Telex: 739952
Fax: 03397 55447

On A93 western end of Ballater, near Balmoral.

The Victorian red sandstone mansion at the heart of this luxury resort hotel was once the Highland retreat of the Keiller family of Dundee. Craigendarroch boasts three restaurants with fine cuisine complementing the splendour of the hotel and countryside surrounding its hillside location. The Oaks and Lochnagar Restaurants are open to non-residents, the other facilities including Cafe Jardin are for members and residents only.

Open all year
Rooms: 50 with private facilities
Dinner (The Oaks) 7 – 10 pm (c-f)
Dinner (Lochnagar) 7 – 10 pm Thu to Sat (b-c)

Credit Card Code		Meal Price Code	
1.	Access/Mastercard/Eurocard	(a)	under £10
2.	American Express	(b)	£10 – £15
3.	Visa	(c)	£15 – £20
4.	Carte Bleu	(d)	£20 – £25
5.	Diners Club	(e)	£25 – £30
6.	Mastercharge	(f)	over £30

Cafe Jardin (members and residents only): Lunch 12 – 2.30 pm (a-b)
Dinner 5 – 10 pm (a-b)
Bed & breakfast £99 – £175
Pan-fried rack of lamb. Confit of wild duck and sautéd sweetbreads. Crayfish tails with strips of fennel, shallots, fine tomato, Pernod and saffron rice. Hot apple and black cherry pancakes.
STB Highly Commended 5 Crowns
Credit cards: 1, 2, 3, 5, 6

DARROCH LEARG HOTEL
Braemar Road, Ballater
Aberdeenshire AB35 5UX
Tel: 03397 55443
Fax: 03397 55443

At the western edge of Ballater on the road to Braemar.
Originally a Victorian country house, the Darroch Learg is now a family owned hotel of 20 bedrooms. There are log fires in the drawing room and a separate smoke room where pre-dinner drinks can be enjoyed in a relaxing and welcoming atmosphere. The dining room is a conservatory with a bright and airy feeling and a wonderful outlook into the Grampian Hills. The head chef and his team use the best of Scottish beef, lamb, game and fish to prepare the interesting and daily changing menu.
Open 28 Dec to 30 Nov
Rooms: 20 with private facilities
Bar Lunch 12.30 – 2 pm (a)
Dining Room/Restaurant Lunch 12.30 – 2 pm Sun only (b): other days – by advance booking only
Dinner 7 – 9 pm (c)
No smoking in dining room
Bed & breakfast £32 – £42
Dinner B & B £44 – £60.50
Home-made pheasant and orange terrine. Saddle of Scotch lamb stuffed with venison forcemeat. Breast of chicken with wild mushrooms. Wild salmon with asparagus mousse. Whisky syllabub.
STB Highly Commended 4 Crowns
Credit cards: 1, 3
Proprietors: The Franks Family

THE GLEN LUI HOTEL
Invercauld Road, Ballater
Aberdeenshire AB35 5RP
Tel: 03397 55402
Fax: 03397 55545

Off A93 in Ballater.
The picturesque little village of Ballater is, of course, the very heart of Royal Deeside, an area in which there is so much to see and do. The Glen Lui Hotel is therefore well placed for those who wish to explore and enjoy the area. It is a small friendly country house in a quiet corner of the village with delightful views over the golf course to Lochnagar. Bedrooms are very comfortable and well equipped and there are a number of executive suites. A great deal of imagination goes into the preparation of the menus and food is first class with a suitably supportive and extensive wine list.
Open Mar to Nov
Rooms: 19 with private facilities
Bar Lunch 12 – 2 pm (a)
Bar Supper 6.30 – 9.30 pm (a)
Dinner 7 – 9.30 pm (d)
No smoking in dining room
Bed & breakfast from £25
Dinner B & B rates on application
Room Rate from £40
Fillet of red snapper in a paper parcel with a julienne of vegetables. Wild Scottish raspberry parfait with a Drambuie sauce.
STB Commended 4 Crowns
Credit cards: 1, 2, 3
Proprietors: Lorraine & Serge Geraud

THE GREEN INN
9 Victoria Road
Ballater AB35 5QQ
Tel: 03397 55701

In centre of Ballater on village green.
A granite-built former temperance hotel overlooking the village green, which is now a small licensed restaurant with three letting bedrooms. The emphasis is on fresh food and maximum use of local produce. The Chef's specials change every night reflecting the best of what is available to him.
Open all year except Christmas Day, 1 Jan + 2 wks Oct
Rooms: 3 with private facilities
Dining Room/Restaurant Lunch (Feb to Oct) 12.30 – 1.30 pm except Thu (a)
Dinner 7 – 9 pm (c)
Bed & breakfast from £20
Dinner B & B from £39.50

Venison, salmon, game in season, baked crab with a chive and cheese sauce, seafood gâteau. Hot strawberries in a Drambuie sauce with home-made vanilla ice-cream. Local cheeses.
STB Commended 3 Crowns
Credit cards: 1, 3, 6
Proprietors: Carol & Jeffrey Purves

Balquhidder

MAP 4

MONACHYLE MHOR FARMHOUSE/HOTEL
Balquhidder, Lochearnhead
Perthshire FK19 8PQ
Tel: 08774 622

North of Callander A84 to Balquhidder. 7 miles beyond village at end of lochside single track road.
In a land of mountains and lochs, Monachyle Mhor sits in its own 2,000 acres of farmland in the heart of The Braes o' Balquhidder. It is a small family run farmhouse/hotel of great character and offers a unique blend of modern comfort and country living. All bedrooms are en suite, and in the restaurant and cosy bar you will find good food and a wealth of hospitality. For those who like to go as they please, the hotel has three luxury cottages each of which sleeps six people.
Open all year
Rooms: 4 with private facilities
Bar Meals 11 am – 10.30 pm (a)
Dining Room/Restaurant Lunch 12 – 2 pm (b)
Dinner 7.30 – 10 pm (b-c)
No dogs
Bed & breakfast £19.50 – £21
Dinner B & B £32 – £35
Mousseline of lemon sole with fresh herbs. Breast of Monachyle grouse with juniper and Madeira, lightly pan-fried. Terrine of Summer fruits. Bread home-baked daily.
STB Commended 3 Crowns
Credit cards: 1, 3
Proprietors: Rob & Jean Lewis

Banchory

MAP 5

HORSE MILL RESTAURANT (NATIONAL TRUST FOR SCOTLAND)

Crathes Castle, Banchory
Kincardineshire AB3 3QJ
Tel: 033044 634
(out of season: 033044 525)
Fax: 033044 797

Royal Deeside (A93) 3 miles east of Banchory.

An attractive and unusual restaurant with helpful staff and a friendly atmosphere. Situated in a converted circular horse mill it is in the grounds of the picturesque 16th century Crathes Castle famous for its painted ceilings, fine furniture and interesting decorations. The walled garden of almost four acres is considered to be among the finest in Britain: it includes a notable collection of unusual plants and has its own plant sales centre. A visitor centre contains permanent exhibitions and a gift shop. The grounds extend to 600 acres, with some 15 miles of well marked woodland trails. Frequent events add to the attraction of this charming property.
Open 1 Apr to 31 Oct
Food service 12 – 5.30 pm (a)
Dinner – booked parties as arranged (b)
Private room available
Facilities for the disabled
No smoking in restaurant
Coffee or tea with home-baked scones and cakes. Lunch from an à la carte menu with a Scottish flavour includes soup, traditional dishes and sweets, or freshly made sandwiches and salads – all home-made.
Credit cards: 1, 3

INVERY HOUSE HOTEL

Bridge of Feugh, Banchory
Kincardineshire AB3 3NJ
Tel: 03302 4782 • Telex: 73737
Fax: 03302 4712

B974, 1 mile south of Banchory.

A superb country house hotel set in acres of wooded grounds on the banks of the River Feugh on Royal Deeside. It is furnished tastefully throughout, and to a very high standard. The principal bedrooms are quite exceptional with some of the bathrooms almost as large as an average bedroom. There are thoughtful personal touches. The public rooms feature antiques and paintings. The food lives up to the same excellent standards of the rest of the hotel and is clearly prepared with great care and presented with panache. There are lovely local walks, and golf, fishing and shooting can be arranged for guests. Invery House is very much in the 'exceptional' category.
Open all year
Rooms: 14 with private facilities
Dining Room/Restaurant Lunch 12.30 – 1.45 pm (d)
Dinner 7.15 – 9.45 pm (f)
No smoking in restaurant
Bed & breakfast £55 – £95
Dinner B & B £80 – £130
Venison with brambles; game pie, baked sea trout, lobster, salmon en croûte.
STB Deluxe 5 Crowns
Credit cards: 1, 2, 3, 5, 6
Proprietors: Stewart & Sheila Spence

RAEMOIR HOUSE HOTEL

Banchory
Kincardineshire AB3 4ED
Tel: 03302 4884 • Telex: 73315
Fax: 03302 2171

On A890 Royal Deeside.

Beautiful historic house set in 3,500 acres of wooded grounds and parkland. Many rooms and suites face south overlooking the nine hole mini golf course and tennis court, and have tapestried walls and antique furniture. This family owned hotel is proud of its Scottish cuisine carefully prepared by award winning chefs.
Open 18 Jan to 31 Dec
Rooms: 28 with private facilities
Bar Lunch 12.30 – 2 pm except Sun (a)
Dining Room/Restaurant Lunch Sun only (b) – or by arrangement
Dinner 7.30 – 9 pm (d)
Bed & breakfast £55 to £85
Dinner B & B £77 to £108
Cream of pheasant soup, game consommé. Smoked salmon roulade, venison, game, fish pâtés and terrines. Poached Dee salmon, roast venison, grouse, Aberdeen Angus beef, rosetted Scottish lamb.
STB Commended 4 Crowns
Credit cards: 1, 2, 3, 5, 6
Proprietors: Kit Sabin,
Judy & Mike Ollis

Banknock
Bonnybridge

MAP 4

GLENSKIRLIE HOUSE

Kilsyth Road, Banknock
Bonnybridge
Stirlingshire FK4 1UF
Tel: 0324 840201

A803 Bonnybridge-Kilsyth road.

Glenskirlie is a small country house set in lovely gardens. Its restaurant has a cosy comfortable atmosphere and has been earning a fine reputation for the standard of its food. Both à la carte and bar lunches are available and when weather permits the bar lunch can be taken outdoors. There is much emphasis on daily fresh specials depending on the availability of produce from the market and there are some intriguing dishes and imaginative sauces. A well presented sweet trolley and a good selection of cheeses round off the menu.
Open all year except Boxing Day, 27 Dec, 1 + 2 Jan
Bar Lunch 12 – 2 pm (a)
Dining Room/Restaurant Lunch 12 – 2 pm (d)
Dinner 6.30 – 9.30 pm except Mon (d)
Closed Mon evening
Facilities for the disabled
Selection of fish and seasonal game.
Credit cards: 1, 2, 3, 5, 6
Proprietors: John & Linda Macaloney

Beattock

MAP 1

AUCHEN CASTLE HOTEL & RESTAURANT

Beattock, Moffat
Dumfriesshire DG10 9SH
Tel: 06833 407
Fax: 06833 667

Direct access from A74, 1 mile north of Beattock Village, 55 miles south of Edinburgh and Glasgow.

Gracious country house spectacularly situated in 50 acres with fine shrubs and trees. It was built by General Johnston in 1849 and became the home of the William Younger family. The hotel is comfortably furnished and decorated to complement the original features which have been retained. Ten of the 25 bedrooms are in a modern wing. Auchen

Castle is ideally placed for visiting the Border Country. Located almost mid way between Carlisle and Glasgow or Edinburgh, it has long been a popular place at which to break a journey either for an accommodation stop or meal time break. Children welcome. A little French spoken.
Open all year except 3 wks over Christmas + New Year
Rooms: 25 with private facilities
Bar Lunch 12 – 2 pm (a)
Dinner 7 – 9 pm (c)
Bed & breakfast £25 – £35
Dinner B & B £36 – £51
Local lamb, poultry, beef and pork. Game in season. Salmon and shellfish.
STB Commended 4 Crowns
Credit cards: 1, 2, 3, 5, 6
Proprietors: Bob & Hazel Beckh

Beauly

MAP 6

CHRIALDON HOTEL
Station Road, Beauly
Inverness-shire IV4 7EH
Tel: 0463 782336
On A862, 12 miles from Inverness.
Step through the elegant entrance into a timbered hallway of highland charm. Chrialdon is a very Scottish house – elegant, yet informal, small yet spacious, where comfort and enjoyment of good food are of the utmost importance. Set in the village of Beauly, it provides an ideal base for touring the Highlands.
Open Jan to Nov
Rooms: 8 , 5 with private facilities
Dinner 7 – 8.30 pm (b)
No smoking in restaurant
Bed & breakfast £17.50 – £24
Dinner B & B £29 – £36
Residents only
Home-made soups and rolls. Venison, salmon, trout with complementary sauces. Pecan nut tart, home-made pastries and various rich ices.
STB Commended 2 Crowns
Credit cards: 1, 3
Proprietor: Jennifer Bond

PRIORY HOTEL
The Square, Beauly
Inverness-shire IV4 7BX
Tel: 0463 782309
Fax: 0463 782531
A862, 12 miles north-west of Inverness.
The Priory is a bustling local hotel with a reputation for particularly good food and efficient friendly service. Situated in the main square in Beauly – close to the ancient Priory ruins. The hotel, which has been recently refurbished to a very high standard, is an ideal base for touring the beautiful north and west of Scotland. Families with children welcome.
Open all year
Rooms: 24 with private facilities
Bar Lunch 12 – 2 pm (a)
Dining Room/Restaurant Lunch 12 – 2 pm (a)
Bar Supper 5.30 – 9.30 pm (a)
Dinner 7.15 – 9.30 pm (b)
Selection of food available all day
Bed & breakfast £27.50 – £37.50
Dinner B & B £42.50 – £52.50
Haggis, chef's pâté, Orkney herring. Salmon, trout, Scotch lamb, Aberdeen Angus beef, speciality whisky steaks. Extensive sweet trolley. Vegetarian dishes.
STB Commended 4 Crowns
Credit cards: 1, 2, 3, 5, 6
Proprietors: Stuart & Eveline Hutton

Benbecula
Isle of

MAP 7

DARK ISLAND HOTEL
Liniclate, Isle of Benbecula
Western Isles PA88 5PJ
Tel: 0870 2414/2283
Benbecula lies between North and South Uist (Western Isles). Hotel is c. 6 miles from the airport.
This unusually named hotel is of modern low ranch-style construction and is acclaimed as one of the best hotels in the Hebrides. There is a comfortable and spacious residents' lounge and a dining room which caters for everything from intimate dinners to major functions. An ideal spot for exploring the adjacent islands. Fishing, golf, bird-watching and interesting archaeological sites.
Open all year
Rooms: 42, 35 with private facilities
Bar Lunch 12 – 2 pm (a)

Dining Room/Restaurant Lunch 12 – 2 pm (a)
Bar Supper 6 – 9.30 pm (a)
Dinner 6 – 9.30 pm (b)
Bed & breakfast £25 – £60
Dinner B & B £39 – £90
Lobster, crab, scallops and venison.
STB Commended 4 Crowns
Credit cards: 1, 3

Biggar

MAP 2

HARTREE COUNTRY HOUSE HOTEL
Biggar
Lanarkshire ML12 6JJ
Tel: 0899 21027
Fax: 0899 21259
Just off A702 on western outskirts of Biggar.
A fine old baronial building dating back to the 15th century, and now a delightful country house hotel in peaceful and pleasant Lanarkshire countryside. It has been extensively refurbished to provide modern standards of comfort in elegant public rooms and bedrooms. The menu includes many Scottish specialities and there is a wide range of choice from bar lunches to à la carte dinners. Almost equidistant (about 40 minutes) from both Edinburgh and Glasgow, Hartree House makes a very convenient and central base.
Open all year
Rooms: 14 with private facilities
Bar Lunch 12 – 2 pm (a)
Dining Room/Restaurant Lunch 12 – 2 pm (b-c)
Bar Supper 6 – 9 pm (a)
Dinner 6 – 8.30 pm (c)
No dogs
Bed & breakfast £33 – £40
Dinner B & B from £43
Local smoked venison with a malt whisky vinaigrette. Scottish salmon pan-fried with fennel, peppers and onion served with a rich crab sauce. Home-made honey and Drambuie ice-cream.
STB Commended 3 Crowns
Credit cards: 1, 2, 3
Proprietors: John & Anne Charlton, Robert & Susan Reed

SHIELDHILL COUNTRY HOUSE HOTEL
Quothquan, Biggar
Lanarkshire ML12 6NA
Tel: 0899 20035
Fax: 0899 21092

Prestige Award Winner 1990

Signposted off main street (A702) in Biggar, 4 miles west taking B7016 for 2 miles then follow signs to hotel.
Christine Dunstan and Jack Greenwald have created a splendid country house hotel from this historic building dating back to 1199, and situated amidst pleasant rolling hills and farmlands. Great care and good taste are evident in every aspect of its furnishings and fittings. Laura Ashley fabrics and wallpapers are much in evidence. Bedrooms are superb some with jacuzzis and four-posters and all with private bathrooms. The same attention to detail has been given to the food which is of very high standard, thoroughly creative and interesting and demonstrating the skill of a master chef behind the scenes.
Open all year
Rooms: 11 with private facilities
Bar Lunch 12 – 2 pm Sun Sat only (b)
Dining Room/Restaurant Lunch 12 – 2.30 pm Sun Sat only (d) - reservations essential
Dinner 7 – 9 pm (d)
No children
No dogs
No smoking in restaurant
Bed & breakfast £49 – £80
Dinner B & B £69 – £100
Fillet of veal stuffed with strawberries on a strawberry and sage cream sauce. Roast saddle of venison with a raspberry essence topped with a ginger and cream sauce. STB Highly Commended 4 Crowns
Credit cards: 1, 2, 3, 5, 6
Proprietors: C Dunstan & J Greenwald

Blair Atholl

MAP 4

THE LOFT RESTAURANT
Invertilt Road, Blair Atholl
Perthshire PH18 5TE
Tel: 0796 481377
6 miles north of Pitlochry in the heart of Blair Atholl.
In a world where restaurants are often lookalikes it is refreshing to come across places like this. The Loft has been

splendidly converted from a former hayloft and retains all the genuine characteristics of twisted oak beams, stone walls and oak floors. Chef/patron Martin Hollis, is an award winning chef and, with his wife Stella, does his utmost to ensure that customers leave satisfied. Menus are compiled from available fresh local produce and are imaginative. The Loft is popular and advance booking, especially for evening meals, is strongly advised.
Open Mar to Dec, but weekends only in Nov + Dec
Light Meals (Terrace & Gallery menu) available 10 am – 6 pm except Sun (a)
Dining Room/Restaurant Lunch 12.30 – 5 pm Sun only (a)
Bistro Supper 6.30 – 9.30 pm except Sun Fri Sat (b)
Dinner 7.30 – 9.30 pm Sun Fri Sat only (c-d)
Table licence
Children welcome – lunchtime only
A chicken and smoked salmon roulade filled with scampi tails on a lime and pink peppercorn cream. Fresh Oban mussels with herbs, shallots, wine and cream. Fillet of Scotch lamb with a morel and chanterelle mousse on a rosemary and red wine essence.
No credit cards
Proprietor: Martin Hollis

WOODLANDS
St Andrews Crescent, Blair Atholl
Perthshire PH18 5SX
Tel: 0796 481 403
A9, 7 miles north of Pitlochry.
Woodlands was built in 1903 and maintains most original features including service bells. Cheerful and comfortable, the house is situated down a quiet lane, with a sheltered garden. No TV in bedrooms. Good selection of freshly made real teas always available. Guests introduced over a glass before

dinner. Leisurely breakfasts with freshly baked bread. Most important house feature – no hurry! All this while gazing at Ben-y-Vrackie! A tranquil atmosphere prevails.
Open all year
Rooms: 4
Dinner at 7.30 pm (b)
Residents only
Unlicensed
Bed & breakfast £17 – £20
Dinner B & B £27 – £30
Rannoch venison in red wine and juniper berries. All home-made preserves – including rowan jelly. Lewis salmon, jugged Buckie kippers. Nut soups and vegetarian dishes.
No credit cards
Proprietor: Dolina MacLennan

Blairgowrie

MAP 4

GLENISLA HOTEL
nr Blairgowrie
Perthshire
PH11 8PH
Tel: 057 582 223
From Blairgowrie, A93 for 9 miles then B951 into Glenisla – c. 6 miles. From Alyth, B954 – 9 miles to Glenisla.
There is a lot of atmosphere in this old coaching inn that dates back to the late 17th century. The bar with its oak beams and log fires prides itself on hand-pumped real ales and is a splendid place for a chat with the locals over a drink or a good bar meal. The restaurant menu is refreshingly straightforward and unpretentious, yet offering a good choice for each course and real value for money. The place itself is steeped in history and the proprietors, Michael and Kirsten Bartholomew, are intent on retaining all that is best of it. An excellent base or stopping place in the picturesque valley of Glenisla.
Open all year
Rooms: 6 with private facilities
Bar Lunch 12.30 – 3 pm (b)
Dining Room/Restaurant Lunch 12.30 – 2.30 pm (c)
Bar Supper 6 – 9 pm (c)
Dinner 6.30 – 8.45 pm except Sun (c)
Facilities for the disabled
No smoking area in restaurant
Bed & breakfast £25 – £28
Dinner B & B £38 – £43
Whole prawns sautéed in garlic butter. Local lamb cutlets, grilled and served

with Cumberland jelly. Fillet of local
salmon, grilled and served with
Hollandaise sauce.
STB Commended 3 Crowns
Credit cards: 1, 3, 6
Proprietors: Michael & Kirsten
Bartholomew

THE OLD BANK HOUSE
Brown Street, Blairgowrie
Perthshire PH10 6EX
Tel: 0250 872902
Centre of Blairgowrie.
The Old Bank House is a tastefully
restored red sandstone Georgian town
house within beautiful gardens. This is a
family run hotel which has a warm and
hospitable atmosphere and offering fine
food and wines. Roaring log fires are a
feature, and all the bedrooms are en
suite with colour televisions and
tea/coffee making facilities. The Old
Bank House is an ideal base for those
with an interest in golf, fishing, hill-
walking or touring the beautiful
Perthshire countryside.
Open all year except Christmas Day
Rooms: 9 with private facilities
*Dining Room/Restaurant Lunch (a) –
on request*
Dinner 7 – 8.30 pm (b)
No smoking in restaurant
Bed & breakfast £19.50 – £27.50
Dinner B & B £32 – £40
*Home-made soups, pâtés and desserts,
using fresh local produce – tender
Scottish lamb, Tay salmon and Angus
beef.*
STB Commended 3 Crowns
Credit cards: 1, 3
Proprietor: Catherine Pearman

Boat of Garten

MAP 6

HEATHBANK HOUSE
Boat of Garten
Inverness-shire PH24 3BD
Tel: 0479 83 234
Situated in village of Boat of Garten.
Heathbank House was built around 1900
and is set in large gardens, primarily of
heathers (hence the name) and herbs.
Each room is decorated in a different
colour theme and filled with Victoriana –
lace, tapestries, fans, prints, mirrors. The
overall effect is very turn-of-the-century,
with lots of interesting junk to discover!

The dining room is bright with flowers
and candle lamps and there is a large
comfortable lounge with a log fire and
an excellent selection of books. Food is
varied, interesting, of unusually high
standard and excellent value. There is a
strong commitment to Scottish dishes
and produce. There is an obvious anxiety
to satisfy guests every needs.
Open 27 Dec to 31 Oct
Rooms: 8, 4 with private facilities
Dinner at 7 pm (b)
Restricted licence
*Non-residents welcome – by prior
arrangement*
No smoking in dining room + bedrooms
Bed & breakfast £17 – £23
Dinner B & B £29 – £35
*Coulibiac of Spey salmon. Scottish lamb
steak with mint Hollandaise. Ice-cream
éclair with hot butterscotch sauce. Home-
made ice-creams e.g. Gaelic coffee or plum
rum.*
STB Commended 3 Crowns
No credit cards
Proprietor: Graham Burge

Bothwell

MAP 3

THE GRAPE VINE RESTAURANT
& CAFE BAR
27 Main Street, Bothwell
Lanarkshire G71 8RW
Tel: 0698 852014
¹/2 mile off M74 (East Kilbride turn-off).
Situated in the centre of a picturesque
conservation village, yet within easy
access of the motorway. The Grape Vine
is an attractive white painted building
with green canopies and flower barrels.
Whether you are looking for a light meal
in the bar, or a more leisurely experience
in the restaurant, both are available all
day, with the emphasis on fresh local
produce, carefully and creatively
prepared under the guidance of the
owner, Colin Morrison.
*Open all year except Christmas + Boxing
Days, 1 + 2 Jan*
Food Service 9 am – 10.30 pm (a)
Restaurant Lunch (c) à la carte
*Local venison, trout, salmon and cheeses
featured.*
Credit cards: 1, 2, 3
Proprietor: Colin Morrison

Braemar

MAP 5

BRAEMAR LODGE
Glenshee Road, Braemar
Aberdeenshire AB3 5YQ
Tel: 03397 41627
Fax: 03397 41655
*On main A93 Perth-Aberdeen road, on
the outskirts of Braemar.*
Braemar Lodge is a former Victorian
shooting lodge. The new owners, Alec
and Caroline Smith, took over during
1992 and are putting their own mark on
the place. The welcome is friendly and
Caroline prepares interesting menus for
the dining room. Bedrooms are
beautifully furnished and decorated, each
one with mountain views.
Open Dec to Oct
Rooms: 8 , 6 with private facilities
Dinner 7 – 9 pm (c)
No dogs in public rooms
No smoking in dining room
Bed & breakfast £25 – £40
Dinner B & B £40 – £60
*Hot baked avocado stuffed with bacon
and walnuts. Drambuie flavoured haggis
with onion sauce. Grilled salmon steak
with mint and caper butter. Fillet steak
served on a crouton with Port and grape
sauce. Cranachan.*
STB Commended 3 Crowns
Credit cards: 1, 3
Proprietors: Alec & Caroline Smith

Bridge of Allan

MAP 4

ROYAL HOTEL
55 Henderson Street
Bridge of Allan
Stirling FK9 4HG
Tel: 0786 832284
Fax: 0786 834377

A9 Stirling-Dunblane, on main street through Bridge of Allan.
An impressive Victorian hotel built in 1842 just two miles north of Stirling in what was then the Spa town of Bridge of Allan. It is of course right in the heart of one of the most romantic and historical parts of Scotland with Bannockburn, Linlithgow Palace, the Wallace Monument and Rob Roy's grave virtually on the doorstep. The hotel has been carefully restored and completely refurbished to present much of the splendour and elegance of the original building.
Open all year
Rooms: 32 with private facilities
Bar Lunch 12 – 2.30 pm (a)
Dining Room/Restaurant Lunch 12 – 2.30 pm (a)
Bar Supper 5 – 7 pm (b)
Dinner 7 – 9.30 pm (c)
Facilities for the disabled
No smoking area in restaurant
Bed & breakfast £40 – £57
Dinner B & B £58 – £77
Room Rate £32 – £49
Smoked salmon bavarois scented with Drambuie. Mignons of Highland venison with a red wine and forest mushroom sauce. Heather Cream parfait.
STB Commended 4 Crowns
Credit cards: 1, 2, 3, 5, 6

Bridge of Cally

MAP 4

BRIDGE OF CALLY HOTEL
Bridge of Cally , by Blairgowrie
Perthshire PH10 7JJ
Tel: 0250 886 231

6 miles north of Blairgowrie, on A93 to Braemar.
The Bridge of Cally Hotel is a most attractive former coaching inn set in the Perthshire hills. It is family run and exudes an old world homely and comfortable atmosphere. There is usually a huge open fire in the bar adding to that feeling of warm welcome. The hotel is noted for its good food with menus featuring a good selection of Scottish produce, carefully prepared and presented. Also available is free fishing on hotel water and golf, pony trekking and skiing are within easy reach.
Open mid Dec to end Oct except Christmas + Boxing Days
Rooms: 9, 6 with private facilities
Bar Lunch 12 – 2 pm (a)
Dining Room/Restaurant Lunch 12 – 2 pm (a)
Bar Supper 7.30 – 9 pm (b)
Dinner 7.30 – 9 pm (c)
Bed & breakfast £25 – £29
Dinner B & B £39 – £43
STB Commended 3 Crowns
Credit cards: 1, 3, 5
Proprietors: Lindsay & Patricia Tolland

Bridge of Earn

MAP 4

ROCKDALE GUEST HOUSE
Dunning Street, Bridge of Earn
Perth PH2 9AA
Tel: 0738 812281

A90 – 1/2 mile from M90 – 4 miles south of Perth. Off main street in Bridge of Earn.
An old stone terraced house in a quiet side street at the centre of the village of Bridge of Earn which has the best of both worlds – country surroundings but yet only four miles from Perth. Rockdale is a family run guest house and is in an ideal situation for touring or a golf break as there are plenty of the well known beautiful courses all within approximately 30 miles. A caring attitude to guests' comforts. Children and dogs welcome.

Open all year except 26 Dec to 10 Jan
Rooms: 8 , 1 with private facilities
Dinner 5.30 – 7 pm set menu (a)
Restricted hotel licence
Residents only
Bed & breakfast £14.50 – £17.50
Dinner B & B £23 – £26
Reduced Winter rates on request
Trout with mushrooms and Pernod sauce, locally caught grilled Tay salmon with creamy orange sauce or lemon and tarragon sauce, chicken cooked with honey, wine and grapes; beef and peppers with orange.
No credit cards
Proprietor: Adele Barrie

Brig O'Turk

MAP 4

THE BYRE INN
Brig O' Turk, The Trossachs
Perthshire FK17 8HT
Tel: 08776 292

North of Callander on A84, turn onto A821 at Kilmahog: Brig O' Turk 5 miles.
A mellow old farm building in a wooded area, just off the main road, which has been converted into a most attractive timbered bar full of rusticity and charm. A more modern design of dining room leads off from it and the whole effect is restful and pleasing. Good quality country cooking and presentation of wholesome dishes from a fairly extensive menu. A daily vegetarian dish is also available. This is a delightful and popular stopping-off place for people touring The Trossachs.
Open mid Dec to mid Nov
Note: closed Mon Tue Wed until Easter
Bar Lunch 12 – 2.30 pm except Tue (a)
Dining Room/Restaurant Lunch 12 – 2.30 pm except Tue (a)
Bar Supper 5 – 8.45 pm except Tue (a)
Dinner 5 – 8.45 pm except Tue (a)
Closed Tue
Facilities for the disabled
No smoking in restaurant
Demi-rondoules of haggis with coarse mustard sauce. Spinach, potato and cream cheese roulade. Deep fried ice-cream with coconut and almonds on an apricot sauce.
Credit cards: 1, 3
Proprietors: John & Anne Park

Brodie

MAP 5

BRODIE COUNTRYFARE
Brodie, by Forres
Morayshire IV36 0TD
Tel: 03094 555

On A96 between Forres and Nairn.
The restaurant seats over 100 people,
with farmhouse-style dining furniture
indoors and pine picnic benches
outdoors. This country style is enhanced
by charming conservatory windows and
traditional decor. There is additional
seating in the new conservatory area.
Brodie Countryfare forms part of a
shopping complex and diners can find
crafts, produce, exclusive fashions and
designer knitwear all under the same
roof.
*Open all year except Christmas + Boxing
Days, 1 + 2 Jan*
*Food service 12 – 5 pm Mon to Sat: 12 –
5.30 pm Sun (a)*
Facilities for the disabled
*Restaurant is non-smoking with small
smoking area*
*Salad bar a speciality. Home-cooked
dishes using local produce. Home-made
soups. Seasonal soft fruit. Selection of
home-baking and desserts.*
No credit cards
Proprietor: Kathleen Duncan

Brora

MAP 6

ROYAL MARINE HOTEL
Golf Road, Brora
Sutherland KW9 6QS
Tel: 0408 621252
Fax: 0408 621181

*Leave A9 Inverness-Wick at bridge in
Brora, heading towards beach and golf
course.*
A most attractive country mansion built
by Sir Robert Lorimer in 1913 and
converted into a hotel in 1939. Leaded
windows, magnificent woodwork, log
fires, a gracious ambience of yesteryear,
allied to courteous service justify its claim
to be the North's favourite golfing and
fishing hotel. Adjacent to Brora's 18 hole
James Braid links golf course and
overlooking the mouth of the famous
salmon river, the site has much to
commend it. A progressive programme
of refurbishment to high standards is

under way. The food is exactly what the
hungry sportsman or traveller would
want. Good quality, generous portions of
fresh traditional fare, nicely presented
and served with charm.
Open all year
Rooms: 11 with private facilities
Bar Lunch 12 – 2 pm (a)
*Dining Room/Restaurant Lunch (b) –
prior booking only*
*Bar Supper 6.30 – 9 pm: 6.30 – 9.30 pm
in Summer (a)*
Dinner 7 – 9 pm (c)
Bed & breakfast £40 – £50
Dinner B & B £55 – £65
*Summer Isles smoked salmon. Suprême of
wild salmon in tarragon butter sauce.
Fillet steaks. Freshly cooked roasts.
Vegetarian selection. Home-made soups
and desserts.*
STB Commended 4 Crowns
Credit cards: 1, 2, 3, 5.

Cairndow

MAP 3

LOCH FYNE OYSTER BAR
Cairndow
Argyll PA26 8BH
Tel: 04996 217/264

Head of Loch Fyne A83.
Simple oyster bar in converted old farm
building serving local produce including
oysters, langoustines, crab, fresh salmon.
Own smokehouse provides smoked
salmon, trout, eel, mussels etc. Also
seafood shop in smokehouse. Short, very
carefully selected wine list. The
restaurant has been expanded to around
80 seats. There is now a bar where
customers may sit and enjoy their food
and wine.

*Open all year except Christmas + Boxing
Days, 31 Dec + 1 Jan*
*Menu available throughout the day 9 am
– 9 pm (b)*
Note: closes 6 pm Nov to Feb
*Oysters on crushed ice in half shell, baked
oysters in parsley and garlic butter,
langoustines, poached salmon, sea fish
platter, Finnan haddock in milk, Loch
Fyne kippers.*
Credit cards: 1, 2, 3
Proprietors: Andrew Lane & John Noble

Callander

MAP 4

BRIDGEND HOUSE HOTEL
Bridgend, Callander
Perthshire FK17 8AH
Tel: 0877 30130
Fax: 0877 31512

*On A81 – 200 yards from Callander
main street, just over the bridge.*
17th century family run hotel,
comfortably appointed, with its garden
offering a magnificent view of Ben Ledi,
yet within three minutes walk of the town
centre. Bedrooms en suite, TVs and tea-
makers. Extensive menu in the à la carte
restaurant – including a choice of
traditional Scottish dishes and game in
season. Open fire in lounge, central
heating throughout. Children and pets
welcome.
*Open all year except Christmas Day, 5 to
7 Jan*
Rooms: 7 , 5 with private facilities
Bar Lunch 12 – 2 pm (a)
Bar Supper 6 – 9 pm (a)
Dinner 7 – 9 pm (c)
Note: pipe and cigars only after 9 pm
Bed & breakfast £16.50 – £29.50
Dinner B & B £34 – £47
*A wide range of food from traditional
home-made Scottish soup, prime roast beef
and lamb to local salmon, Scottish
pancakes with ice-cream and syrup.*
STB Commended 3 Crowns
Credit cards: 1, 2, 3
Proprietors: Sandy & Maria Park

Credit Card Code		*Meal Price Code*	
1.	Access/Mastercard/Eurocard	(a)	under £10
2.	American Express	(b)	£10 – £15
3.	Visa	(c)	£15 – £20
4.	Carte Bleu	(d)	£20 – £25
5.	Diners Club	(e)	£25 – £30
6.	Mastercharge	(f)	over £30

HIGHLAND HOUSE HOTEL
South Church Street, Callander
Perthshire FK17 8BN
Tel: 0877 30269

Just off A84 in town centre.
Small Georgian house beautifully
furnished offering warm and
comfortable accommodation. Intimate
bar with wide range of malt whiskies.
Tasteful dining room and lounge.
Immaculate bedrooms with drink-
making facilities. Colour TV and en suite
facilities. Full central heating in all
rooms. The proprietors strive to offer a
warm welcome and personal service to all
guests.
Open Mar to Nov
Rooms: 9 , 8 with private facilities
Dinner 7 – 7.30 pm (b)
No smoking in dining room + bedrooms
Dogs accepted at proprietors' discretion
Bed & breakfast £18 – £21
Dinner B & B £29.75 – £35
Home-made soups, pâtés, kippers,
herring. Fresh local produce including
salmon, trout, venison. Delicious desserts.
Children's menu available.
STB Commended 3 Crowns
Credit cards: 1, 2, 3
Proprietors: David & Dee Shirley

ROMAN CAMP HOTEL
Callander
Perthshire FK17 8BG
Tel: 0877 30003

Signposted off main route through
Callander (A84).
Originally built in 1625 as a hunting
lodge for the Dukes of Perth, this
charming country house hotel on the
edge of the Trossachs is a superb centre
from which to tour. It is set in 20 acres of
beautiful gardens which sweep down to
the River Teith. The public rooms are
gracious and relaxing, and the restaurant
enjoys a fine reputation for good food.
Open all year
Rooms: 14 with private facilities
Dining Room/Restaurant Lunch 12 –
2 pm (c)
Dinner 7 – 9 pm (e) 4 course menu
Facilities for the disabled
No smoking in restaurant
Bed & breakfast £35 – £65
Dinner B & B £65 – £95
Local fresh fish – salmon, trout – and
seafood. Game in season.
STB Commended 4 Crowns
Credit cards: 1, 2, 3, 5
Proprietors: Eric & Marion Brown

Campbeltown

MAP 6

SEAFIELD HOTEL
Kilkerran Road, Campbeltown
Argyll PA28 6JL
Tel: 0586 554385

On the shores of Campbeltown Loch – 4
minutes walk from town centre.
This Victorian villa overlooking the shore
was built by the founders of the
Springbank Distillery. There is a garden
court annexe in the walled garden at the
rear of the hotel which offers quiet
peaceful accommodation.
Open all year
Rooms: 9 with private facilities
Snacks available in restaurant
Dining Room/Restaurant Lunch 12.30
– 2 pm (a-b)
Dinner 7 – 8 pm (c-d)
Bed & breakfast £30 – £40
Dinner B & B £45 – £60
Local fresh seafoods and salmon. Scottish
beef, lamb and game.
STB Commended 3 Crowns
Credit cards: 1, 3
Proprietors: Alastair & Elizabeth Gilchrist

WHITE HART HOTEL
Main Street, Campbeltown
Argyll PA28 6AN
Tel: 0586 552440/553356
Fax: 0586 554972

On main street in centre of town.
Attractive white painted old world hotel
on a corner site in the centre of
Campbeltown, a busy fishing port and
market town. A well established hotel.
Plans are underway for 1993 to add a 40
seat bistro/conservatory for informal
meals. The White Hart is an ideal base
for the famous Machrihanish golf links,
the Mull of Kintyre and Campbeltown
Loch.
Open 7 Jan to 30 Dec
Rooms: 17 with private facilities
Bar Lunch 12 – 2 pm except Sun (a)
Dining Room/Restaurant Lunch 12 –
2 pm except Sun (a)
Bar Supper 7 – 9 pm except Sun Sat:
5.30 – 8.30 pm Easter Sun to 1 Nov (b)
Dinner 7 – 9.30 pm except Sun (c)
Bed & breakfast £25 – £34.95
Dinner B & B £40 – £49.95
Serving the best of local fresh seafood,
game and meat products.
Credit cards: 1, 3
Proprietors: P Stogdale & B Kennedy

Carnoustie

MAP 4

"11 PARK AVENUE"
11 Park Avenue, Carnoustie
Angus DD7 7JA
Tel: 0241 53336

On A930 east of Dundee.
A substantial Victorian building with
ornate ceilings in the centre of
Carnoustie is the setting for this licensed
restaurant. The open fireplace and
traditional furnishings combine with the
rich colour scheme to create a warm
informal atmosphere. The modern style
menu makes good use of the best of
fresh local produce. Golf courses and the
beautiful Angus glens are virtually on the
doorstep.
Open all year except Christmas + Boxing
Days
Dining Room/Restaurant Lunch 12 –
2 pm except Sun (a)
Dinner 6.30 – 9.30 pm except Sun (b-c)
Closed Sun
Prime Scottish beef and lamb. Local
seafood including crab, lobster and
Arbroath smokies. Home-made bread,
pasta, pastries and soups. Selection of
freshly made desserts.
Credit cards: 1, 2, 3, 5, 6
Proprietors: Stephen Collinson &
Caroline Mitchell

Carradale

MAP 6

CARRADALE HOTEL
Carradale
Argyll PA28 6RY
Tel: 058 33 223
Fax: 058 33 638

Off B842 on B879, about 17 miles north
of Campbeltown, Argyll.
Over sixty years in same family
ownership, this hotel is situated in the
fishing village of Carradale, and stands in
its own gardens above the quaint
harbour. The hotel offers squash courts,
sauna, solarium, and has recently had
some tasteful refurbishment. The golf
course is next to the hotel and there are
safe sandy beaches nearby.
Open 15 Mar to 31 Dec
Rooms: 20 , 18 with private facilities
Bar Lunch 12.30 – 2.15 pm (a)
Dining Room/Restaurant Lunch 12.30
– 2 pm (a)

Bar Supper 5 – 7 pm (a)
Dinner 7.30 – 9 pm (c)
No smoking area in restaurant
Bed & breakfast £26 – £49
Dinner B & B £44 – £59
Kintyre Hill lamb, Carradale oak-smoked
salmon, house kippers.
STB Commended 3 Crowns
Credit cards: 1, 3
Proprietors: John & Katherine Martin

Carrbridge

MAP 6

DALRACHNEY LODGE HOTEL
Carrbridge
Inverness-shire PH23 3AT
Tel: 047984 252
Fax: 047984 382
On A938 to Dulnain Bridge, c. 400
yards from Carrbridge.
Set in 16 acres of peaceful surroundings,
on the banks of the Dulnain River, is
Dalrachney Lodge, a former Victorian
shooting lodge. With its careful blend of
old and new, this hotel offers 11
generously proportioned and tastefully
furnished bedrooms. In addition there
are five comfortable rooms available in
the Keeper's House. Relax by the log fire
in the cosy Stalkers Bar and perhaps try
one of the selection of 45 malt whiskies.

The Lodge Restaurant has gained a
reputation for its fine food and service,
and there is a wide range of wines and
liqueurs.
Open all year
Rooms: 16 with private facilities
Bar Lunch 12 – 2 pm (a)
Dining Room/Restaurant Lunch 12 –
2 pm (a)
Bar Supper 5.30 – 9.30 pm (a)
Dinner 7 – 8.30 pm (c)
No smoking area in restaurant
Bed & breakfast £23 – £32.95
Dinner B & B £39.95 – £49.50
Home-made soups, pâtés and desserts.
Spey Valley salmon, Highland venison,
beef, Scotch lamb beautifully prepared
and served with fresh vegetables in
season.
STB Commended 4 Crowns
Credit cards: 1, 2, 3
Proprietor: Helen Swanney

ECCLEFECHAN BISTRO
Main Street, Carrbridge
Inverness-shire PH23 3AJ
Tel: 047 984 374
Main road Carrbridge, on Carrbridge by-
pass off A9 north of Aviemore.
Informal family run bistro invoking the
best of the Auld Alliance: Scottish food
in a French atmosphere, freshly
prepared the way you like it, from scones
to scallops, steaks to strudel – and coffee
that tastes like coffee.
Open all year except last 2 wks Nov, first
2 wks Dec + Christmas Day
Open for meals 10 am – 3 pm (snacks till
4 pm) + 6.30 – 9.45 pm except Tue (a-b)
Closed Tue
Facilities for the disabled
Venison in claret, Hebridean skink,
haggis and clapshot, local smoked
salmon, Scottish prawns with dill.
Ecclefechan tart, Blairgowrie raspberry
trifle.
Credit cards: 1, 3
Proprietors: Duncan & Anne Hilditch

FEITH MHOR COUNTRY HOUSE
Station Road, Carrbridge
Inverness-shire PH23 3AP
Tel: 047 984 621
One mile west of village of Carrbridge on
road signed to Dalnahaitnach.
This charming 19th century country
house is pleasantly furnished, and has a
warm friendly atmosphere, set in one
acre of delightful gardens and

surrounded by peaceful unspoilt
countryside. The comfortable well
appointed en suite bedrooms enjoy
beautiful views. There is an attractive
dining room and comfortable lounge.
Excellent home-cooked fare including
local and garden produce in season.
Vegetarian dishes are available by
arrangement. This is a wonderful area
for those who enjoy walking, bird-
watching or touring.
Open all year
Rooms: 6 with private facilities
Dinner at 7 pm (b)
No smoking in dining room + lounge
No children under 14 years
Bed & breakfast £20 – £21
Dinner B & B £29 – £32
Fruity spiced gammon, roast Scotch lamb
and beef, poached fresh salmon.
Vegetarian lentil bake, leek and
dumpling casserole. Desserts include
meringue sunrise, pavlova with
raspberries, fresh fruit crumbles.
STB Commended 3 Crowns
No credit cards
Proprietor: Penny Rawson

Castle Douglas

MAP 1

LONGACRE MANOR HOTEL
Ernespie Road, Castle Douglas
Dumfriesshire DG7 1LE
Tel: 0556 3576
Off A75 on northern boundary of Castle
Douglas.
Charming small hotel, personally run,
offering warm welcome and service.
Situated in 1½ acres of woodland
gardens with magnificent views to Screel
and Galloway hills. Television, direct dial
telephone, radio and tea-making
facilities in each room. Premises are fully
central heated.
Open all year except 24 Dec to 4 Jan
Rooms: 4 with private facilities
Dinner 7 – 9 pm (b)
Bed & breakfast £25 – £30
Dinner B & B £37 – £42
Daily changing menu using locally
produced fish, beef, lamb, pork and game
with fresh vegetables. Home-made desserts
a speciality.
STB Highly Commended 3 Crowns
No credit cards
Proprietors: Elizabeth & Walter Meldrum

Chapel of Garioch

MAP 5

PITTODRIE HOUSE HOTEL
Chapel of Garioch, nr Pitcaple
Aberdeenshire AB51 9HS
Tel: 0467 681444 • Telex: 739935
Fax: 0467 681648

Off A96 just north of Pitcaple, 21 miles north of Aberdeen, 17 miles north of airport.
A beautiful turreted Scottish baronial style mansion, standing in its own extensive grounds at the foot of Bennachie, which was originally the home of the owner, Theo Smith. Although the hotel was extended in 1990 to give additional bedrooms and a function room, this was done skilfully and sympathetically. The original character of the public rooms with their antiques and family portraits has been maintained. There is a beautifully kept three acre walled garden.
Open all year
Rooms: 27 with private facilities
Bar Lunch 12.30 – 2 pm (a)
Dining Room/Restaurant Lunch 12.30 – 2 pm (c)
Dinner 7.30 – 9 pm (e)
Bed & breakfast £50 – £85
Dinner B & B £45 – £110
Room Rate £85 – £105
Menu changes daily featuring fresh game and salmon.
STB Commended 4 Crowns
Credit cards: 1, 2, 3, 5, 6
Proprietor: Theo Smith

Cleish
nr Kinross

MAP 4

NIVINGSTON HOUSE
Cleish
Kinross-shire KY13 7LS
Tel: 0577 850216
Fax: 0577 850238

In country, 2 miles from Junction 5 on M90.
A Victorian mansion set in 12 acres of mature gardens and commanding superb views over the rolling countryside. Comfortable furnishings contribute to the relaxed, friendly atmosphere in this country house. Log fires burn in the Winter and candles flicker in the evenings. The best of local produce features on the menus created by the chef, accompanied by delightful unusual sauces.
Open all year except first 2 wks Jan
Rooms: 17 with private facilities
Bar Lunch 12 – 2 pm (a)
Dining Room/Restaurant Lunch 12 – 2 pm (c)
Dinner 7 – 9 pm (e)
Bed & breakfast from £40
Dinner B & B from £60
Oak-smoked salmon. Cream of carrot and apple soup. Roast saddle of lamb with fresh thyme. Bramble brûlée.
STB Commended 4 Crowns
Credit cards: 1, 2, 3, 6
Proprietors: Allan & Pat Deeson

Coll
Isle of

MAP 7

COLL BISTRO
Arinagour, Isle of Coll
Inner Hebrides
Tel: 08793 373

In the main street of Arinagour village.
A quaint little house overlooking Arinagour Bay, which has retained its charm with its black beams, open peat fires, and dinners by candlelight. During the day, the Coll Bistro is open for teas and coffees with delightful home-baking, as well as serving lunches. In the evening guests revel in its warm cosy atmosphere while enjoying the simple but tasteful menus, based on fresh local produce. Sailors will be happy to note that there are shower and laundry facilities available.
Open Easter to Oct
Dining Room/Restaurant Lunch 12 – 3 pm (a)
Dinner 7 – 10 pm (b)
Table licence
Lobster thermidor. Fresh salmon steak. Venison cooked in red wine and cranberry. Home-made beef Bourguignonne. Local crab.
No credit cards
Proprietor: Jan Driver

Colvend

MAP 1

CLONYARD HOUSE HOTEL
Colvend, Dalbeattie
Dumfriesshire DG5 4QW
Tel: 055 663 372
Fax: 055 663 422

4 1/2 miles south of Dalbeattie on A710 Solway coast road. 18 miles west of Dumfries.
Victorian country house hotel in six acres of wooded grounds. Typical 19th century dining room overlooking lawns. Also pleasant large cocktail bar for informal meals. Ground floor bedroom wing with full facilities. One room fitted for disabled guests. Safe grounds for children. French and some German spoken. Dogs welcome (small charge).
Open all year
Note: Accommodation closed 24 to 26 Dec
Rooms: 15 with private facilities
Bar Lunch 12 – 2 pm (a)
Bar Supper 6 – 9.30 pm (a)
Dinner 7 – 9 pm (c)
Facilities for the disabled
Bed & breakfast £30 – £40
Dinner B & B £42 – £56
Solway salmon, Kirkcudbrightshire scallops, Galloway beef and lamb, venison. Luscious home-made sweets of many varieties. Scottish goats cheeses.
STB Commended 4 Crowns
Credit cards: 1, 3
Proprietors: N M Thompson & D Thompson

Comrie

MAP 4

THE DEIL'S CAULDRON LOUNGE BAR & RESTAURANT
27 Dundas Street, Comrie
Perthshire PH6 2LN
Tel: 0764 70352

On A85 west end of Comrie.
The Deil's Cauldron, created from a 200 year old Listed building, takes its name from a well known local beauty spot. The attractive black and white exterior leads to a comfortable lounge and two dining rooms (smoking and non-smoking) featuring original stone walls and decorated with fine water colours, old photographs and prints. From the lounge one can enter the garden to find an interesting fish pond and lots of

heathers and shrubs. There is a good selection of malt whisky available. Reservations advisable.

Open all year except Christmas Day, 1 + 2 Jan, 2 wks Mar + 2 wks Nov
Bar Lunch 12 – 2.30 pm except Tue (a)
Dining Room/Restaurant Lunch 12 – 2.30 pm except Tue (b)
Bar Supper 6 – 9 pm except Tue (b)
Dinner 7 – 9 pm except Tue (c)
Closed Tue
Separate dining room for non-smokers
The menu features local beef, lamb, fish, home-grown vegetables and game in season. Auld Alliance cooking.
Credit cards: 1, 2, 3
Proprietors: Robert & Judith Shepherd

TULLYBANNOCHER FARM FOOD BAR
Comrie
Perthshire PH6 2JY
Tel: 0764 70827

Just outside Comrie on A85 Lochearnhead road.

This is a very popular stopping place for people enjoying the drive along Loch Earn. A solid timber construction, it stands on a prominent knoll among trees and lawns just outside the pretty village of Comrie and with plenty of parking alongside. The self-service restaurant offers a wide choice of freshly prepared meats, fish and quiche with simple but varied salads. There is a refreshing aura of healthy eating and home-baking about the place. Freshly brewed coffee and tea and a selection of wines, beers and soft drinks are available. In fine weather people enjoy eating outside on the rustic tables on the lawns, but there is lots of dining space inside for those who prefer it.

Open late Mar to Oct
Meals available from 9.30 am – 7 pm (a)
Table licence
Dogs allowed outside only
Home-baked ham. Local smoked trout. Coronation chicken, Quiches. Salmon. Fresh strawberry flan.
No credit cards
Proprietor: Peter Davenport

Contin
by Strathpeffer

MAP 6

COUL HOUSE HOTEL
Contin, by Strathpeffer
Ross-shire IV14 9EY
Tel: 0997 421487
Fax: 0997 421945

On A835 to Ullapool, 17 miles north-west of Inverness.

The ancient Mackenzies of Coul picked an incomparable setting for their secluded Highland country mansion, with fine views over forest and mountain. There are log fires, elegant public rooms and the candlelit "Mackenzie's Taste of Scotland Restaurant". All bedrooms are en suite, equipped with colour tele-text TV, radio, direct dial telephone, hospitality tray, hairdryer and trouser press.

Open all year
Rooms: 21 with private facilities
Bar Lunch 12 – 2 pm Mon to Sat: 12.30 – 2 pm Sun (a)
Dining Room/Restaurant Lunch 12.30 – 2 pm (b) – by arrangement only
Bar Supper 6 – 9 pm Mon to Sat: 6.30 – 9 pm Sun (a)
Dinner 7 – 9 pm (d)
Bed & breakfast £31 – £53
Dinner B & B £48 – £74.50
Sauté of Summer Isles scallops. Venison saddle chops. Smoked Conon salmon. Prawns in Highland garlic butter. Pan-fried suprême of chicken with shallots, mushrooms and served in a whisky cream. Fillet steaks. Scottish Maiden's Kiss.
STB Commended 4 Crowns
Credit cards: 2, 5
Proprietor: Martyn Hill

Corsemalzie

MAP 1

CORSEMALZIE HOUSE HOTEL
Corsemalzie, Port William
Newton Stewart
Wigtownshire DG8 9RL
Tel: 098 886 254

Off A714 Newton Stewart-Port William, take B7005 Wigtown-Glenluce road.

A 19th century Scottish mansion house, now a sporting country house hotel, set in 40 acres of woodland and gardens, with its own extensive game, fishing and shooting rights. Dogs accepted (small charge).

Open 6 Mar to 9 Jan except Christmas + Boxing Days
Rooms: 15 , 14 with private facilities
Bar Lunch 12.30 – 2 pm (a)
Dining Room/Restaurant Lunch 12.30 – 2 pm (b)
Bar Supper 7.15 – 9.15 pm (a)
Dinner 7.30 – 9.15 pm (c)
Bed & breakfast £31.50 – £39.50
Dinner B & B £39.50 – £55
Fresh and smoked Bladnoch salmon and trout. Game in season, steaks and roasts a speciality; home-grown vegetables. Scottish sweet table and cheese board with oatcakes (Friday and Saturday evenings).
STB Commended 4 Crowns
Credit cards: 1, 3
Proprietor: Peter McDougall

Coupar Angus

MAP 4

BURRELTON PARK INN
High Street, Burrelton
Perthshire PH13 9NX
Tel: 08287 206

On A94 Perth-Coupar Angus, 3 miles south of Coupar Angus, within 10 minutes of Perth or 25 minutes of Dundee.

Not so much an hotel, more a restaurant with attractive rooms, where personal attention and service enhance first class food. Set in the village of Burrelton, a farming community renowned for its soft fruit and potato growing. A perfect centre for daily touring, north, south, east and west. For the sports enthusiast the best golfing, fishing (salmon), shooting, skiing and walking.

Open all year except 1 Jan
Rooms: 6 with private facilities
All day menu served 11 am – 10.30 pm (a)
Dinner 6.30 – 10.30 pm (b)
No smoking area in restaurant
Bed & breakfast £22.50 – £30
Dinner B & B £30 – £42.50
Special dishes highlighted on blackboard daily, including fresh Tay salmon served in a variety of ways.
STB Commended 3 Crowns
Credit cards: 1, 3
Proprietors: Malcolm & Karen Weaving

Craigellachie

MAP 5

CRAIGELLACHIE HOTEL
Craigellachie
Banffshire AB3 9SS
Tel: 0340 881204
Fax: 0340 881253

On A941, 12 miles south of Elgin.
Set in its own grounds just off the main
square in the village and with the famous
Spey walk at the foot of the garden, this
famous old hotel has been transformed
through alterations and refurbishment
by its owners into something quite
special. The public rooms have been
furnished with taste and elegance and
the whole place exudes an atmosphere of
care and attention. While predominantly
in fishing and shooting country it is also
very much on the famous whisky trail
with several nearby distilleries. The
excellent quality of food matches, and
indeed complements, the high standards
elsewhere. French, Swedish and Danish
spoken.
Open all year
Rooms: 30 with private facilities
Dining Room/Restaurant Lunch 12.30
– 2 pm (a) buffet service
Dinner 7.30 – 9.30 pm (d)
No smoking in dining room
Bed & breakfast £43.50 – £76.50
Dinner B & B £68.25 – £101.25
Crayfish chowder with brandy, steamed
Spey salmon with apricot and thyme
sauce, warm pigeon breast with roast
parsnips and claret sauce. Poached
strudel with gooseberry compote. Scottish
cheese and home-made oatcakes.
STB Highly Commended 4 Crowns
Credit cards: 1, 2, 3, 5, 6
Proprietor: Tomas Gronager

Crail

MAP 4

CAIPLIE GUEST HOUSE
53 High Street, Crail
Fife KY10 3RA
Tel: 0333 50564

High Street, Crail.
A comfortable and neatly maintained
guest house situated in the centre of the
historic and quaint little fishing town of
Crail. Guests' sitting room with TV.
Open 1 Mar to 30 Oct
Rooms: 7
Dinner at 7 pm (b)
It is requested that guests select their
menu by 4 pm
Residents only
No smoking area in dining room
Bed & breakfast £15 – £16.50
Dinner B & B £27 – £28.50
Scottish and continental dishes prepared
from fresh local produce. Cloutie
dumpling, cranachan.
STB Commended 2 Crowns
No credit cards
Proprietor: Jayne Hudson

HAZELTON GUEST HOUSE
29 Marketgate, Crail
Fife KY10 3TH
Tel: 0333 50250

In town centre opposite tourist office and
Tolbooth.
The Hazelton is one of an imposing
terrace of Victorian merchants houses in
the centre of Crail. All rooms have
central heating, colour television, tea
and coffee-making facilities and wash-
hand basin. The relaxed friendly atmosphere and attention to detail ensure a
pleasant stay in this charming little
fishing town in the East Neuk of Fife.
Open Feb to Dec
Rooms: 7
Dinner at 7 pm (b) except Mon Tue –
unless by prior arrangement
It is requested that guests select their
menu by 4 pm
Residents only
No dogs
Bed & breakfast £14 – £17
Dinner B & B £26 – £29
Daily changing menu using local
produce. Fish, seafood and game
featured. Home-smoked specialities.
Vegetarians catered for by arrangement.
STB Commended Listed
No credit cards
Proprietors: Alan & Rita Brown

Crianlarich

MAP 4

ALLT-CHAORAIN COUNTRY HOUSE
Crianlarich
Perthshire FK20 8RU
Tel: 08383 283

Off A82, 1 mile north-west of Crianlarich.
Situated in an elevated position within its
own grounds, Allt-Chaorain has
picturesque views of Benmore and
Strathfinnan from the south-facing sun
lounge. The traditional wood-panelled
dining room caters for three tables of six
people. In the lounge log fires burn
throughout the year.
Open 29 Mar to 30 Oct
Rooms: 9 with private facilities
Dinner 7 – 8 pm (b)
Residents only
No smoking in dining room, bedrooms +
main lounge
A sun lounge is set aside for those who
wish to smoke
Dinner B & B £42 – £45
Wide range of traditional fresh fare.
Game pie, pork fillets, braised steaks,
breasts of chicken, beef olives stuffed with
haggis. Cloutie dumpling.
STB Commended 3 Crowns
Credit cards: 1, 3
Proprietor: Roger McDonald

Crieff

MAP 4

CRIEFF VISITORS CENTRE
Muthill Road, Crieff
Perthshire PH7 4AZ
Tel: 0764 4014

On A822 leading out of Crieff to the south.
Quality self-service restaurant,
showroom, audio-visual room and
garden centre complex alongside two
rural factories producing thistle pattern
Buchan pottery and high quality
Perthshire Paperweights. Within one
hour of Glasgow, Edinburgh and St
Andrews, close by Gleneagles amidst fine
Highland scenery. Serves a range of
popular dishes and snacks.
Open all year except Christmas + Boxing
Days, 1 + 2 Jan
Self-service restaurant and all facilities
open 7 days, 9 am – 5.30 pm: 9 am –
4.30 pm Oct to Mar (a-b)
Facilities for the disabled
Credit cards: 1, 2, 3, 6

MURRAYPARK HOTEL
Connaught Terrace, Crieff
Perthshire PH7 3DJ
Tel: 0764 3731
Fax: 0764 5311

A85 to residential part of town.
Pink-stoned large Victorian house
standing in attractive gardens in the
residential part of town. A comfortable
restaurant with uncrowded atmosphere
overlooks a pleasant garden. Based on
established Scottish foods with many
interesting variations. French spoken.
Children and dogs welcome.
Open all year
Rooms: 13 with private facilities
Bar Lunch 12 – 2 pm (a)
*Dining Room/Restaurant Lunch 12.30
– 2 pm (b)*
Bar Supper 7.30 – 9.30 pm (b)
Dinner 7.30 – 9.30 pm (d)
No smoking in restaurant
Bed & breakfast £33 – £36
Dinner B & B £65 – £70
*Scampi wrapped in bacon and grilled on
a skewer. Chicken in a light curry cream
with banana and pineapple served on
rice. Mushrooms with Stilton, cream and
Port.*
STB Commended 4 Crowns
Credit cards: 1, 2, 3, 5, 6
Proprietors: Ann & Noel Scott

SMUGGLERS RESTAURANT
Glenturret Distillery, The Hosh
Crieff
Perthshire PH7 4HA
Tel: 0764 2424

Prestige Award Winner 1989

A85 north-west of Crieff.
Self-service restaurant (130 seats)
situated in an 18th century converted
whisky warehouse within Scotland's
oldest Highland malt distillery. Award
winning visitors centre. Audio visual
presentation and 3-D exhibition. Whisky
tasting bar – taste different ages of
Glenturret, 8, 12, 15, and 21 years old,
and the Glenturret Malt Liqueur. Whisky
Shop. Children welcome. New disabled
access.
*Open all year except Christmas + Boxing
Days, 1 + 2 Jan*
*Bar Lunch (Smugglers) 12 – 2.30 pm
except Sun (a)*
*Dining Room/Restaurant Lunch (Pagoda
Room) 12 – 2.30 pm except Sun (b)*
Dinner – by arrangement only
Closed Sun

*No smoking area in Smugglers
Restaurant*
No smoking in Pagoda Room
*Glenturret flavoured pâté, smoked
salmon, venison steak, Hosh haggis and
vegetarian haggis. Cranachan and
gâteaux.*
Credit cards: 1, 2, 3
Proprietor: Peter Fairlie

Crinan

MAP 6

CRINAN HOTEL
Crinan, Lochgilphead
Argyll PA31 8SR
Tel: 054 683 261
Fax: 054 683 292

Prestige Award Winner 1991

*A82 Glasgow-Inveraray, then A83 to
Lochgilphead. Follow A816 (Oban) for c.
5 miles, then B841 to Crinan.*
Magnificent views over Loch Crinan, the
sea and islands. There are two
restaurants at the hotel: the renowned
Lock 16 which specialises solely in fresh
seafood, particularly shellfish which is

landed daily at the Canal entrance, and
the Westward Restaurant which has an
equally fine reputation. Both restaurants
enjoy the breathtaking sunsets and
stunning views. The bedrooms have been
individually designed by Frances Ryan,
each with sea views and some with their
own private balconies.
*Open all year except Christmas Eve,
Christmas + Boxing Days*
Rooms: 22 with private facilities
Bar Lunch 12.30 – 2 pm (a)
*Dinner (Westward Restaurant) 7 –
9 pm (e)*
*Dinner (Lock 16 mid Apr to Sep only) at
8 pm except Sun Mon (f) – booking
essential*
Bed & breakfast £50 – £75
*Jumbo Prawns Corryvreckan, Scottish
beef, local wild salmon.*
STB Commended 4 Crowns
Credit cards: 1, 3
Proprietors: Nick & Frances Ryan

SEALGAIR
c/o Wave Yacht Charters
1 Hazel Drive
Dundee DD2 1QQ
Tel: 0382 68501
Fax: 0382 201776

*Yacht based at Bellanoch, by Crinan,
Argyll*

Beauty and craftsmanship combine in
this 46 foot wooden ketch "Sealgair".
The only cruising yacht in the Taste of
Scotland Guide, she offers you a great
holiday experience. Equipped to the
highest standards for comfort,
performance and safety, she can take you
from her base on the Crinan Canal to
meander round secluded bays, or taste
adventure on a trip to St Kilda. The
skipper ensures that you can relax
without worry, while from the galley the
cook offers an imaginative menu based
on fresh ingredients. French spoken.
Open 1 Apr to 30 Sep
Cabins: 4
*Unlicensed – guests welcome to take own
wine*
No children
No dogs
No smoking in dining area + cabins
*Daily rate (all meals + accommodation)
per person £48 – £188*
*Tasty soups, Scottish lamb, venison and
fresh fish. Vegetarian dishes. Home-
baking.*
No credit cards
Proprietor: Wave Yacht Management Ltd

Cromarty

MAP 6

ROYAL HOTEL
Marine Terrace, Cromarty
Ross-shire IV11 8YN
Tel: 03817 217

*On A832, 20 miles north-east of
Inverness.*

This white-painted hotel is situated
overlooking the beach and harbour in
the ancient and historic village of
Cromarty. It has a comfortable and high
standard of furnishing and decor. All the
well appointed bedrooms have views of
the sea and Ross-shire mountains. The
reputation for excellent food and value
for money plus traditional Scottish
hospitality is guarded with pride by the
staff.
*Open all year except Christmas Eve,
Christmas + Boxing Days, 31 Dec,
1 to 3 Jan
Rooms: 10 with private facilities
Bar Lunch 12 – 2 pm Mon to Sat: 12.30
– 2.30 pm Sun (a)
Dining Room/Restaurant Lunch 12 –
2 pm (b)
Bar Supper 5.30 – 9 pm Sun to Thu:
5.30 – 9.30 pm Fri Sat (a)
Dinner 7 – 8.30 pm (c)
No smoking in restaurant
Bed & breakfast £25 – £30
Wide range of traditional Scottish fare.
Farmhouse crêpe. T-bone steaks. Crab salads.
STB Commended 3 Crowns
Credit cards: 1, 2, 3
Proprietor: Stewart Morrison*

Cullen

MAP 5

BAYVIEW HOTEL
Seafield Street, Cullen
Banffshire AB5 2SU
Tel: 0542 41031

*A98 between Banff and Fochabers –
overlooking Cullen Harbour.*

A really charming little hotel splendidly
converted to provide interesting public
rooms and well equipped bedrooms.
Cullen is a pleasant small harbour town
and the Bayview commands excellent
views over the harbour, the beaches and
Moray Firth. Menus are based on the
quality local products most readily
available which of course includes fresh
seafish and shellfish.

*Open all year except Christmas
Rooms: 6 , 5 with private facilities
Bar Lunch 12 – 1.45 pm (a)
Dining Room/Restaurant Lunch 12.30
– 1.45 pm Sun only (b)
Bar Supper 6.30 – 9 pm (b)
Dinner 6.30 – 9 pm (c)
No dogs
Bed & breakfast £27.50 – £35
Cullen skink. Poached fillet of salmon,
garnished with fresh mussels. Fillet steak
stuffed with game pâté served with a
Cognac and cream sauce.
STB Commended 4 Crowns
Credit cards: 1, 3
Proprietor: David Evans*

Cumbernauld

MAP 4

WESTERWOOD HOTEL, GOLF &
COUNTRY CLUB
St Andrews Drive
Cumbernauld G68 0EW
Tel: 0236 457171
Fax: 0236 738478

*A80 to Wardpark exit. Follow to
roundabout, take Dullatur exit. At mini
roundabout, turn right – road leads to
hotel entrance.*

A very spacious and luxurious hotel
situated 13 miles from Glasgow city
centre near Cumbernauld. Its location
on the A80 makes Westerwood within
easy reach of the key road networks.
There are three restaurants within the
hotel and high standards of food
preparation and presentation are evident

throughout. The 18 hole par 73 golf
course was designed by Seve Ballesteros
and Dave Thomas. Other sporting
facilities include a swimming pool,
tennis, squash, snooker, gymnasium etc.
French, German, Swiss, Dutch, Italian
and Spanish spoken.
*Open all year
Rooms: 49 with private facilities
Bar Lunch 12 – 3 pm (a)
Dining Room/Restaurant Lunch (Club
House) 12 – 3 pm (a)
Bar Supper (Club House) 6 – 10 pm
Dinner 7 – 10 pm except Sun (c)
Facilities for the disabled
Bed & breakfast £47.50 – £95
Dinner B & B £67.50 – £115
West Coast scallops with a lemon butter
sauce. Loin of Scottish lamb with maize-
fed chicken parfait and tarragon essence.
Seasonal berries with Drambuie sabayon.
Home-made chocolates.
STB Highly Commended 5 Crowns
Credit cards: 1, 2, 3, 5, 6*

Cupar

MAP 4

OSTLERS CLOSE
Bonnygate, Cupar
Fife KY15 4BU
Tel: 0334 55574

Prestige Award Winner 1989

A92 in Cupar town centre.

This is a gem of a place. A small intimate
and entirely unpretentious restaurant
situated in a small lane off the main
street in Cupar. Jimmy Graham the
chef/proprietor produces some of the
best food in Fife utilising, especially, east
coast fish and shellfish with skill and
imagination. His wife Amanda presides
over the dining room with great charm
and friendliness. The combination of the
two is irresistible.
*Open all year except 1 wk Oct + 1 wk Jun
Dining Room/Restaurant Lunch 12.15
– 2 pm except Sun Mon (c)
Dinner 7 – 9.30 pm except Sun Mon (e)
Closed Sun Mon
Cream of Tay salmon soup, Pittenweem
seafood, e.g. turbot, halibut and lobster;
prawns with garlic and fresh herb butter.
Selection of game in season with home-
made jellies.
Credit cards: 1, 3
Proprietors: Jimmy & Amanda Graham*

Dalbeattie

MAP 1

AUCHENSKEOCH LODGE
by Dalbeattie
Kirkcudbrightshire DG5 4PG
Tel: 038 778 277

5 miles south-east of Dalbeattie on B793.
Former Victorian shooting lodge
personally run by the proprietors. Period
furnishings throughout ensure a genuine
country house atmosphere, whilst
woodlands, formal gardens and
rhododendron walks provide privacy and
tranquillity. Facilities include fishing on
own loch, billiard room and croquet
lawn. Great emphasis is put on the
quality and freshness of the food. To this
end the menu is kept small with a choice
of two dishes at each course; it changes
daily and makes full use of the excellent
meat and fish available locally. Wherever
possible the vegetables, salads, herbs and
soft fruit are fresh from the garden.
Open Easter to Oct
Rooms: 5 with private facilities
Dinner 7.30 – 8 pm (b)
Booking essential for non-residents
Bed & breakfast £22 – £32
Dinner B & B £34 – £45
*Small menu, changing daily. Emphasis
on fresh local produce.*
STB Commended 3 Crowns
Credit cards: 1, 3
*Proprietors: Christopher & Mary
Broom-Smith*

Daviot
nr Inverness

MAP 6

DAVIOT MAINS FARM
Daviot
Inverness IV1 2ER
Tel: 0463 772215
Fax: 0463 772215

*On B851 (B9006) to Culloden/Croy, 5
miles south of Inverness.*
Comfortable early 19th century Listed
farmhouse in quiet situation five miles
from Inverness, under the personal
supervision of Margaret and Alex
Hutcheson. Relax in the warm
atmosphere of this friendly home where
delicious meals are thoughtfully
prepared for you and where log fires
burn in both sitting room and dining

room. Dogs accepted by arrangement.
Open all year except 23 Dec to 4 Jan
Rooms: 3, 2 with private facilities
Dinner at 6.30 pm except Sun (b)
*Note: Jun to Sep dinner not served Sat
also*
*Unlicensed – guests welcome to take own
wine*
No smoking in dining room
Bed & breakfast £14 – £20
Dinner B & B £23 – £30
*According to season – home-made soups,
fresh local salmon and trout, Scottish
meats, vegetables and cheeses. Local fruits
and home-made puddings.*
STB Commended 2 Crowns
No credit cards
Proprietors: Margaret & Alex Hutcheson

Dirleton

MAP 4

OPEN ARMS HOTEL
Dirleton
East Lothian EH39 5BG
Tel: 0620 85 241
Fax: 0620 85 570

*Off A198 between Gullane and North
Berwick.*
Some families are now into their third
generation as guests of the Open Arms, a
much loved up market inn set in the
charming East Lothian coastal village of
Dirleton, overlooking the 13th century
castle and the village green and only
about half an hour's drive from
Edinburgh. Arthur Neil is a host par
excellence and a much respected figure
in the hotel and catering business. It falls
almost automatically that he knows and
understands his customers'
requirements. The menus take full
advantage of the excellent seafood and
agricultural produce so readily available
and food is both prepared and presented
with the panache one would expect from
a successful operation which has been in
the same family's hands for over 40 years.
French and German spoken.
Open all year
Rooms: 7 with private facilities

Bar Lunch 12.30 – 2 pm except Sun (b)
*Dining Room/Restaurant Lunch 12.30
– 2.30 pm Sun only (b)*
Dinner 7 – 9.30 pm (d)
Bed & breakfast £50 – £80
Dinner B & B £70 – £90
*A seafood pastry of prawns, mussels and
scallops. Veal with a lime and mushroom
sauce garnished with fresh thyme.*
STB Commended 4 Crowns
Credit cards: 1, 3, 6
Proprietor: Arthur Neil

Dornoch

MAP 6

DORNOCH CASTLE HOTEL
Castle Street
Dornoch IV25 3SD
Tel: 0862 810216
Fax: 0862 810981

*In the centre of the cathedral town of
Dornoch, 2 miles off A9.*
This imposing former Bishop`s Palace,
some of which dates back to the 14th
century, stands in the centre of the
peaceful town of Dornoch opposite the
13th century cathedral. The street in
which it lies is tree lined giving an air of
ancient tranquillity. The majority of the
comfortable bedrooms overlook the
sheltered garden. The elegant coffee
lounge opens onto the terrace. The
panelled bar is welcoming for a pre-
dinner drink or guests may simply enjoy
relaxing in the comfortable no smoking
lounge. The Bishop`s Room Restaurant –
once the palace kitchen – is one of the
finest in the area, with a wine list to
match.
Open mid Apr to end Oct
Rooms: 17 with private facilities
*Bar Lunch 12.15 – 2 pm Mon to Sat:
12.30 – 2 pm Sun (a)*
*Dining Room/Restaurant Lunch 12.15
– 2 pm Mon to Sat: 12.30 – 2 pm Sun (a)*
*Dinner 7.30 – 8.45 pm Sun to Fri: 7 –
8.45 pm Sat (c)*
No smoking in restaurant
Bed & breakfast £29.50 – £38
Dinner B & B £46 – £54.50
*Local venison, salmon, trout and lobster.
Aberdeen Angus steaks. Home-made
soups, e.g. Brochan Buidhe, and chef's
pâtés.*
STB Commended 4 Crowns
Credit cards: 1, 2, 3
Proprietor: Michael Ketchin

THE MALLIN HOUSE HOTEL
Church Street, Dornoch
Sutherland IV25 3LP
Tel: 0862 810335
Fax: 0862 810810

Down to centre of town, turn right.
A family run hotel with a pleasant bar featuring a malt of the month and an exceptionally good range of bar meals which even includes lobster – and there aren't too many bar menus offering that! The spacious restaurant is adorned with stags heads and has magnificent views of the Dornoch Firth and Struie Hills. It has a well balanced à la carte menu which changes quarterly and features local fish, shellfish and game, and excellent steaks.
Open all year
Rooms: 11 , 6 with private facilities
Bar Lunch 12.30 – 2.30 pm (a)
Dining Room/Restaurant Lunch 12.30 – 2.30 pm (b)
Bar Supper 6.30 – 9 pm (a)
Dinner 6.30 – 9 pm (c)
Kennel for dogs
Facilities for the disabled
Bed & breakfast £19.95 – £25
Dinner B & B £35 – £40
Duck breast in Drambuie and fresh raspberry sauce. Partridge with courgette and red wine sauce. Escalope of salmon with fresh herbs, prawns and caviar sauce.
Credit cards: 1, 2, 3
Proprietors: Malcolm & Linda Holden

Drymen
by Loch Lomond

MAP 3

BUCHANAN HIGHLAND HOTEL
Main Street, Drymen
by Loch Lomond, Stirlingshire
G63 0BQ
Tel: 0360 60588
Fax: 0360 60943

A811 Balloch (Loch Lomond)/Stirling. Drymen is c. 7 1/2 miles east of Balloch.
This has long been a favourite hotel for those who enjoy lovely scenery of the Trossachs and Loch Lomond and when you have finished seeing the countryside there is so much to return to. This attractive old 18th century building has a fully equipped leisure club with swimming pool, sauna, solarium, gymnasium and squash courts. It also has a bowling green and can arrange tennis, golf or fishing for

those so inclined. Public rooms are spacious and comfortably furnished, and there are two good restaurants: Tapestries, with an excellent menu of well presented food, and the Granary, for less formal eating. The staff have been well trained and it shows in polite, attentive and informed service. Breakfasts are quite something, with a great range of choice.
Open all year
Rooms: 50 with private facilities
Bar Lunch (Granary) 12.30 – 2.30 pm (a)
Dining Room/Restaurant Lunch (Tapestries) 12.30 – 2.30 pm (b)
Bar Supper (Granary) 5.30 – 9.30 pm (b)
Dinner (Tapestries) 7 – 9.30 pm (c)
Facilities for the disabled
Bed & breakfast £80 – £88
Dinner B & B £50 – £71 (min 2 nights stay)
Roast monkfish with bacon, thyme and Noilly Prat. Venison with celeriac and a Glayva cream.
STB Commended 4 Crowns
Credit cards: 1, 2, 3, 5

Dufftown

MAP 5

A TASTE OF SPEYSIDE
10 Balvenie Street, Dufftown
Banffshire AB5 4AB
Tel: 0340 20860

50 yards from Tourist Infomation Centre on Elgin road (A941).
Situated in Dufftown, the malt whisky capital of the world, this small independent restaurant and whisky tasting centre aims to promote the best of Speyside food and fine Speyside malts, of which there is an unrivalled selection. Proprietors Joe Thompson and Raymond McLean are on hand to assure a warm welcome. Group bookings out of season can be arranged.
Open 1 Mar to 31 Oct
Bar Meals 11 am – 6 pm (a)
Dinner 6 – 9 pm (b)
Taste of Speyside Platter, roast loin of Scottish lamb, venison and red wine pie, home-made pâtés, soups, bread. Whisky cake. Heather honey and malt whisky cheese cake.
Credit cards: 1, 2, 3
Proprietors: J Thompson & R McLean

Dulnain Bridge

MAP 6

AUCHENDEAN LODGE HOTEL
Dulnain Bridge, Grantown-on-Spey
Morayshire PH26 3LU
Tel: 047 985 347

On A95, 1 mile south of Dulnain Bridge.
An Edwardian hunting lodge, now a comfortable country hotel, furnished with antiques and elegant furnishings, whilst retaining its homeliness. Relax informally with Highland hospitality and log fires. Marvel at some of the finest views across the River Spey and Abernethy Forest towards the Cairngorm Mountains. Then enjoy the award winning home-cooked dinners, with specialities using wild produce from the woods and countryside. The extensive cellars have over 100 wines and 30 malt whiskies. Numerous walks in the woods behind the hotel. Pets welcome. French spoken.
Open all year
Rooms: 7 , 5 with private facilities
Dinner 7.30 – 10.30 pm (d) 4 course menu with choices
No smoking in dining room + one of the lounges
Bed & breakfast £15 – £37.50
Dinner B & B £36.50 – £59
Arbroath smokies in ale and cream, shaggy ink cap soup, wild mushroom pâté, venison steak in rowan jelly sauce, mallard with blaeberries, apple-stuffed pheasant breast with Calvados sauce. Black and white chocolate truffle cake.
STB Commended 3 Crowns
Credit cards: 1, 2, 3, 5
Proprietors: Eric Hart & Ian Kirk

MUCKRACH LODGE HOTEL
Dulnain Bridge, Grantown-on-Spey
Morayshire PH26 3LY
Tel: 047 985 257
Fax: 047 985 325

*On A938, 1/2 mile west of Dulnain
Bridge.*

Former shooting lodge located in ten
secluded acres; the Dulnain River is
adjacent to the hotel. This tastefully
furnished lodge has a warm friendly
atmosphere. You may relax with a drink
by the log fire in the elegantly furnished
cocktail bar before dining in the
extended and refurbished restaurant,
where the emphasis is on the best of
local produce and friendly efficient
service. Muckrach Lodge offers both
table d'hôte and à la carte dinners and
an extensive wine list. All rooms have
colour TV, telephone, tea/coffee-making
facilities and are fully centrally heated.
Open all year except Nov
Rooms: 12 with private facilities
Bar Lunch 12 – 2 pm (a)
*Dining Room/Restaurant Lunch 12 –
2 pm (b)*
Dinner 7.30 – 9 pm (d)
Facilities for the disabled
Bed & breakfast £39 – £47
Dinner B & B £61 – £69
*Special weekly rates for Dinner B & B
available*
Aberdeen Angus beef, Morayshire lamb,
Spey salmon, sea trout. West coast
shellfish, Aberdeen fresh fish. Scottish
cheese board. Home-made soups, pâtés
and desserts. Lunchtime – Muckrach
'substantial' sandwiches.
STB Commended 4 Crowns
Credit cards: 1, 2, 3, 5, 6
Proprietors: Roy & Pat Watson

Dumfries

MAP 1

CAIRNDALE HOTEL
English Street, Dumfries
Dumfriesshire DG1 2DF
Tel: 0387 54111 • Telex: 777530
Fax: 0387 50555
*Situated close to centre of town, on A75
Dumfries-Carlisle route.*

Privately owned and managed by the
Wallace family, this well established hotel
offers all the comfort expected from one
of the region's leading three star hotels.
Originally three Victorian town houses,
the Cairndale now has 76 rooms all with
private facilities, TV, radio, direct dial
telephone, hairdryer and hospitality tray
as standard. Executive rooms and suites
have queen size double beds, mini-bars,
trouser presses and jacuzzi spa baths. In
1991 the Cairndale opened a purpose-
built leisure centre – the Barracuda
Leisure Club – with a heated indoor
swimming pool, sauna, steam room, spa
bath, gymnasium, health/beauty salon,
toning tables, sunbed. There is a carvery
restaurant and continental cafe bar
within the Club.
Open all year
Rooms: 76 with private facilities
Bar Lunch 12 – 2.30 pm (a)
*Dining Room/Restaurant Lunch 12 –
2.30 pm (a)*
Dinner 7 – 9.30 pm: 7 – 10 pm
Carvery (c)
Bed & breakfast £30 – £65
Dinner B & B £45 – £80
*Special rates available for midweek,
weekend + golf breaks*
Smoked salmon mousse with tayberry
cream sauce. Noisettes of Border lamb
with apricots and brandy sauce. Scampi
in Chef Hoefkens' own style. Roast sirloin
of Galloway beef. Hot butterscotch
pancake with pear.
STB Commended 4 Crowns
Credit cards: 1, 2, 3, 5
Proprietors: The Wallace Family

STATION HOTEL
Lovers Walk, Dumfries
Dumfriesshire DG1 1LT
Tel: 0387 54316
Fax: 0387 50388
*Just outside town centre opposite railway
station.*

The hotel offers a delightful combination
of modern guest comfort and facilities
within the maintained character of a
Listed fine red sandstone building. It is
conveniently situated close to the
commercial and shopping centre of this
charming historic town, yet is only one
mile from the attractive Borders
countryside and Burns heritage trail.
*Open all year except Christmas + Boxing
Days, 2 Jan*
Rooms: 32 with private facilities
Bar Lunch 12 – 2 pm (a)

Bar Supper 5 – 10 pm (a)
Dinner 7 – 9.30 pm (b)
*Taste of Scotland applies to main
restaurant only*
No smoking area in restaurant
Bed & breakfast £38 – £63
Dinner B & B £53 – £78
STB Commended 4 Crowns
Credit cards: 1, 2, 3, 5, 6

Dunbar

MAP 4

THE COURTYARD HOTEL &
RESTAURANT
Woodbush Brae, Dunbar
East Lothian EH42 1HB
Tel: 0368 64169
*A1 to Dunbar, 28 miles east of
Edinburgh. Take road off south end of
town's main street towards seashore.*

The water washes against the walls of
these fishermen's cottages which have
been sympathetically converted to a
small hotel and restaurant. Superb views
from the first floor restaurant over the
Forth estuary. The Courtyard is set in the
heart of golf country and is also ideal for
touring the Border country with its wild
and beautiful coastline – yet only 28
miles from the Edinburgh city lights. The
proprietor has built up a good regular
clientele and a sound reputation for
interesting, imaginative – and
inexpensive – food.
Open all year
Rooms: 7 , 2 with private facilities
*Dining Room/Restaurant Lunch 12 –
2 pm (a)*
Dinner 7 – 9.30 pm (b)
Bed & breakfast £21.50 – £39
Dinner B & B £34.50 – £52
*Home-made pâtés and soups. Locally
landed fish and shellfish e.g scallops with
a light white wine and tomato sauce,
dressed crab, monkfish with garlic,
haddock with spiced cream sauce. Steaks
with home-made sauces, chicken with
wild mushroom sauce. Home-made desserts.*
STB Commended 2 Crowns
Credit cards: 1, 3
Proprietor: Peter W Bramley

Credit Card Code		*Meal Price Code*	
1.	Access/Mastercard/Eurocard	(a)	under £10
2.	American Express	(b)	£10 – £15
3.	Visa	(c)	£15 – £20
4.	Carte Bleu	(d)	£20 – £25
5.	Diners Club	(e)	£25 – £30
6.	Mastercharge	(f)	over £30

Dunblane

MAP 4

STAKIS DUNBLANE HYDRO
Perth Road, Dunblane
Perthshire FK15 0HG
Tel: 0786 822551 • Telex: 776284
Fax: 0786 825403

The Stakis Dunblane Hydro is situated
on the fringe of the rural town, from
which it takes its name, within 44 acres of
private mature grounds and
commanding a magnificent view. Built in
1878 as a hydropathic, this splendid
Victorian hotel retains many of its
original features within the facade and
has been modernised and refurbished to
a high standard of comfort. There are
extensive leisure facilities both indoors
and outdoors, and regular entertainment.
Open all year
Rooms: 219 with private facilities
*Dining Room/Restaurant Lunch 12.30
– 2.15 pm (b)*
Afternoon Tea 3 – 5.30 pm
Dinner 6.30 – 9.30 pm (c)
No smoking area in restaurant
Bed & breakfast £39 – £49
*Dinner B & B £49 – £59 (min 2 nights
stay)*
*Terrine of Perthshire pheasant, pigeon
and pistachio. Steamed fillet of Tay
salmon with fresh spinach and pine kernels.*
STB Commended 4 Crowns
Credit cards: 1, 2, 3, 5, 6

Dundee

MAP 4

THE OLD MANSION HOUSE HOTEL
Auchterhouse
by Dundee DD3 0QN
Tel: 082 626 366

*On A923, 7 miles west of Dundee, then
B954 past Muirhead.*
A small luxury hotel converted by the
present owners from a 16th century
baronial home, within 10 acres of
beautiful gardens and woodlands. The
lands around the house steeped in
Scottish history have been in the
ownership of several noted families,
namely the Ogilvies, Strathmores, and
the Earls of Buchan. Superb dining and
excellent wine cellar.
*Open all year except Christmas/New Year
period*

Rooms: 6 with private facilities
Bar Lunch 12 – 2 pm (a)
*Dining Room/Restaurant Lunch 12 –
2 pm (a-b)*
Dinner 7 – 9.30 pm (d)
Bed & breakfast from £40
*Cullen skink, collops in the pan, venison
terrine.*
STB Commended 4 Crowns
Credit cards: 1, 2, 3, 5
Proprietors: Nigel & Eva Bell

THE SANDFORD COUNTRY HOUSE HOTEL
Newton Hill, Wormit
nr Dundee, Fife DD6 8RG
Tel: 0382 541802
Fax: 0382 542136

*Near to B946 junction with A914 route
which links Forth Road Bridge,
Edinburgh with Tay Bridge, Dundee.*
This is one of the Kingdom of Fife's most
picturesque Listed country house hotels.
It is renowned for its fine Scottish and
European cuisine and comfortable
accommodation. Seasonal dishes in
particular, served in the oak-beamed
restaurant, are the hallmark of Chef
Steven Johnstone. An extensive wine list
has been carefully chosen in order to
complement the variety of dishes on the
à la carte and table d'hôte menus. The
hotel is located near to both St Andrews
and Dundee and provides an excellent
venue for those touring, fishing, golfing
or shooting in this region of Scotland.
Since taking over during 1991, the new
owners and the new chef have made a
very considerable impact on standards
which have been uplifted throughout the
building. German spoken.
Open 1 Feb to 31 Dec
Rooms: 16 with private facilities
Bar Lunch 12 – 2 pm (b)
*Dining Room/Restaurant Lunch 12 –
1.45 pm (b)*
Bar Supper 6 – 8 pm (b)
Dinner 7 – 9 pm (c-d)
No smoking in restaurant
Facilities for the disabled
Bed & breakfast from £44
*Ravioli of East Neuk seafood in a chervil
butter sauce with ginger and leek. Pan-
seared fillet of salmon with caramelised
red cabbage in a sauce perfumed with
fennel and tarragon. Medallion of Angus
beef fillet in a red wine sauce with a
confit of shallots and garlic. Apple and
almond tart with an iced prune and
Armagnac parfait and caramel sauce.*
STB Commended 4 Crowns
Credit cards: 1, 2, 3, 5

STAKIS DUNDEE EARL GREY HOTEL
Earl Grey Place
Dundee DD1 4DE
Tel: 0382 29271 • Telex: 76569
Fax: 0382 200072

City location on the waterfront.
Situated on Dundee's waterfront,
commanding magnificent views over the
River Tay. Only minutes from the city
centre, this luxurious hotel promotes the
very highest standards of service and
accommodation. Leisure interests are
well catered for too – the hotel's own
leisure suite incorporates a pool, exercise
area, whirlpool and sauna.
Open all year
Rooms: 103 with private facilities
Bar Lunch 12.30 – 2.30 pm Sat only (a)
*Dining Room/Restaurant Lunch 12.30
– 2.30 pm except Sat (a)*
*Dinner 6.30 – 9.30 Sun: 6.30 – 10 pm
Mon to Thu: 6.30 – 10.30 pm Fri Sat
(c)*
Bed & breakfast £40 – £95
*Dinner B & B £43 – £60 (min 2 nights
stay)*
Room Rate £51.50 – £85
*Highland venison in honey and
Drambuie sauce, breast of pheasant in
whisky sauce. Cranachan, Atholl brose,
Drambuie cream.*
STB Commended 5 Crowns
Credit cards: 1, 2, 3, 5

STRATHDON HOTEL
277 Perth Road, Dundee
Tayside DD2 1JS
Tel: 0382 65648

*On main Perth road, in Dundee's west
end – close to Ninewells Hospital,
Dundee Airport and the University.*
The Strathdon Hotel is in an attractive
Edwardian terrace and many of its rooms
enjoy delightful views over the River Tay.
It is personally run by chef/proprietor
Ian Hornsby and his wife, Carole, who
take pride in ensuring their guests are
made to feel welcome and at home
during their stay. The Strathdon's
popular restaurant is steadily gaining a
reputation for exceptional cuisine using
fresh local produce, complemented by a
fine selection of wines.
Open all year
Rooms: 8 with private facilities
Dinner 7 – 8.45 pm except Sun (b)
Restricted hotel licence
No dogs
No smoking in restaurant
Bed & breakfast £19.50 – £30

Dinner B & B rates on application
Fish stews with king prawns, scallops,
lemon sole and Tay salmon. Noisettes of
lamb and venison. Savoury pancake
glazed with an Arran mustard sauce.
Raspberry crème brûlée with almond
shortbread.
No credit cards
Proprietors: Ian & Carole Hornsby

Dundonnell

MAP 6

DUNDONNELL HOTEL
Dundonnell, by Garve
Ross-shire IV23 2QR
Tel: 085 483 204

On A832 south of Ullapool.
Set by the shores of Little Loch Broom in
the spectacular wilderness of Wester Ross
this three star hotel renowned for its
quality and comfort has been in the
ownership of the Florence family for the
past 30 years. Mid-way between Ullapool
and Gairloch this is the ideal place from
which to explore the surrounding hills
and glens as well as the better known
attraction of Inverewe Gardens.
Open Apr to Oct
Rooms: 24 with private facilities
Bar Lunch 12.15 – 2 pm (b)
Bar Supper 6 – 8.15 pm (b)
Dinner 7 – 8.30 pm (d)
Bed & breakfast £32.50 – £43.50
Dinner B & B £54 – £65
Home-made soups, scallops Moniack,
Drambuie prawn, seafood, chicken,
salmon in dill, cranachan, Scottish
flummery, Caledonian cream.
STB Commended 4 Crowns
Credit cards: 1, 3, 6
Proprietors: Selbie & Flora Florence

Dunfermline

MAP 4

PITFIRRANE ARMS HOTEL
Main Street, Crossford
nr Dunfermline KY12 8NJ
Tel: 0383 736132 • Telex: 728255
Fax: 0383 621760

A994 west of Dunfermline, i.e. Glasgow
road.
The Pitfirrane Arms Hotel is one of the
few original coaching inns left in the
country which has been restored and
extended to meet the modern demand
for excellent cuisine and high standards.
Situated in the pleasant village of
Crossford, on the main Dunfermline-
Glasgow road (A994), the hotel is within
easy access of M90.
Open all year
Rooms: 38 with private facilities
Bar Lunch 12 – 2.15 pm (a)
Dining Room/Restaurant Lunch 12 –
2.15 pm (b)
Bar Supper 5.30 – 9.15 pm (a)
Dinner 7 – 9.15 pm (b)
Bed & breakfast £20 – £53
Dinner B & B £23.75 – £68
Locally available fresh produce.
STB Commended 4 Crowns
Credit cards: 1, 2, 3
Proprietor: M McVicars

Dunkeld

MAP 4

HILLHEAD OF DUNKELD
Brae Street, Dunkeld
Perthshire PH8 0BA
Tel: 0350 728996/728851
Fax: 0350 728705

Exit to Dunkeld from A9, 12 miles north
of Perth. Cross bridge into Dunkeld and
take second road on right. Entrance is first
on left.
Dunkeld is the ancient capital of
Scotland, and Hillhead is situated high
above the town, overlooking the
cathedral and the River Tay. This is
Macbeth country of wooded parkland
and distant mountains, and this country
house sits comfortably serene in six acres
of terraced lawns, trees and herbaceous
beds. It is beautifully decorated
throughout and equipped with fine
china, glassware and napery. A bar lunch
menu which includes such items as
baked avocado wrapped in a puff pastry
trellis, and crisp tulip basket filled with
vanilla ice-cream on a pool of raspberry
purée, gives clear indication that the food
throughout is of a very high standard as
indeed is the service.

Open all year
Rooms: 6 with private facilities
Bar Lunch 12.30 – 2 pm (a)
Dining Room/Restaurant Lunch 12.30 –
2 pm (b)
Dinner 7.15 – 9 pm (d)
Restricted licence
Dogs by arrangement
Facilities for the disabled
No smoking in restaurant + bedrooms
Bed & breakfast £36 – £53
Dinner B & B £50 – £76
A medley of langoustine, sole and prawn
in a piquant white wine sauce. Gently
grilled fillet of wild Tay salmon with a
cucumber and Vermouth sauce.
STB Highly Commended 4 Crowns
Credit cards: 1, 3
Proprietors: Malcolm & Claire Mair

STAKIS DUNKELD HOUSE
HOTEL
Dunkeld
Perthshire PH8 0HX
Tel: 0350 727771 • Telex: 76657
Fax: 0350 728924

A9 to Dunkeld, hotel lies c. 1 mile beyond
village.
A superbly elegant hotel, Dunkeld House
is set in its own 280 acre estate on the
banks of the River Tay, one of Scotland's
finest salmon rivers. Originally built as a
dower house at the turn of the century
by the seventh Duke of Atholl, it is now a
five star luxury hotel but manages to
retain the aura of a country house. The
hotel has been sympathetically extended
and has a private two mile salmon beat
on the river, a world class shooting
academy and first class leisure facilities. It
is also a haven for bird-watchers and
walkers.
Open all year
Rooms: 92 with private facilities
Bar Lunch 12 – 2 pm (b)
Dining Room/Restaurant Lunch 12.30 –
2 pm (b)
Dinner 7 – 9.30 pm (d)
Bed & breakfast £45 – £77.50
Dinner B & B £65 – £97.50 (min 2
nights stay)
Breast of Perthshire wood pigeon served
on pickled red cabbage with a lime and
redcurrant sauce. Medallions of beef
topped with a herb crust and served with
a red wine and shallot sauce. Rich
orange chocolate mousse with chocolate
shortbread. Raspberry crème brûlée.
STB Commended 5 Crowns
Credit cards: 1, 2, 3, 5, 6

Dunoon

MAP 3

ARDFILLAYNE HOTEL
BEVERLEY'S RESTAURANT
Bullwood Road, Dunoon
Argyll PA23 7QJ
Tel: 0369 2267
Fax: 0369 2501

At west end of Dunoon (A815).
A fine country house nestling in 16 acres of wooded grounds overlooking the old town of Dunoon and the Clyde estuary. The hotel is a treasure trove of antique furniture. Beverley's Restaurant with fresh flowers, lace, candlelight and silver, creates an atmosphere of Victorian sophistication. A large à la carte menu features some of the most famous French dishes, using Aberdeen Angus beef, lobster, fish and shellfish, direct from the west coast islands. An extensive wine list, old malts, brandies and ports complete a memorable meal. Altogether a top class restaurant, strongly recommended in many leading guides including AA Top 500 Restaurants in Great Britain.
Open all year
Rooms: 8 with private facilities
Dinner 7 – 9 pm (d)
Restaurant closed Sun evening in Winter
No smoking in restaurant
Bed & breakfast £35 – £45
Dinner B & B £56 – £67
Venison Lady Mary of Guise – an old recipe for dressing venison, with spices, claret, lemons, butter and walnut ketchup. Steak Glengoyne – grilled, with smoked Orkney cheese and flamed with whisky. Halibut steak poached in milk with a light lemon and cream sauce. Scallops St Veronique. Cream of mussel soup. Loch Fyne oyster and champagne soup. Baked Loch Fyne crab.
STB Highly Commended 4 Crowns
Credit cards: 1, 2, 3, 5, 6
Proprietors: Bill & Beverley McCaffrey

CHATTERS
58 John Street, Dunoon
Argyll PA23 8BJ
Tel: 0369 6402

On John Street, Dunoon, opposite the cinema.
Chatters is relatively small but it has added new and exciting dimensions to the eating out scene in Dunoon and from the moment it opened Taste of Scotland received a regular stream of correspondence from the public warmly recommending it. Rosemary MacInnes had earned a fine reputation at Stathlachlan and has clearly taken with her to Dunoon the same personal qualities of charm and warmth that made her such a welcoming hostess. Chatters is an all day establishment serving morning coffee, lunches, afternoon tea and à la carte dinners of superb quality and excellent presentation. Tasteful decor and carefully selected staff provide the right atmosphere for the full enjoyment of really good food.
Open mid Feb to 22 Dec
Bar Lunch 11.30 am – 2.30 pm except Sun (a)
Dining Room/Restaurant Lunch 11.30 am – 2.30 pm except Sun (b)
Bar Supper 6 – 9.30 pm except Sun (a)
Dinner 6 – 9.30 pm except Sun (c)
Closed Sun
Table licence
Smoking discouraged
Loch Fyne shellfish including langoustines, mussels, oysters and scallops etc. Saddle of Inveraray venison with Crème de Cassis sauce. Wide selection of home-made desserts.
No credit cards
Proprietor: Rosemary Anne MacInnes

ENMORE HOTEL
Marine Parade, Kirn, Dunoon
Argyll PA23 8HH
Tel: 0369 2230
Fax: 0369 2148

Seafront between Dunoon and Hunters Quay.
Charming Georgian country house hotel situated on the seafront between Dunoon and Hunters Quay. It was originally built as a Summer house for a wealthy cotton merchant and is now lovingly tended and cared for by the resident proprietors, David and Angela Wilson. Local and own garden produce feature on the imaginative menus, with Scottish delicacies from Loch Fyne and Argyll.
Open Feb to Dec
Rooms: 11 with private facilities
Bar Lunch 12 – 2.30 pm (a)
Dining Room/Restaurant Lunch 12 – 2.30 pm (b)
Bar Supper 5 – 10 pm (b)
Dinner 7.30 – 9.30 pm (d)
Bed & breakfast £29 – £55
Dinner B & B £50 – £75
Loch Fyne fish dishes, local venison and salmon.
STB Highly Commended 4 Crowns
Credit cards: 1, 3, 6
Proprietors: David & Angela Wilson

Eddleston

MAP 2

BARONY CASTLE HOTEL
Blackbarony, Eddleston
Peebles EH45 8QW
Tel: 07213 395
Fax: 07213 275

12 miles south of Edinburgh, 4 miles north of Peebles.
The Barony Castle has a truly impressive appearance – so reminiscent of a French chateau that one almost looks for the vineyards. The building goes back to the early 16th century and it is claimed that King James VI and Sir Walter Scott have stayed there. Bedrooms are large and comfortable with all the modern accessories one expects. There are 65 acres of grounds, an indoor heated swimming pool, sauna and jacuzzi.
Open all year
Rooms: 33 with private facilities
Bar Lunch 12 – 2.30 pm (a)
Dining Room/Restaurant Lunch 12 – 2.30 pm (a)
Bar Supper 7 – 9.30 pm (a)

Credit Card Code		Meal Price Code	
1.	Access/Mastercard/Eurocard	(a)	under £10
2.	American Express	(b)	£10 – £15
3.	Visa	(c)	£15 – £20
4.	Carte Bleu	(d)	£20 – £25
5.	Diners Club	(e)	£25 – £30
6.	Mastercharge	(f)	over £30

Dinner 7 – 9.30 pm (c)
Facilities for the disabled
No smoking area in restaurant
Bed & breakfast £33 – £83
Dinner B & B £49 – £99
Pan-fried breast of quail on a bed of
savoy cabbage. Roast rack of Border lamb.
STB Approved 3 Crowns
Credit cards: 1, 2, 3, 5

Edinburgh

MAP 4

ABBOTSFORD RESTAURANT & BAR
3 Rose Street
Edinburgh EH2 2PR
Tel: 031 225 5276

Rose Street, behind Jenners.
The Abbotsford is a good example of a traditional pub. It has a separate restaurant upstairs, where, in an atmosphere of Victorian charm, good honest inexpensive meals are served. It has been acclaimed in the United States as one of the best hostelries in Scotland. Small parties are catered for, by arrangement, in the restaurant.
Open all year except Christmas Day +
1 Jan
Bar Lunch 12 – 2 pm except Sun (a)
Dining Room/Restaurant Lunch 12 –
2.15 pm except Sun (a)
Dinner 6.30 – 10 pm except Sun (b)
Closed Sun
Seafood platter. Baked suprême of salmon
with Hollandaise sauce. Steaks with a
choice of sauces, e.g. pickled walnut, wild
mushroom.
Credit cards: 1, 3, 6
Proprietor: Colin Grant

THE BALMORAL EDINBURGH
Princes Street
Edinburgh EH2 2EQ
Tel: 031 556 2414 • Telex: 727282
Fax: 031 557 3747

East end of Princes Street at corner of
North Bridge.
Long a dominating feature at the junction of Princes Street and North Bridge, the old NB hotel has been splendidly and expensively renovated, restored and improved and has emerged as the Balmoral to play its role once again as a focal point in the social life of the city. The sumptuous and luxurious Grill Restaurant with its calm dignified atmosphere has imaginative and impressive menus. There is also a busy continental-style brasserie called The Bridges, and the NB Bar which lays claim to being the only pub on Princes Street and serves a limited snack menu. The grand function rooms of the hotel have been face-lifted and, mercifully, unaltered. There is also a well equipped new leisure complex. In addition, there is the Palm Court which is a formal yet relaxed setting for afternoon tea.
Open all year
Rooms: 189 with private facilities
Bar Snacks 11 am – 11 pm (a)
Brasserie Lunch (Bridges) 12 –
2.30 pm (a)
Dining Room/Restaurant Lunch (The
Grill) 12 – 2.30 pm except Sun Sat (c)
Dinner (Bridges) 6 – 11 pm (b)
Dinner (The Grill) 6 – 10.30 pm except
Sun (e)
No dogs
Facilities for the disabled
No smoking area in restaurants
Room Rate £105 – £550
NB Bar: hot roast beef sandwich roll.
Bridges: rosti with smoked salmon or cobb
salad. The Grill: salad of fresh shellfish
on mixed lentils, flavoured with balsamic
vinaigrette; poached salmon on julienne
of leeks with a tangy red and white wine
sauce; puff pastry filled with white
chocolate mousse, served with a rosette of
strawberries.
STB Highly Commended 5 Crowns
Credit cards: 1, 2, 3, 6

CALEDONIAN HOTEL
Princes Street
Edinburgh EH1 2AB
Tel: 031 225 2433 • Telex: 72179
Fax: 031 225 6632

West end of Princes Street.
This magnificent five star deluxe hotel has dominated the Edinburgh scene for most of this century and is truly the 'Grand Dame' of the city, known to and loved by people from all over the world. It is constantly being improved and upgraded in some sector. The dignified and gracious Pompadour Restaurant offers the very best experience in elegant eating with superb menus featuring Scottish specialities and reflecting the high culinary skills of a well trained and experienced kitchen brigade. The Carriages Restaurant on the ground floor offers a simpler menu than that in The Pompadour, but nevertheless carries a fine range of classic dishes with a leavening of international cuisine both at lunchtime and in the evening. For those in a desperate hurry, or a restful hour to spare, there is also an all day long service of coffee, sandwiches, afternoon tea etc in the foyer lounge. This is a hotel with it all and an Edinburgh without the Caley, as it is affectionately known, is unthinkable.
Open all year
Rooms: 240 with private facilities
Bar Lunch (Platform 1) 12 – 2 pm
except Sun (a)
Lunch (Carriages) 12 – 2.30 pm (c)
Lunch (Pompadour) 12.30 – 2 pm
except Sun Sat (c)
Afternoon Tea (Lounge) 3 – 5.30 pm
Dinner (Carriages) 6.30 – 10 pm (d)
Dinner (Pompadour) 7.30 – 10.30
pm Mon to Sat: 7.30 – 10 pm Sun (f)
No smoking area in restaurants
Bed & breakfast £139 – £161.50
Dinner B & B £169 – £191.50
Room Rate £125 – £675
Musselburgh pie, mussel and onion
brose, asparagus strudel, hot smoked
salmon with cinnamon and plum tea,
Tobermory smoked sea trout.
STB Deluxe 5 Crowns
Credit cards: 1, 2, 3, 5, 6

CARLTON HIGHLAND HOTEL
North Bridge
Edinburgh EH1 1SD
Tel: 031 556 7277 • Telex: 727001
Fax: 031 556 2691

City centre – North Bridge links the east end of Princes Street with the Royal Mile.
The Carlton Highland Hotel is a handsome Victorian building standing proud against the Edinburgh skyline, overlooking Princes Street and the historical Royal Mile. It prides itself on offering traditional Scottish hospitality, courtesy and a friendly welcome to all its guests. Its excellent facilities include 197 bedrooms and suites, each with every modern comfort, superb leisure centre, gift shop, hair and beauty salon, patisserie, tapas bar and nightclub. Fine cuisine of the highest quality is to be enjoyed in the hotel's two restaurants, Quills and the Carlton Court, where both table d'hôte and à la carte menus include dishes with a truly Scottish flavour.
Open all year
Rooms: 197 with private facilities
Bar Lunch 12 – 2.30 pm (a)
Dining Room/Restaurant Lunch 12 – 2.30 pm (c)
Bar Supper 6 – 10.30 pm (a)
Dinner 7 – 11 pm (c)
Facilities for the disabled
Bed & breakfast £74 – £116
Dinner B & B £92 – £134
Oak-smoked Scottish salmon. Ragout of Scottish seafood. Noisettes of venison, pan-fried with partridge breasts.
STB Highly Commended 5 Crowns
Credit cards: 1, 2, 3, 5, 6

CRAMOND GALLERY BISTRO
4 Riverside Cramond
Cramond Village, Edinburgh
EH4 6NY
Tel: 031 312 6555

Follow Cramond Glebe Road down to harbour front.
With its narrow wynds, steep steps and huddle of cottages, Cramond still looks the lovely little fishing village it had been for centuries and it is difficult to believe that one is still within the city of Edinburgh. There are even the foundations of a Roman fort clearly visible alongside Cramond Kirk. This is, therefore, a clever spot for Alan and Evelyn Bogue to have established a charming little bistro in one of the old buildings right on the quayside. Yachts nod gaily on the tide outside and there are glorious views across the Firth of Forth. Cramond Bistro, with its low timbered ceilings and lace tablecloths, exudes an entirely appropriate atmosphere. Sensibly, the menu is kept short, changes frequently depending on the availability of fresh produce, and concentrates on excellent local fish, shellfish and steaks. As the premises are unlicensed, guests are welcome to take their own wine.
Open all year except Christmas Day + 1 Jan
Dining Room/Restaurant Lunch 12 – 2.30 pm Sun to Sat, Jul to Sep (a)
Afternoon Tea available Jul to Sep
Dinner 7 – 9.30 pm except Mon Tue (b)
Note: closed Mon Tue from Oct to Jun
Unlicensed – guests welcome to take own wine
No smoking in restaurant
Wild duck with onion, shallots, oranges and brandy. Lobster tails with scallop sauce. Fresh salmon in dill and lemon cream. Special home-made puddings.
No credit cards
Proprietors: Alan & Evelyn Bogue

DALMAHOY HOTEL, GOLF & COUNTRY CLUB
Kirknewton
nr Edinburgh EH27 8EB
Tel: 031 333 1845
Fax: 031 335 3203

On A71 Edinburgh-Kilmarnock, 7 miles from Edinburgh city centre.
Set in rolling acres of beautiful little lochs, burns and trees, Dalmahoy has had a distinguished past and has now emerged as a first class country club hotel of character with a promising future. There are two challenging golf courses, the east course being of championship standards, and there are delightful distant views of Edinburgh and the Castle across the loch. The Pentland Restaurant with its stately regency columns has a varied menu of classic cuisine with specialities based on prime Scottish produce.
Open all year
Rooms: 115 with private facilities
Bar Meals 11 am – 11 pm (b)
Dining Room/Restaurant Lunch 12 – 1.45 pm except Sat (b-c)
Dinner 7 – 9.45 pm Mon to Sat: 7 – 9.15 pm Sun (d)
No dogs
Facilities for the disabled
Bed & breakfast £66 – £115
Dinner B & B £75 – £95
Pressed terrine of lobster, leek and Scottish salmon. Saddle of venison thinly sliced on a potato rosti. Hot soufflé flavoured with mirabelle plums and apricot brandy.
STB Commended 5 Crowns
Credit cards: 1, 2, 3, 5

DUBH PRAIS RESTAURANT
123B High Street
Edinburgh EH1 1SG
Tel: 031 557 5732

Edinburgh Royal Mile.
The frontage to Dubh Prais (Gaelic for cauldron) is only the width of a doorway and you can walk past it without being aware of it so use the Scandic Crown Hotel as a marker. The restaurant is right opposite. Stairs lead directly down to the small cosy and intimate cellar restaurant where James McWilliams, the genial chef/proprietor keeps an attentive watch over his guests. The menu has a light international touch to it but the ingredients are the pick of the Scottish markets and the presentation is of a high standard. Dubh Prais is now well established as a favourite restaurant for both locals and visitors alike. It is especially busy during the tourist season so do book in advance if you can.
Open all year except 2 wks Christmas + 2 wks Easter
Dining Room/Restaurant Lunch 12 – 2 pm except Sun Mon Sat (a)
Dinner 6.30 – 10.30 pm except Sun Mon (c)
Closed Sun Mon
Light pheasant and watercress mousse, saddle of hare, duck and bramble sauce, poached wild salmon, Mallaig scallops and Aberdeen Angus steak – just a few of the dishes you could expect to find on the menu.
Credit cards: 1, 2, 3
Proprietors: James & Heather McWilliams

THE GEORGE HOTEL INTER-CONTINENTAL
George Street
Edinburgh EH3 2PB
Tel: 031 225 1251

City centre of Edinburgh.
Listed amongst Edinburgh's premier hotels, the George enjoys a fine reputation. There are 195 comfortable bedrooms, many with superb views over the city. Le Chambertin Restaurant offers

the finest cuisine and the Carvers Table offers traditional roasts. The Clans Bar has a Scottish theme, decorated with artifacts and curios of the whisky trade.
Open all year
Rooms: 195 with private facilities
Bar Lunch 12 – 2.30 pm (a)
Dining Room/Restaurant Lunch 12.30 – 2.15 pm (c)
Dinner 6.30 – 10 pm (d)
No smoking area in restaurant
Bed & breakfast £87.50 – £147.50
Dinner B & B £102.50 – £162.50
Room Rate £125 – £150
STB Commended 5 Crowns
Credit cards: 1, 2, 3, 5, 6

GRINDLAYS RESTAURANT
8 - 10 Grindlay Street
Edinburgh EH3 9AS
Tel: 031 229 5405
Grindlays is an excellent new addition to the up market Edinburgh restaurant scene. The location has everything going for it – a few yards from Saltire Court, the new financial heart of the city, adjacent to the Lyceum Theatre and Usher Hall, a few hundred yards from the Lothian Road cinemas on one side and Castle Terrace multi-storey car park on the other. And if the location is right, so are the premises. Skilfully laid out to create the impression of small and intimate dining rooms rather than a large impersonal one. The menu is interestingly different with some traditional favourites alongside a good range of well prepared but not over-fussy dishes created from good daily fresh market produce. Full marks too to Grindlays for being open from 6 pm so that you may eat before a theatre show or concert – or even have one or two

courses and come back after the show for a dessert or cheese and coffee.
Open all year
Dining Room/Restaurant Lunch 12 – 2.30 pm (b)
Dinner 6 – 11 pm (c)
Parsleyed rack of lamb. Chicken in a basil and mustard sauce.
Credit cards: 1, 2, 3, 6
Proprietors: Lady Peta Linlithgow & David Jackson

HENDERSON'S SALAD TABLE
94 Hanover Street
Edinburgh EH2 1DR
Tel: 031 225 2131
2 minutes from Princes Street under Henderson's wholefood shop.
Established for over 25 years, Henderson's is a well known and popular rendezvous for healthy eaters. It offers a continuous buffet of fresh salads, savouries and sweets prepared with care and served in an informal cosmopolitan atmosphere. The restaurant specialises in wholefood, vegetarian and vegan dishes. Seating for up to 200. Live music in the evenings. Innovators of healthy eating.
Open all year except Christmas + Boxing Days, 3 + 31 May
Open 8 am – 10.30 pm; salads available throughout day
Breakfast 8 – 11.30 am except Sun (a)
Lunch 11.30 am – 3 pm except Sun (a)
Dinner 4.30 – 10.30 pm except Sun (a)
Closed Sun except during Edinburgh Festival
No smoking area in restaurant
Wide selection of herb teas, freshly squeezed juice, wines from growers using organic methods, hand-made bakery items made with stoneground flour, free range eggs.
Credit cards: 1, 2, 3, 5
Proprietors: The Henderson Family

THE HOWARD
32/36 Great King Street
Edinburgh EH3 6QH
Tel: 031 557 3500
Fax: 031 557 6515
Great King Street is off Dundas Street, the continuation of Hanover Street – 5 minutes from Princes Street.
An elegant and luxurious town house hotel situated in a quiet Georgian terrace in Edinburgh's New Town, yet within easy reach of Princes Street. The very highest standards are evident in every

aspect of the operation of this hotel. The No 36 Restaurant reflects the same pursuit of excellence; its daily changing lunch menu concentrates on presenting the best of freshly available produce from the markets, and for leisurely eating in the evening the chefs excel in the skilful preparation and presentation of excellently balanced well planned dishes which should satisfy the most exacting diner.
Open all year
Rooms: 16 with private facilities
Dining Room/Restaurant Lunch 12 – 2.30 pm except Sun (b)
Dinner 7 – 10 pm (c)
No dogs
Bed & breakfast £70 – £110
Dinner B & B £85 – £150
Room rate £70 – £255
A crisp parcel of Scottish seafood on seasonal leaves with a dill butter sauce. Fillet of Aberdeen Angus stuffed with herb mousse and chicken liver parfait.
STB Highly Commended 4 Crowns
Credit cards: 1, 2, 3, 5, 6

IGG'S RESTAURANT
15 Jeffrey Street
Edinburgh EH1 1DR
Tel: 031 557 8184
Off the Royal Mile.
This is a very interesting restaurant in a street just off the Royal Mile which has a reputation for its small interesting shops. The unusual name is derived from the first name of the proprietor, Ignacio Campos, who runs the restaurant personally. He has a wealth of catering experience behind him and this is a dignified yet relatively relaxed restaurant, with a bright interior and good standards of food preparation and presentation. "Specials" on the menu change daily dependent on the availability of produce in the market. Spanish and French spoken.
Open all year
Dining Room/Restaurant Lunch 12 – 2 pm except Sun Mon (a)
Dinner 6 – 10.30 pm except Sun Mon (b)
Closed Sun Mon
No smoking area in restaurant
Venison in a berry sauce. Lobster with crayfish sauce. Scallops in a white wine and mustard sauce.
Credit cards: 1, 2, 3, 5, 6
Proprietor: Ignacio Campos

JACKSON'S RESTAURANT
209-213 High Street
2 Jackson Close, Royal Mile
Edinburgh EH1 1PL
Tel: 031 225 1793/220 0620

An interesting cellar restaurant at the entrance to the historic Jackson Close, in the famous Royal Mile of old Edinburgh. Popular amongst both Scots and visitors, Jackson's restaurant offers excellent Scottish cuisine with a subtle French flair. In addition there is a private dining room available for parties of 15 to 45. Friendly service and a unique ambience make dinner in Jackson's a night to remember.
Open all year except Christmas + Boxing Days, 1 Jan
Dining Room/Restaurant Lunch 12 – 2 pm except Sun Sat (a)
Dinner 6 – 11 pm (d)
Extended hours during Edinburgh Festival
Haggis balls served in a whisky cream sauce, smoked salmon, Aberdeen Angus steaks with speciality sauces, fresh salmon, game and seafoods.
Credit cards: 1, 2, 3, 6
Proprietor: Lynn MacKinnon

KEEPERS RESTAURANT
13B Dundas Street
Edinburgh EH3 6QG
Tel: 031 556 5707
Dundas Street is to north of Princes Street and the continuation of Hanover Street.
Set in a delightful Georgian basement on the site of Scotland's first wine bar, this restaurant comprises three cellar rooms and a wine/coffee bar. The cellar rooms, with their original stone walls and floors, provide a relaxing atmosphere in which to dine. They may also be reserved for business meetings and private functions.
Open all year except Boxing Day + 1 Jan
Bistro bar upstairs open all day from 10.30 am
Bar Lunch 12 – 2.30 pm except Sun Sat (a)
Dining Room/Restaurant Lunch 12 – 2.30 pm except Sun Sat (a)
Pre-theatre 6 – 7 pm (a) any two courses à la carte
Dinner 6 – 10 pm except Sun (a-b)
Closed Sun except during Edinburgh Festival
No smoking area in restaurant
Imaginative game and poultry dishes – duck in wine and honey sauce garnished with grapefruit; venison collops with red

wine and cranberry sauce. Haggis and leek parcels. Extensive range – fish, steak, vegetarian dishes.
Credit cards: 1, 2, 3, 5, 6
Proprietor: Sheena Marshall

KELLY'S RESTAURANT
46 West Richmond Street
Edinburgh EH6 9DZ
Tel: 031 668 3847
West Richmond Street is off Clerk Street (continuation of North Bridge from east end of Princes Street) convenient for the Queen's Hall.
A really delightful and friendly little restaurant which has established itself very firmly as a favourite eating place for discerning diners looking for something special in the way of food, and a warm comfortable atmosphere in which to enjoy it. The Kellys are a charming couple, very much in evidence, and exercising close personal supervision of their restaurant. Jacque Kelly, sensibly, operates a limited but well balanced menu emphasising prime Scottish produce and the fact that it is almost impossible to get a table without booking in advance, speaks for itself. A place to which you will almost certainly want to return.
Open Nov to Sep except Christmas Day
Private lunches by prior arrangement only (b)
Dinner 6.45 – 9.30 pm except Sun Mon (d)
Closed Sun Mon
Diners requested not to smoke until after 9 pm
Smoked Scottish salmon with mushrooms in Pernod sauce. Border lamb cutlets with orange Grand Marnier and rosemary glaze. Scallops poached in cream, spring onion and whisky sauce. Chocolate box surprise.
Credit cards: 1, 3
Proprietor: Jacque Kelly

KING JAMES THISTLE HOTEL
Leith Street
Edinburgh EH1 3SW
Tel: 031 556 0111 • Telex: 727200
Fax: 031 557 5333
East end of Princes Street.
Restaurant St Jacques at the King James Thistle Hotel serves a modern style cuisine using the best of Scottish and continental produce in both à la carte and table d'hôte menus. The limed oak,

gleaming marble and glistening brass make it impressive for business lunches or intimate for a special occasion. Italian, French, German and Spanish spoken.
Open all year
Rooms: 147 with private facilities
Bar Lunch (Boston Bean Co) 12 – 3 pm (a)
Dining Room/Restaurant Lunch (St Jacques) 12 – 2 pm except Sun (b)
Dinner (St Jacques) 6.30 – 10.30 pm (c)
No dogs except guide dogs
Bed & breakfast £88 – £109
Room Rate £80 – £95
Salmon and monkfish terrine flavoured with saffron jelly and marinated ginger scallops. Fillet of venison rolled in poppy seeds, served with a rich raspberry sauce. Salmon suprême, poached with ginger and seaweed, in lemon and tarragon butter sauce. Loin of lamb with a mint and leek mousse on a rosemary glaze sauce. Chocolate cap filled with cranachan on a Glayva sabayon.
STB Highly Commended 5 Crowns
Credit cards: 1, 2, 3, 5, 6

LIGHTBODY'S RESTAURANT & BAR
23 Glasgow Road
Edinburgh EH12 8HW
Tel: 031 334 2300
On main Corstorphine road out of Edinburgh towards the airport and Glasgow.
Family run business with friendly warm atmosphere and consistent standards. A popular business rendezvous at lunchtime and light bar meals are also available for lunch and evening (week days only). More leisurely meals chosen from an à la carte menu which changes regularly using the best of fresh Scottish produce.
Open all year except Christmas + Boxing Days, 1 + 2 Jan
Bar Lunch 12 – 2 pm except Sun (a)
Dining Room/Restaurant Lunch 12 – 2 pm except Sun (a)
Bar Supper 6 – 9.30 pm except Sun (a)
Dinner 6 – 10 pm except Sun (c)
Closed Sun
Fresh soups made with Scottish seafoods. Salmon, mussels and lobsters. Scotch beef, lamb, venison in a variety of sauces. Duck, freshwater trout, and white fish bought locally.
Credit cards: 1, 2, 3
Proprietors: Malcolm & Norman Lightbody

MARTINS RESTAURANT
70 Rose Street North Lane
Edinburgh EH2 3DX
Tel: 031 225 3106

In the north lane off Rose Street between Frederick Street and Castle Street.
Do not be deterred by the location of this restaurant which stands in splendid isolation in a service lane in the city centre. It is not easy to find but you will be delighted when you do so. It is a favourite rendezvous of the Edinburgh business community and intelligentsia, and Martin and Gay Irons are excellent hosts and genuine in their welcome to this crisp clean well appointed small restaurant. Chef Forbes Stott's fine cooking continues to earn favourable plaudits, and the cheese trolley is exceptional; Martin can practically tell you the name of the cows from which the milk came!
Open all year except 22 Dec to 21 Jan (incl) + 10 days Sep/Oct
Dining Room/Restaurant Lunch 12 – 2 pm except Sun Mon Sat (b-d)
Dinner 7 – 10 pm except Sun Mon (d)
Closed Sun Mon
No smoking in dining areas
Menus are based on the availability of fresh local produce, are regularly changed and specialise in fresh Scottish seafish, shellfish and game.
Credit cards: 1, 2, 3, 5
Proprietors: Martin & Gay Irons

OLD BORDEAUX COACH HOUSE
47 Old Burdiehouse Road
Edinburgh EH17 8BJ
Tel: 031 664 1734
Just off A720 city bypass (Straiton junction), on A701 heading into Edinburgh.
This district of Edinburgh developed at the time when Mary Queen of Scots arrived from the French Court with her retinue. Burdiehouse is a corruption of 'Bordeaux House'. The Old Bordeaux Coach House was at one time the abode of exiled French silk weavers. Today it is a warm welcoming old world inn of character. There is indeed a fine old world feel to it and it has been furnished in appropriate style with attention to traditional comforts. This is a popular venue for citizens of Edinburgh, set in well kept gardens. You can enjoy eating by the log fire in the cosy lounge, or

watching the world go by from the conservatory. French and German spoken.
Open all year except Christmas + Boxing Days, 1 + 2 Jan
Food service 9.30 am – 10 pm (a-b)
Facilities for the disabled
Dunsyre Blue cheese croquettes. Haggis and neeps. Avocado Hebridean. Steaks, duck, Scottish salmon. Vegetarian dishes. Daily specials from best of local produce.
Credit cards: 1, 2, 3, 5
Proprietors: Alan & Linda Thomson, Adrian Dempsey

SCANDIC CROWN HOTEL
80 High Street, Royal Mile
Edinburgh EH1 1TH
Tel: 031 557 9797 • Telex: 727298
Fax: 031 557 9789
Centre of the Royal Mile tourist area.
Edinburgh's newest luxury four star hotel is situated right on the Royal Mile in the heart of the city, ideal for exploring the Old Town. The traditional exterior gives way to a spacious modern interior which combines the best of Scotland and Scandinavia to good effect. Food in The Jewel Restaurant is of high standard, specialising in produce of distinctly Scottish origin, but of course as befits the name of the hotel there is another restaurant where you can ring the changes and indulge in traditional Smorgasbord. There is a well equipped leisure centre and – exceptional in a city centre hotel – a large undercover and on site car park, giving direct access to the hotel.
Open all year except 3 + 4 Jan
Rooms: 238 with private facilities
Dining Room/Restaurant Lunch 12 – 2.30 pm (b)
Dinner 6.30 – 10.30 pm (c-d)
Facilities for the disabled
No smoking area in restaurant
Bed & breakfast from £74
Room Rate £89 – £155
Pockets of finest smoked Scottish salmon filled with marinated salmon, dill, capers and shallots accompanied by a light mustard dressing. Prime fillet of Angus beef, pan-fried with whole shallots and surrounded by a truffle sauce, topped with a garlic cream. Poached loin of Border lamb with crispy savoy cabbage served with creamy horseradish sauce and studded with redcurrants.
STB Commended 5 Crowns
Credit cards: 1, 2, 3, 5, 6

SHERATON EDINBURGH
1 Festival Square
Edinburgh EH3 9SR
Tel: 031 229 9131 • Telex: 72398
Fax: 031 229 6254
Lothian Road opposite Usher Hall and only 5 minutes from Princes Street.
The modern luxurious Sheraton Edinburgh Hotel, ideally situated in the heart of the city, and within walking distance of theatres and concert halls, has embarked on an exciting renovation and refurbishment programme. In May 1993, there will be a completely new look. From the outside, it will be the familiar facade of the Sheraton Edinburgh but the interior will be traditional in flavour and this will be reflected in the warmth and richness of natural wood, and the designs and colours associated with Scotland. By the end of February 1993, two new outstanding restaurants will have been created. The first, with stunning views of Festival Square and the Castle above, will have a friendly and informal atmosphere, and the other, smaller and designed for elegant dining, will specialise in the very best of Scottish produce. For those who wish to relax, there is a leisure centre with pool, sauna, whirlpool and fully equipped gymnasium. Children are welcome. French, Italian, German and Spanish spoken.
Open all year
Rooms: 263 with private facilities
All day dining in the Winter Garden 11 am – 11 pm
Scottish Grill Room Lunch 12 – 2.30 pm except Sun Sat
Scottish Grill Room Dinner 7 – 10.30 pm except Sun
Coffee and afternoon teas served in Winter Garden
No smoking areas in restaurants + lounge
Bed & breakfast rates on application
Dinner B & B rates on application
Weekend rates on application
Poached oysters on a buckwheat and spinach pancake with a vermouth and Scottish caviar butter sauce. Medallions of venison with rhubarb and ginger compote, on a Glayva flavoured game stock.
STB Highly Commended 5 Crowns
Credit cards: 1, 2, 3, 5, 6

SKIPPERS BISTRO
1A Dock Place, Leith
Edinburgh EH6 6UY
Tel: 031 554 1018

Leith, Edinburgh
The historic Port of Leith has always
needed a place like this and Allan
Corbett has provided it. Very much in
the style of a French bistro but with a
character all of its own, Skippers has a
well earned reputation as a leading fresh
seafood restaurant – but it is much more
than that. There is a friendliness and
conviviality about this informal place that
make a meal there one of those pleasant
experiences that one likes to remember.
Open all year
*Dining Room/Restaurant Lunch 12.30
– 2 pm (a-b)*
Dinner 7.30 – 10 pm (b-c)
*Specialises in fresh seafood. Oysters,
gravadlax, potted crab, sirloin steak with
smoked salmon and rosemary butter, sole
with noodles and saffron cream, halibut,
salmon etc.*
Credit cards: 1, 2, 3, 6
Proprietors: Allan & Jennifer Corbett

THE TATTLER
23 Commercial Street, Leith
Edinburgh EH6 6JA
Tel: 031 554 9999

*On corner of main road in Leith port
area (north Edinburgh).*
A cosy Victorian style pub and restaurant,
in an area now enjoying a resurgence of
bustle and interest and in which some
highly acclaimed eating places have
become established. The Tattler's menu
is extensive, covering a wide range of
seafood, meat, poultry and vegetarian
dishes. Dessert items have not always
been a strong point but more attention is
now being given to these. The Tattler
enjoys a good reputation locally and is a
popular lunch time rendezvous for Leith
business people while in the evening it
attracts clientele from a much wider area.
*Open all year except Christmas + Boxing
Days, 1 + 2 Jan*
Bar Lunch 12 – 2 pm (a)
*Dining Room/Restaurant Lunch 12 –
2 pm (b)*
Bar Supper 6 – 10 pm (a)
Dinner 6 – 10 pm (c)
*Some dishes unique to The Tattler, on
extensive restaurant menu with emphasis
on use of first class local produce. Bar
menu is particularly interesting.*
Credit cards: 1, 2, 3, 5
Proprietors: Alan & Linda Thomson

THE WITCHERY BY THE CASTLE
Castlehill, Royal Mile
Edinburgh EH1 1NE
Tel: 031 225 5613
Fax: 031 220 4392

*Situated at the entrance to Edinburgh
Castle.*
The Witchery survives the tourist crush
to remain intimate, friendly and quite
unique. Already steeped in eight
centuries of history, it claims once to
have been the very centre of witchcraft in
the Old Town and the Witchery
restaurant captivates this atmosphere.
The Secret Garden restaurant was
formerly a school playground which has
been carefully converted to retain the
atmosphere of bygone days, but is fully
contemporary in regard to style and
presentation of food.
Open all year except Christmas Day
Bar Lunch 12 – 3 pm (a)
*Dining Room/Restaurant Lunch 12 –
4 pm (a)*
Dinner 4 – 11 pm (c)
Reservations advisable
*Warm salad of wild mushrooms and
toasted pine kernels with a honey
dressing. Collops of venison in a red berry
sauce.*
Credit cards: 1, 2, 3, 5, 6
Proprietor: James Thomson

Elgin

MAP 5

THE MANSION HOUSE HOTEL
The Haugh, Elgin
Morayshire IV30 1AN
Tel: 0343 548811

*Located ¹/4 mile from main road, on
north-east side of Elgin.*
The Mansion House seems to go on
being improved year by year and is very
firmly established as the leading hotel in
Elgin. Although practically in the centre
of the town, it is located in quiet
parkland surrounded by mature trees.
The fine old 19th century mansion has
some lovely architectural features, but
rooms have every modern comfort and
there is even a leisure centre and
swimming pool. The menu is well
compiled and balanced, both in the bar
and the dining room, and service is
responsive, polite and efficient. Elgin is a
nice old town from which to discover the
whisky trails and castles for which the
locality is so well known.

Open all year
Rooms: 22 with private facilities
Bar Lunch 12.15 – 1.45 pm (a)
*Dining Room/Restaurant Lunch 12.15
– 1.45 pm (a)*
Bar Supper 5.30 – 10 pm (b)
Dinner 7.30 – 9.30 pm (c)
Bed & breakfast £65 – £70
Dinner B & B £77.50 – £95
*Fresh local produce – fish, game, fruit
and vegetables, talented presentation and
natural flavours of the cuisine match the
most demanding expectations.*
STB Highly Commended 4 Crowns
Credit cards: 1, 2, 3, 5, 6
Proprietor: Fernando de Oliveira

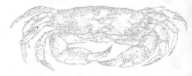

Elie

MAP 4

BOUQUET GARNI RESTAURANT
51 High Street, Elie
Fife KY9 1BZ
Tel: 0333 330374

A delightful little restaurant in the centre
of this charming East Neuk town. With
ample supplies of fresh fish and seafood
on its doorstep the Bouquet Garni
naturally specialises in high quality fish
dishes but with a complementary range
of other typical Scottish fare. The
intimate and cosy candlelit dining room
is almost certain to appeal to the
connoisseur of good food. Well worth a
detour. A little French spoken.
Open all year except first wk Feb
Bar Lunch 12 – 2 pm except Sun (a)
*Dining Room/Restaurant Lunch 12 –
2 pm except Sun (b)*
Dinner 7 – 9.30 pm except Sun (c)
Closed Sun
No smoking area in restaurant
*Rich langoustine and tomato flavoured
bisque; fillet of salmon with langoustine
mousse, creamed leeks, on Muscadet
sauce of potato, chives and cheese.
Strawberry shortcake with Glayva liqueur
cream and sweet butterscotch sauce.*
Credit cards: 1, 3
Proprietors: Andrew & Norah Keracher

Elrick
by Aberdeen

MAP 5

THE COURTYARD RESTAURANT
Elrick
by Aberdeen AB32 6TL
Tel: 0224 742540
Fax: 0224 742796

*A944 Aberdeen-Alford, Elrick is c. 7 miles
from centre of Aberdeen. (Restaurant is
behind Broadstraik Inn)*
The converted stable block of an old
country inn has been refurbished and
comfortably decorated to house the
Courtyard Restaurant. The Broadstraik
Inn has been a popular landmark for
years but the restaurant is an innovation
which offers the best of fresh seasonal
produce cooked in a light modern style
and served in an ambience distinctly
country house in appearance and atmosphere, with soft candlelight, an open
fire, impressive table settings, restful
colours and original watercolours on the
wall. The best kind of country restaurant.
Open all year
*Dining Room/Restaurant Lunch 12.30
– 2 pm except Mon Tue (b)*
*Dinner 6.30 – 9.45 pm except Mon
Tue (d)*
Closed Mon Tue
*Loin of local venison with cherry tomato
compote. Ravioli of langoustine with
lemon oil dressing. Caramelised pear tart
with toffee sauce.*
Credit cards: 1, 2, 3
Proprietor: Tony Heath

Erbusaig
by Kyle of Lochalsh

MAP 6

THE OLD SCHOOLHOUSE RESTAURANT
"Tigh Fasgaidh"
Erbusaig, Kyle
Ross-shire IV40 8BB
Tel: 0599 4369

*Outskirts of Erbusaig on Kyle-Plockton
road.*
In an idyllic setting, standing alone, this
charming old schoolhouse, built in the
1820s as the main school for the area
around Erbusaig, now offers an
education of a different sort. You can

enjoy seafood to steaks, vineyards to
vegetarian, Bach to Beethoven,
candlelight to carnations – offered in the
comfortable mellow atmosphere of a
building where generations of local
families have learned the three 'Rs'.
Booking advisable.
*Open Easter to end Oct: Nov to Easter
open Fri Sat by prior arrangement only
Rooms: 2 with private facilities
Dinner 7 – 10.30 pm (b-d)
Bed & breakfast £20 – £23
Home-cooked dishes using local seafood
and finest Scottish meats. Specially
prepared dessert selections.
Credit cards: 1, 3
Proprietors: Calum & Joanne Cumine*

Falkirk

MAP 4

INCHYRA GRANGE HOTEL
Grange Road, Polmont
Falkirk FK2 0YB
Tel: 0324 711911 • Telex: 777693
Fax: 0324 716134

*Junction 4 or 5, M9 motorway. Situated
on border of Polmont/Grangemouth.*
A fine example of a Scottish country
house set in eight acres of private
grounds, which has been modernised
and extended to provide comfort and
every modern amenity. The leisure club
has a fitness suite, beauty therapist, spa
bath, sauna and steam room. In the
restaurant you can choose from the
varied à la carte or table d'hôte menus,
carefully prepared and featuring local
favourites.
*Open all year
Rooms: 43 with private facilities
Bar Lunch 12 – 2 pm (a)
Dining Room/Restaurant Lunch 12.30
– 2 pm (a)
Bar Supper 6 – 10 pm (a)
Dinner 7 – 9.30 pm (c)
Bed & breakfast £25 – £60
Dinner B & B £40 – £49
Room Rate £71 – £88
Lobster and bacon chowder. Oven roasted
fillet of lamb with a redcurrant and
Glayva sauce.
STB Commended 4 Crowns
Credit cards: 1, 2, 3, 5, 6*

STAKIS FALKIRK PARK HOTEL
Camelon Road
Falkirk FK1 5RY
Tel: 0324 28331 • Telex: 776502
Fax: 0324 611593

On A803 west of town centre.
Set back from the road on a hill
overlooking a quiet park, is the Stakis
Falkirk Park Hotel. It is ideally located
less than one hour from Glasgow and
Edinburgh. The well appointed
bedrooms all include private facilities,
radio, TV, telephone and hospitality tray.
For the business user, function facilities
from five to 200. The hotel's restaurant
boasts à la carte menus specialising in
'Taste of Scotland' dishes.
*Open all year
Rooms: 55 with private facilities
Bar Lunch 12.30 – 2 pm except Sun (a)
Dining Room/Restaurant Lunch 12.30
– 2.30 pm except Sat (a)
Dinner 7 – 10 pm (b)
Bed & breakfast £48 – £77.50
Dinner B & B £61.95 – £91.45 (min 2
nights stay)
Room Rate £39.50 – £69
STB Commended 4 Crowns
Credit cards: 1, 2, 3, 5, 6*

Falkland

MAP 4

COVENANTER HOTEL
The Square, Falkland
Fife KY7 7BU
Tel: 0337 57224

Centre of Falkland.
This 17th century coaching inn – almost
opposite Falkland Palace – has been run
for 14 years by George and Margaret
Menzies who have established a fine
reputation for good food and warm
hospitality. There is a choice of the
traditional restaurant or informal bistro.
*Open all year except 1 Jan + first wk Jan
Rooms: 4 with private facilities
Bar Lunch 12 – 2 pm except Mon (a)
Dining Room/Restaurant Lunch 12 –
2 pm except Mon (a)
Bar Supper 7 – 9.30 pm except Mon (a)
Dinner 6 – 9 pm except Mon (b)
Table d'hôte dinner available as well as
à la carte
Closed Mon
No dogs
Bed & breakfast from £22.50
Dinner B & B from £34
A selection of made to order dishes with*

emphasis on home produce. *Scampi Falkland, Tay salmon, and Scottish beef dishes.*
STB Commended 3 Crowns
Credit cards: 1, 2, 3, 5, 6
Proprietors: George & Margaret Menzies

KIND KYTTOCK'S KITCHEN
Cross Wynd, Falkland
Fife KY7 7BE
Tel: 0337 57477

Off main street in village.
In many respects, historic village of Falkland is an architectural gem with some fascinating buildings and certainly merits a leisurely walk around either before or after you have visited the Palace. It also seems to be a frequent winner of Best Kept Village Awards. Entirely in keeping with the village and the background is Kind Kyttock's Kitchen, a really delightful little restaurant and tea room specialising in delicious home-baking in the traditional Scottish manner. There are too few places like this around nowadays and this one is certainly deserving of a visit and was a worthy winner of The Tea Council's Award for Excellence both in 1991 and 1992.
Open all year except Christmas Day to 3 Jan
Food service 10.30 am – 5.30 pm except Mon (a)
Closed Mon
No smoking throughout
Home-baked pancakes, scones, fruit squares, shortbread, wholemeal bread, stovies, cloutie dumpling. Locally grown vegetables used in Scotch broth and at salad table. Selection of teas available.
No credit cards
Proprietor: Bert Dalrymple

TEMPLELANDS FARM
Falkland
Fife KY7 7DE
Tel: 0337 57383

Off A912, 1/2 mile south of Falkland village.
Set on a hill, this comfortable modernised farmhouse on a small working farm overlooks the Lomond Hills and Falkland. It makes an ideal touring centre. There are 20 golf courses within 20 miles, including St Andrews, and National Trust properties nearby. Other facilities in the area include swimming pools, tennis and bowling.

Templelands offers an abundance of home-made food with soups and sweets a speciality. Coffee/tea facilities, clock radio, hairdryer and electric blanket in bedrooms. Children welcome – reduced rates if sharing with parents. Dogs accepted in bedrooms only.
Open Easter to Oct
Rooms: 2
Dinner at 7 pm (a)
Advance booking preferred
Residents only
Unlicensed – guests welcome to take own wine
No smoking except in lounge
Bed & breakfast £14.50 – £15
Dinner B & B £21.50 – £22
STB Commended 2 Crowns
No credit cards
Proprietor: Sarah McGregor

Fintry

MAP 4

CULCREUCH CASTLE
Culcreuch Castle Country Park, Fintry
Stirlingshire G63 0LW
Tel: 036 086 228/555
Telex : 557299 • Fax: 036 086 555

From Stirling take A811 west for 10 miles to junction with B822. Turn left to Fintry – 6 miles. From Glasgow, take A81 to Killearn then turn right on B818 to Fintry – 6 miles.
There are castles aplenty in Scotland and while some may lay claim to individual distinction, here is one with it all! Culcreuch has romance – in its close proximity to that most romantic of lochs, Loch Lomond; history – in its 700 years of existence as a fortress home for the Clan Galbraith; ghosts – human, animal and musical – but be re-assured, they are benevolent; and grace, beauty and dignity in the way in which it has been restored to the elegant country house hotel it is today. Set in a tranquil 1600 acre estate, there are log fires, a cosy dungeon bar, four poster beds and candlelit dinner; and the chef responds to the atmosphere by basing his menus on traditional Scottish fare.
Open all year
Rooms: 8 with private facilities + 16 lodges
Bar Lunch 12.30 – 3 pm (a)
Dining Room/Restaurant Lunch (b) – booking required
Bar Supper 5 – 9 pm (a)
Dinner 7 – 8.30 pm (c)

Bed & breakfast £32 – £60
Dinner B & B £52 – £80
Smoked trout fillet with citrus cream. Salmon steak oven-baked with white wine, prawns and capers.
Credit cards: 1,2,3,5,6

Fochabers

MAP 5

GORDON ARMS HOTEL
80 High Street, Fochabers
Morayshire IV32 7DH
Tel: 0343 820508
Fax: 0343 820300

A96 between Inverness and Aberdeen.
A lovely old coaching inn with roots going back over 200 years. It is conveniently located for all the activities for which Speyside is famous – whisky trails, golf, fishing on the Spey. Although extensively modernised the hotel retains a lot of the character and atmosphere of bygone days. It offers warm hospitality and good food. There is an interesting à la carte menu com-plemented by a well balanced wine list.
Open all year
Rooms: 12 with private facilities
Bar Lunch 12 – 2.30 pm (a)
Dining Room/Restaurant Lunch 12 – 2.30 pm (a)
Bar Supper 7 – 9.30 pm (a)
Dinner 7 – 9.30 pm (b)
Facilities for the disabled
Room Rate £45 – £65
Special rates available
Cornets of smoked salmon with a lime sauce. Langoustines. Noisettes of lamb served with a purée of mint cream sauce. Fillets of venison filled with prunes.
Credit cards: 1, 2, 3

Forfar

MAP 4

IDVIES HOUSE
Letham, by Forfar
Angus DD8 2QJ
Tel: 030 781 787
Fax: 030 781 8933

4 miles east of Forfar. Hotel is signposted.
Victorian country mansion set in spacious wooded grounds with fine views of the Angus countryside. The well appointed en suite bedrooms offer a high standard of comfort. A well stocked

bar features 150 Scottish malt whiskies and the two dining rooms have menus which reflect the fine quality and variety of Scottish produce. Idvies is personally run by the resident owners, assisted by friendly local staff.

Open all year
Rooms: 10 with private facilities
Bar Lunch 12 – 2 pm (a)
Dining Room/Restaurant Lunch 12 – 2 pm (b)
Bar Supper 6.30 – 9.30 pm except Sun Sat (a)
Dinner 7 – 9.30 pm except Sun (b-c):
7 – 8 pm Sun – residents only
Bed & breakfast £30 – £55
Dinner B & B £45 – £70
Home-smoked Tay salmon, Arbroath smokie mousse and pâté. Local crab and lobster. Home-cured gravadlax. Local venison, game and Angus steak dishes with Scottish liqueur and whisky sauces.
STB Commended 4 Crowns
Credit cards: 1, 2, 3, 5, 6
Proprietors: Pat & Fay Slingsby, Judy Hill

Forres

MAP 5

KNOCKOMIE HOTEL
Grantown Road, Forres
Moray IV36 0SG
Tel: 0309 673146
Fax: 0309 673290

On A940 just south of Forres on Grantown road.
Standing overlooking the Royal Burgh of Forres, the Knockomie Hotel is approached by a driveway just long enough to ensure that guests are away from the hustle and bustle of the main road. The restaurant endeavours to

provide the best of Scottish produce, including salmon, venison and Aberdeen Angus beef, complemented by an extensive wine list. There is a selection of over 70 distinctive malt whiskies in the bar.

Open all year
Rooms: 7 with private facilities
Bar Lunch 12.30 – 2 pm (a)
Dining Room/Restaurant Lunch 12.30 – 2 pm (b)
Dinner 7 – 9 pm (d)
Bed & breakfast £42.50 – £50
Dinner B & B £63 – £70
Scottish produce – scallops, salmon, rib of Aberdeen Angus beef, venison.
STB Commended 4 Crowns
Credit cards: 1, 2, 3
Proprietor: Gavin Ellis

Fort Augustus

MAP 6

LOVAT ARMS HOTEL
Fort William Road, Fort Augustus
Inverness-shire PH32 4DU
Tel: 0320 6204/6
Fax: 0320 6677

Set back from the main Fort William-Inverness road (A82), almost exactly half way between these two famous Highland towns.
Only those in a tremendous hurry will resist the temptation to tarry a while in Fort Augustus when travelling between Fort William and Inverness, and those who do will no doubt repair to the Lovat Arms – the dominant hotel in the village. The original 18th century Fort Augustus barracks were erected in what are now the grounds of the hotel and remnants remain in the huge wall alongside the car park. This spacious Victorian hotel in 2½ acres of grounds is redolent of a more leisurely age and is relaxed, comfortable and welcoming. The restaurant relies heavily, and rightly, on a wide range of west coast fish and shellfish together with local game and beef. Food is prepared to a high standard and bar meals are available in a large old lounge bar.

Open Mar to early Jan
Rooms: 21 with private facilities
Bar Lunch 12.30 – 2 pm (a)
Dining Room/Restaurant Lunch (a-b) – by arrangement
Bar Supper 6.30 – 8.30 pm: 6.30 – 9 pm Jul Aug (a)

Dinner 7 – 8.30 pm: 7 – 9 pm Jul Aug (c-d)
Bed & breakfast £26.50 – £33.50
Mussels Lovat Arms. Seafood cornucopia. Selection of salmon and beef dishes. Noisettes of lamb. Pheasant. Home-made sweets.
STB Commended 4 Crowns
Credit cards: 1, 3
Proprietors: Hector & Mary MacLean

Fort William

MAP 6

CRANNOG SEAFOOD RESTAURANT
Town Pier, Fort William
Inverness-shire PH33 7NG
Tel: 0397 705589/703919
Fax: 0397 705026

Fort William town pier – off A82 Fort William town centre bypass.
It would be lovely to think that every city had a Crannog Seafood Restaurant, but then much of the magic would be lost. This is a really special little restaurant and one that Fort William has long needed. It is located on the town pier and its bright red roofs make it starkly visible on the main road running along the waterfront. A wonderfully integrated business where you can watch the catch being off-loaded directly into the kitchen and shortly afterwards enjoy some of the finest and freshest shellfish you have ever tasted. From the same pier you can then set off on a cruise to Seal Island. This is a speciality restaurant concentrating on wonderfully good seafood; the decor is simple if not spartan so you do not pay for frills but get splendid value for money.

Open all year except Christmas Day + 1 Jan
Dining Room/Restaurant Lunch 12 – 2.30 pm (b)
Dinner 6 – 9.30 pm: 6 – 10.30 pm Jun to Sep (c)
Note: opening times may vary in Winter months
No smoking area in restaurant
Crannog bouillabaisse, smoked mussels and aioli, langoustine with hot garlic butter, salmon en croûte with spinach sauce, walnut tart and cream.
Credit cards: 1, 3

GLEN NEVIS RESTAURANT
Glen Nevis, Fort William
Inverness-shire PH33 6SX
Tel: 0397 705459

2¹/₂ miles along Glen Nevis from Fort William.
A long low ranch-style building, this restaurant is set amidst the scenic splendour of one of Scotland's loveliest glens, at the foot of mighty Ben Nevis. It is situated just outside Fort William and has ample parking. Large windows give every table a view of river and mountains.
Open mid Mar to mid Oct
Dining Room/Restaurant Lunch from 12 noon (a-b)
High Tea from 2.30 pm
Dinner from 5.30 pm (a-c)
Speciality menu changed each week – always features local produce.
Credit cards: 1, 3

THE MOORINGS HOTEL
Banavie, Fort William
Inverness-shire PH33 7LY
Tel: 0397 772 797
Fax: 0397 772 441

Situated off A830, 3 miles from Fort William.
Standing beside the Caledonian Canal at Neptune's Staircase, the Moorings has splendid panoramic views of Ben Nevis and surrounding mountains. The Jacobean-styled restaurant concentrates on Scottish specialities including west coast seafood and prime Scottish beef, complemented by fresh herbs from the hotel garden.
Open all year except Christmas + Boxing Days
Rooms: 24 with private facilities
Dining Room/Restaurant Lunch – by prior arrangement
Dinner 7 – 9.30 pm Mon to Sat: 7 – 8.30 pm Sun (d)
Taste of Scotland applies to main restaurant
Bed & breakfast £25 – £45
Dinner B & B £48 – £68
Marinated scallops, gravadlax, Loch Linnhe prawns, wild salmon, pin-hake. Seasonal local game dishes. Scottish beef, lamb and chicken prepared in an imaginative traditional manner. Fine Scottish cheeses.
STB Commended 4 Crowns
Credit cards: 1, 2, 3, 5, 6
Proprietor: Norman Sinclair

Gairloch

MAP 6

THE MOUNTAIN RESTAURANT & MOUNTAIN LODGE GUEST HOUSE
Strath Square, Gairloch
Ross-shire IV21 2BX
Tel: 0445 2316

In the main (Strath) square, Gairloch's centre.
Gairloch is remote and enchanting, and when one gets there the rest of the world seems a long way off. The Mountain Restaurant claims to be the village's liveliest and busiest restaurant, and uses to the full its splendid lochside setting to present some of the wonderful views out across the bay to the jagged Torridon mountains beyond. Its sun terrace and Alpine conservatory are especially popular in daytime. A wonderful range of no less than 30 different teas and coffees is offered with the daytime cafe menu. The scene changes in the evening for dinner by candlelight but with a degree of informality and fun. A recent addition to the establishment is 'The Nature Shop' displaying natural Scottish merchandise mainly from the highlands and islands.
Open Mar to first wk Jan except Christmas + Boxing Days
Rooms: 3, 2 with private facilities
Food service 9 am – 5.30 pm (a)
Dinner (26 Mar to mid Nov only) 6.30 – 10.30 pm (b)
No smoking area in restaurant
Dogs accepted outside terrace + guest house only
Bed & breakfast £15.75 – £19.95
Dinner B & B rates on application
Room Rate £14.50 – £20
Orkney cheese, herb and garlic croissant with fresh strawberry salad. Scotch salmon steak in Highland champagne butter. Glencairn Highland Beef Wellington. Home-made cinnamon and apple tart. Scottish Christmas pudding (served all year round!). Other desserts include 'Torridon Toboggan Run' and 'Northern Lights'.
STB Commended 2 Crowns
Credit cards: 1, 3
Proprietors: Andrew Rudge & Alison Reid

THE STEADING RESTAURANT
Achtercairn, Gairloch
Ross-shire IV21 2BP
Tel: 0445 2449

On A832 at junction with B802 in Gairloch.
Coffee shop/restaurant located in converted 19th century farm buildings retaining their old world atmosphere, adjoining the prize winning Gairloch Museum of West Highland Life. Local produce, seafood fresh from the loch, home-baked cakes and scones are on offer and there are special dishes for children. Self-service by day and waitress service in evenings. As the complete menu is available all day it is possible to choose what is wanted when it is wanted. The price ranges shown are therefore what a smaller (lunch) or a larger (dinner) meal might cost. Some French and German spoken. Dogs not allowed in restaurant but may be tied up outside in courtyard with water and shade.
Open Easter to end Sep
Food service all day 9.30 am – 9 pm except Sun (a-c)
Dinner 6 – 9 pm except Sun (c)
Closed Sun
Seafood platter – at least six varied seafoods presented with salad and a variety of dressings. Venison casseroled with red wine, mushrooms and spices. Haddock thermidor, baked in squat lobster sauce.
No credit cards

Galashiels

MAP 2

WOODLANDS COUNTRY HOUSE HOTEL & RESTAURANT
Windyknowe Road, Galashiels
Selkirkshire TD1 1RQ
Tel: 0896 4722
Fax: 0896 4722

Just off A7, take A72 towards Peebles. Turn left up Hall Street – Windyknowe Road is second on right.
The Scottish Border countryside is, of course, quite beautiful: full of stately homes, old abbeys and gentle rolling hills and woodland. Perhaps that is why Woodlands is so named, but whatever the origin, here is a lovely Victorian Gothic mansion in two acres of picturesque garden and splendidly situated for the entire Borders area yet within an hour of Edinburgh. Kevin

and Nicki Winsland are caring hosts, keen to ensure that their guests every comfort is looked after. They have been careful to preserve the original ambience and character of the building which has several fine architectural features. The dining room is elegant and comfortable and has a good reputation for fine food and interesting menus.

Open all year
Rooms: 9 with private facilities
Bar Lunch 12 – 2 pm (a)
Dining Room/Restaurant Lunch 12 –
2 pm (b)
Bar Supper 6 – 9.30 pm (a)
Dinner 7 – 9.30 pm (c)
Bed & breakfast £36 – £68
Dinner B & B £50 – £82
Scottish smoked salmon filled with a
mackerel mousse. Smoked oysters wrapped
in bacon and grilled, served in pastry
horns with a mustard sauce. Charcoal
grilled prime steaks.
Credit cards: 1, 3
Proprietors: Kevin & Nicki Winsland

Garve

MAP 6

INCHBAE LODGE HOTEL
by Garve
Ross-shire IV23 2PH
Tel: 09975 269

On A835 Inverness-Ullapool, 6 miles
west of Garve village.
This former Victorian hunting lodge, now a delightful country house hotel, nestles on the banks of the River Blackwater, surrounded by forests and mountains, six miles from the nearest village. Secluded, but not remote, in the very heart of the northern Highlands, Inchbae Lodge is ideally located for exploring this beautiful unspoilt part of Scotland. Over the years Les and Charlotte Mitchell, who are jointly responsible for the cooking, have built a reputation for high quality food, concentrating on local produce, prepared with care and imagination, and served in a relaxing and undemanding atmosphere. There is free trout fishing at the bottom of the garden, and clay pigeon shooting in the grounds. Children are welcome and accommodated free.
Open all year except Christmas + Boxing
Days
Rooms: 12 , 9 with private facilities
Bar Lunch 12 – 2 pm (a)

Bar Supper 5 – 8.30 pm (a)
Dinner 7.30 – 8.30 pm (c)
Facilities for the disabled
No smoking area in restaurant
Bed & breakfast £25 – £35
Dinner B & B £40 – £50
Halibut with smoked salmon sauce. Hill
lamb with orange and mint. Lightly
smoked sirloin with wild mushrooms.
Cloutie dumpling with whisky and
marmalade sauce.
STB Commended 3 Crowns
No credit cards
Proprietors: Les & Charlotte Mitchell

Gatehouse-of-Fleet

MAP 1

CALLY PALACE HOTEL
Gatehouse-of-Fleet
Dumfries & Galloway DG7 2DL
Tel: 0557 814341
Fax: 0557 814522

30 miles west of Dumfries, 1 mile from
A75 (main Dumfries-Stranraer road).
A magnificent and imposing four star hotel in an idyllic setting of 100 acres of forest, parkland and loch. The public rooms are particularly elegant and reflect the grandeur of the original 18th century mansion. The hotel has a core of regular devotees who would not dream of going anywhere else. The 55 bedrooms, suites and family rooms are tastefully furnished

all with private facilities, colour TV, trouser press, hairdryer etc. Indoor leisure facilities include a heated swimming pool, jacuzzi, sauna and solarium, and outdoors there is putting, tennis and croquet. The restaurant concentrates on using the best of local fresh produce, attractively presented. The hotel is superbly managed and caring well mannered staff are quick to respond to the guest's every need.
Open Mar to Dec
Rooms: 55 with private facilities
Dining Room/Restaurant Lunch
12.30 – 2 pm (b)
Dinner 6.30 – 9.30 pm (d)
No smoking in dining room
Bed & breakfast £45.50 – £49.50
Dinner B & B £50 – £62
Menus regularly feature prime Galloway
beef, venison, Cree salmon. All dishes
served with fresh vegetables in season.
STB Highly Commended 4 Crowns
Credit cards: 1, 3

Glasgow

MAP 3

THE BRASSERIE
176 West Regent Street
Glasgow G2 4RL
Tel: 041 248 3801

Approach via Bath Street from city centre;
turn left into Blythswood Street then left
into West Regent Street. From outwith
city, follow one way systems via
Blythswood Square to West Regent Street.
The Brasserie exudes an instant air of quality. An imposing pillared entrance leads in to a dining area that gives the impression of an exclusive club. The food is first class with some unusual items on the menu, and skill and flair demonstrated in its presentation. A courteous and quickly attentive staff have established the Brasserie as a lunchtime favourite for the business community while in the evening it appeals to a wider section of the population looking for a good destination restaurant.
Open all year except public holidays
Bar Lunch 12 – 3 pm except Sun (a)
Dining Room/Restaurant Meals 12 –
11 pm except Sun (b-c)
Bar Supper 5 – 11 pm except Sun (a)
Closed Sun
Wild mushrooms in garlic butter.
Suprême of duck with orange and honey
sauce. Creme brûlée.
Credit cards: 1, 2, 3, 5

THE BUTTERY

652 Argyle Street
Glasgow G3 8UF
Tel: 041 221 8188
Fax: 041 204 4639

Junction 19, M8 – approach by St Vincent Street and Elderslie Street.

This is a very unusual and, to its devoted clientele, a very special restaurant. Situated on the ground floor level of a renovated old tenement block – inside it is a joy. There are lovely touches of Victoriana and a demolished church has obviously contributed its pews and furniture to the construction of the bar. There is an excellent atmosphere of yesteryear in this quiet oasis of comfort and elegance. The high standards of food and polite and unobtrusive service make this one of Glasgow's very best restaurants, which in 1993 celebrates its tenth anniversary.

Open all year except bank holidays
Bar Lunch 12 – 2.30 pm except Sun Sat (b)
Dining Room/Restaurant Lunch 12 – 2.30 pm except Sun Sat (c)
Dinner 7 – 10.30 pm except Sun (e)
Closed Sun
Warmed oysters with smoked bacon and kita olive oil. Mignons of venison filled with haggis and pigeon with saffron barley. Layers of white and dark chocolate wafers, with a praline mousse.
Credit cards: 1, 2, 3, 5

CRANNOG SEAFOOD RESTAURANT

28 Cheapside Street
Glasgow G3 8BH
Tel: 041 221 1727
Fax: 041 221 1727

Off Broomielaw by River Clyde. At north end of Kingston Bridge. Accessible from Clydeside expressway.

Tucked away inconspicuously in Cheapside Street, Finnieston, the Crannog is not a restaurant that you chance upon or one that is dependent on passing trade. This is one you mark and remember. The simple, almost spartan, decor reassures you straight away that you will not be paying for an extravagant 'theme' and expensive furnishings. Time and money is not wasted on frills, yet the restaurant is comfortable enough and the ambience appropriate and pleasing. This is an establishment where seafood is king. The menu is built around really fresh fish and

shellfish cooked to perfection in straightforward traditional style so that it agitates the tastebuds the moment it is set before you. The Crannog formula started in Fort William where it has been a tearaway success, and has been introduced to Glasgow with the same care for quality that marks the original.

Open all year
Dining Room/Restaurant Lunch 12 – 2.30 pm except Sun Mon (a)
Dinner 6 – 9.30 pm Tue to Thu: 6 – 10.30 pm Fri Sat (c)
Closed Sun Mon
Fresh langoustines with garlic butter. Crannog bouillabaisse. Smoked salmon, mussels, trout smoked in own smokehouse in Fort William.
Credit cards: 1, 3

THE GLASGOW MARRIOTT

Argyle Street
Glasgow G3 8RR
Tel: 041 226 5577
Fax: 041 221 9202

At Junction 19 of M8 in centre of city, close to Central Station, Bus and Air Terminal, main shopping/commercial areas, and only 10 minutes by road from Glasgow Airport.

The Glasgow Marriott may have a new name, but this is a hotel that has been a focal point in the social and commercial life of the city for several years as the former Holiday Inn. The new Marriott can be relied on to bring in even higher standards and to continue the constant improvements that have been a characteristic of the hotel. There are two restaurants: L'Academie, a superb up market à la carte restaurant, and The Terrace, where you can make your selection from the produce of the day. The Cafe Rendezvous also offers snacks and light meals throughout the day. There is courtesy coach service to and from Glasgow Airport available to hotel guests.

Open all year
Rooms: 298 with private facilities
Cafe Rendezvous 10 am – 6 pm (a)
Terrace Restaurant 11 am – 10.30 pm (b-d)
Cafe Rendezvous 5 – 6.30 pm except Sun Sat (a)
Dinner (L'Academie Restaurant) 7 – 10.30 pm except Sun (c-f)
No smoking area in restaurant
Bed & breakfast rates on application
Dinner B & B rates on application
Credit cards: 1, 2, 3, 5, 6

MOAT HOUSE INTERNATIONAL

Congress Road
Glasgow G3 8QT
Tel: 041 204 0733 • Telex: 776244
Fax: 041 221 2022

Situated on the banks of the River Clyde, next to the SECC.

The Moat House International must surely have one of the most desirable sites in Glasgow, right on the bank of the River Clyde, adjacent to the Scottish Exhibition Centre and with generous parking. Externally it is towering glass but inside it is dramatically different with its open atrium-style court area dominated by the magnificent mural of Clydeside Glasgow. The bedrooms have magnificent panoramic views and are luxuriously equipped. Food in the Mariner Restaurant is outstanding with menus designed to titillate and excite even the most jaded appetite. Presentation is superb and the restaurant staff are polite, well trained and well managed. The Moat House International has not taken long to establish itself as one of Glasgow's best. On current standards it is likely to go on being so.

Open all year
Rooms: 300 with private facilities
All day dining 12 – 11 pm (Pointhouse)
Dining Room/Restaurant Lunch 12 – 3 pm (b)
Dinner (Pointhouse) 6.30 – 11 pm (b)
Dinner (Mariner) 6.30 – 11 pm except Sun (d)
No dogs
Facilities for the disabled
No smoking in restaurant
Bed & breakfast £50 – £120
Dinner B & B rates on application
Room Rate £40 – £100
STB Highly Commended 5 Crowns
Credit cards: 1, 2, 3, 5, 6

ROGANO RESTAURANT & CAFE ROGANO

11 Exchange Place
Glasgow G1 3AN
Tel: 041 248 4055
Fax: 041 248 2608

Glasgow city centre, near Buchanan Street precinct and Queen Street/George Square.

Since 1876, Rogano has been famed worldwide for its seafood and ambience. It was remodelled in 1935 in similar 'art deco' style to the 'Queen Mary' which was at the time being built on the Clyde. Rogano today maintains the same ambience and high standards on which its reputation was founded. Elegant restaurant on ground floor. Cafe Rogano is situated downstairs and has a bistro atmosphere.

Open all year except public holidays
Bar Lunch 12 – 2.30 pm except Sun (a)
Cafe Rogano 12 – 11 pm Mon to Thu:
12 – 12 midnight Fri Sat (b)
Dining Room/Restaurant Lunch 12 –
2.30 pm except Sun (c-f)
Dinner 7 – 10.30 pm (f)
Specialist fish restaurant. Feuillette of lobster and mussels in a dill cream. Steamed fillet of brill with lobster and Cognac sauce. Also venison, lamb etc dishes with interesting and inventive sauces. Home-made desserts, e.g. chocolate marquise, walnut parfait, tarte tatin, lemon tart, crème brûlée.
Credit cards: 1, 2, 3, 5

STAKIS GLASGOW GROSVENOR HOTEL

Great Western Road
Glasgow G12 0TA
Tel: 041 339 8811 • Telex: 776247
Fax: 041 334 0710

On A82 Great Western Road.

Discreetly elegant, the Stakis Glasgow Grosvenor Hotel is without question one of the most impressive buildings in Glasgow's fashionable West End. Directly opposite the city's Botanical Gardens, the hotel is one mile from the motorway network, and two miles from the city centre.

Open all year
Rooms: 95 with private facilities
Bar Lunch 12.30 – 2.30 pm (a)
Dining Room/Restaurant Lunch
12.30 – 2 pm (b)
Dinner 5.30 – 10.30 pm (c)
Bed & breakfast £45 – £52
Dinner B & B £55 – 62

Arbroath smokie salad. Roast haunch of venison and game sauce.
STB Commended 5 Crowns
Credit cards: 1, 2, 3, 5, 6

THE UBIQUITOUS CHIP

12 Ashton Lane
Glasgow G12 8SJ
Tel: 041 334 5007

A secluded lane in the heart of Glasgow's West End.

A white-washed Victorian mews stable down an old fashioned cobbled street is the setting for one of Glasgow's most renowned restaurants. The wealth of local Scottish produce is polished by traditional and original recipes, to make this restaurant "a wee gem". The 'Chip' as it is affectionately known, boasts one of the UK's most celebrated, extensive and modestly priced wine lists.

Open all year except Christmas Day,
31 Dec, 1 + 2 Jan
Bar Meals 12 – 11 pm (a)
Dining Room/Restaurant Lunch 12 –
2.30 pm except Sun (c)
Dinner 5.30 – 11 pm (d)
Shellfish bisque with cream and fresh ginger. Fillets of Oban landed turbot in a pine kernel and green peppercorn crust with a rich red wine sauce. Aberdeen Angus steaks. Heather honey and Scotch whisky parfait. Rich chocolate marquise with fresh orange syrup. Good selection of Scottish cheeses.
Credit cards: 1, 2, 3, 5, 6
Proprietor: Ron Clydesdale

VICTORIA & ALBERT

159 Buchanan Street
Glasgow G1 2JX
Tel: 041 248 6329

Approach via Buchanan Street pedestrian precinct towards St Vincent Street or from West George Street, short distance from George Square.

A much patronised and very popular establishment with the business community of Glasgow city centre, the Victoria and Albert is primarily an up market bar restaurant. There is a Victorian charm and elegance about it which is very appealing and the dining areas are entirely harmonious. Its central location near the Royal Concert Hall and the Theatre Royal, make it a suitable rendezvous for dining before or after performances, but you can enjoy morning coffee or light meals

throughout the day. For more serious eating there are first class fixed price menus of two or three courses representing good value for money.

Open all year
Bar Meals 12 – 10.30 pm except Sun (a)
Restaurant Lunch/Dinner 12 –
10.30 pm except Sun (b)
Closed Sun
Children welcome in restaurant only
Smoked chicken and orange salad. Halibut steak en papilote. Fresh fruit sabayon.
Credit cards: 1, 2, 3, 5

Glenelg

MAP 6

GLENELG INN

Glenelg Bay
Glenelg, nr Shiel Bridge
Ross-shire IV40 8AG
Tel: 059 982 273
Fax: 059 982 373

Access to Glenelg via unclassified road west of A87 at Sheil Bridge, 1 mile from Kylerhea-Skye ferry which runs April to October.

The Glenelg Inn has been newly refurbished to a high standard from an old coaching mews with cobbled courtyard, on the shores of Glenelg Bay. It has six bedrooms offering the best in comfort. There is a bar where guest, crofter and fisherman alike may relax in the genuine atmosphere of the ceilidh. The restaurant offers fine Scottish cuisine using local seafood, game and other fresh produce. It is several miles along a single track road to get to the Glenelg Inn, but most people find it well worth the effort. Boat trips available.

Open Easter to Oct
Rooms: 6 with private facilities
Bar Lunch 12.30 – 2.30 pm (a)
Dining Room/Restaurant Lunch 12.30
– 2.30 pm (a)
Bar Supper 6.30 – 9 pm except Sun (a)
Dinner 7.30 – 9 pm (c)
Facilities for the disabled
Bed & breakfast £28 – £45
Dinner B & B £45 – £60
Kylerhea oysters and mussels. Local lamb with lentil and cardamom purée. Wild salmon. Organic strawberries. Walnut and rum tart.
Credit cards: 1, 3
Proprietor: Christopher Main

Glenfinnan

MAP 6

THE STAGE HOUSE
Glenfinnan
Inverness-shire PH37 4LT
Tel: 0397 83 246
Fax: 0397 83 307

15 miles west of Fort William on A830
'Road to the Isles' – 1/2 mile on right past
Glenfinnan monument.
This is a historic location for Scots – the place at which Bonnie Prince Charlie landed from France in 1745 to claim the Scottish throne. The Stage House dates back to the 17th century and this old coaching inn has been tastefully modernised to provide comfortable accommodation and an informal relaxed atmosphere. There is an extensive wine list, real ale, log fire in Winter and scope for lots of outdoor activities like fishing and walking. Boats and mountain bikes may be hired, and there are beaches nearby.
Open Mar to 20 Dec + 29 Dec to 3 Jan
Rooms: 9 with private facilities
Bar Lunch 12.30 – 2.30 pm (a)
Bar Supper 5 – 9 pm (a)
Dinner 6.30 – 8.30 pm (c)
No smoking in restaurant or rooms
Bed & breakfast £25.95 – £32.95
Dinner B & B £41.95 – £48.95
Fresh and smoked local seafood a speciality. Home-made soups, local game, interesting and varied vegetables. Scottish cheeseboard.
STB Commended 3 Crowns
Credit cards: 1, 3
Proprietors: Robert & Carole Hawkes, Peggy Mills

Glenlivet

MAP 5

MINMORE HOUSE
Glenlivet, Ballindalloch
Banffshire AB3 9DB
Tel: 08073 378
Fax: 08073 472

On B9136, off B9008, 9 miles from Tomintoul. Adjacent to The Glenlivet Distillery.
Minmore House was the home of the founder of The Glenlivet Distillery. It is situated above the River Livet, amidst four acres of gardens with glorious views. There are ten comfortable en suite bedrooms, each named after local Speyside malts. The dining room specialises in the best of Scottish produce and the menu changes daily. A marvellous location for walking, fishing, bird-watching etc, and a good base from which to follow the whisky and castle trails.
Open 1 May to 31 Oct
Rooms: 10 with private facilities
Bar and Picnic Lunches can be arranged for residents
Dinner at 8 pm (d) – set 5 course meal
No smoking in dining room
Bed & breakfast from £30
Dinner B & B from £48
Fresh Lossiemouth langoustine, roast Highland rack of lamb with fresh mint and honey glaze, Cullen skink, venison and game, Lochin Ora burnt cream.
STB Commended 4 Crowns
Credit cards: 1, 3
Proprietor: Belinda Luxmoore

Glenluce

MAP 1

KELVIN HOUSE HOTEL
53 Main Street, Glenluce
Wigtownshire DG8 0PP
Tel: 05813 303

Just off A75, 10 minutes from Stranraer ferry terminals.
Kelvin House is the centre of social life in the pleasant and tranquil little village of Glenluce, not so far from the shores of Luce Bay. The hotel is an unpretentious traditional two storey building on the main street, dating back to c. 1825. An interesting bar menu is available all day in the lounge or public bar, with a much wider range of good food than one normally experiences under the heading of 'bar menu'. It is for the Cranachan Restaurant that chef/proprietor Gary Conlan is able to demonstrate his skill to the full. Here you can enjoy a splendid choice of fresh local fish, anything from Luce Bay scallops to lobster, together with a selection of seasonal game or meat courses. Nor is the vegetarian forgotten. This out of the way corner of south-west Scotland has lots of outdoor pursuits for sportsmen.
Open all year
Rooms: 6, 5 with private facilities
Bar Lunch 12 – 3 pm (a-b)
Dining Room/Restaurant Lunch 12 – 3 pm (a-b)
Bar Supper 5 – 10.30 pm (a-b)
Dinner 7 – 10.30 pm (b-d)
Bed & breakfast £18.50 – £25
Luce Bay lobster, scallops, turbot, halibut, Cree salmon, local trout. Pigeon, pheasant, venison, duck. All imaginatively cooked.
STB Commended 3 Crowns
No credit cards
Proprietors: Gary Conlan & Karen Howden

Glenrothes

MAP 4

BALBIRNIE HOUSE HOTEL
Balbirnie Park, Markinch
by Glenrothes, Fife KY7 6NE
Tel: 0592 610066
Fax: 0592 610529

Prestige Award Winner 1991

On A92, 1 1/2 miles north-east of Glenrothes.
Balbirnie has been around in one form or another since the time of Robert the Bruce. Parts of the present building go back to 1642 when it became the home of the Balfour family who subsequently improved and extended it in the 18th and 19th century. It is now a magnificent and impressive building with its soaring Ionic portico and classical lines, and it is difficult to accept that it – and its beautiful landscaped grounds – are only a mile or so from Glenrothes. Internally it is superb. The unique long gallery being particularly noteworthy and giving access to graciously proportioned drawing room, library and dining room. Balbirnie House is now a deluxe hotel of very high standard and a great asset to Fife and to Scotland. The appeal, however, is not just in the building. The staff are proud of the establishment and seem to share the owners' urge for excellence. Executive Chef, George Mackay, creates imaginative menus, where the focus is on good quality produce, prepared and presented with skill.
Open all year
Rooms: 30 with private facilities
Bar Lunch 12 – 2.30 pm (a)
Dining Room/Restaurant Lunch 12.30 – 2.30 pm (b)
Dinner 7 – 9.30 pm (d)
Bed & breakfast £60 – £170
Dinner B & B £87 – £197
Room Rate £80 – £160

Macallan smoked salmon salad with toasted brioche and a brown butter vinaigrette. Fillet of halibut coated with mixed herbs and grain mustard, set on a tomato and basil sauce.
STB Deluxe 5 Crowns
Credit cards: 1, 2, 3, 5

RESCOBIE HOTEL & RESTAURANT
Valley Drive, Leslie
Glenrothes, Fife KY6 3BQ
Tel: 0592 742143
Fax: 0592 620231

8 miles from M90 – just off A911 in the village of Leslie.

Rescobie is a country house converted to a small hotel. The owners and staff are welcoming and the atmosphere is relaxed and friendly. There are two comfortable and uncrowded dining rooms and a beautiful lounge with deep armchairs and a log fire. Food is freshly prepared by the chefs from the best of Scottish produce. The table d'hôte menu changes daily and offers four choices of starter and main course. The à la carte menu is small but selective and there is always a full vegetarian menu. Pasta is home-made and sweets are freshly prepared to order. Children very welcome, appropriate reductions. French and German spoken.
Open all year except Christmas + Boxing Days, 27 Dec
Rooms: 10 with private facilities
Bar Lunch 12 – 2 pm (a)
Dining Room/Restaurant Lunch 12 – 2 pm (a)
Dinner 7 – 9.30 pm (c)
No dogs
Bed & breakfast £30 – £50
Dinner B & B £40 – £55 (min 3 day stay)
Cullen skink, game terrine, monkfish wrapped in bacon served with scampi ravioli. Scottish steak cooked with mushrooms and onions, flamed with whisky and finished with cream. Raspberry cranachan, strawberry shortcake, almond meringue.
STB Commended 4 Crowns
Credit cards: 1, 2, 3, 5
Proprietors: Tony & Wendy Hughes-Lewis

Grange
by Errol

MAP 4

WATERYBUTTS LODGE
Grange, by Errol
Perthshire PH2 7SZ
Tel: 0821 642894
Fax: 0821 642523

A85 Perth-Dundee, 9 miles out of Perth take road for Grange. Then after 1¹/₂ miles turn left, immediately before railway crossing.

The original building was a 15th century friary attached to Coupar Angus Abbey though the lectern style doocot and small turreted stone stair is all that remains. The main Georgian building was erected in 1802 and later added to in the Victorian era. Today it is now a beautiful Georgian lodge set in lovely grounds, and with en suite accommodation. A unique herb garden, which provides fresh herbs for the kitchen, was formed originally from Dutch soil shipped as ballast on boats returning from Holland after delivering potatoes. The atmosphere at Waterybutts is distinctly 'house party' and guests wine and dine in style around a 16 foot Charles I refectory table, enjoying good conversation, good food, and an ambience of yesteryear.
Open all year
Rooms: 7 with private facilities
Dinner 6.30 – 10.30 pm (b)
Non-residents – by prior arrangment
Restricted licence
No children
Bed & breakfast £20 – £25
Dinner B & B £32 – £37
Fresh trout pâté. Moules marinière. Haunch of roe venison. Tay salmon poached in herbs. All game in season.
STB Highly Commended 3 Crowns
Credit cards: 1, 2, 3
Proprietors: Barry & Rachel Allenby-Wilcox

Grantown-on-Spey

MAP 5

CULDEARN HOUSE
Woodlands Terrace
Grantown-on-Spey
Moray PH26 3JU
Tel: 0479 2106

On A95, south-west entry to Grantown-on-Spey.

This Victorian house set in its own grounds of lawns and mature trees, combines character with tastefully appointed modern amenities to provide a high degree of comfort and a distinctly Scottish atmosphere. It is ideally situated for touring the Highlands as well as having interest for golfers, anglers, walkers and bird-watchers. Log and peat fires blaze in the public rooms.
Open 1 Mar to 31 Oct
Rooms: 9 with private facilities
Picnic Lunches to order
Dinner 6.45 – 7.30 pm (b)
Residents only
Restricted licence
No dogs
No smoking in dining room
Dinner B & B £38 – £50
Traditional Scottish fare using lamb, beef, venison and trout, is complemented by a modestly priced wine list and range of malt whiskies.
STB Highly Commended 3 Crowns
Credit cards: 1, 3, 6
Proprietors: Alasdair & Isobel Little

Credit Card Code		*Meal Price Code*	
1.	Access/Mastercard/Eurocard	(a)	under £10
2.	American Express	(b)	£10 – £15
3.	Visa	(c)	£15 – £20
4.	Carte Bleu	(d)	£20 – £25
5.	Diners Club	(e)	£25 – £30
6.	Mastercharge	(f)	over £30

GARTH HOTEL

The Square, Grantown-on-Spey
Moray PH26 3HN
Tel: 0479 2836/2162

On the Square of Grantown-on-Spey.
The Garth Hotel commands a view of the
picturesque Square of Grantown-on-Spey
and sits amidst four acres of landscaped
gardens. This three star hotel dates from
the 17th century and offers old world
charm with every modern comfort and
convenience. Seventeen individually
furnished bedrooms – all en suite – with
direct dial telephone, colour TV and
tea/coffee-making facilities. Extensive
and selective menu with an accent on
fresh local produce. French and German
spoken.
Open all year
Rooms: 14 with private facilities
Bar Lunch 12 – 2 pm (a)
Dinner 7.30 – 8.30 pm (c)
No dogs
No smoking in restaurant
Bed & breakfast from £36
Dinner B & B from £55
Highland game pâté. Salmon soup.
Monkfish tails flamed with brandy served
with a fresh cream and peppercorn sauce.
Local venison pan-fried and served with
Port and bramble sauce.
STB Highly Commended 4 Crowns
Credit cards: 1, 2, 3, 5
Proprietor: Gordon McLaughlan

RAVENSCOURT HOUSE HOTEL

Seafield Avenue
Grantown-on-Spey
Moray PH26 3JG
Tel: 0479 2286
Fax: 0479 3260

Just off main Square.
A country house hotel which exudes an
atmosphere of quality and elegance.
Dining is in the conservatory with tasteful
decor and beautiful table appointments.
The drawing rooms, where there are fine
original oil paintings and water colours,
have been furnished sumptuously.
Menus are well balanced, the standard of
cooking and presentation is high and
service was described by our inspector as
faultless. Judging by the remarks in the
visitors book there is a very satisfied
clientele. There are excellent value
house wines and generally a wine list
catering for all tastes and pockets.
Open 8 Feb to 31 Oct
Rooms: 9 with private facilities
Dinner 7 – 9.30 pm except Sun Mon (d)
set 4 course menu

Dinner residents only Sun Mon
No dogs
No smoking area in conservatory
Bed & breakfast £28.50 – £35
Dinner B & B £48.50 – £55
Fresh fish daily. Scottish and French
dishes feature equally. Menu changes
every third day, with a traditional roast
meal on Sunday. Sirloin steaks 'New
York' cut. Rack of lamb for two.
STB Deluxe 3 Crowns
No credit cards

Gullane

MAP 4

GOLF INN HOTEL

Main Street, Gullane
East Lothian EH31 2AB
Tel: 0620 843259
Fax: 0620 842066

18 miles east of Edinburgh, 4 miles west
of North Berwick.
Originally an old coaching house, the
Golf Inn Hotel is now an established
family run business, catering both for the
golfer and non-golfer. The emphasis is
on personal and friendly service coupled
with excellent food and good beer!
Recently refurbished to a high standard
and offering facilities for weddings,
conferences, dinner dances etc. For the
resident, golf packages can be tailored to
requirement. The Carriage Lounge has
an interesting range of light snack dishes
and the Saddlers Restaurant menu, for
the serious diner, has just the right touch
of choice and quality.
Open all year
Rooms: 18 , 11 with private facilities
Bar Lunch 12 – 2.30 pm (a)
Dining Room/Restaurant Lunch 12 –
3 pm (a)
Bar Supper 5 – 10 pm (a-b)
Dinner 6.30 – 10 pm (b-c)
Dogs by arrangement
Restricted parking
Bed & breakfast £30 – £40
Dinner B & B £42 – £52
Roast Scotch beef Blair Atholl. Roast
chicken with skirlie. Scampi Isle of May.
Credit cards: 1, 3, 5
Proprietors: Tom & Kathleen Saddler

GREYWALLS

Muirfield, Gullane
East Lothian EH31 2EG
Tel: 0620 842144
Fax: 0620 842241

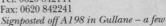

Signposted off A198 in Gullane – a few
miles from A1.
This exquisitely proportioned country
house was designed at the turn of the
century by the renowned architect Sir
Edwin Lutyens and retains all of the
grace and grandeur of the times. Its
gardens are equally magnificent and
look out over the famous Muirfield
Golf Course. The house is almost a
time capsule, but incorporating the
elegance of the Edwardian era with
modern comfort and amenities. The
cuisine is outstanding and Chef Paul
Baron's deft touch makes every meal a
special occasion. The whole atmosphere of Greywalls is of luxury and
relaxation.
Open 20 Apr to 31 Oct
Rooms: 23 with private facilities
Bar Lunch 12.30 – 2 pm except Sun (a)
Dining Room/Restaurant Lunch
12.30 – 2 pm (c)
Dinner 7.30 – 9.30 pm (f)
Facilities for the disabled
Bed & breakfast £75 – £90
Room Rate £85 – £150
Finest Highland smoked salmon and
home-cured gravadlax. Best end of lamb
roasted in oven, served on bed of grated
courgette with tarragon sauce. Rich
bitter chocolate mousse in a brandy
snap basket with fresh raspberries and
raspberry sauce.
STB Highly Commended 4 Crowns
Credit cards: 1, 2, 3, 5, 6
Proprietors: Giles & Ros Weaver

Harris
Isle of

MAP 7

ALLAN COTTAGE GUEST HOUSE

Tarbert
Isle of Harris PA85 3DJ
Tel: 0859 2146

Upper road overlooking ferry road, c. 600
yards from ferry.
Formerly the telephone exchange for the
Isle of Harris, Allan Cottage has been

extended and brought up to a high standard of comfort while faithfully preserving all the traditional features which make it a house of unusual charm and character. The dining room is furnished with antiques and gleaming copper and brass, and there is a cosy lounge where you can relax by an open coal fire after your meal. This is a small establishment and gives Bill and Evelyn Reed the opportunity to cosset their guests and display their culinary skill in imaginative and interesting menus.
Open Apr to Oct
Rooms: 3 , 1 with private facilities
Dinner 6.30 – 8.30 pm (b)
Residents only
Unlicensed
No smoking in dining room
Bed & breakfast £15 – £17.50
Dinner B & B £27.50 – £30
Harris venison with walnuts, Port and Guinness. Local lamb with apricots, orange and walnut stuffing. Aberdeen Angus steak with fresh ginger and horseradish. Wild salmon in season.
STB Highly Commended 2 Crowns
No credit cards
Proprietors: Bill & Evelyn Reed

ARDVOURLIE CASTLE
Aird A Mhulaidh
Isle of Harris PA85 3AB
Tel: 0859 2307

On A859, 10 miles north of Tarbert.
Ardvourlie Castle is a Victorian hunting lodge built by the Earl of Dunmore in a beautiful setting on the shores of Loch Seaforth in the mountains of North Harris. Carefully restored, in period, without change to architectural detail and using many fine antiques, the Castle now forms a guest house of unusual distinction.
Open all year except Christmas + Boxing Days
Rooms: 4
Dinner by arrangement (d)
Residents only
Restricted licence
Bed & breakfast £34.07 – £39.95
Dinner B & B £51.70 – £57.57
Food based on blend of traditional Scottish and innovation, using local and free-range ingredients when available. Home-made bread.
No credit cards
Proprietors: Paul & Derek Martin

SCARISTA HOUSE
Isle of Harris PA85 3HX
Tel: 0859 85 238
Fax: 0859 85 277

On A859, 15 miles south-west of Tarbert (Western Isles).
Scarista House is a charming Georgian dwelling and occupies an imposing position overlooking a three mile long shell-sand beach on the magnificent Atlantic coast of Harris. The seven bedrooms, all with views over the sea, are comfortably and traditionally furnished, with bathrooms en suite. There are two lawned gardens, a walled herb garden and a vegetable garden. With no television or radio, but an extensive library, the hotel offers an atmosphere of complete tranquillity, complemented by excellent cuisine – in which local fish and shellfish feature prominently – and a carefully selected wine list. Children over eight years welcome.
Open Apr to mid Oct
Rooms: 7 with private facilities
Dinner at 8 pm (d)
Residents licence
No smoking in dining room
Bed & breakfast £39 – £52
Dinner B & B £62- £75
Razor-shell clams. Prawn soufflés. Fillet of wild venison with a blackcurrant and cassis sauce. Vegetables from the garden. Praline ice-cream with raspberry and almond biscuits. Various Scottish cheeses. Home-made oatcakes and chocolate fudge.
STB Commended 3 Crowns
No credit cards
Proprietors: Ian & Jane Callaghan

SIAMARA GUEST HOUSE
6 Leacklee
Isle of Harris PA85 3EH
Tel: 085 983 314

South of Tarbert (c. 5 miles) take fourth road on left, signposted for Rodel via east. After c. 1¹/2 miles take first left for Stockinish, 150 yards on right.
Siamara is a small cosy guest house on the shores of Loch Stockinish where herons, buzzards, seals and otters are frequently to be seen from guest rooms. If your interest is sea fishing, Tony Dolby will arrange to take you out in his 16 foot boat at a nominal cost. For those who just want to enjoy peace and quiet there is plenty of it available and Tony and his wife, Penny, are trying to develop the concept of a word 'Harris-ed' as being exactly the opposite to 'harassed'. This is a place where you can enjoy good

company, high quality food and accommodation and revel in the tranquillity.
Open all year except Christmas, 2 wks Feb + 2wks Oct
Rooms: 3 with private facilities
Dinner at 7 pm (b)
Residents only
Unlicensed
Children over 12 years welcome
Bed & breakfast from £23
Dinner B & B from £34
Local salmon and beef. Lamb with rosemary. Venison with Port and walnuts. Steamed puddings. Home-made meringues etc.
STB Highly Commended 3 Crowns
No credit cards
Proprietors: Penny & Tony Dolby

TWO WATERS GUEST HOUSE
Lickisto
Isle of Harris PA85 3EL
Tel: 085983 246

C79 single track road between Stockinish and Geocrab.
A modern comfortable bungalow situated just 15 yards from the sea in wild mountainous scenery. If you are lucky you may well spot otters and seals nearby. John and Jill Barber have concentrated on making this a home from home and guests look forward eagerly to the imaginative evening meals which feature local seafoods and some of John's own smoked products. The choice of fish for breakfast is quite exceptional but standard normal breakfast fare is of course also available. All rooms are en suite with tea/coffee-making facilities and thoughtful little touches like home-made biscuits. There is free trout fishing and a sea boat is available. A lovely spot from which to indulge in some hill-walking, angling, sailing or bird-watching.
Open 1 May to 30 Sep
Rooms: 4 with private facilities
Dinner at 7 pm (b) 4 course menu
Residents only
Unlicensed
No children
No smoking in dining room
Bed & breakfast from £22
Dinner B & B from £34
Hot smoked salmon and trout. Shellfish. Scottish beef, venison and pheasant. Home-made soups and sweets. Fresh vegetables from garden.
STB Highly Commended 3 Crowns
No credit cards
Proprietors: Jill & John Barber

Hawick

MAP 2

MANSFIELD HOUSE HOTEL
Weensland Road, Hawick
Roxburghshire TD9 9EL
Tel: 0450 73988
Fax: 0450 72007

On A698 approximately 1 mile from centre of Hawick.

The MacKinnon family own and run this Victorian country house hotel in 10 acres of terraced lawns and wooded grounds. The large public rooms feature high ornately plastered ceilings, magnificent fireplaces of Italian marble and elegant brass chandeliers. Bedrooms en suite with TV and tea/coffee-making facilities.

Open all year except Boxing Day + 1 Jan
Rooms: 12 with private facilities
Bar Lunch 12 – 1.45 pm (a)
Dining Room/Restaurant Lunch 12 – 1.45 pm except Sun Sat (b)
Bar Supper 5.30 – 9 pm Mon to Fri: 5.30 – 8 pm Sun (a)
Dinner 7 – 9 pm: 7 – 8 pm Sun (c)
No smoking area in restaurant
Bed & breakfast £30 – £52
Dinner B & B £45 – £70
All meals individually prepared by prize winning chef using the best local produce. Home-made desserts a speciality. Extensive range of Scottish cheeses, malt whiskies and liqueurs.
Credit cards: 1, 2, 3, 5, 6
Proprietors: Sheila & Ian MacKinnon

WHITCHESTER CHRISTIAN GUEST HOUSE
Borthaugh, Hawick
Roxburghshire TD9 7LN
Tel: 0450 77477
Fax: 0450 371080

1/4 mile off A7, 2 miles south of Hawick on B711 to Roberton.

A former Dower House of the Buccleuch Estate set in 3½ acres of garden. David and Doreen Maybury relocated from Duns to this quiet beautiful spot. The house has been refurbished in a comfortable and relaxing style. All food including the bread is cooked on the premises and local produce is widely used. Full board includes a traditional Scottish afternoon tea. A wide range of soups are made such as carrot and coriander and lemon and yoghurt, sweets include brûlées, pavlovas, sorbet concoctions and many others, a large

Scottish cheese board is kept.
Open all year except 2 wks mid Jan
Rooms: 8 , 4 with private facilities
Dining Room/Restaurant Lunch 12.30 – 2 pm except Sun (a)
Tea 4.30 – 5 pm
Dinner 7 – 8.30 pm (b)
Unlicensed
No smoking in dining room, bedrooms + conservatory
Bed & breakfast £18 – £20
Dinner B & B £26 – 28
Home-made soups and bread. Rowan poached trout. Grouse, pheasant, venison, local lamb. Nut meringue gâteau, cranachan, syllabubs.
STB Commended 3 Crowns
No credit cards
Proprietors: David & Doreen Maybury

Helmsdale

MAP 6

NAVIDALE HOUSE HOTEL
Helmsdale
Sutherland KW8 6JS
Tel: 043 12 258

1/2 mile north of Helmsdale on A9.

A former Victorian shooting lodge of the Dukes of Sutherland, Navidale is now a comfortable country house hotel. It stands in seven acres of garden on a cliff top overlooking the Moray Firth. There is an air of spacious elegance about the public rooms which have superb panoramic views and open fires. There are fine sea views from most of the bedrooms. The kitchen makes good use of the fine supply of local seafish and shellfish.

Open 11 Jan to 18 Nov
Rooms: 15 with private facilities
Dinner 6.45 – 8.45 pm (c)
No smoking in restaurant
Dinner B & B £50 – £55
Fresh Skye oysters. Steamed mussels with garlic butter. Wing of skate with prawn and caper butter. Caithness rack of lamb with garlic and red wine sauce.
Credit cards: 1, 3
Proprietor: Marcus Blackwell

Humbie
nr Edinburgh

MAP 4

JOHNSTOUNBURN HOUSE HOTEL
Humbie
East Lothian EH36 5PL
Tel: 087533 696
Fax: 087533 626

From A68 Edinburgh-Jedburgh 2 miles south of Pathhead, turn at Fala (hotel is signposted) – 2 miles on right.

A beautifully kept large country mansion, approached by a long tree-lined drive and surrounded by acres of lawns, gardens and picturesque farmland at the foot of the Lammermuir Hills. The visitor to Johnstounburn would hardly imagine that he or she is only 15 miles away from bustling Edinburgh. And once inside the 17th century stone walls, warmed by the open fires and treated to an outstanding menu made with fresh local produce, one begins to appreciate the depth of Scotland's heritage. Johnstounburn has 20 well appointed bedrooms, conference rooms for as many delegates, an exquisite pine-panelled dining room, and a singularly relaxing wood-panelled lounge.

Open all year
Rooms: 20 with private facilities
Bar Lunch 12 – 2 pm (a-b)
Dining Room/Restaurant Lunch 12 – 2 pm (c)
Dinner 7 – 9 pm (e)
Bed & breakfast £60 – £95
Dinner B & B £85 – £120
Seafood terrine wrapped in smoked salmon, roast saddle of venison and peppered duck breast.
STB Commended 4 Crowns
Credit cards: 1, 2, 3, 5

Huntly

MAP 5

THE OLD MANSE OF MARNOCH
Bridge of Marnoch
by Huntly AB54 5RS
Tel: 0466 780873

On B9117, 1 mile off Huntly-Banff A97 route.

The Old Manse of Marnoch is a lovely secluded Georgian country house set in three acres of mature gardens on the River Deveron. Well appointed bedrooms, elegant lounges, and dining room set with silver and crystal, combine to provide an experience of true Scottish hospitality where guests are encouraged to feel genuinely at home. The set four course dinner changes daily and everything is prepared in The Old Manse kitchen, whilst herb parterre and walled kitchen garden supply organic produce in season. A destination for the discerning traveller. Fluent German spoken. Dogs welcome, but not in the dining room.

Open all year except 2 wks Nov
Rooms: 5 with private facilities
Packed lunch – as requested (a)
Dining Room/Restaurant Lunch as requested (a)
Afternoon tea – as requested (a)
Dinner 7.30 for 8 pm or by arrangement (d) 4 courses
Reservations essential for non-residents
No smoking in dining room + one of two lounges
Bed & breakfast from £35
Dinner B & B from £50
Fine Scots cooking, traditional and contemporary. Award winning breakfast menu includes three different sausages, Scotch woodcock, devilled ham, home-baked breads, home-made preserves and marmalades.
STB Deluxe 3 Crowns
No credit cards
Proprietors: Patrick & Keren Carter

Innerleithen

MAP 2

TRAQUAIR ARMS HOTEL
Traquair Road, Innerleithen
Peeblesshire EH44 6PD
Tel: 0896 830229
Fax: 0896 830260

On A72 mid-way between Peebles and Galashiels. Turn off Innerleithen High Street on B709, Traquair Road 150 yards.
An attractive traditional 19th century Scottish inn, just a half hour from Edinburgh and ten minutes from Peebles, in a delightful Borders valley. Hugh and Marian Anderson run it as a relaxing, friendly, family run hotel with genuine concern for the comfort of their guests. Imaginative menus utilise the best local produce and, in appropriate weather, can be enjoyed beside a blazing log fire in the dining room or al fresco in

the secluded garden. The bar prides itself on its real ales.
Open all year
Rooms: 10 with private facilities
Bar Meals 12 – 9 pm (a)
Dinner 7 – 9 pm (b)
Bed & breakfast £27 – £35
Dinner B & B £41 – £51
Grilled river trout. Poacher's Salmon with Drambuie and cream sauce. Venison steaks in red wine sauce. Traquair lamb cutlets with fresh ginger and lemon sauce. Spiced beef and chestnut casserole. Vegetarian dishes.
STB Commended 3 Crowns
Credit cards: 1, 3
Proprietors: Hugh & Marian Anderson

Inverkeilor
by Arbroath

MAP 4

GORDON'S RESTAURANT
Homewood House, Main Street
Inverkeilor, by Arbroath
Angus DD11 5RN
Tel: 02413 364

Just off A92 Arbroath-Montrose, at north end of Main Street.
A cosy little village restaurant, Gordon's occupies the end of a row of terraced properties forming Main Street and dates back to 1850. The restaurant is attractively decorated in a traditional cottage style. Chef/ proprietor Gordon Watson's cooking is imaginative and unpretentious making full use of quality fresh ingredients from the locality and fresh herbs from their own garden. His wife, Maria, looks after the customers and sets a tone of friendly and efficient service.
Open all year except last 2 wks Jan
Rooms: 2
Bar Lunch 12 – 2.30 pm except Mon (a)
Bar Supper 6.30 – 9.15 pm except Mon Sat (a)
Dinner 7 – 9.15 pm except Sun Mon (b)
Closed Mon
Facilities for the disabled
No smoking area in restaurant
Bed & breakfast from £15
Dinner B & B from £30
Seafood bisque with Cognac. Smoked duck with a warm salad. Medallions of beef with shallots and button mushrooms, flamed with vodka in a cream sauce. Noisettes of Scotch lamb, marinated in

lemon, oregano and bay leaves, pan-fried and served on a potato pancake. Home-made desserts.
STB Approved 1 Crown
Credit cards: 1, 3
Proprietors: Gordon & Maria Watson

Invermoriston

MAP 6

GLENMORISTON ARMS HOTEL
Invermoriston, Glenmoriston
Inverness-shire IV3 6YA
Tel: 0320 51206

At junction of A82 and A887 in Invermoriston.
This 200 year old coaching inn nestles at the foot of Glenmoriston, one of Scotland's loveliest glens, a few minutes from world famous Loch Ness. An ideal base for touring the West Highlands and Skye. An acclaimed restaurant serving local venison, Angus steaks and wild salmon in season. There is a superb selection of malt whiskies to complement your meal.
Open all year except Christmas Day
Rooms: 8 with private facilities
Bar Lunch 12 – 2 pm (a)
Bar Supper 5.30 – 8.30 pm (a)
Dinner 6.30 – 8.30 pm (c)
Bed & breakfast £25.50 – £39.50
Dinner B & B £40.50 – £45.50
Suprêmes of pheasant cooked with tomatoes, mushrooms and cream, finished with Talisker Whisky. Grilled noisettes of Scottish lamb with stilton and pear butter.
STB Commended 4 Crowns
Credit cards: 1, 3, 6
Proprietor: Alan Draper

ANCHOR & CHAIN RESTAURANT

Coulmore Bay, North Kessock
Ross-shire IV1 1XB
Tel: 0463 73313

Off A9, 5 miles north of Inverness.
Superb location on the water edge with
magnificent views of the Beauly Firth.
Fresh local produce is used in the
preparation of meals and the same care
and attention is taken be it for a bar meal
or an à la carte dinner. The site of the
restaurant is such that there is not too
much "passing traffic", and for survival it
is necessary to ensure that customers go
away completely satisfied and willing to
recommend it to their friends. What
better basis for a successful restaurant.
Open Apr to Oct
Bar Lunch 12 – 2 pm except Sun (a)
Dining Room/Restaurant Lunch
12.30 – 2.30 pm Sun only (b)
Bar Supper 6 – 7.30 pm (a)
Dinner 6 – 9 pm (d)
*Deep-fried mushrooms stuffed with
haggis, with a whisky chive and cream
sauce. Lightly poached fillet of sole with a
lobster and Pernod sauce.*
Credit cards: 1, 3
Proprietor: Iain MacPherson

BUNCHREW HOUSE HOTEL

Bunchrew
Inverness IV3 6TA
Tel: 0463 234917
Fax: 0463 710620

*On A862 Inverness-Beauly, c. 10
minutes from centre of Inverness.*
Bunchrew House is a Scottish mansion
dating back to 1621, set amidst 18 acres
of landscaped gardens and woodland on
the shores of the Beauly Firth. This is a
place to forget the hustle and bustle of
everyday life and relax in an informal
ambience more akin to a private country
house. The traditional cuisine includes
prime Scottish beef, fresh lobster and
salmon, locally caught game and venison
and freshly grown vegetables. Special
pride is taken in the wine list which is
designed to complement the menu.
Some French, Italian, Japanese and
German spoken.
Open all year
Rooms: 11 with private facilities
Bar Lunch 12 – 2 pm (a)

*Dining Room/Restaurant Lunch 12 –
2 pm (b)*
Dinner 7 – 9 pm (d)
Facilities for the disabled
No smoking in dining room
Bed & breakfast £30 – £60
Dinner B & B £50 – £80
*Avocado and prawn mousse with dill
mayonnaise. Smoked salmon with
quenelles of cream cheese. Assorted
seafood in a cream sauce, served in a hot
croissant. Baked gigot of lamb. Roast
Highland grouse in a redcurrant and
honey sauce. Grape crème brûlée.*
STB Commended 4 Crowns
Credit cards: 1, 2, 3
Proprietors: Alan & Patsy Wilson

CRAIGMONIE HOTEL & LEISURE SPORTIF

Annfield Road, Inverness
Inverness-shire IV2 3HX
Tel: 0463 231649
Telex: 94013304
Fax: 0463 233720

*1/2 mile from town centre. At top of Castle
Street turn left into Old Edinburgh Road
(one way). At crossroads, forward keeping
left into Annfield Road.*
A 'Town House' style hotel, built in 1880
by William MacKay, a Gaelic scholar
whose ancestors fought alongside
'Bonnie Prince Charlie' at Culloden. The
Craigmonie has been tastefully
transformed by Derek Moffat, his wife
Jane and son Iain who is Chef de
Cuisine. The Angus steaks are a
speciality, perhaps not surprising as the
same butcher has been supplying them
for over 21 years. White fish and shellfish
come from the west coast and game in
season from local estates. Bedrooms are
well equipped and the public rooms are
comfortable and furnished to a high
standard. There are also leisure facilities.
*Open all year except Christmas Day, 1 +
2 Jan*
Rooms: 35 with private facilities
Bar Lunch 12 – 2 pm except Sun (a)
*Dining Room/Restaurant Lunch 12 –
2 pm (a)*

Bar Supper 5 – 9 pm (a)
Dinner 6.30 – 9 pm (c)
No smoking in restaurant
Bed & breakfast £48 – £68
Dinner B & B £64 – £79
*Lamb and vegetable soup flavoured with
mint. Medallions of venison with
strawberries, Drambuie and ginger sauce.
Braised salmon steak with white wine
and chives.*
STB Commended 4 Crowns
Credit cards: 1, 3, 5, 6
Proprietor: Derek Moffat

CULLODEN HOUSE HOTEL

Culloden
nr Inverness IV1 2NZ
Tel: 0463 790461

*Off A96, 3 miles from Inverness, 5 miles
from Inverness Airport.*
Culloden House must surely be
Inverness's most magnificent building,
an architectural gem with an historic and
romantic association with Bonnie Prince
Charlie and the Battle of Culloden which
was fought nearby. It has acres of
parkland, fine lawns and trees and is an
oasis of exceptional quiet. Discerning
guests choose Culloden for its comfort,
dignity and luxury. The public rooms are
magnificent and bedrooms and
bathrooms are spacious and splendidly
equipped and furnished. The food is of
exceptionally high standard, served by
attentive staff in an imposing dining
room. As if all this wasn't enough, Ian
and Marjory McKenzie have had
constructed in a discreet area of the
wooded grounds just 200 yards from the
hotel, a most impressive Palladian
mansion with four suites which represent
the ultimate in luxury and will serve as an
additional facility to the main building.
Open all year
*Rooms: 23 with private facilities +
4 Garden Suites*
*Dining Room/Restaurant Lunch
12.30 – 2 pm (d)*
Dinner 7 – 9 pm (e)
Room Rate £150 – £190
*Mousse of Scottish blue cheese served with
salad and a hazelnut vinaigrette. Terrine
of duck liver and venison served with an
apple compote and rich Madeira sauce.
Marinated loin of venison wrapped in
pastry with spinach and mushrooms,
served with a rich game sauce.*
STB Deluxe 5 Crowns
Credit cards: 1, 2, 3, 5, 6
Proprietors: Ian & Marjory McKenzie

DUNAIN PARK HOTEL
Dunain Park
Inverness IV3 6JN
Tel: 0463 230512
A82, 1 mile west of Inverness.
Ann and Edward Nicoll give a warm
welcome and offer fine food in this
beautiful small hotel, secluded in six
acres of gardens and woodland. They
maintain high standards of cuisine,
comfort and service while retaining the
aura of a country house. An atmosphere
enhanced by log fires, antiques and oil
paintings. The hotel has 14 rooms, six of
which are suites, and all with private
facilities. Centrally heated throughout.
Two acres vegetable garden. Indoor
heated swimming pool and sauna. Award
winning restaurant is also recommended by
Egon Ronay and other guides.
Open all year except 2 wks Feb
Rooms: 14 with private facilities
Dinner 7 – 9 pm (d)
No smoking in dining room
Bed & breakfast £55 – £95
Dinner B & B £75 – £115
Special low season rates available
Saddle of venison, lamb, Highland Cattle
steaks, Guinea fowl, duck, quail, salmon,
seafood and extensive sweet buffet.
STB Deluxe 4 Crowns
Credit cards: 1, 2, 3, 5
Proprietors: Ann & Edward Nicoll

GLEN MHOR HOTEL & RESTAURANT
Ness Bank
Inverness IV2 4SG
Tel: 0463 234308
Fax: 0463 713170
On river bank below castle.
Superbly situated on the south bank of
the River Ness near the town centre. All
bedrooms have en suite facilities. Freshly
prepared local produce is featured in
modern Taste of Scotland menus in the
up market Riverview Restaurant which is
open for dinner and Sunday lunch.
Nico's Bistro Bar is an interesting
alternative and informal venue for
traditional Highland dishes and snacks,
day and night.
Open all year except 1 + 2 Jan
Rooms: 30 with private facilities
Bar Lunch 12 – 2 pm (a)
Dining Room/Restaurant Lunch 12.30
– 2 pm Sun only (a)
Bar Supper 5 – 9.30 pm (a-b)
Dinner 6.30 – 9 pm (c-d)
Bed & breakfast £35 – £45

Salmon in various styles. Langoustines,
oysters, mussels, fresh fish, beef, lamb.
STB Commended 4 Crowns
Credit cards: 1, 2, 3, 5
Proprietor: J Nicol Manson

INVERMOY HOUSE PRIVATE HOTEL & CARRIAGES RESTAURANT
Moy, by Tomatin
Inverness-shire IV13 7YE
Tel: 080 82 271
On B9154, 11 miles south of Inverness.
Recently taken over by Catherine and
Mike Brady, this is a charming converted
Highland railway station surrounded by
pine forests, yet only 15 minutes from
Inverness. The red sandstone hotel has
two restaurants – the Station Dining
Room and the à la carte Carriages
Restaurant, converted from two railway
carriages and furnished in Edwardian
style. A range of Scottish foods from the
Western Isles to the Borders is cooked in
both traditional and contemporary style,
encompassing fish, shellfish, game, lamb,
beef and poultry dishes. Vegetarian
dishes are always available and special
diets catered for by arrangement. Highly
trained kitchen staff exercise the strictest
standards. From Spring 1993 the
accommodation will comprise a family
suite of two rooms with private facilities
and a self-catering apartment sleeping
two to four persons, as well as two rooms
with private facilities.
Open mid Jan to 24 Dec
Rooms: 2 with private facilities + family
suite
Dinner 7 – 9.30 pm (c)
Dinner (Carriages) 7.30 – 9 pm (c)
No smoking in restaurants
Bed & breakfast from £19
Dinner B & B from £37
Credit cards: 1, 3
Proprietors: Catherine & Mike Brady

WHINPARK HOTEL
17 Ardross Street
Inverness IV3 5NS
Tel: 0463 232549
By Eden Court Theatre.
Whinpark is a restaurant with rooms,
within easy walking distance of the town
centre and near to Eden Court Theatre
on the River Ness. The restaurant offers
'something special' to the discerning
diner and features local produce such as
Ness salmon, game and Aberdeen Angus

steaks. A relaxed house party atmosphere
with a truly Highland welcome.
Open all year
Rooms: 8 , 4 with private facilities
Lunch (Lounge) 12 – 2 pm except Sun
Sat (a)
Dining Room/Restaurant Lunch 12 –
2 pm except Sun Sat (a)
Pre/After Theatre Suppers by
arrangement
Dinner 6.30 – 9.30 pm (b-c)
Bed & breakfast £17.50 – £27.50
Dinner B & B £27.50 – £39.50
Lightly baked tartlet of seafood mousse.
Shetland herring fillets prepared in a
variety of marinades. Wild Highland
game. Scotch beef.
STB Commended 3 Crowns
Credit cards: 1, 3
Proprietor: Stephen MacKenzie

Inverurie

MAP 5

THAINSTONE HOUSE HOTEL
Thainstone Estate, Inverurie
Aberdeenshire AB5 9NT
Tel: 0467 21643
Fax: 0467 25084
On A96 north of Aberdeen (8 miles from
airport).
The impressive facade of Thainstone
House remains unchanged, but behind it
has been completely transformed and
has become a sumptuous and luxurious
hotel and leisure centre. Architects and
designers have done a wonderful job in
retaining the character of the old
palladian building whilst introducing
gracious new public rooms and well
equipped bedrooms. International award
winning chef Bill Gibb – winner of the
Taste of Scotland Scotch Lamb
Challenge 1992 – presides in the kitchen
and the food is of an exceptional
standard of excellence. Thainstone in its
present form is a splendid addition to
the quality country house hotels of
Scotland.
Open all year
Rooms: 48 with private facilities
Cammies Grill Lunch 12 – 2 pm (a)
Dining Room/Restaurant Lunch
(Simpsons) 12.30 – 2.30 pm Sun only
(b)
Jazz Brunch 11 am – 2 pm Sun only (b)
Cammies Grill 5 – 10 pm (b)
Dinner (Simpsons) 7.30 – 9.30 pm (d)
No dogs
Bed & breakfast £52.50 – £82

Dinner B & B £75 – £93.50
Room Rate £75 – £125
Special weekend rates available
Charlotte of leek, chicken and asparagus
with coriander butter and black trumpets.
Rosette of beef with a herb crust, served
with a fricassé of mushrooms and a
Madeira and truffle sauce. Raspberry
brûlée with Summer berries.
STB Highly Commended 5 Crowns
Credit cards: 1, 2, 3, 5, 6

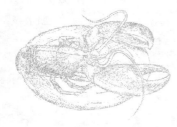

Islay
Isle of

MAP 7

KILCHOMAN HOUSE RESTAURANT
by Bruichladdich, Isle of Islay
Argyll PA49 7UY
Tel: 049 685 382

At end of B8018, off A847 Bridgend-
Bruichladdich. Beyond Kilchoman
Church, on the Atlantic side of the
Rhinns of Islay, 6 miles from
Bruichladdich.

A Listed Georgian building, formerly a
manse, Kilchoman House sits in a little
hollow, overlooked by majestic crags and
open farmland, and is the Taylor family's
home. Their attractive and relaxed 20
seat dining room is admirably hosted by
Stuart whilst Lesley applies imagination
in creating daily changing menus with
the help of superior local produce. A
very pleasant way to spend an evening.
The five self-catering cottages are open
all year, minimum three nights stay, early
booking advised.

Open Easter to Oct, but available to
booked parties Nov to Easter
Dinner 7.30 – 9 pm except Sun Mon (c)
Reservations essential
Closed Sun Mon
Drunken bullock. Venison McHarrie.
Lobster Thermidor (pre-ordered). Stir-
fried Islay scallops. Vegetarian and
special diets by request.
No credit cards
Proprietors: Stuart & Lesley Taylor

TAIGH-NA-CREAG
7 Shore Street
Port Charlotte, Isle of Islay
Argyll PA48 7TR
Tel: 049 685 261

Loch side, Port Charlotte village almost
opposite pier.

Not everyone goes off to the islands in
search of peace and quiet. But that is
what you will find in Islay. Little more
than the soft murmur of the sea in a
place where 'getting away from it all'
really means that. There are no five star
hotels here but what there is may well be
preferable; unpretentious, scrupulously
clean little B&Bs such as Carole and
David Harris operate in tiny Port
Charlotte getting on for 200 years old
but architecturally virtually unchanged.
In the little private dining room
overlooking Loch Indaal the Harrises
serve good breakfasts and interesting
dinners using only fresh meat, fish and
vegetables and if you are having a day
out walking or bird-watching they will
pack you a generous lunch and look
after your special needs if you are a
vegetarian. This is the real way to live in
the islands.
Open all year
Rooms: 2
Dinner at 7 pm (b)
Residents only
Unlicensed – guests welcome to take own
wine
Dogs – by arrangement
No smoking throughout
Bed & breakfast £16 – £18.50
Dinner B & B £26 – £28.50
Lobster bisque. Cock-a-leekie soup.
Mussels in white wine and garlic.
Venison pie with red wine, cream and
mushrooms. Islay lamb with apricot
sauce. Fresh fish always available.
Hommity pie (vegetarian). Home-made
bread and chocolates.
No credit cards
Proprietors: Carole & David Harris

Jedburgh

MAP 2

WILLOW COURT
The Friars, Jedburgh
Roxburghshire TD8 6BN
Tel: 0835 63702

From Market Place, Jedburgh, take
Exchange Street – The Friars is first road
on right.

Though a mere two minutes walk from
the centre of this historic old Borders
town, Willow Court has a fine panoramic
view over Jedburgh and is quietly situated
in two acres of gardens. The bedrooms of
this delightful guest house are
charmingly decorated and have a
pleasant airy feel to them. The garden
provides almost all of the fruit and
vegetables needed in the kitchen and fills
the house with flowers. Jane McGovern is
much acclaimed for her cooking and
rightly so, and she and her husband are
very welcoming hosts and establish an
immediate rapport with their guests.
Open all year
Rooms: 4 with private facilities
Dinner 6 – 7 pm (a)
Unlicensed
Facilities for the disabled
No smoking in restaurant + bedrooms
Bed & breakfast £16 – £18
Dinner B & B £24 – £30
Best Border beef, lamb and game. Fresh
and smoked Tweed trout and salmon.
Home-grown fruit and vegetables. Special
local cheeses.
STB Highly Commended 3 Crowns
No credit cards
Proprietor: Jane McGovern

Keiss

MAP 6

SINCLAIR BAY HOTEL
Main Street, Keiss
Caithness KW1 4XA
Tel: 0955 83 233

On main A9, 7 miles from John o'
Groats.

Sinclair Bay Hotel is situated just seven
miles south of John o' Groats and eight
miles north of Wick on the A9. The hotel
is fully licensed and is well appointed
and pleasingly decorated throughout.
Most bedrooms have spectacular views
over sea and cliffs, and all have wash
basins with continuous hot water, tea and

coffee-making facilities and television. There is also a comfortable lounge with television. For those who enjoy eating – farm-reared fowls, roasts and grills (only the finest of Scotland's beef) and fresh seafood are your choice from a daily changing menu. Free golf for all residents. Fishing and sea angling by arrangement.
Open all year
Rooms: 7 , 1 with private facilities
Bar Lunch 12.30 – 2 pm (a)
Bar Supper 7 – 9.30 pm (a)
Dinner 7 – 9.30 pm (b)
No smoking in dining room
Bed & breakfast £14.50 – £23
Prawn and crab platter. Venison cream pâté. Lemon sole in prawn and mushroom sauce. Prime Scottish beef and lamb. Vegetarian dishes.
Credit cards: 1, 3
Proprietors: David & Margaret Angus

Kelso

MAP 2

FLOORS CASTLE
Kelso
Roxburghshire TD5 7RW
Tel: 0573 23333
A699 west of Kelso.
Floors is the magnificent and imposing Border home of the Duke of Roxburghe much of which is open to the public. The self-service restaurant which caters for visitors is plainly but comfortably furnished and has a well sheltered open courtyard in which you may eat out in good weather. The restaurant makes good use of available fresh produce from the castle gardens, salmon from the River Tweed, and there is some good home-baking.
Open May to Oct plus Easter
Food service all day Sun to Thu: also Fri Sat in Jul + Aug
Restaurant Lunch (a)
No smoking area in restaurant
Floors kitchen pheasant pâté, Tweed salmon, smoked Tweed salmon, home-baking from Floors Castle kitchens.
Credit cards: 1, 3

SUNLAWS HOUSE HOTEL
Heiton, Kelso
Roxburghshire TD5 8JZ
Tel: 05735 331 • Telex: 728147
Fax: 05735 611
On A698 Kelso-Jedburgh in the village of Heiton.
A magnificent 18th century Scottish baronial gentleman's home owned by the Duke of Roxburghe. Situated in beautiful expansive grounds and superb gardens, it offers the charm and comfort of a stylish period and luxurious country house, whether fishing, shooting, relaxing or enjoying the countryside.
Open all year
Rooms: 22 with private facilities
Bar Lunch 12.30 – 2 pm (a)
Dining Room/Restaurant Lunch 12.30 – 2 pm except Sun Sat (b)
Dinner 7.30 – 9.30 pm (d)
Bed & breakfast £41 – £82
Dinner B & B £66 – £107
Breast of wild Border duck with leek and apricot timbale. Pure heather honey and Glayva ice-cream.
STB Highly Commended 4 Crowns
Credit cards: 1, 2, 3, 5, 6

Kenmore

MAP 4

CROFT-NA-CABER
Garden Restaurant, Kenmore
Perthshire PH15 2HW
Tel: 0887 830 236
Fax: 0887 830 649
A827 to Kenmore, then take unclassified road along south shore of the loch for 1/2 mile.
With its indoor flower beds and hanging baskets, there really is an airy garden feeling about the aptly named Garden Restaurant at Croft-na-Caber. Adjacent is a comfortable lounge for aperitifs and coffee. There are some lovely views out over Loch Tay and the hills beyond. The Swiss-trained head chef and his team present a varied and interesting menu combining the best of traditional and modern Scottish fare, with an intriguing element of continental cuisine.
Open all year
Rooms: 6 , 2 with private facilities plus 17 chalets
Bar Meals 12 – 10 pm (a)
Dining Room/Restaurant Lunch 12 – 2.30 pm (a)
Dinner 7 – 9.30 pm (c)

Taste of Scotland applies to Garden Restaurant
Facilities for the disabled
No smoking in restaurant
Bed & breakfast £17.50 – £32
Dinner B & B from £23
Smoked Tay salmon and smoked scallops served with a cream mayonnaise. Sirloin steak served with a herb and red wine sauce. Home-made apple and bramble pie. Cranachan.
Credit cards: 1, 3
Proprietor: A C Barratt

KENMORE HOTEL
Kenmore
Perthshire PH15 2NU
Tel: 0887 830 205
Fax: 0887 830 262
Off A9 on A827, 16 miles west of Ballinluig, 17 miles east of Killin. Kenmore at the head of Loch Tay is designated as one of Scotland's prettiest villages and it also boasts Scotland's oldest inn. Built in 1572 the Kenmore Hotel is the focal point in the village and has a splendid reputation for the excellence of its facilities and the courteous good manners of an attentive staff. Bedrooms are comfortable, very well equipped and en suite. The dining room offers lovely panoramic views over the River Tay, and the chef is well supported by a good kitchen staff and makes intelligent and creative use of a plentiful supply of really fresh local produce. Golfers and fishermen enjoy 50% reduced rates at Taymouth Castle Golf Course and a two mile stretch of the River Tay, but if your preference is for a quietly luxurious and relaxing stay, this would be the place for you.
Open all year
Rooms: 38 with private facilities
Bar Lunch 12.30 – 2.30 pm (a)
Bar Supper 7.30 – 9.30 pm (a)
Dinner 7.30 – 9.30 pm (c)
Dogs by arrangement
No smoking in dining room
Bed & breakfast £28 – £58.75
Dinner B & B £40.25 – £73
Crispy breast of duck served on a bed of braised cabbage with a honey and lemon sauce.
STB Commended 4 Crowns
Credit cards: 1, 2, 3
Proprietor: Andrew MacTaggart

Kentallen of Appin

MAP 6

ARDSHEAL HOUSE
Kentallen of Appin
Argyll PA38 4BX
Tel: 063 174 227

On A828, 4 miles south of Ballachulish Bridge.
Set in 900 acres of woods and meadows overlooking Loch Linnhe, this 1760 house – once the home of the Stewarts of Appin – has oak panelling, open fires and is furnished with antiques. The relaxed congenial atmosphere is conducive to enjoying the superb meals and fine wines, and offers a true taste of the best of Scotland.
Open wk before Easter to early Nov
Rooms: 13 with private facilities
Dining Room/Restaurant Lunch 12 – 2 pm (a-c)
Dinner 8.15 – 8.30 pm (f)
No smoking in restaurant
Dinner B & B £64 – £90
Ramekin of Loch Linnhe prawns and Colonsay oysters in rose jelly with garden herbs. Mangetout and ginger soup. Medallions of venison with blackcurrant vinegar. Rosette of beef with sage butter, chestnut purée and thyme.
Credit cards: 1, 3
Proprietors: Bob & Jane Taylor

Kilchrenan

MAP 6

ARDANAISEIG HOTEL
Kilchrenan, by Taynuilt
Argyll PA35 1HE
Tel: 086 63 333
Fax: 086 63 222

Prestige Award Winner 1990

3¹/2 miles off B845 at Kilchrenan.
It is easy to fall in love with a place like Ardanaiseig. Everything about it seems just right. It is set in a renowned shrub and woodland garden on the shores of Loch Awe with really magnificent views. This is a country house hotel that is beautifully appointed. The kitchen reflects the same high standards that prevail throughout this peaceful haven, food is imaginative and prepared and

presented with panache.
Open Easter to mid Oct
Rooms: 14 with private facilities
Bar Lunch 12.30 – 2 pm (a)
Dining Room/Restaurant Lunch 12.30 – 2 pm (c)
Dinner 7.30 – 9 pm (f)
No smoking in dining room
Bed & breakfast £41.50 – £71.50
Dinner B & B £75 – £105
Warm home-smoked scallops with snow peas and chives. A symphony of west coast shellfish pan-fried and accompanied by a saffron butter sauce. Crisp brandy snap basket filled with fresh garden fruits.
STB Highly Commended 4 Crowns
Credit cards: 1, 2, 3, 5
Proprietors: Tom & Carmen Robbins

TAYCHREGGAN HOTEL
Kilchrenan, by Taynuilt
Argyll
PA35 1HQ
Tel: 086 63 211

Leave A85 at Taynuilt on to B845 on loch side past Kilchrenan.
There was a time when sturdy Highland cattle going to market were made to swim across Loch Awe and land at Taychreggan where they rested for the night. It is not surprising therefore, that this hotel started off as a drovers' inn. It is now a very comfortable, delightful small hotel in a most peaceful and secluded site with splendid views across the loch. There are still echoes of the past in the cobbled courtyard – a pleasant place in which to sit out and enjoy a cool drink, and there are three well equipped public rooms. The dining room is attractively laid out and there is a strong emphasis on fresh local products, well presented and served. Various theme weekends in Autumn and Winter.
Open Mar to Dec
Rooms: 15 with private facilities
Bar Lunch 1 – 2.15 pm (a)
Dining Room/Restaurant Lunch 1 – 2.15 pm (b)
Dinner 7.30 – 9.15 pm (d)
Bed & breakfast rates on application
Dinner B & B rates on application
Local fresh fish, prawns, turbot, halibut, salmon, venison, beef, etc – served in an enterprising and interesting manner.
Credit cards: 1, 2, 3, 5

Kildrummy

MAP 5

KILDRUMMY CASTLE HOTEL
Kildrummy, by Alford
Aberdeenshire AB3 8RA
Tel: 09755 71288 • Telex: 94012529
Fax: 09755 71345

On A97 Ballater-Huntly, 35 miles west of Aberdeen.
The castle itself could not have looked more imposing than does this grand mansion house overlooking the ruins of the original 13th century castle. The grounds are superb – acres of beautiful gardens and woodland. Internally there is original wood panelling, and tapestries dating from the turn of the century. The whole building exudes character and atmosphere; the food and service are of a standard to enhance the overall grandness of the place and the bedrooms have every modern comfort and convenience.
Open Feb to Dec
Rooms: 16 with private facilities
Dining Room/Restaurant Lunch 12.30 – 1.45 pm (b)
Dinner 7 – 9 pm (d)
No smoking in dining room
Bed & breakfast £48 – £60
Dinner B & B £55 – £85
Salmon terrine on a saffron sauce lightly laced with Scotch whisky. Warm salad of Kildrummy game. Loin of veal with a light almond and rosemary sauce with a timbale of wild rice.
STB Deluxe 4 Crowns
Credit cards: 1, 2, 3, 6
Proprietor: Thomas Hanna

Kilfinan

MAP 3

KILFINAN HOTEL
Kilfinan, nr Tighnabruaich
Argyll PA21 2EP
Tel: 070 082 201
Fax: 070 082 205

B8000, on the eastern side of Loch Fyne.
An ancient coaching inn which has been modernised to very high standards without losing any of its traditional character. It is set in breathtaking countryside on the eastern shore of Loch Fyne. Rolf and Lynne Mueller have settled in very quickly here and have already earned commendations for the

excellence of the cuisine. Chef Mueller is a member of the Master Chefs of Great Britain. Trained in Switzerland, he brings an international touch to the best of local produce – salmon, trout, venison, pheasant and wild duck from the surrounding Kilfinan Estate are often featured on the menu.
Open Mar to end Jan
Rooms: 11 with private facilities
Bar/Restaurant Lunch 12 – 2 pm (a)
Dinner 7.30 – 9.30 pm (d)
Bed & breakfast £34 – £39
Dinner B & B £55 – £60
Ragoût of venison with redcurrant sauce. Roast saddle of lamb with rosemary. Smoked haddock sausage and halibut fillet in a sorrel sauce. Drambuie parfait.
STB Highly Commended 3 Crowns
Credit cards: 1, 2, 3

Killiecrankie

MAP 4

KILLIECRANKIE HOTEL
Killiecrankie, by Pitlochry
Perthshire PH16 5LG
Tel: 0796 473220
Fax: 0796 472451

On old A9, 3 miles north of Pitlochry.
A converted Dower House, set in four acres of well kept gardens overlooking the historic Pass of Killiecrankie. Furnished to a high standard to reflect the expected small country house atmosphere and comfort requirements of the most fastidious guest.
Open Mar to Dec
Rooms: 11 with private facilities
Bar Lunch 12.30 – 2 pm (a)
Bar Supper 6.30 – 9.30 pm (b)
Dinner 7 – 8.30 pm (d)
No smoking in dining room
Bed & breakfast £44 – £45
Dinner B & B £67.50 – £68.50
Sautéd king prawns with garlic and fresh samphire, finished with cream and saffron. Tournedos of Scotch beef on a mustard and mint sauce with pickled walnuts. Grilled whole lemon sole with citrus fruits and smoked oysters. Fresh raspberry tart. Lemon parfait on a coconut coulis.
STB Commended 4 Crowns
Credit cards: 1, 2, 3
Proprietors: Colin & Carole Anderson

Kilmarnock

MAP 1

THE COFFEE CLUB
30 Bank Street, Kilmarnock
Ayrshire KA1 1HA
Tel: 0563 22048

In town centre.
Situated in one of the oldest streets in Kilmarnock opposite the Laigh Kirk. Offering something for everyone – quick service, snack meals and a large varied menu including grills and vegetarian dishes, and dinner from the interesting Rosemaling menu. All food is produced to order using fresh produce where practicable and bakery items are a speciality. The ambience is relaxed and friendly, and you may take your own wine.
Open all year except Christmas + Boxing Days, 1 + 2 Jan
Coffee and meals served from 9 am – 10 pm (a-b)
Closed Sun for meals but coffee lounge open 12 – 5.30 pm
Unlicensed – guests welcome to take own wine
No smoking area in air-conditioned restaurant
Fish, omelettes, chicken dishes and grills. Slimmers special. Vegetarian dishes. Children's menu. Sandwiches and salads etc.
Credit cards: 1, 3
Proprietors: Svend Kamming & William MacDonald

Kilmelford

MAP 6

CUILFAIL HOTEL
Kilmelford
Argyll PA34 4XA
Tel: 085 22 274 • Fax: 085 22 264

A816 midway between Oban and Lochgilphead, at top of Loch Melfort.
A traditional Scottish country hotel with a good west of Scotland atmosphere, and which is a very popular overnight or meal time stopping place on the Oban-Lochgilphead road. It is a good base for touring or exploring the Firth of Lorn and well known to hill-walkers, fishermen and sailors. There is lots of character about the place and the recent programme of refurbishment and renovation had done much to improve the standard of bedrooms and public rooms. It has delightful gardens just across the road – splendid for a relaxing

Summer evening's cool drink as you watch the world go by.
Open all year
Rooms: 12 with private facilities
Bar Lunch 12 – 2.30 pm (a)
Bar Supper 6.30 – 9.30 pm (a)
Dinner 6.30 – 9.30 pm (b)
Bed & breakfast £27.50 – £30
Home-made pies with crisp puff pastry. Chicken in pastry with various fillings and sauces. Pork and beef en croûte. Local salmon. Prawns and lobster. All dishes freshly prepared.
STB Commended 3 Crowns
Credit cards: 1, 3
Proprietor: David Birrell

Kilmun

MAP 3

FERN GROVE
Kilmun
Argyll PA23 8SB
Tel: 036984 334

6 miles from Dunoon on A880 on the side of the Holy Loch.
The former family home of the 'Campbells of Kilmun' is on a site overlooking the Holy Loch. The welcoming warm hospitality of hosts Ian and Estralita Murray creates a very comforting and friendly atmosphere in this attractive Victorian house. It is not a large building and it emanates an air of relaxation and cosy family living. Estralita presides in the kitchen and prepares daily menus using only fresh local and home-grown produce and creates interesting and appealing meals. There is a sensibly priced wine list. The recent introduction of a seafood and salad all day dining option is proving popular.
Open all year
Rooms: 4 with private facilities
All day dining 11 am – 8.30 pm
Dining Room/Restaurant Lunch 12.30 – 2 pm (c) – by prior arrangement
Bar Supper 7 – 11 pm (b)
Dinner 7 – 9.30 pm (c)
No dogs
No smoking in restaurant + bedrooms
Bed & breakfast £20 – £25
Dinner B & B £34 – £40
Special Winter rates on application
Home-baked assorted breads. Unusual soups and pâtés. Best of home-produced beef and lamb. Imaginative vegetarian dishes (by request). No rules 'sweetaholics' dessert trolley! Only the best of Scottish cheeses.
STB Commended 3 Crowns
Credit cards: 1, 2, 3, 5
Proprietors: Ian & Estralita Murray

Kilwinning

MAP 1

MONTGREENAN MANSION HOUSE HOTEL

Montgreenan Estate
Torranyard, Kilwinning
Ayrshire KA13 7QZ
Tel: 0294 57733 • Telex: 778525
Fax: 0294 85397

Off A736 Glasgow-Irvine near Torranyard.

This lovely old mansion house can trace its origins back to the 14th century, though the present building is primarily 18th century and still retains attractive features from that period including marble and brass fireplaces and decorative ceilings. Set in acres of peaceful garden and woodland it is difficult to realise that it is only about 20 minutes away from Glasgow airport. Perhaps the latter factor has contributed to its growing reputation as a centre for executive conferences. There is even a heliport facility! Bedrooms are excellently equipped and the dining room is not only elegant but displays high standards of food presentation and service.

Open all year
Rooms: 21 with private facilities
Bar Lunch 12 – 2.30 pm (c)
Dining Room/Restaurant Lunch 12 – 2.30 pm (c)

Dinner 7 – 9.30 pm (d)
Bed & breakfast £46 – £66
Dinner B & B £70 – £90
Scottish lobster Montgreenan, Montgreenan game and whisky pie. Locally caught salmon, trout and shellfish.
STB Highly Commended 4 Crowns
Credit cards: 1, 2, 3, 5, 6
Proprietors: The Dobson Family

Kincraig

MAP 6

MARCH HOUSE GUEST HOUSE

Feshiebridge, Kincraig
Kingussie
Inverness-shire PH21 1NG
Tel: 0540 651 388

Off A9 at Kincraig. Follow B970 for 2 miles to Feshiebridge. Past red telephone box, turn right. Half mile on left down gravel drive.

This very comfortable family run guest house is situated in the tranquillity of beautiful unspoilt Glenfeshie. Surrounded by mature pine trees it enjoys outstanding views of the Cairngorm Mountains. Perfect for all outdoor pursuits including skiing, gliding, watersports and golf (six courses within easy reach) and a naturalist and bird-watcher's paradise. Local attractions include the Wildlife Park, Highland Folk Museum and Inchriach Alpine Nursery. All rooms have private facilities and tea/coffee etc. Home-baking and cooking with imagination using the best of local produce including salmon, trout, lamb, Angus beef and venison, and fresh herbs from the garden. Friendly relaxed atmosphere.

Open 27 Dec to Oct except 1 to 14 May
Rooms: 6 with private facilities
Dinner at 7 pm (b)
Reservations essential for non-residents
Unlicensed – guests welcome to take own wine
Bed & breakfast £16 – £22
Dinner B & B £26.50 – £32.50
Spicy vegetable soup. Soda bread rolls with walnuts. Venison with pickled walnuts and red wine. Local trout and salmon. Carbonnade of beef. Raspberry and apple pie. Hot pancakes with pears, cream and chocolate sauce.
STB Commended 1 Crown
No credit cards
Proprietors: Caroline & Ernie Hayes

Kingussie

MAP 6

THE CROSS

Tweed Mill Lane, Kingussie
Inverness-shire PH21 1TC
Tel: 0540 661166
Fax: 0540 661080

Prestige Award Winner 1989

2 hours north of Edinburgh, in centre of Kingussie.

In March 1993 Tony and Ruth Hadley are scheduled to re-locate their renowned restaurant to a former tweed mill a mere 250 yards from their original location, providing extended dining and accommodation facilities. Devotees need not worry – to make life easy it will retain its name and telephone number. The Hadleys will continue to look after their guests with the same high standards of food and personal service that have gained them so much praise in the past. But do note that until March the original establishment in the High Street will still be open.

Open Mar to Nov 1993
Rooms: 9 with private facilities
Dining Room/Restaurant Lunch 12.30 – 2.30 pm except Tue (b)
Dinner 7 – 9 pm except Tue (e-f)
Closed Tue
Dinner B & B £55 – £75
Credit cards: 1, 3
Proprietors: Tony & Ruth Hadley

THE OSPREY HOTEL

Ruthven Road, Kingussie
Inverness-shire PH21 1EN
Tel: 0540 661510

In Kingussie village, on corner of main road.

An attractive small Highland hotel where the owners, Robert and Aileen Burrow, put great emphasis on personal service and providing a relaxing and informal atmosphere for their guests. The imaginative menu features the best of local produce, home-baking and interesting vegetarian dishes, and there is an extensive wine list. An ideal base from which to tour, or for those wishing to take advantage of the numerous sporting and outdoor pursuits in the area.

Open all year except 2 wks Nov
Rooms: 8, 4 with private facilities
Dinner 7.30 – 8 pm (c)

No smoking in dining room
Bed & breakfast £20 – £34
Dinner B & B £37 – £52
North Sea bake. Wild mushroom brioche.
Prince of Wales salmon. Fillet steak with
blue stilton and Port sauce. Mulled wine
sorbet. Chocolate and chestnut roulade.
STB Commended 2 Crowns
Credit cards: 1, 3
Proprietors: Robert & Aileen Burrow

Kinlochbervie

MAP 6

THE KINLOCHBERVIE HOTEL
Kinlochbervie , by Lairg
Sutherland IV27 4RP
Tel: 097 182 275
Fax: 097 182 438

On B801, via A838 from Lairg.
An imposing modern hotel set on the
hillside with superb views of
Kinlochbervie harbour and Loch Clash.
Somewhat naturally, therefore, a
selection of locally landed fish features
prominently on the menus in the
candlelit dining room. In addition there
is a bistro for informal eating. The hotel
has been refurbished to a high standard
and is personally supervised by the
owners, Rex and Kate Neame.
Open 1 Apr to 31 Oct
Rooms: 14 with private facilities
Bar Lunch 12 – 1.45 pm (b)
Restaurant Lunch (bistro) 12 – 1.45 pm
(b)
Bar Supper 6.30 – 8.30 pm (b)
Dinner 7.30 – 8.30 pm (e)
No smoking in dining room
Bed & breakfast £42 – £54
Dinner B & B £66 – £78
Locally caught white fish, king prawns,
salmon and lobster are prepared and
cooked with skill and pride.
STB Highly Commended 4 Crowns
Credit cards: 1, 2, 3, 5
Proprietors: Rex & Kate Neame

Kinloch Rannoch

MAP 4

BUNRANNOCH HOUSE
Kinloch Rannoch
Perthshire PH16 5QB
Tel: 0882 632407

Turn right after 500 yards on
Schiehallion road, just outside Kinloch
Rannoch off B846.
Bunrannoch is a family run former
hunting lodge nestled at the foot of the
'sleeping giant' mountain close by Loch
Rannoch. The cosy lounge, log fires and
uninterrupted Highland views
complement the delicious aromas from
the kitchen. Walk the mountain glens,
ramble on Rannoch Moor or catch a
trout in the loch, then return to
Bunrannoch House to relax and savour
the delights of Highland cooking.
Open all year except Christmas + New Year
Rooms: 7 , 5 with private facilities
Dinner 7 – 9.30 pm (b)
No smoking in dining room
Bed & breakfast £16 – £18
Dinner B & B £28 – £32
Fillet of venison in redcurrant and Port.
Best Scotch fillet in whisky cream sauce.
Apple and walnut cake with butterscotch
and rum sauce.
STB Approved 2 Crowns
Credit cards: 1, 3
Proprietor: Jennifer Skeaping

CUILMORE COTTAGE
Kinloch Rannoch
Perthshire PH16 5QB
Tel: 0882 632218

Small is Beautiful Award 1990

100 yards from east corner of Loch
Rannoch.
Anita Steffen has made a tremendous
success of this cosy little 18th century
croft and the standard and style of her
food has been lauded and publicised to a
degree that is remarkable for such a
small establishment. Much of the
produce is grown in the cottage garden
and the rest is carefully sourced to
ensure freshness and quality. Thereafter
Anita displays her own skill and flair to
the great satisfaction of her diners.
Cuilmore is delightfully secluded and
guests have the complimentary use of
mountain bikes, dinghy and canoe to
explore the locality.
Open all year except Christmas + New Year

Rooms: 2 with private facilities
Dinner 7 – 9 pm (c)
Prior booking essential for non-residents
Unlicensed – guests welcome to take own
wine
No children
No smoking in dining room
Bed & breakfast from £17.50
Dinner B & B from £32.50
Terrine of salmon with herb mayonnaise.
Mousseline of sole with lime and
almonds. Saddle of venison in chanterelle
cream sauce. Breast of pheasant with
grapes, nuts and orange. Chocolate
teardrop. Fruit parfaits.
STB Highly Commended Listed
No credit cards
Proprietor: Anita Steffen

Kinnesswood

MAP 4

THE LOMOND COUNTRY INN
Kinnesswood, by Loch Leven
Perthshire KY13 7HN
Tel: 0592 84 253 • Fax: 0592 84 693

4 miles from Kinross. From south, M90
Junction 5, B9097 via Scotlandwell.
From north, M90 Junction 7, A911 via
Milnathort.
Situated in the historic village of
Kinnesswood, by the Lomond Hills, this
cosy family run hotel offers magnificent
views over Loch Leven. Only fresh food is
served – simply prepared and very tasty –
good wines and real ale. Twelve en suite
bedrooms all with colour TV, telephones,
tea and coffee-making facilities. Only 45
minutes from Edinburgh, Perth and St
Andrews, and at the hub of all the
sporting, leisure and cultural
opportunities that abound in the area.
Open all year
Rooms: 12 with private facilities
Bar Lunch 12 – 2.30 pm (a)
Dining Room/Restaurant Lunch 12 –
2.30 pm(a)
Bar Supper 6 – 9 pm (a)
Dinner 6 – 9 pm (b)
Light snacks (scones, sandwiches and
tea) served all day
Bed & breakfast £23.50 – £28.50
Dinner B & B £30 – £35
Loch Leven trout – this distinctive local
trout is simply grilled in butter to retain
its special flavour and served with fresh
local vegetables.
STB Commended 3 Crowns
Credit card: 1, 2, 3, 6
Proprietors: David Adams & Neil Hunter

Kinross

MAP 4

CROFTBANK HOUSE HOTEL
30 Station Road, Kinross
Fife KY13 7TG
Tel: 0577 63819

Junction 6, M90 on approach to Kinross.
Chef/Patron Bill Kerr and his wife Diane
run this old Victorian mansion house as
a small and friendly hotel and restaurant,
serving creative and imaginative food.
Ideally situated for shooting, fishing and
golf – surrounded by world famous golf
courses – and with good access to
Edinburgh, Perth, Stirling and St
Andrews. Chef appointed to Master Chef
Institute of UK.
*Open all year except Christmas + Boxing
Days*
Rooms: 3 with private facilities
Bar Lunch 12 – 2 pm except Mon (a)
*Dining Room/Restaurant Lunch 12 –
2 pm except Mon (b)*
Bar Supper 6 – 9 pm except Mon (b)
Dinner 6.30 – 9 pm except Mon (d)
Closed Mon
No smoking in restaurant
Bed & breakfast £32 – £36
Dinner B & B £44 – £52
Room Rate £36 – £48
*Seafood parcel, warm monkfish salad,
breast of wild pigeon.*
STB Commended 2 Crowns
Credit cards: 1, 3
Proprietors: Bill & Diane Kerr

THE GROUSE & CLARET RESTAURANT
Heatheryford
Kinross KY13 7NQ
Tel: 0577 864212
Fax: 0577 864212

*Junction 6, M90, opposite the Granada
Services.*
Only 200 yards from the M90 at Exit 6
with its entrance drive exactly opposite
the motorway service area yet a world
apart in style and standard. Taking its
unusual name from a fishing fly this
really is a special place with a peaceful
atmosphere, serving delightful food and
wine. The decor is charming and the old
sandstone buildings are filled with
unusual antique furniture, old rugs and
lovely pictures. There are many examples
of fine local craftwork for sale in the art
gallery, which also caters for special
parties of up to 70 guests and is popular

for birthdays, anniversaries and business
meetings. Meriel Cairns takes pride in
floral table decorations and garlands the
beams with flowers and ivy for special
occasions. The delicious home-made
food is beautifully presented with lots of
fresh herbs and garnished with tiny wild
flowers. It is a bit like dining with a good
friend and one who is an exceptional
cook. The comfortable ground floor
rooms overlook the water. Also available
is fly-fishing for the enthusiastic
fisherman.
Open all year except Feb
Rooms: 4 , 3 with private facilities
Bar Lunch 11.30 am – 3 pm (a)
*Dining Room/Restaurant Lunch 12 –
2.30 pm (a)*
Dinner 7 – 9 pm (b-c)
Table licence
Facilities for the disabled
No smoking in restaurant
Bed & breakfast £18.50 – £24
*Seasonal game and shellfish e.g. lobster,
crayfish, cooked to order with wine and
herbs. Delicious home-made puddings –
rose petal tart, hazelnut meringue.*
STB Award Pending
Credit cards: 1, 3
Proprietors: John & Meriel Cairns

Kippen

MAP 4

CROSS KEYS HOTEL
Main Street, Kippen
by Stirling FK8 3DN
Tel: 078 687 293

*On B822 Callander-Fintry and just off
A811 Stirling-Erskine Bridge, only 8
miles west of Stirling.*
An attractive old 18th century village inn,
now a small family run hotel, set in the
peaceful and picturesque village of
Kippen, near Stirling. The hotel has
retained its old world character which is
enhanced by log fires in the bars during
Winter. In addition to informal meals in
the bar and family room, there is a small
restaurant where the interesting menu
offers a good selection of freshly
prepared dishes.
*Open all year except evening 25 Dec +
1 Jan*
Rooms: 3
*Bar Lunch 12 – 2 pm Mon to Sat:
12.30 – 2 pm Sun (a)*
*Dining Room/Restaurant Lunch 12 –
2 pm Mon to Sat: 12.30 – 2 pm Sun (a)*
Bar Supper 5.30 – 9.30 pm (a)

Dinner 7 – 8.45 pm (c)
Bed & breakfast £19.50 – £21.50
*Home-made soups and pâtés. Roast
venison and fresh raspberry and red wine
sauce. Medallions of fillet of beef with a
peppered brandy and cream sauce. Fillet
of salmon with a lemon and rosemary
cream sauce. Athole brose with Kippen
honey.*
Credit cards: 1, 3
Proprietors: Angus & Sandra Watt

Kirkcudbright

MAP 1

AULD ALLIANCE RESTAURANT
5 Castle Street
Kirkcudbright DG6 4JA
Tel: 0557 30569

Kirkcudbright town, opposite the castle.
Black and gold fronted Listed building
with a display of shells and other seaside
paraphernalia in the bay window. In this
small restaurant Anne serves and Alistair
cooks the quality produce of Scotland
prepared in the French culinary style.
The menu features local seafood and
Galloway beef.
Open 1 Mar to 31 Oct + Christmas wk
*Dining Room/Restaurant Lunch 12 –
2 pm (a)*
Dinner 6.30 – 9 pm (c)
*House speciality – Kirkcudbright queen
scallops fried in garlic butter with smoked
Ayrshire bacon, finished in Galloway
cream.*
No credit cards
Proprietors: Alistair & Anne Crawford

SELKIRK ARMS HOTEL
High Street, Kirkcudbright
Kirkcudbrightshire DG6 4JG
Tel: 0557 30402
Fax: 0557 31639

Off A75, 27 miles west of Dumfries.
Historic 18th century hotel with Burns
connection in the picturesque harbour
town of Kirkcudbright, with its own large
secluded garden. Although recently
refurbished the hotel still manages to
retain its character. There are extensive à
la carte and daily changing table d'hôte
menus. Marvellous walking, fishing, bird-
watching and beaches nearby.
Open all year
Rooms: 15 with private facilities
Bar Lunch 12 – 2 pm (a)
*Dining Room/Restaurant Lunch 12 –
2 pm (a) – booking essential*

Bar Supper 6 – 9.30 pm (a)
Dinner 7 – 9.30 pm (c)
Bed & breakfast £34 – £42
Dinner B & B £51 – £59
Seafood, scallops, salmon, Dover sole,
plaice, lobster. Galloway beef and lamb.
Pheasant in a cream and lemon sauce.
Duck breast in an orange and brandy
sauce.
STB Highly Commended 4 Crowns
Credit cards: 1, 2, 3, 5, 6
Proprietor: John Morris

Kirkintilloch

MAP 3

THE LADY MARGARET
CANALBOAT
Scotland in View Ltd
c/o 10 Bankhead Road, Waterside
Kirkintilloch, Glasgow G66 3LH
Tel: 041 776 6996 or 0836 607755

**Canalboat based at Glasgow Road
Bridge Jetty, on A803 between
Bishopbriggs and Kirkintilloch, near
The Stables.**

Calm water canal cruises on the northern
outskirts of Glasgow, in country scenery,
with floodlights and central heating for
all year round operation. The purpose-
built canalboat is tastefully appointed.
Crystal glasses and Wedgwood crockery
enhance attractive table settings, with
pink linen and fresh flowers. A relaxing
experience, unrivalled in Scotland.
Available for group bookings at any time,
any day. The boat provides a quality
venue which is especially suitable for
business entertainment, family
gatherings and weddings – as well as for
individual table bookings on weekend
cruises for that special occasion.
Operates all year except Christmas Day + 1 Jan
Lunch (Sun only) sailing at 1 pm (b)
Dinner sailing at 7.30 pm Thu Fri Sat (e)
Advance booking essential
Imaginative set menus incorporating the
best in fresh Scottish produce and dishes
with an emphasis on quality and
presentation.
Credit cards: 1, 2, 3, 5
Contact: Patrick Le Pla

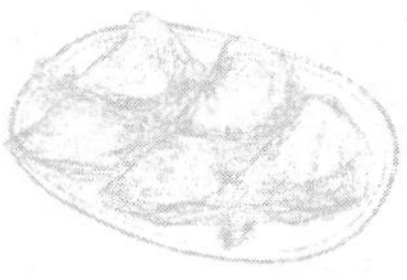

Kirkmichael

MAP 4

THE LOG CABIN HOTEL
Kirkmichael, by Blairgowrie
Perthshire PH10 7NB
Tel: 0250 881288
Fax: 0250 881402
Signposted off A924 in Kirkmichael.
Uniquely built of whole Norwegian pine
logs, the Log Cabin Hotel nestles high in
Glen Derby with some wonderful
panoramic views. The hotel is centrally
heated and double glazed so guests are
assured of a warm welcome. Lovely views
from the restaurant where the menus
change each evening to reflect the
availability of local produce. An ideal
centre for touring Perthshire. Also
popular with hill-walkers and convenient
for skiing in Glenshee.
Open all year
Rooms: 13 with private facilities
Bar Lunch 12 – 1.45 pm (a)
Bar Supper 6 – 8.45 pm (b)
Dinner 7.30 – 8.45 pm (c)
Bed & breakfast £22 – £27
Dinner B & B £34 – £39
Home-produced dishes using tender game
and local produce including salmon and
trout. Delicious desserts for those on and off
diets(!) with a selection of home-made ice-
creams.
STB Award Pending
Credit cards: 1, 2, 3, 5
Proprietor: A F Finch

Kyle of Lochalsh

MAP 6

BIADH MATH RESTAURANT
Railway Platform, Kyle of Lochalsh
Ross-shire IV40 8XX
Tel: 0599 4813
At Kyle of Lochalsh railway station on
platform 1. Parking on slipway to
station.
You have to know exactly where you are
going to find Biadh Math the good food
cafe which is right on the railway
platform, but do not be deterred by that.
For holiday-makers on a budget and
lovers of good homely food this is a find.
It specialises in the abundance of fresh
local seafood, langoustine, scallops and
monkfish, served up in interesting ways,
but for those who prefer red meat there
are usually good lamb and steak

alternatives. Jams, chutneys and cakes are
home-made as is the fudge with your
coffee. On cold nights a coal fire burns
bright and creates a snug little haven
overlooking the harbour, the Cuillin
Hills and the ferry to Skye. In the peak
season, the restaurant is open for
breakfast and for light snacks all day.
Open Easter to Oct
Note: please telephone to check opening
times during off-peak season.
Meals available 10 am – 4.30 pm (a):
6.30 – 9 pm (b)
Table licence
Langoustines in garlic butter. Seafood
crêpes on a tarragon sauce. Queen
scallops in a white wine sauce. Local
oysters in season. Lamb kebabs and
whisky steaks. Cranachan. Banana rum
crêpes.
Credit cards: 1, 3
Proprietors: Andrea Matheson &
Jann MacRae

WHOLEFOOD CAFE, HIGHLAND
DESIGNWORKS
Plockton Road
Kyle of Lochalsh IV40 8DA
Tel: 0599 4388
On Kyle-Plockton road.
The Wholefood Cafe is situated in what
was the old village school which is on the
outskirts of Kyle, facing the sea. All the
food served is prepared and cooked on
the premises using best quality fresh and
local produce. Anything from a coffee to
a full meal is available all day. There is
also an outside terrace and garden.
Open Easter to Oct
Lunch (Spring & Autumn) 12 –
2.30 pm except Mon Sat (a)
Lunch (Summer) 12 – 6 pm (a)
Dinner (Spring & Autumn) 7 – 9 pm
Sun Fri only (b)
Dinner (Summer) 7 – 9 pm (b)
No smoking in restaurant
Home-made soups: parsnip and apple;
mushroom, brown ale and fresh thyme.
Herring in oatmeal with mixed salad;
leek, carrot and stilton cheese quiche.
Wild Loch Duich salmon. Fresh spinach,
pasta shell and cashewnut bake;
buckwheat pancakes filled with spiced
stir-fried vegetables served with local
yoghurt and cucumber sauce. Fresh
strawberry cheesecake; bramble, apple and
gooseberry crumble. Local cheeses with
oatcakes.
Credit cards: 1, 3
Proprietor: Fiona Begg

Kylesku

MAP 6

LINNE MHUIRICH
Unapool Croft Road
Kylesku, by Lairg
Sutherland IV27 4HW
Tel: 0971 502227

3/4 mile south of the new Kylesku Bridge on A894.
Fiona and Diarmid MacAulay welcome non-smokers to their modern crofthouse which is peacefully situated overlooking Loch Glencoul with panoramic views of hills and lochs. The Handa Island Nature/Bird Reserve and lovely, lonely sandy beaches are nearby. Directions and maps for many local walks are provided. The dinner menus change daily and are discussed with guests after breakfast. Vegetarian dishes are enthusiastically prepared. Guests are welcome to take their own wine as the premises are not licensed to provide alcoholic beverages. In the evening at 10 pm guests are offered a choice of hot drink and something tasty to eat. French spoken.
Open Easter to mid Nov
Rooms: 3 , 1 with private facilities
Dinner at 7.30 pm except Sun Sat (a)
Residents only
No smoking throughout
Bed & breakfast £16.50 – £21.50
Dinner B & B £26 – £29
Local fish and seafood – Kylesku prawn vol au vents; smoked haddock au gratin; salmon baked with lemon and herbs. Home-made quiches and pâtés. Casseroles. Vegetarian dishes. Unusual salads. Tempting desserts and home-baking. Filter coffee. Scottish honey and cheeses.
STB Commended 2 Crowns
No credit cards
Proprietors: Fiona & Diarmid MacAulay

Laggan

nr Newtonmore

MAP 6

THE GASKMORE HOUSE HOTEL
Laggan, nr Newtonmore
Inverness-shire PH20 1BS
Tel: 05284 250
Fax: 05284 350

On A86 Newtonmore-Fort William: 8 miles from Newtonmore, 10 minutes from A9.
The Gaskmore House Hotel is situated in a beautiful historical part of the Spey Valley. Set amidst some of the most splendid scenery in the Highlands and with a wide range of sporting activities practically on the doorstep. If all you want to do is get away from it all and relax in comfort with the peace and tranquillity Gaskmore offers, then this could be an excellent hideaway. This is a family run country house hotel distinguished by exceptional cuisine and offering friendly efficient service.
Open all year
Rooms: 24 with private facilities
Light Lunch 12.30 – 2 pm (a)
Dining Room/Restaurant Lunch 12.30 – 2 pm (b)
Dinner 7 – 9.30 pm (e)
Facilities for the disabled
No smoking in restaurant
Bed & breakfast £41 – £52
Dinner B & B £59 – £70
Pigeon sausage with a marmalade of shallots. Scottish Spring lamb with an apricot flan, served with a pearl barley and thyme sauce. Warm puff pastry box of berries with a blackberry sorbet. Hand-made chocolates.
STB Commended 4 Crowns
Credit cards: 1, 3
Proprietors: John & Janet Grover

Langbank

MAP 3

GLEDDOCH HOUSE
Langbank
Renfrewshire PA14 6YE
Tel: 0475 54 711 • Telex: 779801
Fax: 0475 54 201

Off M8 Glasgow-Greenock at Langbank (B789).
Beautifully situated in 360 acres overlooking the River Clyde and Loch Lomond hills, this hotel offers all the advantages of gracious living and distinctive cuisine. Amenities include 18 hole golf course within the grounds and Clubhouse facilities of squash, sauna, snooker and horse-riding. In addition off-road driving and clay pigeon shooting can be arranged. Gleddoch was formerly a family residence and has been tastefully converted still retaining the features of a private home, with service and accommodation of the highest standard.
Open all year
Rooms: 33 with private facilities
Bar Lunch (Clubhouse) 12 – 2.30 pm except Sun Sat (a)
Dining Room/Restaurant Lunch 12.30 – 2 pm (b)
Bar Supper (Clubhouse) 6 – 9.30 pm except Sun Sat (a)
Dinner 7.30 – 9 pm (e)
Bed & breakfast £65 – £105
Dinner B & B £70 – £80 (weekend break)
Room Rate £81.50 – £96.50
Marinated Scottish salmon on radicchio lettuce with a saffron dressing. Poached fillet of brill with a light orange and watercress sauce.
STB Highly Commended 4 Crowns
Credit cards: 1, 2, 3, 5, 6

Credit Card Code	Meal Price Code	
1. Access/Mastercard/Eurocard	(a)	under £10
2. American Express	(b)	£10 – £15
3. Visa	(c)	£15 – £20
4. Carte Bleu	(d)	£20 – £25
5. Diners Club	(e)	£25 – £30
6. Mastercharge	(f)	over £10

Largs

MAP 3

MANOR PARK HOTEL
Skelmorlie, nr Largs
Ayrshire PA17 5HE
Tel: 0475 520832
Fax: 0475 520832

Off A78, c. 2 miles north of Largs.
Gracious Victorian manor situated in its
own grounds on a hillside overlooking
Firth of Clyde. Beautiful gardens with
acres of lawns, shrubs, trees and a water
garden. Panoramic views from all public
rooms towards the islands and
mountains of Argyll, with glorious
sunsets. Family run hotel with first class
cuisine and service. Bedrooms well
appointed, with tea-making facilities and
hairdryers. Unique cocktail bar with
renowned malt whisky collection.
Open all year
Rooms: 23 , 22 with private facilities
Bar Lunch 12.30 – 5 pm (a)
Dining Room/Restaurant Lunch 12.30
– 2.30 pm (b-c)
Bar Suppers 5 – 8.30 pm (b)
Dinner 7 – 9.15 pm (c-d)
Bed & breakfast from £35
Dinner B & B from £50
The best of local meat and fish
predominate, with fresh vegetables.
Scampi Laphroaig, venison Macallan.
STB Commended 4 Crowns
Credit cards: 1, 2, 3, 5

WHAM'S &
THE PLATTER
80 Main Street
Largs KA30 8DH
Tel: 0475 672074

A78 west coast route between Ardrossan
and Greenock.
Situated in a building dating from 1887,
these two restaurants operate similar self-
service menus over lunchtime, but in the
evening the style changes to a more
relaxed table service – Wham's offering
seafood as its speciality while The Platter
specialises in steaks. Dine in the
conservatory-style Wham's, or in The
Platter's Victorian ambience.
Open all year
Dining Room/Restaurant Lunch
11.45 am – 2.45 pm except Sun
Dinner 5 – 8.45 pm except Sun (c)
Closed Sun
Menu and seasonal daily specials
including Cullen skink, Arbroath

smokies, Loch Fyne kippers, mussels,
oysters, crayfish, lobster. Platter fillet of
beef, Scottish lamb chops, home-made
steak pie.
Credit cards: 1, 3

Letham

MAP 4

FERNIE CASTLE HOTEL
Letham, Cupar
Fife KY7 7RU
Tel: 033 781 381
Fax: 033 781 422

Off A914 Glenrothes-Tay Bridge/
Dundee, 1 mile north of A91/A814
Melville roundabout.
This impressive old building, part of
which goes back to the 16th century, has
a number of attractive and unusual
features. Internally, the unique ambience
of the Keep Bar is striking as is the large
circular ballroom and the original stately
proportioned family dining room when
Fernie was privately owned. There are
comfortable and elegant twin drawing
rooms on the first floor. Outside is one
of the best preserved ice houses in
Scotland in which Winter ice was stored
to serve the castle through the Summer.
Set in 28 acres of pleasant lawn and
woodland and with its own small loch,
Fernie Castle makes a splendid base for
exploring historic Fife. St Andrews is
only 20 minutes away and there are golf
courses and places of interest galore.
Chef Christopher Sandford's creative
menus have raised the level of eating
experience to new heights and meet the
twin objectives of pleasing both palate
and pocket.
Open all year
Rooms: 15 with private facilities
Bar Lunch 12 – 2.30 pm (a-b)
Dining Room/Restaurant Lunch 12 –
2.30 pm (b)

Bar Supper 6.30 – 9.30 pm (a-b)
Dinner 7 – 9.30 pm (c-e)
Bed & breakfast £35 – £50
Dinner B & B £45 – £55
Poached fillet of Tay salmon. Rack of
lamb. Steamed Orkney mussels. Fernie
creel – seafood in a wine stock. Grand
dessert selection.
STB Commended 3 Crowns
Credit cards: 1, 2, 3
Proprietors: Norman & Zoe Smith

Lewis
Isle of

MAP 7

HANDA
18 Keose Glebe (Ceos), Lochs
Isle of Lewis PA86 9JX
Tel: 0851 83334

$1^1/2$ miles off A859, 12 miles south of
Stornoway: last house in village of 'Ceos'.
This is a delightful modern home on a
hilltop which seems hundreds of miles
from anywhere but of course is not. It is a
convenient spot for exploring Lewis and
Harris but much nearer at hand –
virtually on the doorstep – there is hill-
walking, bird-watching, fishing, and otter
sighting if you are lucky. In this small
comfortable haven, island hospitality and
personal attention are very much to the
fore. Alongside traditional recipes there
is innovative home-cooking using fresh
herbs and vegetables from the kitchen
garden. Vegetarian and individual
dietary requirements are catered for.
There is brown trout fishing on the
private loch 100 yards from the house
and a boat and equipment can be hired.
Open 1 Mar to 31 Oct
Rooms: 3 , 1 with private facilities
Dinner 6.30 – 7.30 pm (b)
Unlicensed – guests welcome to take own
wine
No smoking in dining room
Bed & breakfast £16 – £20
Dinner B & B £28 – £32
Home-made breads, soups. Lamb and
dill hotpot. Lemon sole with walnut
stuffed mushrooms. Shellfish platter.
Salmon in orange and vermouth. Wild
brown trout with mint. Fillet steak in
Port and mushrooms.
STB Highly Commended 2 Crowns
No credit cards
Proprietors: Murdo & Christine
Morrison

PARK GUEST HOUSE

30 James Street, Stornoway
Isle of Lewis PA87 2QN
Tel: 0851 70 2485

*1/2 mile from ferry terminal. At junction
of Matheson Road, James Street and
A866 to airport and Eye peninsula.*
A substantial stone built house dating to
around 1883, centrally located in the
town of Stornoway. The old wood of the
interior has been refurbished and the
public rooms and bedrooms are
tastefully decorated. The dining room,
featuring a Glasgow style fireplace, has a
warm, homely atmosphere. Fresh local
produce – shellfish, game, venison, Lewis
lamb – feature on the menu prepared
with care and presented by
Chef/Proprietor Roddy Afrin. Ideal base
for touring, golf, bird-watching, fishing
etc, or just exploring some of the lunar-
like landscapes of Lewis and Harris.
Open all year except 24 Dec to 5 Jan
Rooms: 5
Packed Lunches available (a)
*Dining Room/Restaurant Lunch 12 –
1.45 pm Tue to Fri (a)*
*Dinner at 6 pm (table d'hôte) (b) –
residents only*
*Dinner 7.30 – 8.30 pm (a la carte)
except Sun Mon (c-d)*
Note: Dinner Sun Mon – residents only
No dogs
Bed & breakfast from £19
Dinner B & B from £30
*Home-made soups, pâtés, desserts.
Smoked trout mousse wrapped in oak-
smoked salmon. Hebridean scallops and
crowdie in puff pastry. Noisettes of local
venison in Port wine sauce with
blackcurrants.*
STB Commended 2 Crowns
No credit cards
Proprietors: Catherine & Roddy Afrin

Lochcarron

MAP 6

LOCHCARRON HOTEL

Lochcarron
Ross-shire IV54 8YS
Tel: 05202 226

At east end of village, facing the loch.
This 19th century Highland hostelry has
been delightfully modernised to provide
the facilities expected of an AA two star
hotel. The majority of the
accommodation, which includes two
suites with their own small sitting rooms,
overlook the sea loch. This view is also
shared by the lounge bar and restaurant,
where fish and shellfish from local boats
and game from nearby sporting estates
feature highly on both à la carte and
table d'hôte menus which cater for every
taste.
Open all year
Rooms: 10 with private facilities
Bar Lunch 12 – 2 pm (a)
*Dining Room/Restaurant Lunch 12 –
2 pm (a)*
Bar Supper 6 – 9 pm (a)
Dinner 7 – 9 pm (b)
Bed & breakfast £26 – £34
Dinner B & B £31.50 – £49.50
*Platter of seafood. Poached salmon with
prawns and lemon butter. Breast of duck
in red wine. Beef and venison steaks.*
STB Commended 3 Crowns
Credit cards: 1, 3
Proprietors: Pam & Tony Wilkinson

ROCKVILLA HOTEL &
RESTAURANT

Main Street, Lochcarron
Ross-shire IV54 8YB
Tel: 05202 379

*Situated in centre of village, c. 20 miles
north of Kyle of Lochalsh.*
An oldish stone building, all very neat
and clean looking, on the main street
enjoying a splendid view of the loch and
with a cheerful air of informality which
should appeal to guests. This small family
run hotel and restaurant is situated
between the Kintail and Torridon
mountain ranges and within leisurely
touring distance of Gairloch, the
Applecross Peninsula and the Skye Ferry
terminal. It makes a splendid base from
which to explore some of the most
beautiful scenery in Scotland. After a day
out touring, walking or sightseeing, there
will be a friendly welcome on return and
an interesting selection of dishes to
satisfy the most fastidious appetite, all
prepared from the local harvest of the
sea, rivers and glens.
Open all year except 1 Jan
Rooms: 4, 2 with private facilities
Bar Lunch 12 – 2.30 pm (a)
Bar Supper 6 – 9.30 pm (a)
Dinner 6 – 9.30 pm (c)
No dogs
No smoking in restaurant
Bed & breakfast £20 – £25
Dinner B & B rates on application
*Wide selection of fresh local seafood
including salmon, lobster and prawns as*
available. Venison and steaks. A la carte
changes daily according to availability of
fresh produce.
STB Commended 3 Crowns
Credit cards: 1, 3
Proprietors: Lorna & Ken Wheelan

Loch Earn
St Fillans

MAP 4

ACHRAY HOUSE HOTEL

St Fillans, Loch Earn
Perthshire PH6 2NF
Tel: 076 485 231

A85, 12 miles west of Crieff.
Stunning lochside position in St Fillans –
an area of outstanding natural beauty.
Well established, family run hotel, known
for its wide selection of good food, value
and service, with a caring attitude that
brings people back year after year.
Achray House is centrally placed for
sightseeing and an ideal base for golf,
walking, field and watersports.
Open 1 Mar to 31 Oct
Rooms: 10, 7 with private facilities
Bar Lunch 12 – 2 pm (a)
Bar Supper 6.30 – 9.30 pm (a)
Dinner 6.30 – 9.30 pm (b)
Bed & breakfast from £21
Dinner B & B from £28
*Wide choice of Scottish produce –
pheasant, grouse, steaks, salmon,
venison, trout, lamb, pork and seafood.
Good choice of vegetarian dishes always
available. Large selection of freshly made
desserts (the house speciality).*
STB Highly Commended 3 Crowns
Credit cards: 1, 3
Proprietors: Tony & Jane Ross

THE FOUR SEASONS HOTEL

St Fillans, Loch Earn
Perthshire PH6 2NF
Tel: 076 485 333
Fax: 076 485 333

*On A85, 12 miles west of Crieff, at west
end of St Fillans overlooking Loch
Earn.*
There are few lovelier locations than that
of the Four Seasons at the east end of
Loch Earn in the charming little village
of St Fillans. Huge picture windows in all
the public rooms and most of the
bedrooms offer stunning views across
and down the loch, and there are six

chalets on the wooded hillside behind the hotel. The Scott family are anxious to ensure the comfort of their guests and Chef Andrew Scott has some really interesting and imaginative dishes on his menu. There are not too many places where the bar lunch menu runs to large bowls of Skye mussels cooked in white wine, or Guinea fowl terrine, or Arbroath smokies and poached eggs. That, however, should whet the appetite for a leisurely dinner in the attractive dining room where regularly changing menus emphasise the abundance of game and seafood, but the chef is willing to prepare any special requests, given appropriate notice.
Open Mar to Nov
Rooms: 18 with private facilities
Bar Lunch 12 – 2.15 pm (a)
Dining Room/Restaurant Lunch 12.30 – 2.30 pm (b)
Bar Supper 6.30 – 9.30 pm (b)
Dinner 7 – 9.45 pm (c)
Facilities for the disabled
No smoking in dining room
Bed & breakfast £28 – £38
Dinner B & B £47 – £57
Pastry case of pink wood pigeon and chanterelles. Warm mussels and scallops on a bed of mixed leaves with walnut and saffron dressing. Saddle of lamb with rosemary crust and redcurrants.
Credit cards: 1, 2, 3
Proprietors: Allan & Barbara Scott

Lochearnhead

MAP 4

CLACHAN COTTAGE RESTAURANT
Clachan Cottage Hotel
Lochside, Lochearnhead
Perthshire FK19 8PU
Tel: 0567 830247
Lochearnhead is on A85 Crieff-Crianlarich.
Clachan Cottage Hotel enjoys a spectacular lochside setting on the east side of the village of Lochearnhead. It is well placed for touring central Scotland including the Trossachs, Glencoe, Oban and Scone Palace. For the energetic there are 26 golf courses within an hour, and a good choice of walking, fishing and watersports. The restaurant which is upstairs has good views across the loch. It offers freshly prepared meals using Scottish produce. Many rooms with private facilities, and all with tea and coffee-making facilities. Open fires – range of malts, and friendly service in a relaxed atmosphere. Frequent live entertainment. Special breaks available throughout year.
Open 3 Apr to 31 Dec
Rooms: 21 , 15 with private facilities
Bar Lunch 12 – 2.30 pm (a)
Bar Supper 6 – 9.30 pm (a)
Dinner 7 – 9 pm (c)
Taste of Scotland applies to restaurant only
Smoking not encouraged in restaurant
Bed & breakfast £22.50 – £24.50
Dinner B & B £36 – £38
Smoked mackerel and whisky pâté, served with a light mixed salad and a basil vinaigrette. Suprême of chicken in an orange sauce laced with a light Sherry. Aberdeen Angus steak with mushrooms in a cream sauce.
STB Approved 3 Crowns
No credit cards
Proprietor: Andrew Low

GOLDEN LARCHES RESTAURANT
Balquhidder Station
Lochearnhead
Perthshire FK19 8NX
Tel: 05673 262
Situated on A84, 2 miles south of Lochearnhead.
This is a very attractive little restaurant on the main route between Strathyre and Lochearnhead. There are usually colourful window boxes and hanging baskets. The interior is crisp and clean, with pine furniture. It is family run and specialises in home-made scones, cakes and fruit pies. Meals are plain Scottish fare but cooked to order and feature traditional Scottish soups and good Angus steaks and steak pies. Local Loch Tay trout and fresh vegetables are also available.
Open Easter to Oct
Meals and snacks served all day
Open till 7 pm low season; 9 pm high season (a-b)
Unlicensed
Home-baking of sweets and cakes.
Scottish high tea.
No credit cards
Proprietors: James & Loraine Telfer

Lochgilphead

MAP 6

STAG HOTEL
Argyll Street, Lochgilphead
Argyll PA31 8NE
Tel: 0546 2496
On A83 between Oban and Inveraray.
The Stag Hotel is situated in the centre of Lochgilphead. It is a family run hotel, well placed for visiting Oban, Inveraray and the Mull of Kintyre. It is furnished to the highest standard throughout and all rooms have colour TV, telephone and tea/coffee-making facilities. Residents' lounge for guests. There is also a sauna and solarium available, as well as free golf for hotel guests, at the local nine hole course.
Open all year
Rooms: 17 with private facilities
Bar Lunch 12 – 2 pm (a)
Dining Room/Restaurant Lunch (Aug Sep only) 12 – 2 pm (a)
Bar Supper 5.30 – 8.30 pm (a)
Dinner 7 – 8.30 pm (b)
Bed & breakfast £30 – £32
Dinner B & B £44 – £46
Winter weekend breaks Nov to Apr, also Christmas/New Year breaks.
Loch Fyne salmon, venison steak, Sound of Jura clams, Islay malt whisky syllabub.
STB Commended 3 Crowns
Credit cards: 1, 3
Proprietor: Joyce Ross

Lochinver

MAP 6

THE ALBANNACH

Baddidarroch, Lochinver
Sutherland IV27 4LP
Tel: 05714 407

*From Lochinver follow signs for
Baddidarroch. After 1/2 mile, pass
turning for Highland Stoneware, turn
left for the Albannach.*
A 19th century house of character set in
walled, sheltered, south facing gardens
with mature trees and shrubs and
spectacular views across Lochinver Bay
towards Suilven and Canisp. The
Albannach offers an original style of
cooking, emphasising the best of local
produce particularly game and seafood,
and using home-grown herbs, vegetables,
fruits and mushrooms in season. Meals
are served before an open log fire in the
wood-panelled dining room. Changing,
daily set three course menu with no
choice on main courses unless arranged
in advance. Vegetarians welcome with
prior notification. French spoken.
Children over five years welcome.
Open all year
Rooms: 6 , 3 with private facilities
Dinner at 7 pm (b)
*Non-residents welcome by prior
arrangement*
*Unlicensed – guests welcome to take own
wine*
No dogs
Facilities for the disabled
No smoking throughout
Bed & breakfast £22 – £26
Dinner B & B £37 – £41
*Lochinver monkfish, prawns and sole.
Local lamb and game, with herbs and
sauces. Puddings with seasonal soft fruits
and nuts.*
STB Commended 3 Crowns
Credit cards: 1, 3
*Proprietors: Colin Craig &
                    Lesley Crosfield*

LOCHINVER LARDER'S
RIVERSIDE BISTRO

Main Street, Lochinver
Sutherland IV27 4JY
Tel: 05714 356

*A837 to Lochinver, second property on
right as enter village.*
Polished wooden tables and chairs,
Highland stoneware, good glassware and
attractive table settings, give a pleasing
appearance to this 44 seat restaurant

which you enter through the delicatessen
shop. It is situated on the bank of the
River Inver as it flows into the sea and a
large bay window provides pleasant
panoramic views of the bay and its
activities. With a plentiful supply of
seafood landed directly at the village
harbour, the menu majors on this and
on really good steaks, but there are
sufficient other items to provide
adequate choice. Presentation is good
and the service is pleasant and
unhurried. Very popular and very busy in
the season.
Open Apr to Oct
*Note: also open Nov to Apr, Fri Sat only
Food service 9 am – 9 pm Mon to Sat:
10.30 am – 9 pm Sun
Dining Room/Restaurant Lunch 12 –
2 pm (a)
Dinner 6 – 9 pm (b)
Facilities for the disabled
No smoking in restaurant
Freshly landed seafood and fish from
village harbour. Beef steaks from
Highland cattle.
Credit card: 1
Proprietors: Ian & Debra Stewart*

MACPHAILS'

216 Clashmore
Stoer, by Lochinver
Sutherland IV27 4JQ
Tel: 057 15 295

*B869 (single track), 10 miles north of
Lochinver, West Sutherland.*
A traditional croft house, modernised to
a high standard, but retaining much of
the original character, including roof
beams and peat/log fire. The
atmosphere is welcoming, warm and
friendly. A lochside situation overlooking
the sea to the Hebrides. Sandy beaches
nearby. Peaceful with no passing traffic.
French spoken.
Open May to Oct
*Rooms: 3 , 1 with private facilities
Dinner at 7.30 pm (b)
No dogs
Facilities for the disabled*

*No smoking area in dining room
Unlicensed – guests welcome to take own
wine
Bed & breakfast £13 – £21
Dinner B & B £24 – £32
Home-made bread and oatcakes. A
variety of interesting menus, including
traditional Scottish dishes using local
salmon, venison and seafoods.
Vegetarian by request. Freshly ground
coffee.
No credit cards
Proprietors: Pat & Madeline Macphail*

Loch Lomond

MAP 3

CAMERON HOUSE HOTEL

Loch Lomond, Alexandria
Dunbartonshire G83 8QZ
Tel: 0389 55565
Fax: 0389 59522

Prestige Award Winner 1991

*On A82 near Balloch, on the banks of
Loch Lomond.*
This most impressive location has been
developed carefully and skilfully with due
regard to the aesthetics of the site and is
now a superb luxury resort hotel set in
108 wooded acres on the south west
shore of Loch Lomond. There are
excellent leisure facilities and a choice of
three restaurants. You can choose the
elegance of the Georgian Room or the
Grill Room with its emphasis on local
produce and you can enjoy afternoon tea
overlooking the loch in the tranquillity
of the Drawing Room. The hotel
restaurants are open to non-residents but
leisure facilities are for members and
residents only.
*Open all year
Rooms: 68 with private facilities
Bar Lunch (Clubhouse) 12.30 – 3 pm
(a)
Lunch (Brasserie) 12 – 2 pm (b)
Lunch (Georgian Room) 12 – 2 pm (c)
Lunch (Grill Room) 12.30 – 2 pm Sun
only (c)
Dinner (Brasserie) 7 – 10 pm (b)
Dinner (Georgian Room) 7 – 10 pm (f)
No dogs
Facilities for the disabled
No smoking area in restaurant
Bed & breakfast £69 – £275
Dinner B & B £87.50 – £313.50
STB Deluxe 5 Crowns
Credit cards: 1, 2, 3, 5, 6*

Lockerbie

MAP 1

SOMERTON HOUSE HOTEL

Carlisle Road, Lockerbie
Dumfriesshire DG11 2DR
Tel: 05762 2583

Outskirts of Lockerbie about 300 yards from main A74.
A robust red sandstone Victorian mansion standing in its own grounds, with interesting architectural aspects especially the unusual Kauri timber panelling and plaster cornices. All bedrooms en suite with TV, central heating and direct dial telephone.
Open all year
Rooms: 7 with private facilities
Bar Lunch 12 – 2 pm (a)
Dining Room/Restaurant Lunch 12 – 2 pm (b) – reservations only
Bar Supper 6 – 9 pm (a)
Dinner 7 – 9 pm (c)
No smoking in restaurant
Bed & breakfast £25.75 – £36
Whole grilled sardines and garlic bread. Devil's beef tub soup. Local lamb cooked in yoghurt with apricots. Collops in the pan. Galloway pork and beef. Local salmon and trout.
STB Commended 4 Crowns
Credit cards: 1, 2, 3
Proprietors: Sam & Patricia Ferguson

Lybster

MAP 6

PORTLAND ARMS HOTEL

Lybster
Caithness KW3 6BS
Tel: 059 32 208 • Fax: 059 32 208

On A9, 12 miles south of Wick.
The Portland was built to serve as a staging post early last century. There have been many changes since, but the quality of personal service established then has been maintained. The hotel is fully central heated and double glazed. All rooms have private facilities including colour TV, telephone, tea-making facilities. Four-poster beds available. Executive rooms with jacuzzi baths also available.

Open all year
Rooms: 20 with private facilities
Bar Lunch 12 – 2.30 pm (a)
Dining Room/Restaurant Lunch 12 – 2.30 pm (a)
Bar Supper 5 – 9.30 pm (a)
Dinner 7 – 9.30 pm (c)
Bed & breakfast £24.50 – £32.90
Dinner B & B £41 – £51.35
Succulent Aberdeen Angus steaks, seafood platters, game dishes, fresh cream sweets.
Credit cards: 1, 3
Proprietors: Gerald & Helen Henderson

Mallaig

MAP 6

MARINE HOTEL

Station Road, Mallaig
Inverness-shire PH41 4PY
Tel: 0687 2217

Adjacent to railway station. First hotel on right off A82, and a 5 minute walk from ferry terminal.
Mallaig marks the end of the famous West Highland Line and the equally famous Road to the Isles. It is also a busy fishing port and a ferry terminal. The Marine Hotel is perched overlooking the harbour where you can see most of the action. It is family run and friendly, and most of the bedrooms are en suite and are well appointed with colour TVs and the usual facilities. The menu, sensibly, takes full advantage of the freshly landed fish and shellfish and specialises in it. Those who live in large cities remote from a fishing port have just no idea how good fresh fish can taste!
Open all year except Christmas + New Year
Note: restricted service Oct/Nov to Mar
Rooms: 21, 16 with private facilities
Bar Lunch 12 – 2 pm (a)
Dining Room/Restaurant Lunch – by arrangement only
Bar Supper 6 – 9.30 pm (b)
Dinner 7 – 9 pm (c)
Bed & breakfast from £20
Dinner B & B £35 – £50
Home-made soups and pâté. Local seafood – scallops a speciality. Scottish meats and vegetables. Imaginative desserts. Scottish breakfast with porridge and locally smoked kippers.
STB Commended 3 Crowns
Credit cards: 1, 3
Proprietors: Elliot & Dalla Ironside

by Maybole

MAP 1

LADYBURN

by Maybole
Ayrshire KA19 7SG
Tel: 06554 585
Fax: 06554 580

A77 (Glasgow-Stranraer) to Maybole then B7023 to Crosshill. Turn right at War Memorial (Dailly-Girvan). After exactly 2 miles, turn left and follow signs. 5 miles south of Maybole.
"Peace and tranquillity" are words that are often applied to descriptions of country house hotels and in many cases are overdone – but not here. This is a superb away-from-it-all retreat contiguous to the magnificent Kilkerran Estate which guests are invited to enjoy. Ladyburn is a very gracious house and exemplifies life as it used to be lived, and ought to be lived. Jane and David Hepburn are charming hosts and go out of their way to welcome you as a personal guest to their elegant home. Everything about Ladyburn epitomises gracious living and the food is of the same imposing standard. This is honest cooking at its best: food that does not need, and does not get, the pretentious frills that some adopt to disguise inferior cuisine. The whole experience here will send you home with a warm glow of satisfaction. Italian, French, German and Russian spoken. Children over 12 welcome.
Open all year except Boxing Day
Rooms: 8 with private facilities
Dining Room/Restaurant Lunch 12.30 – 1.45 pm (b)
Dinner 7.30 – 8.45 pm Tue to Sat (d)
Note: Dinner Sun Mon – residents only
Restricted licence
No dogs
No smoking in dining room
Bed & breakfast from £70
Dinner B & B from £95
Jane Hepburn uses fresh local produce, garden vegetables and herbs, and old family recipes. Roast sirloin, Great Aunt May's chicken casserole, Mrs Runcie's pudding.
STB Deluxe 3 Crowns
Credit cards: 1, 2, 3
Proprietors: Jane & David Hepburn

Melrose

MAP 2

BURTS HOTEL
Market Square, Melrose
Roxburghshire TD6 9PN
Tel: 089 682 2285
Fax: 089 682 2870

B6361, 2 miles from A68, 38 miles south of Edinburgh.

A delightful hotel dating back to 1722, situated in this historic town in the heart of the Border country. It is ideally situated for walking, horse-riding, golf, game shooting and salmon fishing. The elegant restaurant offers a choice of Scottish and international cuisine. An extensive lunch and supper menu is also available in the popular lounge bar. There is a secluded garden to the rear of the hotel with tables for fine weather.

Open all year except Boxing Day
Rooms: 21 with private facilities
Bar Lunch 12 – 2 pm (a)
Dining Room/Restaurant Lunch 12.30 – 1.30 pm (b)
Bar Supper 6 – 9.30 pm Mon to Thu: 6 – 10.30 pm Fri Sat: 6.30 – 9.30 pm Sun (b)
Dinner 7 – 9 pm Sun to Thu: 7 – 9.30 pm Fri Sat (c)
Bed & breakfast £39 – £50
Dinner B & B £46 – £50
Mini-break terms available from Nov to May.
Specialities include Tweed salmon, chicken howtowdie, grouse and pheasant, venison and Scottish beef, complemented by an excellent wine list.
STB Commended 4 Crowns
Credit cards: 1, 2, 3, 5
Proprietors: Graham & Anne Henderson

MELROSE STATION RESTAURANT
Palma Place, Melrose
Roxburghshire TD6 9PR
Tel: 089 682 2546

Close to Market Square. Follow signposts to Melrose Station, which is up hill to right of dairy.

A friendly and unpretentious restaurant within the historic Melrose Railway Station building which has been restored and converted to include comfortable and attractive surroundings for diners in a peaceful situation. Simple but imaginative blackboard menus offer a choice of light or more substantial

lunches and a table d'hôte dinner at weekends, all at very reasonable prices. The new proprietors, Claire and Ian Paris, have already gained a reputation for their personal attention and home-style cooking, using only the best of local produce.

Open all year except 3 wks Feb
Morning coffee 10 am – 12 noon except Mon
Dining Room/Restaurant Lunch 12 – 2.30 pm except Mon (a)
Afternoon tea (Summer only) 2.30 – 4 pm except Mon
Dinner 6.45 pm Thu to Sat only (c)
Closed Mon
Home-made soups and pâtés. Interesting filled pancakes and quiches, salad bar at lunchtime. Noisettes of lamb served with a creamy tomato and basil sauce. Selection of home-made desserts.
Credit cards: 1, 3
Proprietors: Ian & Claire Paris

Melvich
by Thurso

MAP 6

THE SHEILING GUEST HOUSE
Melvich, by Thurso
Caithness KW14 7YJ
Tel: 0641 3256

Melvich on A836, 18 miles west of Thurso.

With its outstanding scenic views over the Halladale River and Melvich Bay, the quiet peaceful Sheiling caters for every comfort within its warm friendly atmosphere. Guests return year after year to enjoy home-cooked meals and the personal service of Joan Campbell. There are two spacious lounges and the bedrooms all have tea/coffee-making facilities and electric blankets. The menus change daily and there is a large selection breakfast menu. The Sheiling is an ideal stop for touring Caithness and Sutherland being midway between Wick and Cape Wrath (Durness) and within daily reach of trips to the Orkney Isles.

Open Apr to Sep
Rooms: 3 with private facilities
Dinner at 6.30 pm – or by arrangement – except Fri Sat (b)
Residents only
Unlicensed – guests welcome to take own wine
No smoking in dining room
Bed & breakfast £17 – £20

Dinner B & B £19 – £22
Caithness beef, Sutherland lamb, Melvich Bay salmon and local haddock. Fresh fruit, vegetables from kitchen garden. Sweets and traditional puddings with Scottish cream.
STB Highly Commended 3 Crowns
No credit cards
Proprietor: Joan Campbell

Moffat

MAP 1

COREHEAD FARM
Annanwater, Moffat
Dumfriesshire DG10 9LT
Tel: 0683 20973

From Moffat, turn into Beechgrove Drive and continue for 5 miles to valley end.

A picturesque farmhouse on a large hill farm, situated in the "Devil's Beef Tub" amidst the beautiful Moffat hills, in a secluded and wooded site at the head of the Annan Valley. This makes an ideal base for hill-walking – the farm includes Hart Fell at 2651 feet, one of the highest peaks in southern Scotland – or touring the many attractions of Dumfries and Galloway. There is also a fine golf course and excellent tennis courts in the area, as well as fishing and riding available locally. The proprietor, Berenice Williams, was an award finalist in Farmhouse Cook of the Year 1991.

Open all year except 20 Dec to 6 Jan
Rooms: 2 with private facilities
Dinner 6.30 – 7 pm (b)
Residents only
Unlicensed – guests welcome to take own wine
No smoking in dining room + bedrooms
Dinner B & B £20 – £24
Own naturally reared lamb and beef with locally produced fish and game used with home-grown vegetables. Fruits from own garden included in mouth-watering desserts. Home-made soups a speciality.
STB Highly Commended 3 Crowns
No credit cards
Proprietor: Berenice Williams

HARTFELL HOUSE

Hartfell Crescent, Moffat
Dumfriesshire DG10 9AL
Tel: 0683 20153

One mile off A74.
A delightful, small family run hotel in a 19th century Listed building, situated in a quiet and peaceful rural setting, yet within a few minutes walk from the centre of Moffat. There are fine cornices and beautiful woodwork in its spacious rooms. Hartfell House has a very comfortable and homely atmosphere and is ideally located for visiting the Borders and south-west Scotland.
Open Mar to Nov
Rooms: 9 , 5 with private facilities
Dinner 6 – 7 pm except Mon Tue (b)
Non-residents by prior booking
No smoking in dining room
Bed & breakfast £18 – £23
Dinner B & B £28 – £36
Home-made mousse and soups. Venison casserole, roast loin of Scotch lamb with ginger sauce, wild salmon steaks. Fillet of beef with a mushroom and Drambuie sauce. Fresh fruit and vegetables in season.
STB Commended 3 Crowns
No credit cards
Proprietors: Andrea & Alan Daniel

WELL VIEW HOTEL

Ballplay Road, Moffat
Dumfriesshire
DG10 9JU
Tel: 0683 20184

2 miles off A74,¹/₂ mile from centre of Moffat.
Set in half an acre of garden overlooking the hills and town, this 19th century country house has been extensively converted and refurbished to make it a small comfortable privately run hotel. Rooms are furnished to an excellent standard and are all supplied with fresh fruit, hand-made biscuits and sherry. Deluxe rooms have many additional extras. Creative table d'hôte menus are prepared by the kitchen brigade and there is an extensive wine list to complement your meal. German spoken and also a little French. Children welcome. Dogs accepted by prior arrangement.
Open all year
Rooms: 7 , 5 with private facilities
Dining Room/Restaurant Lunch 12 – 1 pm except Fri Sat (b)
Dinner 6.30 – 8.30 pm (c)

Prior reservation essential for both lunch + dinner
Facilities for the disabled
No smoking in dining room
Bed & breakfast £23 – £40
Dinner B & B £42 – £62
Room Rate £30 – £78
Smoked haddock soufflé, mousseline of turbot, cauliflower and blue cheese soup, fillet of Galloway beef with Kelso mustard sauce, escalope of venison with a blaeberry and mushroom sauce. Carse of Gowrie raspberry and Armagnac brûlée.
STB Deluxe 3 Crowns
Credit cards: 1, 3
Proprietors: Janet & John Schuckardt

Moniaive
nr Thornhill

MAP 1

MAXWELTON HOUSE

Moniaive, nr Thornhill
Dumfriesshire DG3 4DX
Tel: 084 82 385

Entrance on B729, off A76 Dumfries-Thornhill, or A702 New Galloway-Thornhill.
The very name is evocative, and anyone with the slightest claim to Scottish ancestry together with many millions more who have heard the well loved ballad will be drawn to Maxwelton House, the birthplace of Annie Laurie. The house has been magnificently restored by Mr and Mrs Hugh Stenhouse and – together with the chapel and an interesting museum of agricultural and domestic tools – is well worth a diversion on a journey and a few hours of anyone's time. The tearoom is in the Pavilion attached to the house and it serves morning coffee, light and inexpensive lunches, and that rarity now – delicious traditional afternoon teas with freshly made home-baking.
Open Easter to late Sep: 11 am – 5 pm Wed to Sun
Dining Room/Restaurant Lunch except Mon Tue (a)
Closed Mon Tue
Unlicensed
Facilities for the disabled
No credit cards
Proprietors: Maxwelton House Trust

Muir of Ord

MAP 6

GILCHRIST FARM

Muir of Ord
Ross-shire IV6 7RS
Tel: 0463 870243

Follow signs to B9169, off A832 Muir of Ord or A862 Beauly, opposite Black Isle Showground.
Ann Fraser assures you of a warm welcome to this comfortable farmhouse set in an attractive garden. The working farm is ideally situated for touring the Highlands. 18 hole golf course less than a mile away. Inverness 20 minutes away by car.
Open Apr to Oct – advance booking preferred
Rooms: 2
Dinner 6.30 – 7.30 pm except Sun Sat (a)
Residents only
Unlicensed – guests welcome to take own wine
No smoking in dining room
Bed & breakfast £13 – £15
Dinner B & B £21 – £23
Good home-cooking from fresh local produce. Home-made soups and desserts a speciality. Salmon, trout, venison, Scottish beef, lamb etc.
STB Commended 1 Crown
No credit cards
Proprietor: Ann Fraser

ORD HOUSE HOTEL
Muir of Ord
Ross-shire IV6 7UH
Tel: 0463 870492

On A832 Ullapool-Marybank, 1/2 mile west of Muir of Ord.

John and Eliza Allen offer you at Ord House a stay which will be comfortable, relaxed and enjoyable. Table d'hôte and à la carte menus are made up from their own garden produce and local meat, game and fish. Fifty acres of woodlands and beautiful formal gardens, combined with a 17th century laird's house, make Ord something special. All bedrooms have private facilities and many have been recently refurbished. Downstairs, there are log fires in the bar and drawing rooms to enjoy and in the grounds there are croquet and clay-pigeon shooting. Fluent French spoken. Children and dogs are very welcome.

Open May to mid Oct
Rooms: 12 with private facilities
Bar Lunch 12.30 – 2 pm (a)
Dinner 7 – 9 pm (c)
Bed & breakfast £28 – £40
Dinner B & B £46 – £58
Seafood moneybags; west coast scallops 'aux petits legumes'. Breast of Scottish quail lightly flavoured with a watercress and chive sauce. Fillet of fresh wild Conon salmon en papillote with cepes and cream. Baby turnips boulangère; fresh asparagus in a pastry cloud; vegetable tartlets with a Hollandaise sauce.
STB Commended 3 Crowns
Credit cards: 1, 2, 3
Proprietors: John & Eliza Allen

Mull
Isle of

MAP 7

ARDFENAIG HOUSE
by Bunessan, Isle of Mull
Argyll PA67 6DX
Tel: 06817 210
Fax: 06817 210

2 miles west of Bunessan on A849, turn right on private road to Ardfenaig House, 1/2 mile.

Once occupied by the notorious Factor Mor, chamberlain to the Duke of Argyll, and latterly a private shooting lodge, Ardfenaig House stands in a glorious position on the shore of Loch Caol on the Ross of Mull. Surrounded by open moorland and quiet secluded beaches Ardfenaig is perfect for walking, painting, exploring or simply relaxing. The Island of Iona is a short ferry ride away and Fingals Cave on Staffa is easily reached. The house is set amongst 15 acres of woodland and gardens. It is the home of Malcolm and Jane Davidson who offer warm hospitality, good food and fine wine in a country house setting.

Open 1 Apr to 31 Oct
Rooms: 5 with private facilities
Dinner at 8 pm (d)
Restricted licence
No smoking in dining room
Dinner B & B £70 – £80
Home-made bread and soups. Locally caught wild Atlantic salmon. Atholl brose, Ardfenaig chocolate slice, home-made ice-cream. Selection of Scottish cheeses.
STB Highly Commended 3 Crowns
Credit cards: 1, 3
Proprietors: Malcolm & Jane Davidson

ARDRIOCH
Ardrioch Farm, Dervaig
Isle of Mull PA75 6QR
Tel: 06884 264

1 mile from Dervaig on Calgary road.
Ardrioch is a traditionally furnished comfortable cedar wood farmhouse. Guests may relax in the mellow wood-panelled sitting room with its peat fire and extensively filled bookshelves, and enjoy the view of the sea, loch and surrounding hills. All bedrooms have tea-making facilities, wash-basins and room heaters; en suite facilities available. The house is a short stroll to the loch side and two miles from the harbour, where Ardrioch's own sea sailing is available. Ideal for walking, bird-watching and fishing. Multi-activity holidays also available. Working farm – sheep, cows, friendly collies, lambs and calves, enjoyed by children.

Open Apr to Oct
Rooms: 4 , 1 with private facilities
Dinner 6.30 – 7.30 pm (b)
Unlicensed – guests welcome to take own wine
No dogs
No smoking throughout
Bed & breakfast £16 – £18.50
Dinner B & B £26 – £28.50
Room Rate £32 – £37
Home-smoked mackerel pâté; salmon steaks baked in a cream, lemon and dill sauce; venison casseroled with cider,
rowan jelly and mushrooms. Home-made ice-creams – gooseberry and ginger, blackcurrant and cassis, apricot and almond.
STB Commended 2 Crowns
No credit cards
Proprietors: Jenny & Jeremy Matthew

ASSAPOL COUNTRY HOUSE HOTEL
Bunessan, Isle of Mull
Argyll PA67 6DW
Tel: 06817 258
Fax: 06817 445

Follow A849 toward Iona till reach Bunessan. On outskirts of village, turn left after school.

Assapol Country House Hotel is a small unpretentious family run hotel overlooking Loch Assapol, where guests can fish for sea trout and salmon. A former manse and 200 years old, Assapol offers friendly comfortable and attractive accommodation. Traditional cuisine is served using the island's locally produced pork, game, wild salmon, crab etc. Dinner is served in one sitting at 7 pm, but that provides the excuse to spend the rest of the evening trying a dram of the many speciality cask strength malt whiskies whilst relaxing in front of an open log fire. Surrounded by outstanding countryside, this is an ideal base for walking, bird-watching and sightseeing, and convenient for those going on to Staffa for the day.

Open 1 Apr to 31 Oct
Rooms: 7 with private facilities
Dinner at 7 pm (b) – one sitting
Restricted licence
Non-residents welcome when dining space available
No children under 13
No smoking in restaurant
Bed & breakfast £24 – £28
Dinner B & B £37.50 – £41.50
Home-made soups. Wild salmon with lime and chive sauce. Venison MacDuff with Port. Cider and wine syllabub. Atholl brose.
STB Commended 3 Crowns
Credit cards: 1, 3
Proprietors: Harry & Mary Kay

CRAIG HOTEL
Tobermory Road, Salen
Isle of Mull PA72 6JG
Tel: 0680 300347

In Salen village, on Tobermory-Craignure road.
More home than hotel and situated by the Sound of Mull – ideal for exploring the beauties of Mull, Iona and Staffa – the Craig is a typical 19th century Scottish family house with 20th century comforts, including attractive lounge with log fire, magazines and board games.
Open 26 Mar to 4 Oct
Rooms: 6
Dinner at 7.15 pm (b)
Residents only
No smoking in dining room
Bed & breakfast £20 – £24
Dinner B & B £30 – £35
Local seafood and Scottish meats cooked with fresh garden herbs. Home-made soups, pâtés, puddings and conserves. Interesting cheese board.
STB Commended 2 Crowns
Credit cards: 1, 3
Proprietors: James & Lorna McIntyre

DRUIMARD COUNTRY HOUSE & THEATRE RESTAURANT
Dervaig, Isle of Mull
Argyll PA67 6QW
Tel: 06884 345

On B8073, 8 miles west of Tobermory.
Peaceful family run small country house hotel just outside the village of Dervaig, overlooking glen, river and sea loch. It is well situated for touring, boat trips, fishing, walking, and there are sandy beaches nearby. The elegant restaurant is renowned for good food specialising in fresh local produce. Well appointed bedrooms (colour TVs etc), and Britain's smallest professional theatre.
Open Mar to Oct
Rooms: 6 , 4 with private facilities
Dinner 6 – 9 pm (c)
Bed & breakfast £33 – £49.50
Dinner B & B £52.50 – £68.50
Freshly cooked local produce, wild salmon, scallops, crab, venison. Scottish roasts and vegetarian dishes. Home-made soups, individual starters and sweets. Menu changed daily according to availability.
STB Highly Commended 3 Crowns
Credit cards: 1, 3
Proprietors: Clive & Jenny Murray

DRUIMNACROISH
Dervaig, Isle of Mull
Argyll PA75 6QW
Tel: 06884 274 • Fax: 06884 2544

Via ferry from Oban to Craignure. On Salen-Dervaig road, 1¹/2 miles south of Dervaig.
Druimnacroish is an interesting place to stay. Donald McLean virtually converted the buildings himself into an unusual country house hotel in this delightful part of Mull. His wife, Wendy, presides in the kitchen and produces a varied selection of dishes, complemented by vegetables and fruit culled from the hotel's own six acre garden. There is a carefully selected wine cellar. To discover the subtle values of tranquillity and perhaps a new slant on life, it can be a most rewarding experience to join the McLeans in their home at Druimnacroish.
Open mid Apr to mid Oct
Rooms: 6 with private facilities
Packed Lunches to order
Dinner at 8 pm (d)
No smoking in restaurant
Bed & breakfast from £50
Dinner B & B from £70
Specialities include scampi marinated in malt whisky, rib of Aberdeen Angus beef carved at table off the bone. Wild salmon.
STB Commended 4 Crowns
Credit cards: 1, 2, 3, 5, 6
Proprietors: Donald & Wendy McLean

LINNDHU HOUSE
Tobermory
Isle of Mull PA75 6QB
Tel: 0688 2425

On A848 south of Tobermory.
A most comfortable, traditional Highland hotel set in 35 acres of glorious woodland two miles south of Tobermory. Linndhu offers superb cuisine, spacious accommodation and outstanding views. There is a trout stream in the grounds, and fishing, walking, bird-watching, golf, deer-stalking and pony-trekking can be arranged for guests.

Open all year
Rooms: 8 , 5 with private facilities
Dining Room/Restaurant Lunch 12.30 – 2.30 pm (c) – by arrangement
Dinner 8 – 9 pm (c)
Bed & breakfast £30 – £50
Dinner B & B £50 – £70
Room Rate £30 – £140
Scallops in saffron sauce, carbonade venison, cranachan.
STB Commended 3 Crowns
No credit cards
Proprietors: Ian & Jennifer McLean

THE PUFFER AGROUND
Main Road, Salen, Aros
Isle of Mull PA72 6JB
Tel: 068 0300 389

On A849 Craignure-Tobermory road.
The quaint name of this restaurant derives from the old days when the 'puffer' – the local steamboat – ran right on to the shore to unload its cargo and went off on the next high tide. The restaurant has a maritime theme and usually features an exhibition of oil paintings during July and August.
Open mid Apr to mid Oct
Dining Room/Restaurant Lunch 12 – 2.30 pm except Sun Mon until Jul (a)
Dinner 7 – 9 pm except Sun Mon until Jul (a-b)
Closed Sun Mon until Jul
Scottish and Mull produce used whenever possible to create 'home-type' cooking in a friendly atmosphere.
No credit cards
Proprietors: Graham & Elizabeth Ellis

STRONGARBH HOUSE & RESTAURANT
Tobermory
Isle of Mull PA75 6PR
Tel: 0688 2328
Fax: 0688 2142

Upper town – well signposted.
A welcome addition to the limited number of quality establishments in Tobermory, Strongarbh has lovely gardens and delightful views over the Bay. It is one of the earliest of the fine Victorian houses built in the 19th century and has recently been completely and comfortably refurbished without detriment to the character of the building. The restaurant, rightly, concentrates on offering the best of the bountiful supply of fresh local seafood and other island specialities.

►

Open all year
Rooms: 4 with private facilities
Dining Room/Restaurant Lunch
12.30 – 2 pm (b)
Dinner 7 – 9.30 pm (c)
Restricted licence
Bed & breakfast £32 – £36
Dinner B & B £52 – £56
Room Rate £59 – £67
Suprême of Mull salmon en papillote
with thyme and julienne vegetables.
Sautéd Mull scallops en croûte with
herbs. Rack of Mull lamb with garlic and
rosemary. Home-made sticky toffee
pudding.
STB Highly Commended 3 Crowns
Credit cards: 1, 3, 6
Proprietors: Ian & Mhairi McAdam

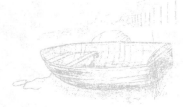

TIRORAN HOUSE
Tiroran
Isle of Mull PA69 6ES
Tel: 06815 232

Prestige Award Winner 1988

From Craignure, A849 towards Iona,
turn right onto B8035 at head of Loch
Scridain until signposted to Tiroran.
A remote and enchanting country house
hotel, beautifully situated on Loch
Scridain, offering the highest standards
of comfort for those seeking to explore
the lovely islands of Mull, Iona and
Staffa. Set in over 50 acres of grounds,
the lovely gardens include lawns,
shrubberies and woodlands which slope
down to the loch. The food is highly
acclaimed and dinners are elegantly
served by candlelight in the dining room
overlooking gardens and sea loch.
Open Jun to early Oct
Rooms: 9 with private facilities
Lunch as required – residents only
Dinner from 7.45 pm (e)
No smoking in dining room
Dinner B & B £84 – £103
Fresh seafood, including scallops and
crab, Hebridean smoked trout and own
gravadlax are regular starters. Main

courses using lamb and beef from the
estate and island venison, with fresh
vegetables.
No credit cards
Proprietors: Robin & Susan Blockey

WESTERN ISLES HOTEL
Tobermory
Isle of Mull PA75 6PR
Tel: 0688 2012
Fax: 0688 2297

Tobermory is a 40 minute drive from
Oban/Craignure ferry.
A magnificent Gothic style building
enjoying a truly remarkable situation on
the cliff overlooking Tobermory Bay.
The views from the dining room, terrace
lounge and many of the bedrooms are
breathtaking and must surely be
regarded as some of the best in Scotland.
Bedrooms have been extensively
refurbished and are now more in
keeping with the general standard of the
hotel. All have private bathrooms, TV,
tea/coffee-making facilities. Dogs are
accepted by prior arrangement, at a
small charge.
Open 1 Feb to 1 Jan except 19 to 27 Dec
Rooms: 28 with private facilities
Bar Lunch 12 – 1.45 pm (a)
Bar Supper 7 – 8 pm (a)
Dinner 7 – 8.30 pm: 7 – 8 pm Winter (d)
No smoking in dining room
Bed & breakfast £32 – £55
Dinner B & B £50 – £75
Home-made soups. Many specialities
using local products including trout,
venison, salmon, prawns, scallops and
lobster.
STB Commended 4 Crowns
Credit cards: 1, 3
Proprietors: Sue & Michael Fink

Nairn

MAP 6

GOLF VIEW HOTEL
Seabank Road
Nairn IV12 4HD
Tel: 0667 52301 • Telex: 75134
Fax: 0667 55267

At west end of Nairn.
An imposing Victorian hotel in a
commanding position overlooking the
Moray Firth and the hills of the Black
Isle. A full range of leisure centre
facilities and a heated outdoor pool.
Near to the championship golf course.

The chef has earned renown for the
standard of preparation and
presentation of food.
Open all year
Rooms: 48 with private facilities
Dining Room/Restaurant Lunch 12 –
2 pm Mon to Sat: 12.30 – 2 pm Sun (b)
Dinner 7 – 9.15 pm (c-d)
Bed & breakfast rates on application
Dinner B & B rates on application
Baked fillet of salmon, topped with
garden herbs and puff pastry, served with
a smoked salmon sauce. Breast of
woodpigeon and medallion of venison on
a bed of spaghetti vegetables, with a Port
wine rosemary sauce.
STB Commended 5 Crowns
Credit cards: 2, 3, 5, 6

Newbigging

MAP 3

NESTLERS HOTEL
Dunsyre Road, Newbigging
Lanark ML11 8NA
Tel: 0555 840 680

On A721 midway between Edinburgh
and Glasgow, 18 miles north of Peebles.
This traditional stone built house has all
the character of the old village inn and
has a happy and welcoming atmosphere
provided by the friendly and attentive
staff. It is now an intimate and
unpretentious family hotel with lots of
character well situated in rural
Clydesdale, almost equidistant from
Edinburgh and Glasgow. The menu is
sensibly planned with good home-
cooking the order of the day. The
desserts particularly are renowned
locally. Elaine and Nick Anderson go to
great trouble to ensure their guests enjoy
good hospitality as well as good food.
Open all year
Rooms: 3, 2 with private facilities
Meals available from 8 am –
9.30 pm (a-b)
Bar Lunch (a)
Dining Room/Restaurant Lunch (a)
Bar Supper (a)
Dinner (b)
No smoking in restaurant
Bed & breakfast £22.50 – £26.50
Dinner B & B £35 – £39
Home-cooked ham baked in Pentland
honey with cloves and served with a fresh
parsley sauce.
STB Commended 3 Crowns
Credit cards: 1, 3
Proprietors: Elaine & Nick Anderson

Newburgh

Aberdeenshire

MAP 5

UDNY ARMS HOTEL

Main Street, Newburgh
Aberdeenshire AB41 0BL
Tel: 03586 89444 • Fax: 03586 89012
On A975, 2 1/2 miles off A92 Aberdeen-Peterhead, 15 minutes from Aberdeen.
The Craig family, who own and run this fine old country hotel, put the comfort of their guests right to the front in their operating of the Udny Arms. Bedrooms are individually styled and decorated, and all have private facilities, TV, coffee/tea-making, hairdryers, trouser presses etc. There is a restful air of Victorian charm about the dining room which has a first class menu specialising in the excellent fresh seafood so readily available locally, but if you wish to dine less formally there is the lively friendly Bistro or the Cafe Bar as alternatives. The Garden Suite in the grounds of the hotel is much in demand for small conferences, weddings etc.
Open all year
Rooms: 26 with private facilities
Bar Lunch 12.30 – 2 pm (a)
Dining Room/Restaurant Lunch 12.30 – 2 pm (b)
Dinner 6.30 – 9.30 pm (c)
Bed & breakfast from £50
Room Rate £45.50
The Udny Creel: salmon, scallops, mussels, squid, king prawn and crab, cooked in fish and lobster stock, finished with cream, brandy, tomato and tarragon. Lamb steak marinated in lemon and garlic, and chargrilled. Sticky toffee pudding.
STB Commended 3 Crowns
Credit cards: 1, 2, 3
Proprietor: J D Craig

Newtonmore

MAP 6

ARD-NA-COILLE HOTEL

Kingussie Road, Newtonmore
Inverness-shire PH20 1AY
Tel: 054 03 214
At northern end of Newtonmore village.
Ard-na-Coille is an Edwardian shooting lodge situated on an elevated position in two acres of woodland. Each room, individually and tastefully furnished to retain the period features, has a spectacular view of the Spey Valley and surrounding mountains. The informal and relaxing atmosphere encourages guests to enjoy the widely acclaimed high standard of cuisine. Menus are based on the finest regional produce and are complemented by an extensive cellar.
Open 29 Dec to 14 Nov except 1 wk Apr + 1 wk Sep
Rooms: 7 with private facilities
Dinner at 7.45 pm (e) 5 course set menu
No smoking in dining room
Dogs accepted by prior arrangement
Bed & breakfast £40 – £50
Dinner B & B £60 – £70
Warm mousse of smoked trout with a lime vinaigrette. Celery and Dunsyre Blue soup. Roast Ayrshire Guinea fowl with a chanterelle sauce. Coffee and praline parfait with an apricot and rum sauce.
Credit cards: 1, 3
Proprietors: Nancy Ferrier & Barry Cottam

Newton Stewart

MAP 1

CREEBRIDGE HOUSE HOTEL

Minnigaff, Newton Stewart
Wigtownshire DG8 6NP
Tel: 0671 2121
From roundabout signposted Newton Stewart on A75, through the town, bear left over the River Cree, 250 yards on left is Minnigaff.
At one time home of the Earl of Galloway this fine old country house has the best of both worlds. Not only is it set peacefully in acres of well kept gardens but it is also just three or four minutes walk from the busy market town of Newton Stewart. The public rooms are gracious, the drawing room with a particularly fine mahogany fireplace, and the cosy atmospheric bar has a fine reputation for its bar meals – and its large range of malt whiskies. Food in the dining room, which overlooks the gardens, is personally supervised by proprietor Chris Walker and is highly acclaimed.
Open all year
Rooms: 18 with private facilities
Bar Lunch 12 – 2 pm (a)
Bar Supper 6 – 9 pm (b)
Dinner 7 – 8.30 pm (c)
No smoking in dining room
Bed & breakfast £25 – £40
Dinner B & B £42 – £58
Fillet of beef in a green peppercorn sauce. Medallions of venison in a gin and redcurrant sauce. Whole grilled lemon sole. Prawns with garlic butter. Grilled local lamb cutlets.
STB Commended 4 Crowns
Credit cards: 1, 3
Proprietors: Chris & Sue Walker

THE KIRROUGHTREE HOTEL

Newton Stewart
Wigtownshire DG8 6AN
Tel: 0671 2141
Fax: 0671 2425
Signposted 1 mile outside Newton Stewart on A75.
The McMillan family are outstanding hoteliers in south-west Scotland and the news that they had acquired the Kirroughtree Hotel would delight their many thousands of satisfied guests and fans who constitute their clientele. Douglas McMillan's personality and experience will be evident in the Kirroughtree as will the exceptional standards of quality, service and value which are such a marked feature of the family's other hotels – North West Castle, Stranraer, and the Cally Palace, Gatehouse-of-Fleet. Kirroughtree is a splendid 18th century mansion in immaculately landscaped gardens with an established reputation for the excellence of its cuisine. Free golf is offered at five local courses and also free use of the leisure facilities of the sister hotels mentioned above. Children over 12 years welcome.
Open Feb to 3 Jan
Rooms: 22 with private facilities
Soup and Sandwiches 12 – 2 pm
Dining Room/Restaurant Lunch 12 – 2 pm (b)
Dinner 7 – 9 pm (d)
No smoking dining room available
Dinner B & B £60 – £85
Special rates for over 60s and special weekly terms.
Bavarois of smoked Cree salmon. Noisettes of Kirroughtree Forest venison with local wild mushrooms served on a Grand Veneur sauce.
STB Highly Commended 5 Crowns
Credit cards: 1, 3
Proprietors: The McMillan Family

North Berwick

MAP 4

Newcomer of the Year Award 1992

HARDING'S RESTAURANT
2 Station Road,
North Berwick
East Lothian EH39 4AU
Tel: 0620 4737

Next to railway station.
The building was originally an
Edwardian tea room – slate roofed
and white painted outside and inside
with astragalled windows looking
towards North Berwick Law. Interior
is light and airy with light oak chairs
and checked linen tablecloths.
Simple decor of framed animal prints
and oriental rugs. The restaurant
area looks through to the kitchen
where chef/proprietor Chris
Harding can be seen at work. The
aim is to provide a welcoming
informal atmosphere where someone
enjoying a candlelit dinner will feel
just as at ease as someone who has
been in for warm scones with home-
made jam. There are no dress
restrictions. The wine list is almost
entirely Australian with over 70
different wines, all personally chosen
by Chris Harding who is an
Australian.
Open all year except 3 wks
Christmas/New Year + 1 wk Oct
Dining Room/Restaurant Lunch
12.15 – 2 pm Wed to Sat (a)
Dinner 7.30 – 9 pm Wed to Sat (c)
Restaurant closed Sun Mon Tue
Table licence
Facilities for the disabled
No smoking in restaurant
Smoked salmon with almond and
lime dressing. Pan-fried fillet of
Aberdeen Angus beef coated with a
red wine sauce.
No credit cards
Proprietor: Christopher Harding

North Queensferry

MAP 4

SMUGGLERS RESTAURANT
17 Main Street, North Queensferry
Fife KY11 1JT
Tel: 0383 412567

Take Junction 1 M90, follow B981 into
North Queensferry.
This intimate restaurant has a
spectacular location beneath the Forth
Rail Bridge. The atmosphere in the
candlelit dining room is relaxed and
informal, with fresh flowers in
abundance. Smugglers has earned a high
reputation both north and south of the
Firth of Forth and this is built on the
quality of the food, with a menu that
changes frequently. Carefully selected
ingredients, including beef, lamb, game,
fish and shellfish, are combined with
fresh herbs and particularly interesting
sauces to produce meals of distinction.
Also worth noting are the excellent
selection of freshly baked bread and the
hot sticky toffee pudding.
Open all year
Dinner 7.15 – 10.30 pm Thu Fri Sat
only (d)
Closed Sun to Wed
No smoking in restaurant
Hot Arbroath smokie tureen. Garlic and
herb soup. Skewered aromatic fish. Pigeon
with cider and plum sauce. Potatoes with
garlic and walnut oil.
Credit cards: 1, 3
Proprietors: Ernest Kallus & Judi Short

Oban

MAP 6

MANOR HOUSE HOTEL
Gallanach Road, Oban
Argyll PA34 4LS
Tel: 0631 62087
Fax: 0631 63053

From south side of Oban follow signs to
Gallanach and Kerrera Ferry. Past car
ferry terminal.
Set in an enviable position in its own
grounds on a commanding promontory
above Oban Bay, the Manor House has
long held the reputation for high quality
in the comfort of its accommodation and
the excellence of Scottish and French
cuisine. All bedrooms have en suite
facilities, television, direct dial telephone
and central heating. German and French
spoken.
Open 1 Feb to 25 Dec
Rooms: 11 with private facilities
Bar Lunch 12.30 – 2.30 pm (b)
Dinner 7 – 8.30 pm (c)
No smoking in restaurant
Dinner B & B £42 – £75 (min 2 nights
stay)
Fresh west coast oysters with fennel and
honey. Scampi Laphroaig. Parfait Flora
MacDonald.
STB Highly Commended 4 Crowns
Credit cards: 1, 3
Proprietor: J L Leroy

SEA LIFE CENTRE – SHORELINE RESTAURANT
Barcaldine, Oban
Argyll PA37 1SE
Tel: 063 172 386

On A828 Oban-Fort William, 10 miles
north of Oban.
The Shoreline Restaurant is within the
Sea Life Centre. In this self-service
restaurant a full range of meals and
snacks is available including a salad table
and a small oyster bar. You'll also be
enjoying your meal in comfortable
surroundings which give you the best
possible vantage point to appreciate fully
the majestic splendour of the glorious
views over Loch Creran to the mountains
beyond.
Open Feb to Nov + weekends Dec/Jan
Note: closed Christmas Day + 1 Jan
Coffee Shop open 10 am – 5.30 pm
Meals available 12 – 5.30 pm: 12 –
6.30 pm Jul Aug (a)
Table licence only
No smoking area in restaurant
Seafood lasagne, salmon pie, seafood pie.
Local seafood – oysters (fresh), smoked
salmon and trout. Coffee shop has freshly
ground coffee and home-baked fare.
Credit cards: 1, 3

SOROBA HOUSE HOTEL
Soroba Road, Oban
Argyll PA34 4SB
Tel: 0631 62628

A816 to Oban.
Soroba House stands in a dominant and
beautiful site of nine acres above the
town, yet close enough to the town
facilities, ferry terminal etc. The
accommodation is in the form of suites
and flatlets, some within the gardens

around the hotel, so guests have the option of catering for themselves or experiencing the specialities of the hotel's handsomely appointed dining room.
Open all year
Rooms: 25 with private facilities
Bar Lunch 12 – 2.15 pm (a)
Dining Room/Restaurant Lunch 12 – 2.15 pm (a)
Dinner 7 – 10.15 pm (a-b)
Bed & breakfast from £32
Dinner B & B from £44
Selection of local produce features on menus – seafood, fish, venison, lamb, Scotch beef etc.
Credit cards: 1, 5, 6
Proprietor: David Hutchison

THE WATERFRONT RESTAURANT
No 1 The Waterfront
The Pier, Oban
Argyll PA34
Tel: 0631 63110
The waterfront, Oban.
It would be difficult to get closer to the main source of supply than this. The Waterfront Restaurant has built up its reputation by concentrating on the local seafood arriving at the pier at Oban and likes to boast that it gets it "from the pier to the pan as fast as we can". Lovers of fish and shellfish go here to savour the daily catch at remarkably moderate prices. Part of the same complex but on the ground floor is Creel's Coffee Shop which specialises in home-baking and in a range of sandwiches, including some superb seafood fillings – a very poular rendezvous for a quick and satisfying snack.
Open all year
Creel's Coffee Shop 8.30 am – 6 pm (a)
Dining Room/Restaurant Lunch 12 – 3 pm (a)
Dinner 6 – 10 pm (b)
Specialises in dishes featuring local seafood and fish.
Credit cards: 1, 3
Proprietor: Stuart Walker

WILLOWBURN HOTEL
Clachan Seil, Isle of Seil
by Oban PA34 4TJ
Tel: 08523 276
11 miles south of Oban, via A816 and B844, signposted Easdale, over Atlantic Bridge.
The Willowburn is a small modern privately owned hotel set in two acres of ground on the sheltered north-east shore of the beautiful unspoilt Hebridean island of Seil which is linked to the mainland by the only single span bridge to cross the Atlantic. All bedrooms have full amenities and the restaurant, overlooking Seil Sound, offers table d'hôte and à la carte menus for a relaxing end to your day.
Open Easter to late Oct
Rooms: 6 with private facilities
Bar Lunch 12.30 – 2 pm (a)
Bar Supper 6 – 8.30 pm (a)
Dinner 7 – 8 pm (c)
Dinner B & B £36 – £44
Locally caught Atlantic salmon, squat lobsters, prawns, mussels etc. Herb roast chicken with Drambuie stuffing. Prime Scottish roast beef and steak. Willowburn pâté with whisky and oatmeal.
STB Commended 3 Crowns
Credit cards: 1, 3
Proprietors: Archie & Maureen Todd

Onich
by Fort William

MAP 6

ALLT-NAN-ROS HOTEL
Onich, by Fort William
Inverness-shire PH33 6RY
Tel: 08553 210
Fax: 08553 462
On A82, 10 miles south of Fort William.
The Macleod family welcome you to their Highland country house, in its own gardens on the shores of Loch Linnhe. All the comfortably furnished bedrooms overlook the loch and have private facilities, telephone, colour TV, full controllable heating, hairdryers, and much more. The dining room which also overlooks the loch, has fine views from the picture windows. The cuisine is a blend of French and Highland, utilising the best of local game, salmon and seafood. There is a varied and interesting wine list, and a good range of malt whiskies. A good centre from which to explore the West Highlands and islands.
Open Easter to end Oct
Rooms: 21 with private facilities
Dining Room/Restaurant Lunch 12.30 – 2 pm (a)
Dinner 7 – 8.30 pm (c)
No dogs
No smoking in dining room
Dinner B & B £50 – £66.50
A modern style Taste of Scotland menu with a French influence, featuring fruit, vegetables and herbs from the hotel gardens, supplemented by home-baking and best local produce.
STB Highly Commended 4 Crowns
Credit cards: 1, 2, 3, 5, 6
Proprietor: James Macleod

THE LODGE ON THE LOCH
Onich, by Fort William
Inverness-shire PH33 6RY
Tel: 08553 237/238
Telex: 94013696 • Fax: 08553 463
On A82, 1 mile north of the Ballachulish Bridge.
Everything about the Lodge on The Loch spells good taste and good standards. There is a refined elegance about this acclaimed family run hotel which is immediately apparent and promises to apply to every aspect of it – as indeed it does. The public rooms, the dining room and many of the bedrooms have superb views out over Loch Linnhe to the Morvern mountains beyond. The menus are compiled with the same care and attention as is devoted to the rest of the hotel and meals are of unusually high standard.
Open 1 Feb to 30 Nov + Christmas/New Year
Rooms: 20 , 18 with private facilities
Bar Lunch 12.30 – 2.30 pm (a)
Dining Room/Restaurant Lunch 12.30 – 2.30 pm (a)
Dinner 7 – 9.30 pm (d)
Facilities for the disabled
No smoking in restaurant
Dinner B & B £48 – £78
Scottish smoked salmon with gravadlax and poached Loch Lochy salmon, served with fresh dill and mustard vinaigrette. Local scampi wrapped in Glen Uig smoked salmon. Medallions of venison with game and rowanberry sauce. Sweet crêpe with Drambuie ice-cream and Blairgowrie raspberry sauce.
STB Highly Commended 4 Crowns
Credit cards: 1, 3
Proprietors: Norman & Jessie Young

Orkney
Isles of

MAP 7

CREEL RESTAURANT & ROOMS
Front Road, St Margaret's Hope
Orkney KW17 2SL
Tel: 0856 83 311

13 miles south of Kirkwall, at seafront.
A scenic drive which takes you over the famous Churchill Barriers, relics of World War II, brings you to St Margaret's Hope and the Creel Restaurant. The Creel enjoys a reputation to rival the best. It is busy with Orcadians and visitors from all over the world. The restaurant won the Taste of Britain Award in 1986 and was listed in the AA Top 500 Restaurants in Britain 1989. Alan Craigie, the proprietor/chef, works wonders with fish and shellfish and this highly commended restaurant is one at which it is essential to book in advance. The Craigies have recently completed the upgrading of the accommodation to provide comfortable spacious rooms – with sea views – which complement the high standard and reputation of the food.
Open Feb to Dec
Rooms: 3 with private facilities
Dinner 7 – 9 pm except Mon (c)
Note: closed Mon Jun to Aug, but please check low season opening times
Bed & breakfast £20 – £25
Dinner B & B £30 – £35
A varied and changing menu using a wide range of local seafood, famous Orkney beef, smoked lamb and local vegetables.
STB Commended 3 Crowns
Credit cards: 1, 3
Proprietors: Alan & Joyce Craigie

FOVERAN HOTEL
nr Kirkwall, St Ola
Orkney KW15 1SF
Tel: 0856 872389

On A964 Orphir road, 2 1/2 miles from Kirkwall.
This modern purpose built hotel, all on the one level, is set in 32 acres with spectacular views over Scapa Flow. It has a reputation for its friendly personal atmosphere. Open-fired sitting room for pre-dinner drinks and after-dinner coffee. The Scandinavian-style dining room is bright and attractive. The hotel

has its own private beach.
Open all year except Christmas + Boxing Days, 1 + 2 Jan
Rooms: 8 with private facilities
Dinner 7 – 9 pm except Sun (b-c)
Bed & breakfast £32.50 – £40
Home-made soups and pâtés; prawns, scallops, lobster, sea trout, fresh Orkney lamb, beef, game, farm-cheese – all as available. New dishes from traditional raw materials.
STB Commended 4 Crowns
Credit cards: 1, 3, 6
Proprietors: Ivy & Bobby Corsie

Peat Inn

MAP 4

THE PEAT INN
Peat Inn
Fife KY15 5LH
Tel: 033 484 206

In A Class of Its Own 1989

At junction of B940/941, 6 miles south-west of St Andrews.
An 18th century village inn, situated in the village which bears its name, just six miles from St Andrews. An outstanding restaurant recognised as one of Britain's finest, featuring the very best Scottish produce served stylishly in the intimate, beautifully furnished dining rooms. Well worth a detour.
Open all year except Christmas Day + 1 Jan
Rooms: 8 with private facilities
Dining Room/Restaurant Lunch at 1 pm except Sun Mon (c)
Dinner 7 – 9.30 pm except Sun Mon (e-f)
Closed Sun Mon
No smoking in dining rooms
Bed & breakfast from £65
Dinner B & B £125 – £135
Breast of pigeon in a pastry case with wild mushrooms. Whole lobster in sauce with coriander and ginger. Caramelised apple pastry with a caramel sauce.
Credit cards: 1, 2, 3, 5
Proprietors: David & Patricia Wilson

Peebles

MAP 2

CRINGLETIE HOUSE HOTEL
nr Peebles EH45 8PL
Tel: 072 13 233

A703, 2 1/2 miles north of Peebles.
Cringletie is a perennial favourite of its many enthusiastic patrons and continues to demonstrate high standards in all aspects of hotel-keeping. It is a fine old red sandstone baronial mansion in 28 acres of gardens just off the main Peebles-Edinburgh road, in peaceful serene surroundings. Many of the herbs and vegetables for the kitchen come from its own garden. Aileen Maguire exercises a close personal supervision of food preparation and presentation, and meals are imaginative and exemplify home-cooking at its best.
Open 13 Mar to 1 Jan
Rooms: 13 with private facilities
Light Lunch except Sun (a)
Dining Room/Restaurant Lunch 1 – 1.45 pm Mon to Sat (a): Sun (b)
Afternoon tea 3.30 – 4.30 pm
Dinner 7.30 – 8.30 pm (d)
No smoking in restaurant
Bed & breakfast £43 – £60
Haggis stuffed mushrooms with whisky sauce, hot cheese mousse baked with cream, roast duckling with blackberry and gin sauce, casseroled haunch of venison with red wine and prunes. Toffee cheesecake.
STB Highly Commended 4 Crowns
Credit cards: 1, 3
Proprietors: Stanley & Aileen Maguire

DRUMMORE
Venlaw High Road
Peebles EH45 8RL
Tel: 0721 720336

In a quiet cul-de-sac off the Edinburgh Road (A703), opposite the Citroen garage in Peebles.
Drummore is built on two levels within its own garden among trees on Venlaw Hill, with views over Peebles and the Tweed Valley. It is well sited for walking, exploring the Borders or visiting Edinburgh.
Open Easter to Oct: advance bookings only Apr + May
Rooms: 2
Dinner 6.30 – 7.30 pm (b)
Unlicensed
Bed & breakfast from £13

Dinner B & B from £24
Fresh local poultry, lamb and beef. Trout
fresh from the farm. Variety of salads.
STB Commended 2 Crowns
No credit cards
Proprietor: Jean Phillips

KAILZIE GARDEN RESTAURANT
Kailzie
Peebles EH45 9HT
Tel: 0721 722807

B7062, 2 1/2 miles from town centre.
Situated in 17 acres of beautiful gardens
by the River Tweed this attractive but
unpretentious little restaurant is housed
in the old stable square and has been
carefully converted to retain as many of
the original features as possible. The
main dining area in the old coach room
still has the original wood panelling. The
old stalls and loose boxes form an
extension to this area. The menu is
simple and great emphasis is placed on
good home-cooking and baking using
local produce, fresh fruit and vegetables
from the gardens during the season.
Open Mar to end Oct
Dining Room/Restaurant Lunch
12.15 – 1.45 pm (a)
Afternoon Tea 3 – 5 pm
Dinner at 7.30 pm – last Sat of every
month (c)
Facilities for the disabled
No smoking area in restaurant
Home-made soups, pâté, lamb and fish.
Selection of home-baked sweets including
meringues.
No credit cards
Proprietors: Grace & Ewen Innes

KINGSMUIR HOTEL
Springhill Road
Peebles EH45 9EP
Tel: 0721 720151
Fax: 0721 721795

On quiet south side of Peebles.
Kingsmuir is a century-old house
standing in its own leafy grounds. It is a
family run hotel, specialising in Scottish
cooking, using the best of local produce
in a wide variety of dishes, served in
dining room, lounge or bar, lunchtime
and evenings. Smaller portions of most
dishes can be served for children and
those with smaller appetites. Ideal centre
for touring Edinburgh and stately homes
of the Borders, golfing and fishing.
Open all year except Christmas Day,
1 Jan + 19 Jun

Rooms: 10 with private facilities
Bar Lunch 12 – 2 pm (a)
Dining Room/Restaurant Lunch 12 –
2 pm (a)
Bar Supper 7 – 9.30 pm (a)
Dinner 7 – 9 pm (b)
No smoking in dining room
Bed & breakfast £29 – £40
Dinner B & B £41 – £52
Home-made soups (especially Cullen
skink) and pâtés. Kingsmuir steak pie.
Salmon – Tweed Kettle a speciality –
trout, seafish and shellfish. Roasts of beef,
lamb, venison, chicken with skirlie. Fresh
selection of home-made sweets daily.
STB Commended 3 Crowns
Credit cards: 1, 2, 3
Proprietors: Elizabeth & Norman Kerr

PEEBLES HOTEL HYDRO
Innerleithen Road
Peebles EH45 8LX
Tel: 0721 720602
Fax: 0721 722999

A large, imposing chateau-style hotel
with lofty ceilings, wide corridors and
plenty of space, set in 30 acres of ground
overlooking River Tweed valley and
Border hills. The hotel's bedrooms are
comfortable and up-to-date – all rooms
having private facilities, TV, hospitality
tray, direct dial telephones and most with
hairdryers and trouser presses. Leisure
centre with pool, jacuzzi, saunas,
solarium, steam bath, beauty salon,
gymnasium, etc. Tennis, squash, riding.
Open all year
Rooms: 137 with private facilities
Bar Lunch 12.30 – 3 pm (a)
Dining Room/Restaurant Lunch
12.45 – 2 pm (b)
Dinner 7.30 – 9 pm (c)
Bed & breakfast £35.25 – £60.75
Dinner B & B £48.25 – £73.50
Fresh trout from local fish farm. Best of
Scottish smoked salmon, Border lamb,
beef and other Scottish produce.
STB Commended 4 Crowns
Credit cards: 1, 2, 3, 5, 6

Perth

MAP 4

BALLATHIE HOUSE HOTEL
Kinclaven, by Stanley
Perthshire PH1 4QN
Tel: 0250 883268 • Telex: 76216
Fax: 0250 883396

Off A9 north of Perth through Stanley or
off A93 south of Blairgowrie to
Kinclaven.
A magnificent country house within its
own estate and with lawns rolling right
down to the bank of the River Tay,
famous for its salmon fishing. A steady
process of refurbishment has created
superbly comfortable, elegant and well
equipped public rooms and bedrooms.
There is every conceivable comfort here.
David Assenti's staff are highly trained
and motivated, and their polite attentive
caring service is a pleasure to experience.
Housekeeping is of the highest standard,
while from the kitchen Head Chef
Stephen Robertson and his staff produce
really delicious imaginative meals.
Ballathie of course is well known to
sportsmen, but everyone will enjoy a stay
at this delightful country house, so
centrally located for most of the major
visitor attractions.
Open 21 Feb to 23 Jan except Boxing
Day, 27 Dec, 2 to 4 Jan
Rooms: 27 with private facilities
Bar Lunch 12.30 – 1.45 pm except
Sun (a)
Dining Room/Restaurant Lunch
12.30 – 1.45 pm (b)
Dinner 7 – 8.30 pm (d)
No smoking in dining rooms
Bed & breakfast £42 – £76
Dinner B & B £65 – £98
Daily changing menus featuring the best
of fresh produce, creating a balance of
simpler traditional dishes and modern
cuisine for the discerning palate.
STB Deluxe 4 Crowns
Credit cards: 1, 2, 3, 5, 6

Credit Card Code		Meal Price Code	
1.	Access/Mastercard/Eurocard	(a)	under £10
2.	American Express	(b)	£10 – £15
3.	Visa	(c)	£15 – £20
4.	Carte Bleu	(d)	£20 – £25
5.	Diners Club	(e)	£25 – £30
6.	Mastercharge	(f)	over £30

THE BEIN INN
Glenfarg, nr Perth
Perthshire PH2 9PY
Tel: 057 73 216

*10 minutes south of Perth. Exit M90,
Junction 8 northbound/9 southbound, in
the Glen on old A9.*
An attractive well maintained traditional
coaching inn set in the beautiful Glen of
Glenfarg. Character restaurant serving à
la carte and vegetarian menus. Cosy
lounge bar, "hideaway" snack bar (May to
Oct). Well appointed accommodation,
most en suite.
*Open all year except Boxing Day + 27 Dec
Rooms: 13 , 11 with private facilities
Bar Lunch 12 – 2 pm (a)
Bar Supper 5.30 – 9.30 pm (b)
Dinner 7 – 9.30 pm (d)
Bed & breakfast £21 – £37.50
Dinner B & B £38 – £51
Cullen skink, Scottish smoked trout and
salmon. Highland game soup. Venison
casserole, Tayside salmon, local Scottish
lamb, beef, pheasant Blairgowrie. Cloutie
dumpling.
STB Commended 3 Crowns
Credit cards: 1, 3, 6
Proprietors: Mike & Elsa Thompson*

HUNTINGTOWER HOTEL
Crieff Road
Perth PH1 3JT
Tel: 0738 83771
Fax: 0738 83777

Signposted off A85, 3 miles west of Perth.
Set in 3 ½ acres of beautiful landscaped
gardens, the Huntingtower Hotel acts as
a perfect base as a gateway to the
Highlands. Facilities such as salmon
fishing and game shooting are available
close by. The oak-panelled restaurant
with its high ceiling, quality furnishings
and table appointments creates an
almost grand feeling, whilst retaining the
relaxed and comfortable atmosphere
which pervades this country house.
*Open all year
Rooms: 19 with private facilities
Bar Lunch 12 – 2.30 pm (a)
Dining Room/Restaurant Lunch 12 –
2.30 pm (a)
Dinner 7 – 9.30 pm (c)
Bed & breakfast £42 – £60
Dinner B & B £60 – £78
Room Rate £36 – £52
Locally caught game and salmon. Fresh
local produce prepared carefully and
imaginatively.
STB Commended 4 Crowns
Credit cards: 1, 2, 3, 5, 6*

THE LANG BAR & RESTAURANT
Perth Theatre, 185 High Street
Perth PH1 5UW
Tel: 0738 39136
Fax: 0738 24576

*Perth city centre in pedestrian zone at
middle section of High Street.*
The Lang Bar and Restaurant forms an
integral part of Perth Theatre and is
imbued with the vibrant atmosphere of
live entertainment. Built in 1900, the
Theatre has been beautifully restored
giving a wonderful rich setting for the
Restaurant, Coffee Bar and Bar. Enter
the front door of the Theatre and pass
through the Box Office, and you come to
the Coffee Bar where home-baking and
light meals are available at lunchtime
and in the evening. The Coffee Bar often
plays host to art exhibitions by local
artists. A short flight of stairs leads to the
Restaurant and bar area. Dinner in the
Restaurant is dependent on theatre
productions and consequently there are
occasions when it is not available, so
booking or enquiry in advance is
recommended.
*Open all year except Christmas Day +
1 Jan
Bar Lunch 12 – 2 pm (a)
Dining Room/Restaurant Lunch
11.45 am – 2.15 pm except Sun (a)
Bar Supper 6 – 10 pm (a)
Dinner 6 – 10 pm except Sun (b) –
booking advised
Closed Sun
Facilities for the disabled
Spinach roulade with mushrooms and
walnuts. Beef and artichoke pie. Crusty
bread, ham and prawns. Home-made
soups.
Credit cards: 1, 2, 3*

MURRAYSHALL COUNTRY HOUSE HOTEL
Scone, nr Perth
Perthshire PH2 7PH
Tel: 0738 51171 • Telex: 76197
Fax: 0738 52595

Prestige Award Winner 1988

4 miles out of Perth, 1 mile off A94.
Murrayshall Hotel is a sumptuously
appointed and elegant country house
with high standards of quiet, unobtrusive
efficient service. It is set in 300 acres of
parkland and with a challenging 6,420
yards golf course. With Executive Chef
Bruce Sangster overseeing the kitchens,
David Hunt – his Head Chef – uses

produce from the hotel's four acre
garden to produce a Taste of Scotland
with a hint of French cuisine for the Old
Masters Restaurant. French and Spanish
spoken.
*Open all year
Rooms: 19 with private facilities
Bar Lunch (Club House) 12 – 3 pm (a)
Dining Room/Restaurant Lunch (Club
House) 12 – 3 pm (a)
Bar Supper (Club House) 6 – 9 pm (b)
Dinner 7 – 10 pm (c)
Gourmet evenings + weekends
No dogs
Bed & breakfast £55 – £95
Dinner B & B £75 – £115
Breast of locally shot pigeon with red
cabbage compote. Parcel of wild Tay
salmon and turbot with langoustine tails.
Perthshire raspberries.
STB Highly Commended 5 Crowns
Credit cards: 1, 2, 3, 5, 6*

NEWTON HOUSE HOTEL
Glencarse
nr Perth PH2 7LX
Tel: 073 886 250
Fax: 073 886 717

Off A85 between Perth and Dundee.
This former Dower House (c. 1840) is set
back from the A85, four miles from
Perth and 13 from Dundee, and an ideal
location to explore the dramatic
countryside or visit the numerous places
of interest such as Glamis Castle, Scone
Palace and world famous golf courses.
The Newton House prides itself on a
high standard of "old fashioned
hospitality". The ten recently refurbished
en suite bedrooms overlook the gardens.
It is a keen advocate of Taste of
Scotland's aims and fresh local produce
is presented in the Country House
Restaurant and bar menus. Fluent
French is spoken, also German and
Spanish.
*Open all year
Rooms: 10 with private facilities
Bar Lunch 12 – 2 pm (b)
Restaurant Lunch 12 – 2 pm (c)
Bar Supper 5 – 9.30 pm (b)
Dinner 6.30 – 9.30 pm (d) 4 course
menu
No smoking in restaurant
Bed & breakfast from £40
Dinner B & B from £58
Gourmet Dinner B & B bargain break
from £55 (min 2 nights stay)
Cornets of oak-smoked Scottish trout with
prawns Marie Rose. Fresh ocean halibut
with a lime, blackcurrant and Glayva*

sauce. Marinated loin of Scotch lamb baked into puff pastry, with an elderberry wine and fresh mint sauce.
STB Highly Commended 4 Crowns
Credit cards: 1, 2, 3, 5
Proprietors: Geoffrey & Carol Tallis

NUMBER THIRTY THREE SEAFOOD RESTAURANT
33 George Street
Perth PH1 5LA
Tel: 0738 33771

Perth city centre.
There is a surprising paucity of good independent restaurants in Perth, so Number Thirty Three stands out like a beacon! With its pink and grey art deco theme this is a very smart and stylish restaurant right in the city centre. It specialises in all types of fish and shellfish and is designed so that you may enjoy light meals in the Oyster Bar – even just a coffee and some mussels – or indulge in more serious eating in the restaurant. The attractive ambience of the place, combined with this excellent balance of eating styles and the undoubted quality of its food, makes this a winner.
Open all year except 10 days Christmas/ New Year
Bar Lunch 12.30 – 2.30 pm except Sun Mon (a)
Dining Room/Restaurant Lunch 12.30 – 2.30 pm except Sun Mon (c)
Bar Supper 6.30 – 9.30 pm except Sun Mon (a)
Dinner 6.30 – 9.30 pm except Sun Mon (c)
Closed Sun Mon
Mary's seafood soup. Creamy crab and prawn terrine. Monkfish and spring vegetables parcel. Seafood casserole. Sticky toffee pudding with butterscotch sauce.
Credit cards: 1, 2, 3
Proprietors: Gavin & Mary Billinghurst

PARKLANDS HOTEL & RESTAURANT
St Leonards Bank
Perth PH2 8EB
Tel: 0738 22451 • Fax: 0738 22046
Junction of St Leonards Bank and Marshall Place in centre of Perth adjoining South Inch Park.
Parklands has a commanding site overlooking open parkland and, comfortably ensconced with a drink in the conservatory or the outside terrace, it is difficult to believe that you are in the centre of this historic old city and ancient capital of Scotland. Head Chef Daniel Martelat has a fine reputation locally and his menus are interestingly different with a subtle hint of Gallic culinary tradition showing in the preparation and presentation of his food. Allan Deeson has handled with sensitivity the restoration of this old property and converted it into a very comfortable hotel – an excellent base from which to explore the many interesting and historic places within easy reach of the city.
Open all year except New Year
Rooms: 14 with private facilities
Bar Lunch 12 – 2 pm (a)
Dining Room/Restaurant Lunch 12 – 2 pm (b)
Dinner 7 – 9 pm (d)
Bed & breakfast £30 – £75
Dinner B & B £50 – £95
Special weekend breaks
Speciality – lunchtime seafood buffet.
STB Highly Commended 4 Crowns
Credit cards: 1, 2, 3, 6
Proprietors: Pat & Allan Deeson

SCONE PALACE
Perth PH2 6BD
Tel: 0738 52300
On A93 Braemar road, 2 miles out of Perth.
Ancient crowning place of Scotland's kings – now the historic home of the Earl and Countess of Mansfield. See the antique treasures, explore the grounds, enjoy lunch beside the range in the 'Old Kitchen' restaurant, or a snack in the coffee shop. Take home the excellent produce from the shop. To arrange special off-season visits contact the Administrator.
Open 9 Apr to 11 Oct
Food Service 9.30 am – 5 pm (a)
Dining Room/Restaurant Lunch 11.30 am – 2 pm except Sun (a)

Note: open Sun for Lunch Jul + Aug only Dinner 7 – 8 pm (f) – by arrangement only
Fresh Tay salmon, home-made soup always available on the lunch menu. Home-baking, chutney and marmalade a speciality.
No credit cards

Peterhead

MAP 5

WATERSIDE INN
Fraserburgh Road, Peterhead
Aberdeenshire AB4 7BN
Tel: 0779 71121 • Telex: 739413
Fax: 0779 70670
30 miles north of Aberdeen on A952. 1 mile north of Peterhead.
It comes as a surprise to most people to learn that Peterhead is the most easterly town in mainland Scotland. Another surprise is in store at the Waterside Inn, Peterhead's leading hotel on the northern side of the town but just sufficiently out of it to give a quiet rural setting. The name may suggest a riverside pub but nothing could be further from the truth. The concept is nearer that of a good international chain, with splendid executive and family facilities and extensive conference suites. There is also a leisure complex offering swimming pool, jacuzzi, Turkish steam room, saunas and gymnasium. Ogilvies Restaurant is a sophisticated elegant dining room with a menu to match. Food is imaginative, very well presented and served by courteous well trained staff who seem to take genuine pleasure and pride in their work. The buffet breakfast in the Grill Room is really something!
Open all year
Rooms: 110 with private facilities
Bar Lunch 12 – 2.30 pm (a)
Dining Room/Restaurant Lunch 12 – 2.30 pm (b)
Bar Supper 6 – 9 pm (b)
Dinner 6 – 10 pm (c)
Taste of Scotland applies to Ogilvies Restaurant
Bed & breakfast £28.65 – £79
Dinner B & B from £37.50
Beef and fish dishes from Europe's premier fishing port and rich Buchan hinterland.
STB Commended 5 Crowns
Credit cards: 1, 2, 3, 5

Pitlochry

MAP 4

AUCHNAHYLE FARM

Tomcroy, Pitlochry
Perthshire PH16 5JA
Tel: 0796 472318
Fax: 0796 473657

Off East Moulin Road, at end of Tomcroy Terrace.

Auchnahyle, the delightful secluded 18th century farmhouse home of Penny and Alastair Howman, has featured in Taste of Scotland for over eight years. It is a "Wolsey Lodge" and recommended by Karen Brown and also Chris Gill in his "Charming Small Hotels Guide". Elegant four course candlelit dinners are served for up to six resident guests who are treated as friends and offered every comfort. Fresh farm and garden produce including herbs from the small herb garden feature widely. Booking ahead advisable.

Open all year except Christmas to New Year
Rooms: 3 with private facilities
Picnic Lunches on request
Dinner 6.45 – 8 pm (c)
Unlicensed – guests welcome to take own wine
No children under 12
No smoking in dining room
Bed & breakfast £27 – £39
Dinner B & B £40.50 – £56.50
Quail eggs with smoked venison garnish; chicken stuffed with cream cheese, fresh herbs and courgettes; minted green fruit salad. Chocolate Drambuie marquise.
Credit cards: 1, 3
Proprietors: Penny & Alastair Howman

BIRCHWOOD HOTEL

East Moulin Road, Pitlochry
Perthshire PH16 5DW
Tel: 0796 472477
Fax: 0796 473951

200 yards off Atholl Road on Perth side of Pitlochry.

Birchwood is a beautiful stone built Victorian manor house on a wooded knoll surrounded by four acres of attractive grounds. The hotel is noted for its food and hospitality and there is a choice of à la carte and table d'hôte menus and an extensive wine list. All bedrooms have private facilities, colour TV, telephone and courtesy trays. Dogs accepted by arrangement.

Open Mar to end Oct
Rooms: 16 with private facilities
Dining Room/Restaurant Lunch 12 – 1.30 pm (a)
Dinner 6.30 – 8 pm (c)
No smoking in restaurant
Bed & breakfast rates on application
Dinner B & B £42 – £52
Salmon roulade, Celtic salmon parcels, Highland steak, pork Edradour. Sweet trolley – all made on the premises with local produce and fresh cream.
STB Highly Commended 3 Crowns
Credit cards: 1, 3
Proprietors: Brian & Ovidia Harmon

CASTLEBEIGH HOUSE

Knockard Road, Pitlochry
Perthshire PH16 5HJ
Tel: 0796 472925
Fax: 0796 473473

Just off Pitlochry-East Moulin road.

Castlebeigh is a good example of the large houses built in Pitlochry in the period 1870 to 1880. These were made for confident gracious living. Castlebeigh sits high on the hillside on the north side of Pitlochry and has sweeping views over the Tummel valley. It is well situated and convenient for the many attractions and places of interest that make the town so popular.

Open Feb to Dec
Rooms: 21 , 19 with private facilities
Dinner 6 – 8 pm (c)
No smoking in restaurant
Bed & breakfast £20 – £35
Dinner B & B £28 – £45
Salmon mousse with cucumber sauce. Deep fried Scottish brie with cranberry sauce. Great favourites are the home-made sweets.
STB Commended 3 Crowns
Credit cards: 1, 3
Proprietors: Alistair & Diane McMenemie

CRAIGMHOR LODGE, HOTEL & RESTAURANT

27 West Moulin Road, Pitlochry
Perthshire PH16 5EF
Tel: 0796 472123

Pitlochry – on A924 Braemar road.

Craigmhor, traditional in style, is set in two acres of secluded grounds overlooking the Tummel Valley, with the town of Pitlochry nestling below. The Lodge offers guests comfortable accommodation in en suite bedrooms

with tea/coffee makers and colour TV. It also features a relaxing lounge with open fire, an intimate cocktail bar and restaurant, open from 6.30 pm, enabling guests to enjoy a pre-theatre meal.

Open all year
Rooms: 11 with private facilities
Bar Lunch 12 – 2 pm (a)
Dining Room/Restaurant Lunch (b) – reservations only
Bar Supper 7 – 9 pm (b)
Dinner 7 – 8.30 pm: 6.30 – 8.30 pm during Theatre season (c)
Facilities for the disabled
No smoking in restaurant
Bed & breakfast £25 – £30
Dinner B & B £37 – £47
Roast haunch of wild boar, fresh Tay salmon and local venison served with only the finest of fresh seasonal produce. Home-made desserts.
STB Commended 3 Crowns
Credit cards: 1, 3
Proprietors: Jean Hutton, Ian & Sandra Mackenzie

DUNFALLANDY HOUSE

Logierait Road, Pitlochry
Perthshire PH16 5NA
Tel: 0796 472648

On south side of Pitlochry, signposted off road leading to Festival Theatre.

Originally built for General Archibald Fergusson in 1790, this Georgian mansion house is now a beautifully refurbished country house hotel. It is magnificently situated within the Dunfallandy Estate and has unrivalled views of the glorious Tummel Valley, with the popular highland town of Pitlochry nestling below. This characterful house retains its historical features including marble fireplaces, log fires and the 'General's Bath' – the original Georgian ceramic bath of rather alarming depth! The elegant dining room offers imaginative food expertly prepared and presented, enhanced by fresh flowers, silver cutlery, crystal glasses and candlelight. An extensive wine list features traditional and New World wines.

Open Mar to Oct plus Christmas + New Year
Rooms: 9 with private facilities
Dinner 6.15 – 8 pm (b)
No children
No dogs
No smoking in dining room
Bed & breakfast £25 – £35
Dinner B & B £40 – £50
Wild duck breast poached with local chanterelles, fresh garden herbs and claret. Varied selection of vegetarian dishes always available.
STB Commended 3 Crowns
Credit cards: 1, 2, 3
Proprietors: Jane & Michael Bardsley

EAST HAUGH COUNTRY HOUSE HOTEL & RESTAURANT
East Haugh, by Pitlochry
Perthshire PH16 5JS
Tel: 0796 473121
Fax: 0796 472473
On old A9 road, 1 mile south of Pitlochry.
East Haugh House is a beautiful 17th century turreted stone Clan house, set in two acres of lawned gardens, which has been sympathetically refurbished to offer a high standard of accommodation. The restaurant and conservatory bar are complemented by the individually designed and furnished bedrooms, one featuring an antique pine four-poster bed and and open fire. All rooms have direct dial telephone, colour TV and tea/coffee-making facilities. Neil McGown, the proprietor/chef, takes the greatest pride in preparing his dishes which are becoming renowned, and he may even shoot or catch the ingredients for you himself!
Open Mar to Jan except 24 to 29 Dec
Rooms: 6 with private facilities
Bar Lunch 12 – 2 pm (b)
Dining Room/Restaurant Lunch – private functions by arrangement
Bar Supper 6 – 10.30 pm (b)
Dinner 7 – 10 pm (d)
Bed & breakfast £20 – £62
Dinner B & B £40 – £82
Mix of traditional Scottish and classic French. Game in season, an abundance of fresh fish and shellfish. Original vegetarian dishes.
STB Commended 3 Crowns
Credit cards: 1, 3
Proprietors: Neil & Lesley McGown

KNOCKENDARROCH HOUSE HOTEL
Higher Oakfield, Pitlochry
Perthshire PH16 5HT
Tel: 0796 473473
Fax: 0796 474068
High on hill overlooking village – just off Atholl Road.
Splendidly confident large Victorian house standing squarely on its hill looking over the Tummel Valley and Pitlochry. This small hotel combines modern amenities with the atmosphere of a comfortable home. In 1992 it was named by the RAC as Scotland's Small Hotel of the Year. Bookings advised and essential for non-residents.
Open Apr to Oct
Rooms: 12 with private facilities
Dinner 6.15 – 7.45 pm (b)
Bed & breakfast from £24.50
Dinner B & B from £38
Good home cooking – vegetarian and special diets catered for. Cucumber mousse. Stuffed venison rolls. Brown bread ice-cream. Walnut tart.
STB Commended 3 Crowns
Credit cards: 1, 2, 3, 5
Proprietors: John & Mary McMenemie

MILL POND COFFEE SHOP
Burnside Apartments
19 West Moulin Road
Pitlochry PH16 5EA
Tel: 0796 472203
Around 300 yards north of junction of A924 Pitlochry-Braemar (West Moulin Road) and Atholl Road, Pitlochry.
A delightful little coffee shop within an apartment hotel, with 14 serviced studios/apartments, situated in a convenient quiet location. An imaginative menu is served throughout the day, with home-made soups and hot dishes, cold buffet, tasty snacks and sandwiches, vegetarian dishes, home-

baking and speciality ices. Selection of teas, coffees and health drinks. Children welcome.
Open 1 Apr to 31 Oct
Continuous food service from 10.30 am – 7 pm daily (b)
No smoking in coffee shop
Open sandwiches – Tay salmon, local smoked gammon; from the buffet – smoked trout, salmon, game pâté. Ginger cream meringues, butter shortbread, gateaux with local seasonal fruits, Scottish cheeses.
Credit cards: 1, 3
Proprietors: Bill & Jessie Falconer

PITLOCHRY FESTIVAL THEATRE RESTAURANT
Port-na-Craig, Pitlochry
Perthshire PH16 5DR
Tel: 0796 473054
On south bank of the River Tummel, approx 1/4 mile from centre of town. Clearly signposted.
Scotland's 'Theatre in the Hills' is beautifully situated on the banks of the River Tummel and its glass frontage allows wonderful views from the Brown Trout Restaurant and Coffee Bar. Home-baking is a feature of the Coffee Bar, which also serves generously filled rolls. The lunchtime buffet, with its wide choice of meats, fish and vegetarian salads every day is popular with locals and tourists alike. There is always plenty of food, but seating can become scarce on a matinee day! Dinner is served formally and the imaginative menus make full use of Scotland's best produce. Its popularity reflects the fact that the combination of good food and good theatre makes a very special evening's entertainment. Evening booking essential. French spoken.
Open early Apr to 9 Oct
Dining Room/Restaurant Lunch 12 – 2 pm except Sun (a)
Dinner (from 30 Apr) at 6.30 pm (c) – booking essential
Facilities for the disabled
No smoking in restaurant
Smoking area in Coffee Bar
Breast of chicken filled with haggis in a cream sauce. Glazed roast leg of pork with apple, Drambuie and rosemary sauce. Salmon baked in pastry with currants and ginger served with cream, mustard, chervil and tarragon. Smoked salmon and prawn terrine, with lemon sauce. Mincemeat roulade.
Credit cards: 1, 2, 3, 5, 6

TORRDARACH HOTEL
Golf Course Road, Pitlochry
Perthshire PH16 5AU
Tel: 0796 472136

On road signposted to golf course at north end of town.
Torrdarach is a traditional old Scottish house offering a high standard of personal service and traditional home cooking. The hotel is in a quiet and peaceful woodland setting overlooking Pitlochry. This is a good centre for touring, walking and fishing, and of course, the famous Festival Theatre.
Open Apr to Oct
Rooms: 7 with private facilities
Dinner 6.30 – 7 pm (b)
Residents only
No dogs
No smoking in dining room
Bed & breakfast £25 – £30
Dinner B & B £37 – £42
Kipper pâté, fresh Scottish salmon, home-made soups and desserts, together with local beef and lamb provide interesting and varied menus.
STB Highly Commended 3 Crowns
No credit cards
Proprietors: Richard & Vivienne Cale

WESTLANDS OF PITLOCHRY
160 Atholl Road, Pitlochry
Perthshire PH16 5AR
Tel: 0796 472266
Fax: 0796 473994

On old A9 north of town centre.
Westlands is situated close to the centre of Pitlochry yet enjoys fine views over the surrounding mountains and Vale of Atholl. The proprietors' policy of continual improvement provides 15 bedrooms (all en suite) with colour TV, tea/coffee tray, radio, hairdryers and direct dial telephones, and central heating throughout. Westlands Restaurant offers distinctive cuisine in tasteful surroundings using the best products Scotland has to offer. 'Taste of Scotland' dishes are a particular feature.
Open all year
Rooms: 15 with private facilities
Bar Lunch 12 – 2 pm (a)
Dining Room/Restaurant Lunch (b) – reservations only
Bar Supper 6.15 – 9.30 pm (a)
Dinner 6.15 – 9 pm (c)
Bed & breakfast £28 – £46
Dinner B & B £43.50 – £63.50
Reduced rates available for Spring/Autumn, also Winter + Theatre packages.

Ragoût of mushrooms and prawns bound with Orkney smoked cheese sauce in a filo pastry parcel. Rendezvous of Scottish seafood cooked in a fresh dill cream sauce.
STB Commended 4 Crowns
Credit cards: 1, 3
Proprietors: Andrew & Sue Mathieson

Plockton

MAP 6

THE HAVEN HOTEL
Innes Street, Plockton
Ross-shire IV52 8TW
Tel: 059 984 223

In the village of Plockton.
In the lochside village of Plockton, originally a 19th century merchant's house, The Haven has been carefully converted into a charming small hotel set in the centre of one of Scotland's most beautiful villages. The hotel features three lounges, one with open fire, two "no smoking". Bedrooms are furnished to the highest standard.
Open 10 Feb to 18 Dec
Rooms: 13 with private facilities
Bar Lunch 12.30 – 1.45 pm (a)
Dining Room/Restaurant Lunch 12.30 – 1.45 pm (a) – reservations only
Dinner 7 – 8.30 pm (c)

No smoking in restaurant
Bed & breakfast £31.50 – £33.50
Dinner B & B £42 – £51
Plockton prawns, pheasant, local salmon, venison, haggis, kippers, local black pudding, wild duck, Scottish lamb, beef and pork. Home-made sweets.
STB Highly Commended 4 Crowns
Credit cards: 1, 3
Proprietors: Marjorie Nichols & John Graham

Port of Menteith

MAP 4

LAKE HOTEL
Port of Menteith
Perthshire FK8 3RA
Tel: 08775 258
Fax: 08775 671

On A81 – at Port of Menteith – 200 yards on road to Arnprior.
The Lake Hotel stands right on the shore of Scotland's only lake (the others are all lochs). It has been converted from a 19th century manse and has delightful views over the lake to the hills of the Trossachs. The hotel has been fitted out to a high standard of comfort. There is a large conservatory and an elegant lounge. Altogether this is a most attractive establishment in lovely surroundings serving quality fresh food.
Open all year
Rooms: 14 with private facilities
Bar Lunch (Lake Bistro) 12 – 2 pm (b)
Dining Room/Restaurant Lunch 12 – 2 pm Sun only (c)
Bar Supper (Lake Bistro) 7 – 9.30 pm (b)
Dinner 7 – 9 pm (c)
No smoking area in restaurant
Bed & breakfast £25 – £45
Dinner B & B £42 – £75
West coast smoked fish and shellfish. Loin of Scotch lamb. Shortbread with local berries. Orkney goats cheese.
STB Highly Commended 4 Crowns
Credit cards: 1, 3
Proprietor: J L Leroy

Credit Card Code		Meal Price Code	
1.	Access/Mastercard/Eurocard	(a)	under £10
2.	American Express	(b)	£10 – £15
3.	Visa	(c)	£15 – £20
4.	Carte Bleu	(d)	£20 – £25
5.	Diners Club	(e)	£25 – £30
6.	Mastercharge	(f)	over £30

Portpatrick

MAP 1

THE FERNHILL GOLF HOTEL
Heugh Road, Portpatrick
nr Stranraer DG9 8TD
Tel: 077 681 220
Fax: 077 681 596

Just off main road into Portpatrick.
Portpatrick's leading hotel is
spectacularly situated with magnificent
views over the Irish Sea and the town.
This popular three star hotel is owned
and run by Anne and Hugh Harvie who
are regularly improving and updating to
maintain high standards throughout.
The conservatory is especially attractive
and is a fashionable eating area for à la
carte and bar meals. The restaurant
offers a fine selection of food and wine,
and the patronage of local people is a
pointer to the high quality of the cuisine.
Smoking is discouraged in the restaurant
and conservatory but permitted in the
bar extension. Ample overnight parking
is available within the walled grounds.
*Open all year except Christmas + Boxing
Days*
Rooms: 21 with private facilities
Snacks available all day
Bar Lunch 12 – 2 pm (a)
*Dining Room/Restaurant Lunch 12 –
2 pm (b)*
Bar Restaurant Meals 6 – 10 pm (b)
Dinner 7 – 10 pm (c)
No dogs in public rooms
No smoking in restaurant + conservatory
Bed & breakfast £38 – £85
Dinner B & B £50 – £97
*Only finest meat, fish and local produce
used in season and when available. All
meals are cooked to order.*
STB Highly Commended 4 Crowns
Credit cards: 1, 2, 3, 5
Proprietors: Anne & Hugh Harvie

Rothes

MAP 5

ROTHES GLEN HOTEL
Rothes
Morayshire IV33 7AF
Tel: 034 03 254

*About 1 mile north of Rothes, on A941 to
Elgin.*
An delightful turreted and compact
Victorian mansion, standing in 40 acres
of wood and parkland, maintaining a
herd of long-haired Highland cattle. The
public rooms are imposing, with marble
fireplaces and 18th century furniture.
Open Feb to Dec
Rooms: 16 , 13 with private facilities
Bar Lunch 12.30 – 2 pm (a)
*Dining Room/Restaurant Lunch
12.30 – 2 pm (b)*
Dinner 7.30 – 9 pm (d)
Bed & breakfast from £50.25
Dinner B & B from £69.50
*Fresh fish and shellfish from the Moray
Firth and salmon from the River Spey.*
Credit cards: 1, 2, 3, 5, 6
*Proprietors: Donald & Elaine
Carmichael*

Rum
Isle of

MAP 7

KINLOCH CASTLE
Isle of Rum
Inverness-shire PH43 4RR
Tel: 0687 2037

*The Isle of Rum National Nature Reserve
is on the route taken by the small isles
ferry service operated from Mallaig by
Caledonian MacBrayne.*
Kinloch Castle is one of Scotland's
most remarkable hotels. Situated on an
island nature reserve of spectacular
wildness and beauty, the hotel offers
guests a chance to experience living
history in the Edwardian castle rooms
which have changed little since the turn
of the century. Over your pre-dinner
drink listen to the extraordinary
'orchestrion' – a mechanical organ
reputedly built for Queen Victoria. Enjoy
the best of fresh local fare served at the
original dining table taken from the
owners ocean-going yacht 'Rhouma'
during the Boer War. This is a castle with
a difference in an island with a
difference, and nature lovers will find so
much to enjoy.
Open Mar to Oct
Rooms: 9
Dinner at 7.30 pm (d)
Children over 7 years welcome
No dogs
No smoking in dining room
Dinner B & B £68 – £88
*The best of Mallaig fish and seafood.
Rum venison in season and freshly
caught brown trout from the lochs.*
No credit cards
Proprietors: Kathleen & Iain MacArthur

St Andrews

MAP 4

THE GRANGE INN
Grange Road, St Andrews
Fife KY16 8LJ
Tel: 0334 72670

*Grange Road is off A917 to Crail on exit
from St Andrews.*
Long a favourite rendezvous in St
Andrews, the Grange Inn has changed its
format somewhat in response to
customer demand and now offers a
more informal and relaxed style of
eating. The dining capacity has been
expanded and there are now three
separate dining areas, one of which is for
non-smokers. All of the charm of this
lovely old world inn has been retained
and the deft hand of Christopher
Trotter, a prominent Scottish chef and
now the new partner/ chef at the
Grange, is evident in the carefully
compiled menu, augmented by daily
dishes displayed on a blackboard.
Whether you are looking for a delicious
light lunch or a leisurely gourmet
dinner, you will find it here.
Open all year
Rooms:-2 with private facilities
*Dining Room/Restaurant Lunch
12.30 – 2.15 pm (b)*
Dinner 6.30 – 9.30 pm (d)
No smoking dining area available
Bed & breakfast from £30
Dinner B & B rates on application
*Mussel and onion stew. Smoked wild
Rannoch venison. Cold seafood platter.
Braised duck with red cabbage. Sticky
toffee pudding.*
Credit cards: 1, 2, 3, 5
Proprietors: Ann Russell & Peter Aretz

RUFFLETS COUNTRY HOUSE & GARDEN RESTAURANT

Strathkinness Low Road
St Andrews
Fife KY16 9TX
Tel: 0334 72594
Fax: 0334 78703

On B939, 1¹/2 miles west of St Andrews.
This turreted mansion house is set in beautifully landscaped gardens, 1¹/2 miles west of St Andrews – the mecca of the golfing world – yet only one hour's drive north from Edinburgh. The hotel has been in the same private family ownership since 1952 and is personally managed by proprietor Ann Russell and Peter Aretz, the general manager. Service is friendly and personal within a relaxed ambience. Public rooms are spacious and attractively furnished in contemporary country house style. At the beginning of 1993 a further six bedrooms will come on stream, making a total of 26 en suite bedrooms, all individually and tastefully decorated. The Garden Restaurant has gained an RAC merit award for the past two years. Cooking is light with an emphasis on fresh Scottish produce. Many of the fresh vegetables, herbs and fruits are supplied by the hotel's own gardens.
Open 1 Feb to 31 Dec
Rooms: 26 with private facilities
Bar Lunch 12.30 – 2 pm (a)
Dining Room/Restaurant Lunch
12.30 – 2 pm Sun Sat (b)
Dinner 7 – 9 pm (d)
Bed & breakfast £33.50 – £68
Dinner B & B £50.50 – £88
Fresh salmon and horseradish mousse with avocado pear and baby oatcakes. Fillet of Perthshire lamb oven roasted with basil and rosemary. Rufflets raspberries in an almond cup with Drambuie cream on a coulis of Summer fruits.
STB Highly Commended 4 Crowns
Credit cards: 1, 2, 3, 5
Proprietor: Ann Russell

ST ANDREWS GOLF HOTEL

40 The Scores, St Andrews
Fife KY16 9AS
Tel: 0334 72611 • Telex: 94013267
Fax: 0334 72188

A91 to St Andrews, turn left for golf course.
Situated on the cliffs with magnificent views over the Links and St Andrews Bay, 200 yards from the world famous "Old Course". The building is Victorian, tastefully modernised with most comfortable bedrooms and elegant public rooms. Quality prints of the best of Scottish artists line the walls. The oak-panelled restaurant offers a fine selection of dishes prepared from the best of local produce and complemented by an extensive and carefully selected wine list. Golf arranging is a speciality, either using one of the hotel's packages or having a holiday tailored to your requirements. The hotel is family owned and run. Children welcome. Dogs accepted – small charge. Italian and some French spoken.
Open all year
Rooms: 23 with private facilities
Bar Lunch 12 – 3 pm (a)
Dining Room/Restaurant Lunch
12.30 – 2.30 pm (b)
Dinner 7 – 9.30 pm (d)
No smoking in restaurant
Bed & breakfast from £52.50 – £70
Dinner B & B from £66 – £82
Petite éclairs filled with a delicate trout mousse, served with a natural yoghurt and horseradish dressing. Fresh Tay salmon poached in white wine, finished with orange and vermouth sauce. Strips of Perthshire venison sautéed with a julienne of fresh vegetables, served with smoked oysters.
STB Highly Commended 4 Crowns
Credit cards: 1, 3, 6
Proprietors: Maureen & Brian Hughes

ST ANDREWS OLD COURSE HOTEL

St Andrews
Fife KY16 9SP
Tel: 0334 74371 • Telex: 76280
Fax: 0334 77668

A91 to St Andrews.
This hotel of international reputation is now hailed as one of Scotland's leading resort hotels and was awarded 'Hotel of the Year' 1991 by the Caterer & Hotelkeeper. It overlooks the famous 17th Road Hole and the historic Royal & Ancient Clubhouse, and offers superb views of the city, St Andrews Bay and the distant mountains of the Highlands. There is a range of leisure activities including health spa and swimming pool. Both formal and relaxed dining available and the food is of a high standard to match the overall excellence of the establishment.
Open all year
Rooms: 125 with private facilities
Bar Lunch 11 am – 4 pm (a)
Dining Room/Restaurant Lunch
12.30 – 2.30 pm (b)
Afternoon tea available
Dinner 7 – 10 pm (e)
Facilities for the disabled
Room Rate £170 – £330
Oak-smoked pigeon and artichoke salad. Saddle of hare with lavender glaze. Linguini tossed in pesto sauce with crab and scallops.
STB Deluxe 5 Crowns
Credit cards: 1, 2, 3, 5

St Boswells

MAP 2

DRYBURGH ABBEY HOTEL

St Boswells
Roxburghshire TD6 0RQ
Tel: 0835 22261
Fax: 0835 23945

At St Boswells take B6404 signposted Dryburgh Abbey for 2 miles, then B6356 for just over 1¹/2 miles.
This magnificent baronial building on the banks of the River Tweed has undergone a complete renovation and refurbishment and is now a splendid luxury hotel. The ownership has changed and with it has come a change of policy and of standards. The proprietors, David and Graham Grose, also operate the prestigious Thurlstone Hotel in South Devon and Dryburgh Abbey seems set for the same high quality rating in all departments. Rooms are magnificently equipped and in the kitchen a leading young chef demonstrates originality and imagination in carefully prepared well presented meals. There is an admirable wine list to complement the food.
Open all year
Rooms: 28 with private facilities
Bar Lunch 12.15 – 2.15 pm except Sun (a)
Dining Room/Restaurant Lunch
12.30 – 2 pm (b)
Dinner 7.30 – 9.15 pm (d)
Facilities for the disabled
No smoking in restaurant
Bed & breakfast £40 – £80
Dinner B & B £55 – £95 (min 2 nights stay)
Chef Patrick Ruse prepares traditional dishes with an imaginative touch using local fresh produce.
STB Highly Commended 5 Crowns
Credit cards: 1, 3
Proprietors: David & Graham Grose

Selkirk

MAP 2

PHILIPBURN HOUSE HOTEL
Selkirk
TD7 5LS
Tel: 0750 20747
Fax: 0750 21690

A707 Moffat-Peebles, 1 mile from A7.
An attractive Georgian house, now an award winning country house hotel and restaurant, set in the heart of the romantic Scottish Borders. Imaginative bar meals, home-baked afternoon teas. In the courtyard behind the house is a swimming pool. There are five acres of beautiful grounds and the garden gained a "Grounds for Delight" Award 1989. Special breakaway packages available.
Open all year
Rooms: 16 with private facilities
Bar Lunch 12.15 – 2 pm (a)
Dining Room/Restaurant Lunch 12.15 – 2.15 pm (b)
Bar Supper 6.30 – 9 pm (a)
Dinner 7.30 – 9.30 pm (d)
No smoking area in restaurant
Bed & breakfast £49 – £60
Dinner B & B £52 – £75
Medallions of roe deer with a blueberry sauce and poached pear. Fillet of Border lamb cooked rosy pink on a crisp potato galette with gooseberry and mint sauce.
STB Commended 4 Crowns
Credit cards: 1, 3, 6
Proprietors: Jim & Anne Hill

Shetland
Isles of

MAP 7

BUSTA HOUSE HOTEL
Busta, Brae
Shetland ZE2 9QN
Tel: 080622 506
Fax: 080622 588

On the Muckle Roe road, 1 mile off A970 Hillswick road.
The impressive but slightly severe external appearance of Busta House gives no hint of the charm and elegance of the interior. This is reputedly the oldest continuously inhabited building in Shetland and it enjoys a commanding site overlooking Busta Voe. The public rooms are impressive and have been furnished with good taste while the bedrooms have every thoughtful facility that one would expect from caring hosts. The food lives up to the standard of the rest of the hotel concentrating on the plentiful harvest of good local produce from both land and sea, and there is a well chosen wine list and a stock of over 100 malt whiskies. Peter and Judith Jones can arrange holiday packages including flights or ferry from the UK mainland, and organise car hire, with a car to meet you at the airport or ferry terminal.
Open 3 Jan to 22 Dec
Rooms: 20 with private facilities
Bar Lunch 12 – 2 pm Mon to Sat: 12.30 – 2 pm Sun (a-c)
Bar Supper 7 – 9 pm (a-c): 6.30 pm for children – if required
Dinner 7 – 9 pm (d)
No smoking in dining room
Bed & breakfast £36.50 – £59
Dinner B & B £56 – £81.50 (min 3 nights stay)
Room Rate £56 – £85
Roast leg of Shetland lamb with blackcurrant and ginger wine sauce. Shetland salmon baked with oranges and fresh thyme. Suprême of chicken stuffed with prawns in puff pastry, served with a purée of red pepper.
STB Commended 4 Crowns
Credit cards: 1, 2, 3, 5
Proprietors: Peter & Judith Jones

ST MAGNUS BAY HOTEL
Hillswick
Shetland ZE2 9RW
Tel: 080 623 372
Fax: 080 623 373

36 miles north of Lerwick, on north-west branch of A970.
A timber clad hotel erected at the turn of the century with a most unusual history. It was built in Norway and floated across the North Sea for an international exhibition in Glasgow, then brought again by sea to Shetland. It occupies a splendidly dominating position in the village and must rank as one of the most northerly hotels in the British Isles. The original building has been extended over the years, but retaining the impressive stairway and the pine-lined dining room. In addition there is a separate coffee or supper room and a public bar. The chef relies heavily – and rightly – on a copious supply of fresh fish and local shellfish. Children are welcome.
Open all year
Rooms: 26 with private facilities
Bar Lunch 12.30 – 1.45 pm (a-b)
Dining Room/Restaurant Lunch 1 – 2.30 pm Sun only (b)
Bar Supper 6.30 – 9 pm (a-b)
Dinner 7.30 – 9 pm (c)
Bed & breakfast £35 – £40
Dinner B & B £55 – £60
Room Rate £40 – £70
Fresh seafood – lobster, scallops etc. Smoked salmon roulade with a creamy walnut sauce. Shetland lamb pan-fried with juniper berries. Sherry ginger log.
STB Approved 3 Crowns
Credit cards: 1, 3
Proprietors: Peter & Adrienne Titcomb

Skye
Isle of

MAP 7

ARDVASAR HOTEL
Ardvasar, Sleat
Isle of Skye IV45 8AS
Tel: 047 14 223

At roadside A851, close to Armadale pier (Armadale-Mallaig ferry).
A small white, traditional, whitewashed stone building overlooking mountains and Sound of Sleat water to Mallaig. Cosy small rooms, sitting room with log fire. Traditionally furnished to give warm homely atmosphere.
Open Mar to Dec (accommodation) + all year for meals, except Christmas + New Year
Rooms: 10 with private facilities
Bar Lunch 12 – 2 pm (a)
Bar Supper 5 – 7 pm (a)
Dinner 7.30 – 8.30 pm (c)
Bed & breakfast from £30
Dinner B & B from £50
Room Rate £56 – £65
Fresh lobster, scallops, prawns. Princess scallops. All locally caught – on availability. Daily changing menus.
Credit cards: 1, 3
Proprietors: Bill & Gretta Fowler

ATHOLL HOUSE HOTEL
Dunvegan
Isle of Skye IV55 8WA
Tel: 047 022 219
Fax: 047 022 481

On roadside A863 on outskirts of Dunvegan.

Family run hotel – formerly a manse – ideally situated on the outskirts of the village of Dunvegan with magnificent views of MacLeod's Tables and Loch Dunvegan. The tastefully decorated bedrooms are well equipped with colour TV, direct dial telephone, tea/coffee-making facilities, hairdryers etc. The comfortable lounge has an open fire and a fine range of malt whiskies is stocked.

Open all year except Nov
Rooms: 9 , 7 with private facilities
Morning Coffee 10 – 11.30 am
Dining Room/Restaurant Lunch 12.30 – 2 pm (a)
Afternoon Tea 3 – 4.30 pm
Dinner 7 – 9.30 pm (c)
Restricted licence
No smoking in restaurant
Bed & breakfast £26.50 – £32
Dinner B & B £44 – £49.50
Constantly changing menu, featuring the best of local produce. Fresh Skye oysters, crab, prawns, scallops etc. Fresh fish – Skye salmon, trout. Fresh Scottish beef, local lamb and venison. Home-made soups, pâté, sweets and Highland cheeseboard. Fresh locally grown organic fruit and vegetables during the season.
STB Commended 3 Crowns
Credit cards: 1, 3
Proprietors: Cliff & Barbara Ashton

FLODIGARRY COUNTRY HOUSE HOTEL
& THE WATER HORSE RESTAURANT
Staffin, Isle of Skye
Inverness-shire IV51 9HZ
Tel: 047 052 203
Fax: 047 052 301

A855 north from Portree to Staffin, 4 miles from Staffin to Flodigarry.

Unspoilt by progress, this delightful hotel is a warm sheltered haven amidst the dramatic scenery of northern Skye with views across the sea to the Torridon Mountains and towering pinnacles of the Quiraing providing a remarkable skyline to the views inland. Set in five acres of gardens and mixed woodland, the fine 19th century mansion house is steeped in history and has strong Jacobite

associations. Residents and non-residents can enjoy traditional dishes and other specialities which are prepared using fresh, and where possible, local produce. The standard of food is first class and in addition to the full four course table d'hôte menu, there are excellent bar meals available throughout the day and evening.

Open all year
Rooms: 16 , 11 with private facilities
Bar Meals 11 am – 10 pm (a)
Dining Room/Restaurant Lunch 12 – 2.30 pm Sun only (b)
Dinner 7 – 10 pm (c)
Bed & breakfast £21 – £60
Dinner B & B £38 – £77
Seaweed and nettle soups. Seafood. Game. Wide variety of produce used from gardens and surrounding hills. Home-baked breads, scones and cakes. Hand-made confectionery.
STB Award Pending
Credit cards: 1, 3
Proprietors: Andrew & Pamela Butler

GLENVIEW INN
Culnacnoc, by Portree
Isle of Skye IV51 9JH
Tel: 047 062 248

On A855, 13 miles north of Portree.

This traditional Skye house stands just a few yards off the east coast road from Portree to the north of the island. It has been pleasingly converted to a friendly little rural inn with a cosy bar, an attractive dining room and a comfortable terrace lounge. It has always had a good reputation for the standard of its food, for interesting menus – and for generous portions! Surprisingly perhaps, there are not too many good eating places on the magnificent scenic route from Portree to Staffin, and the Glenview fills the need

and makes a pleasant base from which to enjoy it all.

Open Easter to Dec except Christmas Day
Rooms: 6 , 4 with private facilities
Bar Meals 12 – 10 pm (a)
Dinner 7.30 – 9.30 pm (c)
Bed & breakfast from £26.50
Dinner B & B from £45
Fresh bread, unusual soups and rich pâtés. Skewered scallops, roast lobsters and Skye oysters. Whiskied steaks. Chicken stuffed with crab. Calorie-laden puddings!
STB Commended 3 Crowns
Credit cards: 1, 3
Proprietors: Linda & Alistair Thomson

HARLOSH HOUSE
by Dunvegan
Isle of Skye IV55 8ZG
Tel: 047 022 367

Off A863, 4 miles south of Dunvegan.

This is one of those cosy friendly small hotels that one loves to come across by chance and then indulge in quiet satisfaction at the discovery. Harlosh has a fine open site on the shores of Loch Caroy with fine views of the Cuillins and the small islands of Loch Bracadale. There are excellent cliff top walks. It is a pleasing and comfortable little hotel to which Lindsey Elford will greet you with great charm and courtesy. Husband Peter masterminds the kitchen and makes imaginative use of the excellent fresh produce, particulary fish and shellfish, for which Skye is renowned. The public rooms are small but this all contributes to the friendly warmth and intimate atmosphere of the place. The master bedroom is superb and, though smaller, other bedrooms are well equipped and comfortble. Harlosh is popular with many visitors to the island so, in the season, do not leave things to chance but book in advance.

Open Easter to mid Oct
Rooms: 6 , 5 with private facilities
Dinner 7 – 8.30 pm Tue to Sun (d)
Note: Dinner Mon – residents only
No dogs
No smoking area in restaurant
Bed & breakfast £30 – £39.50
Dinner B & B £50 – £59.50
Local fish and shellfish – fresh whenever possible on a constantly changing menu dependent on what is available. Cooked sympathetically to any requirement.
STB Highly Commended 3 Crowns
Credit cards: 1, 3
Proprietors: Peter & Lindsey Elford

HOTEL EILEAN IARMAIN
Sleat, Isle of Skye
Inverness-shire IV43 8QR
Tel: 04713 332
Fax: 04713 275

Barely 20 minutes drive on A851 Armadale-Kyleakin.

You do not have to have the Gaelic to enjoy the Hotel Eilean Iarmain (Isle Ornsay Hotel) for though its menus are described in Gaelic there is a very clear English translation underneath. What you will experience is that warmth of welcome and hospitality for which the Highlands and islands are so renowned. This is a traditional hotel with good en suite accommodation, in an idyllic setting overlooking the harbour. A good centre from which to enjoy stalking, shooting, walking, fishing, riding, golf or just laze and lap up the tranquillity. Menus are well balanced and interesting and make full use of the excellent shellfish for which local waters are famous, but there is also lots of other choice for non-shellfish eaters.
Open all year
Rooms: 12 with private facilities
Bar Lunch 12.30 – 2 pm (a)
Dining Room/Restaurant Lunch 12.30 – 2 pm (a)
Bar Supper 6 – 9 pm Mon to Sat: 6.30 – 9 pm Sun (a)
Dinner 7 – 9 pm (c)
No smoking in restaurant
Bed & breakfast £35 – £50
Dinner B & B £54.50 – £69.50
Fresh Eilean Iarmain oysters. Stilton and broccoli soup. Local wild salmon with fresh chives and cream. Roast haunch of venison with rowan jelly.
Credit cards: 1, 3
Proprietors: Sir Iain & Lady Noble

LOCHBAY SEAFOOD RESTAURANT
1/2 Macleod's Terrace
Stein, Waternish
Isle of Skye IV55 8GA
Tel: 047083 235

Situated 5 miles down the Waternish Peninsula, in Stein Village. Last house in the village.

Situated in the old fishing village of Stein and located just 30 yards from the jetty and shore with some lovely unspoilt views of the loch and the Outer Isles. It has been converted from two cottages which were built in 1740 and is now a speciality seafood restaurant with accommodation. There is a lot of atmosphere about this friendly little restaurant where you will be made welcome whether formally or informally dressed.
Open Mar to Nov
Rooms: 3
Dining Room/Restaurant Lunch 12 – 3 pm except Sat (a)
Dinner 6 – 9 pm except Sat (c)
Restaurant closed Sat except Easter Sat
Bed & breakfast from £16
Starters of squat lobster, princess scallops, oysters, mussels etc. Seafood platter, lobster, king prawns, scallop, various selection of fresh fish. Clootie dumpling etc.
No credit cards
Proprietors: Peter & Margaret Greenhalgh

ORD HOUSE
Ord
by Teangue, Sleat
Isle of Skye IV43 8QN
Tel: 047 15 294

From Kyleakin, head for Broadford, take road to left signposted for Armadale, Sleat, or 'Garden of Skye'. After passing Isle Ornsay look for road to right, signposted to Ord.

The picture postcard of Ord House says it all. This fine old 18th century Laird's house nestles in a quiet position by the sea with stunning views to the Cuillins and Blaven. Ord House featured in Alexander Smith's book 'A Summer in Skye', first published in 1865, and has extensive connections with the MacDonalds including the famous Flora. The house has been comfortably restored, is full of books and pictures, and makes a warm and friendly base for an island holiday. Iona Noble's cooking is imaginative and has earned her much praise and she and husband Robin really make everyone feel like a personal and greatly welcome guest.
Open Apr to Oct
Rooms: 5 , 2 with private facilities
Dinner at 7.30 pm (c)
Restricted licence
No smoking in dining room
Bed & breakfast £27 – £31
Dinner B & B £43 – £47
Sorrel soup. Home-made herb bread. Potato scone stuffed with Ord scallops in cream and white wine. Gratin of fresh fruit.
No credit cards
Proprietors: Robin & Iona Noble

SKEABOST HOUSE HOTEL
Skeabost Bridge
Isle of Skye IV51 9NP
Tel: 047 032 202

4 miles north of Portree on Dunvegan road.

Turning into the drive to Skeabost House is like entering a new world. In direct contrast to the stark countryside around it, Skeabost is an oasis of cultivated serenity. A former hunting lodge, this delightful country house hotel stands in 12 acres of secluded woodlands and garden, wonderfully positioned on the shore of Loch Snizort. This is a comfortable and relaxing family run hotel with good lounges, a billiard room, cocktail bar and an attractive restaurant. The staff go all out to make guests welcome and to attend to their every need and the chefs make good use of an abundance of fresh produce from sea and farm.
Open Apr to Oct
Rooms: 26 with private facilities
Bar Lunch/Buffet Table 12 – 1.30 pm (a)
Bar Supper 7 – 8.30 except Sun (a)
Dinner 7 – 8.30 pm (d)
Bed & breakfast £38.50 – £49.50
Dinner B & B £61 – £71
Fresh salmon, venison, Skye lamb.
STB Commended 4 Crowns
Credit cards: 1, 3
Proprietors: Stuart/McNab/Stuart

THREE CHIMNEYS RESTAURANT

Colbost, nr Dunvegan
Isle of Skye IV51 9SY
Tel: 047 081 258 (Glendale)
4 miles west of Dunvegan on B884 road to Glendale. Look out for Glendale Visitor Route signs.
The road to the Isles may not end here, at this most westerly point in Skye – but it should. This is a gem of a place right down by the shore of Loch Dunvegan. It is an old crofter's cottage with beamed ceilings, interior stone walls, and open fires. It exudes atmosphere and a candlelit dinner here could not fail to be memorable. Eddie and Shirley Spear are a charming couple, and Shirley who presides in the kitchen is much acclaimed by food writers and has earned a high reputation for her cooking. Naturally she specialises in the abundance of delicious shell fish and fresh fish so readily available in the island but she is equally adept in the preparation and presentation of beef, lamb and venison dishes. The pièce de resistance in the dessert menu is her special marmalade pudding and local legend has it that people go back to Skye just to have another helping! There is excellent accommodation in and around the nearby village of Dunvegan and local B & B. No visit to Skye can be really complete without a meal at the Three Chimneys. Macallan/Decanter Restaurant of the Year 1990.
Open Apr to Oct
Dining Room/Restaurant Lunch 12.30 – 2 pm except Sun (b)
Dinner 7 – 9 pm except Sun (d)
Closed Sun
No smoking in restaurant
Local shellfish – fresh Skye oysters, langoustine and lobster. Fresh fish and wild Skye salmon. Fresh Scottish beef, lamb and venison dishes, including steaks. Vegetarian selection.
Credit cards: 1, 3
Proprietors: Eddie & Shirley Spear

ULLINISH LODGE HOTEL
Struan
Isle of Skye IV56 8FD
Tel: 047 072 214
Off A863 between Sligachan and Dunvegan.
Ullinish Lodge is an 18th century country house beautifully set overlooking the Cuillins and the shores of Loch Bracadale. It is ideally situated for walking and climbing, and there is brown trout fishing in the three lochs, salmon fishing in two rivers and rough shooting over 27,500 acres. John and Claudia Mulford are welcoming hosts. There is a large lounge with open fire and a pleasant restaurant where the menu changes daily and features a fine selection of Scottish produce. The hotel has a fine range of malt whiskies and a good selection of wine including a range of Scottish wines and liqueurs. German spoken.
Open Easter to Oct
Rooms: 8 with private facilities
Dining Room/Restaurant Lunch 12 – 2 pm Mon to Sat: 12.30 – 2 pm Sun (a)
Bar Supper 6 – 9 pm (a)
Dinner 7 – 9 pm (or by arrangement) (c-e)
No smoking area in restaurant
Bed & breakfast £28 – £46
Dinner B & B £44 – £62
Home-made soups and pâtés. Venison in red wine. Pheasant with cranberries and walnuts. King scallops with Talisker sauce and dressed crab. The house speciality is a seafood dish for two, featuring lobster, local prawns and a range of local shellfish.
STB Commended 3 Crowns
Credit cards: 1, 3
Proprietors: John & Claudia Mulford

South Queensferry

MAP 4

THE HAWES INN
Newhalls Road, South Queensferry
West Lothian EH30 9TA
Tel: 031 331 1990
Fax: 031 319 1120
At east end of the village, under the Forth Rail Bridge.
This fine historical building, with its marvellous view across the Firth of Forth, dates from the 16th century. It has literary connections with Sir Walter Scott and was immortalised by Robert Louis Stevenson in 'Kidnapped'. The Hawes Inn is full of character and almost a tourist attraction in its own right. A pleasant 20 minute drive from Edinburgh city centre and only five miles from Edinburgh Airport, it has long been a popular destination restaurant for the city cognoscenti before or after a stroll along the front at South Queensferry. There are eight bedrooms, a quality restaurant, an atmospheric bar with family room attached, and an extensive beer garden.
Open all year except Christmas Day + 1 Jan
Rooms: 8
Bar Meals 12 – 9 pm
Dining Room/Restaurant Lunch 12 – 2 pm (b)
Dinner 6.30 – 10 pm
Bed & breakfast £34 – £51
Warm poached salmon with a tarragon mayonnaise. Mussels. Fillet steak Allen Breck – stuffed with haggis and served with a Glayva, syboe and cranberry sauce. Cranachan.
STB Approved 1 Crown
Credit cards: 1, 2, 3, 5

by Spean Bridge

MAP 6

CORRIEGOUR LODGE HOTEL
Loch Lochy, by Spean Bridge
Inverness-shire PH34 4EB
Tel: 039 781 685
Fax: 039 781 696
Follow A82, 17 miles north of Fort William; 47 miles south of Inverness.
Perhaps the finest location in "The Great Glen", with outstanding views over Loch Lochy, this former hunting lodge is the ideal retreat for a well deserved break. This grand old house has been tastefully restored to provide the atmosphere of yesteryear with the comfort of today. All bedrooms have en suite facilities and are individually furnished with antiques. The Loch View Conservatory offers guests a range of high quality cuisine – all home-made, using local produce. While enjoying a meal in this relaxing setting you can watch the boats sailing Loch Lochy on their way through the Caledonian Canal. The hotel has its own pontoon/jetty. A good place from which to explore the Highlands.
Open Mar to Nov
Rooms: 8 with private facilities

Bar Lunch 12 – 2 pm (a)
Bar Supper 6 – 9 pm (a)
Dinner 6 – 8.30 pm (c)
No dogs
No smoking in restaurant
Bed & breakfast £25 – £36
Dinner B & B £43 – £58
Freshly baked Loch Lochy trout with lemon and herbs. Charcoal grilled Aberdeen Angus steaks. Rack of Highland lamb with rosemary and honey. Braised haunch of venison in red wine.
STB Highly Commended 3 Crowns
Credit cards: 1, 3
Proprietors: Rod & Lorna Bunney

OLD PINES

Gairlochy Road, Spean Bridge
Inverness-shire
PH34 4EG
Tel: 039 781 324
Fax: 039 781 433

From Spean Bridge take A82 to Inverness. One mile north take B8004 next to Commando Memorial 300 yards on right.

The spectacular Commando Memorial at Spean Bridge is a stopping place for most people, not only for the excellence of the sculpture but for the fabulous views across the Great Glen towards Aonach Mor and Ben Nevis. If you have got this far, you are only 300 yards from the delightful little Scandinavian-style home of Niall and Sukie Scott. A really friendly informal atmosphere prevails and guests love it. Much thought goes into the planning of the daily menu and a four course dinner by candlelight in the conservatory dining room is a highlight in most people's day.
Open all year except 2 wks Nov
Rooms: 8 , 6 with private facilities
Dining Room/Restaurant Lunch (a)
Dinner 7 – 9.30 pm (b-c)
Unlicensed
No dogs
Facilities for the disabled
No smoking throughout
Dinner B & B £35 – £40
Fruit and cheese salad. Langoustine. Loch Lochy trout stuffed with leeks and garlic. Wild salmon. Pheasant with grapes, wine and sage. Rhubarb and banana brûlée. Hazelnut and raspberry meringue gâteau. Home-made breads and preserves. Scottish hand-made cheeses.
STB Commended 3 Crowns
Credit cards: 1, 3
Proprietors: Niall & Sukie Scott

Stewarton

MAP 3

CHAPELTOUN HOUSE HOTEL

nr Stewarton
Ayrshire KA3 3ED
Tel: 0560 82696
Fax: 0560 85100

Signed off B769 Stewarton-Irvine (access via A77 or A78).

A delightful country house retreat in lovely Ayrshire countryside, all the better for being a little off the beaten track. It was built in 1900 and features fine plasterwork and friezes of thistles and roses to celebrate the marriage of a Scottish industrialist and his English wife. The splendid panelled and timbered interior of Chapeltoun induces a sense of comfortable relaxation and that is what this place is all about. Bedrooms are spacious and beautifully appointed, as are the public rooms. Food is varied, interesting and of high standard relying largely on the excellence of the abundant local produce, from what is one of the richest farming areas in the country. The proprietors are very much in evidence supervising well-trained staff and attending to the comfort and convenience of their guests.
Open all year
Rooms: 8 with private facilities
Bar Lunch 12 – 2 pm (a)
Dining Room/Restaurant Lunch 12.30 – 2 pm (c)
Dinner 7 – 9 pm (d)
No smoking in restaurant
Bed & breakfast £45 – £84
Best of local meat, fish, game and vegetables.
STB Highly Commended 4 Crowns
Credit cards: 1, 2, 3
Proprietors: Colin & Graeme McKenzie

Stirling

MAP 4

THE TOPPS FARM

Fintry Road, Denny
Stirlingshire FK6 5JF
Tel: 0324 822471

On B818 Denny - Fintry road, off M80.
This much commended working sheep and cashmere goat farm is splendidly sited in central Scotland within easy reach of Edinburgh, Glasgow and Perth. Its huge picture windows give superb views out towards the Fintry and Ochil Hills. So popular has it become that it has now opened a restaurant to complement the guest house facilities. Jennifer Steel's home-cooking is highly praised and covers many traditional favourites as well as really interesting and imaginative dishes. The 'Farmers Breakfast' is quite something, but so too is dinner – as the complimentary comments from satisfied guests confirm.
Open all year except Christmas Day + 1 Jan
Rooms: 8 with private facilities
Dining Room/Restaurant Lunch 12.30 – 2 pm except Mon Tue (a)
Dinner from 7 pm except Mon Tue (b)
Restaurant closed Mon Tue, except pre-Christmas
No smoking throughout
Bed & breakfast from £17
Dinner B & B from £30
Breakfast – trout, porridge, local haggis, black pudding etc. Grumphies and tatties. Wild garlic lamb. Honey poached salmon. Glenmorangie gâteau. Rosewater meringues. Poached spicy pears.
STB Commended 3 Crowns
Credit cards: 1, 3
Proprietors: Jennifer & Alistair Steel

Stonehaven

MAP 5

TOLBOOTH RESTAURANT

Old Pier, Stonehaven Harbour
Stonehaven
Tel: 0569 62287

Off A92, onto A957 to Stonehaven, 10 miles south of Aberdeen.
The Tolbooth – built in the 16th century – is the oldest building in Stonehaven and is set on the harbourside with picturesque views. The restaurant specialises in fresh fish and seafood, but interesting vegetarian and meat dishes are also available. There is a permanent exhibition of Royal Scottish Academy artists on the whitewashed stone walls. Afghan rugs enhance the beautifully polished wooden floors.
Open Apr to Oct: also Nov to Mar for dinner + Sun Lunch only
Dining Room/Restaurant Lunch 12 – 2.30 pm except Mon (b) - Jun to Oct only
Dinner 7 – 9.30 pm except Mon (d)
Closed Mon
Lightly grilled west coast scallops sliced waferthin and served on a watercress salad with tangy lime butter. North Sea

▶

bouillabaisse – local fish, mussels and prawns simmered in a saffron and tomato broth. Monkfish cooked with green peppercorns, tomato and cream, served in a puff pastry case. Organic herbs and vegetables.
Credit cards: 1, 3
Proprietor: Moya Bothwell

Strachur

MAP 3

THE CREGGANS INN
Strachur
Argyll PA27 8BX
Tel: 0369 86 279
Fax: 0369 86 637

1¹/₂ hours from Glasgow on A83 then A815, overlooking Loch Fyne.
The Creggans is an old inn, set at the roadside on the shore of scenic Loch Fyne. A well designed extension harmoniously blends with the original building. This is an inn with a difference. The food is superb and the atmosphere in the friendly comfortable luncheon bars delightful. At night in the attractive dining room looking down the loch, dinner is more formal, with a large selection of original Scottish country house dishes from Lady MacLean's cookbooks.
Open all year
Rooms: 21 , 17 with private facilities
Bar Lunch 12.30 – 2.30 pm (a)
Bar Supper 6.30 – 7.30 pm (a)
Dinner 7.30 – 9 pm (d)
No smoking in dining room
Bed & breakfast £50 – £60

Dinner B & B £70 – £80
Loch Fyne oysters, smoked salmon, local lobster, mussels, prawns and kippers. Fillet of Argyll hill lamb with Port wine and redcurrant sauce.
STB Commended 3 Crowns
Credit cards: 1, 2, 3, 5, 6
Proprietors: Sir Fitzroy MacLean,
The Hon Lady MacLean &
Charles E MacLean

Stranraer

MAP 1

NORTH WEST CASTLE HOTEL
Portrodie
Stranraer DG9 8EH
Tel: 0776 4413
Fax: 0776 2646

Prestige Award Winner 1989

Seafront – opposite harbour.
Anyone who has ever travelled on the Stranraer-Larne ferry – and thousands who have not – will know and love the North West Castle Hotel. A superbly managed resort hotel which seems to incorporate everything that anyone could possibly want. In its own grounds overlooking the harbour it has an indoor swimming pool, jacuzzi, multi-gym, saunas, sunbeds, bowls, a curling rink, table tennis, darts, pool, snooker. It naturally follows that the bedrooms have colour TVs, radio, trouser press, hairdryer and coffee-making facilities. You might like to try one of the new tastefully decorated suites, with views over Loch Ryan. For those on inclusive rates there is even free golf at two local courses. A pianist plays during dinner.
Open all year
Rooms: 70 with private facilities
Bar Lunch 12 – 2 pm except Sun (a)
Dining Room/Restaurant Lunch 12 – 2 pm (c)
Dinner 7 – 9 pm (d)
Bed & breakfast £38 – £78
Dinner B & B £55 – £90
Smoked salmon cornet filled with prawns. Poached escalope of Cree salmon

Hollandaise. Roast fillet of beef with a whisky sauce. Vegetarian dishes available.
STB Highly Commended 5 Crowns
No credit cards
Proprietor: H C McMillan

Strathconon

MAP 6

AN SHEBEEN HIGHLAND INN
Curin, Strathconon
by Muir of Ord
Ross-shire IV6 7QG
Tel: 09976 227

At Tore roundabout (A9), take A835 (Ullapool) then Marybank/ Strathconon road. Restaurant 7 miles along single track road.
'An Shebeen' nestles in the rugged hills overlooking Loch Meig, along the secluded unspoilt glen of Strathconon, 28 miles from Inverness – capital of the Highlands. It is an old 18th century croft which was locally renowned as an illicit drinking house and has now been restored with great care to preserve the stone walls and beamed ceilings which gave the original 'Shebeen' so much of its character. In this traditional atmosphere, good Scots fare is featured in the Phoit Dhubh dining room or in the Bothan Bar.
Open May to Oct: Nov to Apr open Sat Sun only, except Christmas + Easter wks
Bar Lunch 12.30 – 2.30 pm (a)
Dining Room/Restaurant Lunch 12.30 – 2.30 pm (a-b)
Bar Supper 6 – 8 pm (a-b)
Dinner 7.30 – 9 pm (c)
Facilities for the disabled
Kiste of prawns. Mushrooms in oatmeal batter served with home-made rowan jelly. Suprême of chicken served with a silver birch and cream sauce. Marinade of venison. Wild fruits in Scottish mead. Cranachan.
No credit cards
Proprietors: Nairn & Sheila MacEwan

Credit Card Code		Meal Price Code	
1.	Access/Mastercard/Eurocard	(a)	under £10
2.	American Express	(b)	£10 – £15
3.	Visa	(c)	£15 – £20
4.	Carte Bleu	(d)	£20 – £25
5.	Diners Club	(e)	£25 – £30
6.	Mastercharge	(f)	over £30

Strathlachlan

MAP 3

INVER COTTAGE RESTAURANT

Strathlachlan, by Cairndow
Argyll PA27 8BU
Tel: 036 986 396/275

B8000, 7 miles south of Strachur.
Inver Cottage is an attractive little
restaurant in delightful surroundings on
the shores of Loch Fyne, overlooking the
ruins of old Castle Lachlan. Open log
and peat fires add a special touch to the
place, creating a nice relaxed
atmosphere. Tony and Gina Wignell
have now taken over the Inver Cottage
Restaurant and continue to produce the
good standards of food they set at their
previous establishment in Kilfinan.
Open Mar to Oct
Bar Lunch 11.30 am – 2.30 pm except
Tue (a)
Dining Room/Restaurant Lunch
11.30 am – 2.30 pm except Tue (b)
Dinner 6 – 10 pm except Tue (c)
Closed Tue
Fresh local produce including shellfish
and fish, lamb, beef etc. Wide selection of
desserts.
Credit cards: 1, 3
Proprietors: Tony & Gina Wignell

Strathyre

MAP 4

CREAGAN HOUSE

Restaurant with Accommodation
Strathyre
Perthshire FK18 8ND
Tel: 087 74 638

On A84, 1/4 mile north of Strathyre.
In a lovely country setting, Creagan is a
family owned 17th century farmhouse
with five charming bedrooms. The
baronial dining hall with its grand open
fire provides a unique setting in which to
enjoy good food and fine wines. A
mixture of experience, caring and
friendliness contribute to your
enjoyment.
Open Mar to Jan except 8 to 17 Oct
Rooms: 5 , 3 with private facilities
Dining Room/Restaurant Lunch at
1 pm Sun only (b)
Lunch parties on other days by
arrangement
Dinner 7.30 – 8.30 pm (b-c)
Booking essential for all meals

No smoking in dining hall + bedrooms
Bed & breakfast £22.50 – £39
Dinner B & B £26.75 – £58.25
Two set price menus available each
evening and may include – mushrooms
Dunsyre, smokie in a pokie, venison
turbigo, beef and pigeon Vin Santo,
Crabbies apple cake. Fresh local produce
is used wherever possible.
STB Highly Commended 3 Crowns
Credit cards: 1, 3
Proprietors: Gordon & Cherry Gunn

Strontian

MAP 6

KILCAMB LODGE HOTEL

Strontian
North Argyll PH36 4HY
Tel: 0967 2257

Strontian, south-west of Fort William.
There are new owners at this charming
old country house in 30 acres of secluded
grounds on the shores of Loch Sunart.
Natural lawns slope gently down to the
waters edge with the Morvern Hills rising
steeply in the background. The Blakeway
family and the house suit each other and
previous high standards have been
continued and enhanced. The family
brings an additional warmth and
friendliness to the place and good taste is
evident in the personal touches and
flowers, china etc. Food is first class, and
carefully planned and balanced menus
make full use of excellent local produce.
Our inspector ended her report by
saying "so glad I came here". Perhaps
that says it all.
Open Apr to Oct
Rooms: 10 with private facilities
Light Lunch available
Dinner at 7.30 pm (d)
No smoking in dining room
Bed & breakfast from £38
Dinner B & B from £58
Room Rate £32
A light seafood pancake of prawns and
sole. Poached halibut on a bed of spinach
with a Hollandaise sauce. Fillet of lamb
in a herb cream sauce. Sticky toffee sponge
with a rich butterscotch sauce. Selection
of Scottish cheeses.
STB Highly Commended 3 Crowns
Credit cards: 1, 3
Proprietors: Gordon & Ann Blakeway

Swinton

MAP 2

THE WHEATSHEAF HOTEL & RESTAURANT

Main Street, Swinton
Berwickshire TD11 3NB
Tel: 089 086 257

12 miles from Berwick-upon-Tweed on
B6461 to Kelso.
An attractive old hotel in the centre of
Swinton, a popular hostelry for locals
and one to which people travel from
quite some distance to enjoy the good
food. There is a lot of old world charm in
the quaint bar with its black beams, game
birds that have fallen into the hands of
the taxidermist, appropriate furniture
and considerable ambience. The
restaurant menu is extensive and the
food is remarkably good, achieving Julie
and Alan Reid's objective of providing
the best of fresh local produce in a
welcoming but unpretentious
atmosphere – and representing excellent
value for money. Recent renovation has
upgraded the accommodation facilities.
Open all year except mid 2 wks Feb
Rooms: 4 , 2 with private facilities
Bar Lunch 11.45 am – 2 pm except
Mon (a)
Dining Room/Restaurant Lunch
11.45 am – 2 pm except Mon (b)
Bar Supper 6 – 9.30 pm except Mon (a)
Dinner 6 – 9.30 pm except Mon (b)
Closed Mon
Facilities for the disabled
No smoking area in restaurant
Bed & breakfast £20 – £40
Suprême of wild salmon in a light creamy
Hollandaise sauce with chopped dill.
Fillet of halibut on a carrot and
coriander coulis. Medallions of venison
in a blackberry and malt whisky sauce.
STB Award Pending
Credit cards: 1, 3
Proprietors: Alan & Julie Reid

Tain

MAP 6

MORANGIE HOUSE HOTEL
Morangie Road, Tain
Ross-shire IV19 1PY
Tel: 0862 892281

Just off A9 Inverness-Wick.
A fine old Victorian mansion set in its
own beautifully kept grounds, close by
the shores of the Dornoch Firth, on the
northern outskirts of the Highland town
of Tain, Scotland's oldest Royal Burgh.
The hotel has been extensively
modernised but still maintains the
character of the building with its superb
collection of Victorian stained glass
windows. Award winning chefs prepare
meals unsurpassed in the area and served
by the friendly but efficient staff.
Open all year
Rooms: 13 with private facilities
Bar Lunch 12 – 2.30 pm (a)
*Dining Room/Restaurant Lunch 12 –
2 pm (b)*
Bar Supper 5 – 10 pm (a)
Dinner 7 – 10 pm (c)
No dogs
Bed & breakfast £32.50 – £50
Dinner B & B £49 – £66
*Mussel and onion stew. Salmon steak
poached in white wine served with a
lobster and prawn sauce. Slices of prime
Scottish fillet steak cooked in a Port wine
sauce.*
STB Commended 4 Crowns
Credit cards: 1, 2, 3, 5, 6
Proprietor: John Wynne

Tarbert

MAP 6

THE ANCHORAGE RESTAURANT
Quayside
Harbour Street, Tarbert
Argyll PA29 6UD
Tel: 0880 820881

Prestige Award Winner 1991

On A83 – situated on Tarbert quayside.
A small unpretentious but splendid little
bistro restaurant right on the quayside
and a great favourite of the sailing
fraternity. There is not too much elbow
room when it is busy but it does make for
atmosphere. The Anchorage specialises
in freshly caught fish and shellfish from
the local waters of Arran, Islay, Gigha

and Jura, and has a direct line to a
fishing boat that it may earmark its
requirement of the best of the day's
catch. Chef, Olivia Veiber, creates some
memorable dishes and the proprietor,
David Evamy, is an intriguing and attentive host in the restaurant. This should
be a 'must' for those in or near Tarbert.
Open Mar to Dec
*Dining Room/Restaurant Lunch
11.30 am – 2.30 pm (a)*
Dinner 6.45 – 10.30 pm (b-c)
Closed Sun Mon
Facilities for the disabled
*Seafood is the speciality of this restaurant,
all personally selected, direct from boat
and the quayside. Brought in from
Kintyre and the islands. Aberdeen Angus
beef. Vegetarian dishes available.*
Credit cards: 1, 3
Proprietors: David & Fiona Evamy

THE COLUMBA HOTEL
East Pier Road, Tarbert
Argyll PA29 6UF
Tel: 0880 820808

*On East Pier Road, 1/2 mile to the left
around the harbour.*
A family-run hotel in a listed Victorian
building splendidly positioned on the
loch side at the entrance to Tarbert
Harbour where there is always lots of
interest on the waterfront. There are fine
views over Loch Fyne and the hills start at
the back door. There are cosy bars
usually with log fires burning and there is
a sauna, mini gym and solarium.
Restaurant menus place much emphasis
on local produce with a leaning towards
traditional Scottish dishes and
imaginative preparation of other
specialities. As the hotel so delightfully
puts it "children and other pets are
especially welcome".
Open all year
Rooms: 11 , 9 with private facilities
Bar Lunch 12 – 2 pm (a)
*Dining Room/Restaurant Lunch 1 –
3 pm Sun only (a)*
Bar Supper 6 – 8 pm (a)
Dinner 7 – 9 pm (c)
No smoking in restaurant
Bed & breakfast £19.50 – £28.95
Dinner B & B £32.95 – £41.50
*Cullen skink. Medallions of Scottish beef
with Dunsyre Blue cheese and horseradish
sauce. Local wild salmon with fresh dill
and white wine sauce.*
STB Commended 3 Crowns
Credit cards: 1, 2, 3, 5
Proprietors: Gina & Bob Chicken

Thornhill

MAP 1

TRIGONY HOUSE HOTEL
Closeburn, Thornhill
Dumfriesshire DG3 5EZ
Tel: 0848 31211

*Off A76 south of Thornhill, 13 miles
north of Dumfries.*
Trigony House makes an excellent base
for exploring this magnificent
untouched part of Scotland. An
attractive country house hotel situated
just off A76 in over four acres of
secluded gardens and woodlands. The
hotel has a friendly and welcoming
atmosphere together with high standards
of comfort and hospitality. Children over
10 welcome.
Open all year except Christmas Day
Rooms: 9 with private facilities
Bar Lunch 12.30 – 2 pm (a)
Bar Supper 6.30 – 9 pm (a)
Dinner 7 – 8.30 pm (c)
No children under 10
Bed & breakfast £29 – £33.50
Dinner B & B £44 – £48.50
*Roast Galloway beef, local pheasant and
venison, Nith salmon.*
STB Commended 3 Crowns
Credit cards: 1, 3
Proprietors: Frank & Mary Kerr

Tillicoultry

MAP 4

HARVIESTOUN INN
Mains Farm, Tillicoultry
Clackmannanshire FK13 6PQ
Tel: 0259 52522
Fax: 0259 52523

*Just off A91 on eastern edge of
Tillicoultry.*
Transformations and restorations
sometimes do not succeed but this one
comes off brilliantly. The original
character of these old farm steadings has
not only been retained but enhanced.
The buildings form three sides of a
spacious cobbled courtyard with a
delightful elevated patio by the front
entrance. The warm stone frontage is
inviting but gives no clue to the
luxurious layout of the first floor
Brannigan's Brasserie, or the cosy
informality of the Coffee Bean Co coffee
shop and restaurant on the ground floor.
For those with celebration – or

conference – in mind, there is also the elegant Orchid Pavilion. The food is consistently reliable with a carefully balanced but not ridiculously extensive menu, and the presentation indicates experienced and caring chefs in the kitchen.

Open all year
Bar lunch 12 – 2.30 pm (a)
Dining Room/Restaurant Lunch 12 – 2.30 pm Mon to Sat: 12.30 – 3 pm Sun (a)
Bar Supper 5 – 8 pm (a)
Dinner 6.30 – 9 pm Mon to Sat (b–c): 5 – 8 pm Sun (b)
Facilities for the disabled
No smoking area in restaurant
Ravioli of wild mushrooms with chive butter sauce. Fillet of Aberdeen Angus in puff pastry with Perigourd sauce. Medley of steamed fish with lemon and dill sauce. Crème brûlée. Apple and raspberry crumble with a light custard sauce.
Credit cards: 1, 2, 3, 6
Proprietors: Kevin & Sheila Gilmartin

Tiree
Isle of

MAP 7

THE GLASSARY
Sandaig, Isle of Tiree
Argyll PA77 6XQ
Tel: 08792 684
On west coast of island.
Restaurant situated on the picturesque west coast of the island close to white, sandy beaches. Adjacent is the guest house which is all on one level and has a residents' lounge with TV, and tea/coffee-making facilities. The restaurant is a pine-lined converted byre with views of shore and Atlantic Ocean.

Open Easter to Oct
Rooms: 3
Dining Room/Restaurant Lunch 12 – 2 pm (a)
Dinner 7 – 9 pm (b-d)
Bed & breakfast from £15
Dinner B & B from £25
Extensive and imaginative à la carte menu, using Isle of Tiree reared beef and lamb, wild salmon from Mull and Atlantic seafood. Interesting sweet menu, features Carrageen pudding – a traditional island recipe, made from local seaweed.
No credit cards
Proprietors: Mabel & Donnie Macarthur

Tongue

MAP 6

THE BEN LOYAL HOTEL
Main Street, Tongue
Sutherland IV27 4XE
Tel: 0847 55 216
At junction of A838 and A836, mid-way between John o' Groats and Cape Wrath.
Standing in a splendid location overlooking the Kyle of Tongue, the peaks of 'The Queen of Scottish Mountains' and ruined Varrich Castle, this hotel seems to have been designed with the sole intention of enabling guests to enjoy these quite stunning panoramas from the comfortably furnished lounge to the beautifully appointed bedroons with their pine furniture, pretty fabrics and four poster beds. But perhaps the best views can be had from the dining room. However you will find your loyalties torn between relishing the view and savouring the food. Only fresh local produce – much of it home-grown – is used in the preparation of a largely traditional menu.

Open 15 Feb to 31 Dec except Christmas + Boxing Days
Rooms: 18 , 9 with private facilities
Bar Lunch 12 – 2 pm Mon to Sat: 12.30 – 2 pm Sun (a)
Dining Room/Restaurant Lunch – by prior arrangement only (b)
Bar Supper 6 – 8.20 pm Mon to Sat: 6.30 – 8.20 pm Sun (a)
Dinner 7 – 8.15 pm (b)
Facilities for the disabled
Bed & breakfast £16 – £30
Dinner B & B £28.50 – £42.50
Special rates for 3 or 7 nights available
Lentil soup. Suprême of local salmon with lemon and herb butter. Roast haunch of venison with Madeira and cranberry gravy. Bread and butter pudding.
STB Highly Commended 3 Crowns
Credit cards: 1, 3
Proprietors: Mel & Pauline Cook

Troon

MAP 1

HIGHGROVE HOUSE
Old Loans Road
Troon KA10 7HL
Tel: 0292 312511
Fax: 0292 318228
Off A759 near Loans.
If there are three key words in Bill Costley's vocabulary they must be quality, freshness and value. His acquisition and transformation of Highgrove House was an immediate success as he introduced his formula of the pick of the market's produce, beautifully prepared and presented and at remarkably modest prices. Success was well earned and the popularity and appeal of Highgrove has continued unabated. Perched high on a hilltop just outside Troon, with fine views out over the Firth of Clyde to Arran, the location could not be better for those who want to play golf at some of the world's premier courses, sail or fish, wander round the country of Rabbie Burns – or just relax and enjoy the excellent food.

Open all year
Rooms: 9 with private facilities
Bar Lunch 12 – 2.30 pm (a)
Dinner 6 – 9.30 pm (c)
Bed & breakfast from £49
Dinner B & B from £90
Warm salad of langoustines and red snapper with dill butter dressing. Steamed turbot with fresh asparagus, crab and orange mousseline.
Credit cards: 1, 2, 3
Proprietors: William & Catherine Costley

LOCHGREEN HOUSE
Monktonhill Road, Southwood
Troon KA10 7EN
Tel: 0292 313343
Fax: 0292 318661
A79 from Ayr, or A77 from Glasgow to roundabout near Prestwick Airport, take road for Troon (B749). Lochgreen is $^1/_2$ mile on left.
Lochgreen House in Southwood near Troon is a magnificent mansion built in 1905 surrounded by 15 acres of beautiful woodlands, gardens and private tennis court, and situated in the heart of Ayrshire's Burns Country. The hotel is privately owned and managed by one of Scotland's top chefs, Bill Costley, and his wife Catherine, and it naturally follows

▶

that the food is superb, beautifully prepared and presented, and outstanding value for money. It is little wonder that guests come from far and near to sample it and it is therefore always wise to book in advance. This is a hotel with every facility for a relaxing and comfortable stay.
Open all year
Rooms: 7 with private facilities
Dining Room/Restaurant Lunch 12 – 2.30 pm (a)
Dinner 7 – 9.30 pm (d)
No dogs
Facilities for the disabled
No smoking in restaurant
Bed & breakfast £49.50 – £89
Dinner B & B £60 – £75
Roast rack of Ayrshire lamb with creamed leeks and redcurrant sauce. Steamed Doon salmon with a lobster sauce.
Credit cards: 1, 2, 3
Proprietors: William & Catherine Costley

MARINE HIGHLAND HOTEL
Troon
Ayrshire KA10 6HE
Tel: 0292 314444 • Telex: 777595
Fax: 0292 316922
South end of Troon overlooking golf course and sea.
This magnificent four star hotel overlooks the 18th fairway of Royal Troon Championship Golf Course with breathtaking views across the Firth of Clyde to the Isle of Arran. An atmosphere of quiet elegance exists throughout the hotel combined with a standard of service and hospitality second to none. There are excellent leisure facilities within the Marine Leisure and Sports Club. A very special hotel which has admirably blended style and tradition with outstanding facilities.
Open all year
Rooms: 72 with private facilities
Crosbie's Brasserie open all day for meals and snacks
Bar Lunch 12 – 2.30 pm (a)
Dining Room/Restaurant Lunch 12.30 – 2 pm (b)
Bar Supper 6 – 10.30 pm (a)
Dinner 7 – 10 pm (c)
Bed & breakfast from £70
Dinner B & B from £65 (min 2 nights stay)
Wild boar, local wild salmon, fresh scallops, Scotch lamb, fresh vegetables.
STB Commended 5 Crowns
Credit cards: 1, 2, 3, 5, 6

PIERSLAND HOUSE HOTEL
Craigend Road, Troon
Ayrshire KA10 6HD
Tel: 0292 314747
Fax: 0292 315613
South corner of Troon.
Piersland House was built around 1899 for Sir Alexander Walker of Johnnie Walker whisky fame. It is set in four acres of grounds and gardens. The interior wood panelling is a special feature. The Tapestry Room is a country house style dining room decorated and furnished in keeping with the period nature of the Listed building. The hotel has always had a good reputation for its food.
Open all year
Rooms: 19 with private facilities
Bar Lunch 12 – 2.30 pm (a)
Dining Room/Restaurant Lunch 12 – 2.30 pm (a)
Bar Supper 7 – 9.30 pm (a)
Dinner 7 – 9.30 pm (c)
Bed & breakfast £43 – £53
Dinner B & B £61 – £71
Room Rate £36 – £59
Baked leg of lamb in a red wine and rosemary essence. Grilled rainbow trout on a bed of vegetables, served with parsley sauce. Selection of home-made desserts.
STB Commended 4 Crowns
Credit cards: 1, 2, 3, 5, 6

Turnberry

MAP 1

MALIN COURT HOTEL
Turnberry, Girvan
Ayrshire KA26 9PB
Tel: 0655 31457/8 • Fax: 0655 31072
On A719 Ayr-Girvan, south of Maidens.
Malin Court is situated between Ayr and Girvan, on the west coast of Scotland, and is an ideal base for touring the 'Burns Trail'. It is central to a lot of major golf courses, including the famous Turnberry. The restaurant, which has an excellent view of Arran and the hills beyond, offers both table d'hôte and full à la carte menus. A programme of development during 1992 has increased the hotel's accommodation to 17 rooms with private facilities.
Open all year
Rooms: 17 with private facilities
Bar Lunch 12.15 – 2.15 pm (a)
Dining Room/Restaurant Lunch 12.15 – 2.15 pm (b)
Afternoon Tea 2 – 5 pm
Bar Supper 5 – 9.30 pm (a)

Dinner 7.30 – 9.30 pm (c)
Bed & breakfast £45 – £55
Dinner B & B £55 – £65
Fresh local beef, lamb and pork, salmon and fresh sea produce.
STB Commended 4 Crowns
Credit cards: 1, 2, 3, 5, 6

TURNBERRY HOTEL, GOLF COURSES & SPA
Turnberry
Ayrshire KA26 9LT
Tel: 0655 31000 • Telex: 777779
Fax: 0655 31706

Prestige Award Winner 1990

A77 – 17 miles south of Ayr.
A magnificent hotel on a unique elevated site overlooking Scotland's south-west Ayrshire coast. Within its 360 acres are a luxury 132 bedroom hotel of international reputation, two championship golf courses, all weather tennis courts, conference suites and a splendid spa and leisure centre. The new golf clubhouse opens in May 1993 and will incorporate a restaurant on the first floor, with superb views over the 18th green of the Ailsa Championship golf course. This is a hotel where elegance and gracious service are obvious throughout, and especially so in the superb restaurants renowned for their food, and where a meal looking out over Ailsa Craig and Arran, becomes an unforgettable occasion. Awarded RAC five star Hotel of the Year 1990.
Open all year
Rooms: 132 with private facilities
Bar Meals (Clubhouse Restaurant) 8 am – 8 pm Summer: 8am – 6 pm Winter (b)
Lunch (Bay at Turnberry Restaurant) 12 – 4 pm (c)
Dining Room/Restaurant Lunch (Hotel) 1 – 2.30 pm Sun only (c)
Dinner (Bay at Turnberry Restaurant) 6 – 10 pm (f)
Dinner (Hotel Restaurant) 7.30 – 10 pm (f)
Bed & breakfast £75 – £97.50
Lobster and scampi terrine flavoured with Cognac. Suprême of halibut oven baked with a dill brioche crust, served with a thyme sauce. Roast rack of lamb with baby vegetables, redcurrants and mint flavoured pan juices. Loin of venison with skirlie, on a peppered game sauce with buttered blueberries.
Credit cards: 1, 2, 3, 5, 6

Tyndrum

MAP 4

CLIFTON COFFEE HOUSE & CRAFT CENTRE

Tyndrum
Perthshire FK20 8RY
Tel: 08384 271
Fax: 08384 330

On A85 just east of junction with A82.
A popular staging post at the eastern end of Glen Coe. A family run roadside restaurant and shopping complex surrounded by scenic splendour. The busy self-service restaurant has special facilities for the disabled and there are adjacent speciality shops in which to browse. Renovations taking place over Winter 1992 will provide extended facilities for the 1993 season.
Open mid Mar to late Dec
Meals and snacks served all day from end Mar to end Dec (a)
No smoking area in restaurant
No dogs except guide dogs
Fresh local produce, vegetables, salmon, brought together to give good food at budget prices.
Credit cards: 1, 2, 3, 5
Proprietors: L P Gosden,
D D, L V & I L Wilkie

Udny Station

MAP 5

MUFFIN & CRUMPET BISTRO

Main Street, Udny Station Village
Aberdeenshire AB41 0QJ
Tel: 06513 2210
Fax: 06513 2965

From Bridge of Don boundary, 8 miles on B999 to Tarves, ¹/₂ mile off this road up into village. Or off A92 Aberdeen-Ellon, 4 miles on Culter Cullen Village road.
An interesting conversion of what had been a row of shops, with an equally interesting concept inside. The split level room retains its old pine panelling and has pretty wallpaper on the ceiling and lots of memorabilia on the high shelf. Peter and Marilyn Rattray have created a style of their own with some unusual combinations of food utilising muffins and crumpets in many dishes. Children are made specially welcome and there is special provision and a special menu for them. This is an establishment that will appeal to all tastes and overall an

enterprising business that seems likely to expand. Bookings are advisable, especially at weekends.
Open all year except Christmas Day, 1 Jan + last 2 wks Jan
Dining Room/Restaurant Lunch available for group bookings only
Dinner 6.30 – 9 pm except Mon Tue; later Sat (a-b)
Closed Mon
Booking advisable
Table licence
Trout fillet poached in a whisky and ginger court bouillon served with a little salad. Mussels with wine, onion, garlic and cream, served with crusty bread. Fillet steak with a toasted oatmeal topping, finished in a red wine, black peppercorn and mushroom sauce.
Credit cards: 1, 3
Proprietors: Marilyn & Peter Rattray

Uphall

MAP 4

HOUSTOUN HOUSE HOTEL & RESTAURANT

Uphall
West Lothian EH52 6JS
Tel: 0506 853831
Fax: 0506 854220

Just off A89 Edinburgh-Bathgate at Uphall.
The core of this hotel is the old 16th century Tower House, of which the vaulted bar with its great open fireplace is the most striking reminder. Over the years the building has been adapted and extended to provide the comfortable hotel accommodation which is a feature of today. Three adjacent dining rooms on the first floor provide flexibility and create an atmosphere of quietness and intimacy – so much better than one large room. There are 26 acres of grounds, and herbs and vegetables for the kitchen are grown in the garden. Well balanced menus change daily; food is interesting and well presented and there is an extensive and carefully chosen wine list – and a fine range of malt whiskies.
Open all year
Rooms: 30 with private facilities
Bar Lunch 12 – 2 pm (a)
Dining Room/Restaurant Lunch 12.30 – 2 pm except Sat (c)
Dinner 7.30 – 9.30 pm (e)
No smoking dining room available
Bed & breakfast £55 – £90

Dinner B & B £45 – £120 (weekend break)
Crayfish and scallops with a leek tartlet on a basil flavoured sauce. Creative desserts.
STB Commended 4 Crowns
Credit cards: 1, 2, 3, 5

Walkerburn

MAP 2

TWEED VALLEY HOTEL & RESTAURANT

Walkerburn
nr Peebles EH43 6AA
Tel: 089 687 636
Fax: 089 687 639

A72 at Walkerburn – 7 miles east of Peebles and 7 miles west of Galashiels. 32 miles south of Edinburgh.
Built in 1906 by Henry Ballantyne as a wedding present for his son, the present day Tweed Valley Hotel retains much of the original character of the building with its oak panelling, carvings and an ornate dining room ceiling. The hotel overlooks the River Tweed and has scenic views of the hills. It has its own walled garden which produces vegetables and herbs, and the recent acquisition of a smoker means home-smoked products now feature on the menus. An ideal base for sightseeing, golf and country pursuits, including fishing and bird-watching.
Open all year except Christmas + Boxing Days
Rooms: 15 with private facilities
Bar Lunch 12 – 2 pm (a)
Dining Room/Restaurant Lunch 12 – 2 pm (a)
Bar Supper 6.30 – 8.30 pm (a)
Dinner 7 – 8.30 pm (c)
No smoking in restaurant
Bed & breakfast £40 – £55
Dinner B & B £45.50 – £59
Trout, salmon, venison and game dishes including grouse, pheasant, duck in season and as available.
STB Commended 4 Crowns
Credit cards: 1, 3
Proprietor: Charles Miller

West Linton

MAP 2

THE LEADBURN INN
Leadburn, West Linton
Peeblesshire EH46 7BE
Tel: 0968 72952

On the junction of A701, A702 and A720.

Small family run hotel, set in beautiful countryside between Edinburgh and the Borders. One of the oldest inns in Scotland – records date back to August 1777. A menu which is as extensive as any in the Borders is served all day, every day in the lounge, the conservatory or the bar. In the evening dinner is served in the attractive Carriage Restaurant – a luxuriously converted railway carriage. Carefully planned table d'hôte menu includes a selection of traditional Scottish dishes.

Open all year except Christmas + Boxing Days, 1 + 2 Jan
Rooms: 6 , 2 with private facilities
Bar Meals 12 – 10 pm (a-b)
Dinner 6 – 10 pm (b)
Bed & breakfast £20 – £25
Dinner B & B £28 – £40
Border game pie. Roast rack of Border lamb with a light heather honey and mint glaze. Smoked haddock crumble.
Credit cards: 1, 2, 3, 5, 6
Proprietors: Linda & Alan Thomson

Whitebridge

MAP 6

KNOCKIE LODGE
Whitebridge
Inverness-shire IV1 2UP
Tel: 045 63 276

Prestige Award Winner 1990

On B862, 8 miles north of Fort Augustus. 26 miles south of Inverness.
For those who like to really get away from it all there are few more blissful spots than this delightful country house hotel in idyllic countryside high above Loch Ness. Formerly a shooting lodge, Ian and Brenda Milward have converted and furnished it with great attention to the comfort and well-being of their guests. Bedrooms are splendidly appointed and the excellent public rooms include a reading/writing room and a billiard room. Menus change daily and the food is of exceptionally high standard. A stay here is a special experience and will make you reluctant to return to the bustle of everyday life.

Open 2 May to 24 Oct
Rooms: 10 with private facilities
Bar Lunch 12.30 – 1.45 pm for residents only
Dinner at 8 pm (d)

Note: dinner for non-residents by prior arrangement only
Restricted licence
No smoking in dining room
Dinner B & B £62 – £95
Brochette of langoustine with a tomato coulis. Gressingham duck breast with apples and a Port wine sauce. Roast lamb fillet with a kidney and mushroom stuffing. Gooseberry ice-cream with nutty curls.
STB Deluxe 3 Crowns
Credit cards: 1, 2, 3, 5, 6
Proprietors: Ian & Brenda Milward

THE TASTE OF SCOTLAND

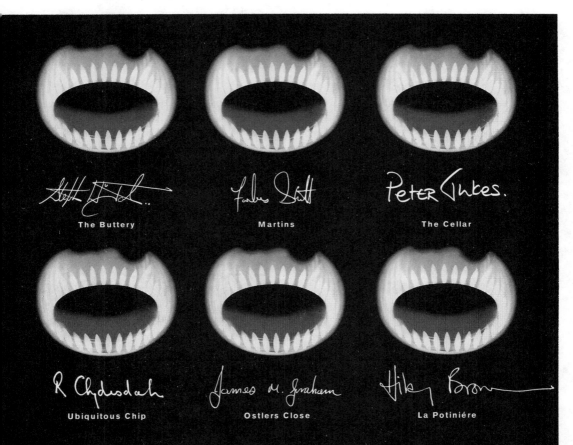

The Buttery

Martins

The Cellar

Ubiquitous Chip

Ostlers Close

La Potiniére

More top chefs are at home on our range.

There's one ingredient most top chefs recommend: controllable, economical gas.

And British Gas in Scotland has a whole menu of ways to get you cooking. Just call our Industrial and Commercial Sales Department on 031 559 5000.

Don't y<u>ou</u> just love being in control.

British Gas
Scotland

EXPRESS FOODSERVICE

Unit E, Fallside Road, Bothwell,
Lanarkshire G71 8HB
Telephone 0698-817326

Suppliers of:

CHEESE, BUTTER, OTHER CHILLED DAIRY PRODUCTS TO CATERERS, CASH & CARRYS & WHOLESALERS

see entry page 63

The air of a dream seems to haunt this mansion house, set amidst wild cherry trees, against the imposing backdrop of the Ochil Hills. The Gean has been caringly reappointed to the grandeur of its halcyon days when dinner parties in the magnificent walnut panelled dining room and conversations echoing in the vaulted ceiling of the Boardroom and Grand hall would breathe life into the serene opulence of this beautiful country home.

The luxury guest bedrooms retain an air of individuality with a dignified sense of a common heritage.

Magnificent Discoveries

Although the beauty of the building and the grand setting is an aesthetic feast for the soul, the Gean's reputation for fine contemporary continental cuisine and traditional Scottish country-house fare completes the cycle!

We would like to share some of this with you soon.

THE GEAN HOUSE

GEAN PARK ALLOA SCOTLAND FK10 2HS TELEPHONE: 0259 219275 FAX: 0259 213827
RATED AMONG THE TOP 10 SCOTTISH HOTELS BY THE EGON RONAY GUIDE.

see entry page 42

EST.1775

Scotland's Oldest Distillery
& Award-Winning Visitor Centre
Crieff, Perthshire

☆ Guided Tour and Audio-Visual Presentation, 3-D Exhibition.

☆ FREE taste of The Glenturret Single Highland Malt Scotch Whisky.

☆ Whisky Tasting Bar-taste older Glenturret 8, 12, 15, 21 years old and The Glenturret Malt Liqueur.

☆ Smugglers Restaurant and Pagoda Room, Caithness Glass Taste of Scotland Prestige Award.

☆ Whisky and souvenir shop.

☆ One of Scotland's top attractions.

OPEN

MARCH TO DECEMBER
Monday to Saturday 9.30 am to 4.30 pm
Sundays 12 noon to 4.30pm

JANUARY & FEBRUARY
Monday to Friday 11.30 am to 2.30 pm

GLENTURRET DISTILLERY LIMITED

THE HOSH, CRIEFF, PERTHSHIRE, PH7 4HA. TELEPHONE 0764-2424 (8 LINES) FACSIMILE 0764-4366

INVERARAY JAIL

Open every day

**Winner of
the 'Europa Nostra Silver Medal of Honour' and
'The Best Scottish Attraction of the Decade'**

Experience 19th Century prison life with guides dressed as Warders, Prisoners & Matron.

Torture death & damnation exhibition.

Sit & listen to trials in the 1820 Courtroom among lifelike models.

Try the Cranking Machine, Whipping Table, Hammocks & take a stroll in the Prison Exercise Yard.

Translations & Guide Books are available in French, German & Italian.

Superb selection of books, Scottish crafts & many unusual souvenir items.

Tel 0499-2381 • Fax 0499-2195

If you're looking for good food, our world is your oyster.

The Highlands and Islands of Scotland is one of the best eating places on earth. The unspoilt environment helps to create not only the finest local produce, but the freshest too. While spectacular scenery provides the perfect place setting.

And no matter where you go, from village tea-room to up-market restaurant, a rare blend of proud heritage and traditional warmth is sure to await you.

Highlands & Islands
OF SCOTLAND

Millport

Goatfell from Brodick

Rhu, Gareloch

Sunset over Arran from Largs

Cassillis Castle, nr Maybole

Dunure Castle, Ayrshire

Scott's View, Borders

Peebles, Borders

Kelso, Borders

Abbotsford, Borders

When quality counts - only Scotch Beef and Lamb will do

Prime quality beef and lamb from Scotland

Taste of Scotland
Scotch Lamb Challenge

Scotch Lamb
So creative and versatile

The delicate taste and flavour of Scotch lamb has long been recognised by caterers as perhaps the finest in the world, and now thanks to schemes such as Farm Assured Scotch Lamb and Quality Assured Scotch Lamb, the wholesomeness and quality is guaranteed.

The Taste of Quality

Last year saw the introduction of an exciting and prestigious recipe competition, run by the Scotch Quality Beef and Lamb Association in conjunction with the Taste of Scotland Scheme Ltd, open to all cooks and chefs employed by Taste of Scotland members.

Entrants were required to devise their own three course meal (starter, main course and dessert) using original recipes, with Scotch lamb as the main course.

The winner of the 1992 Taste of Scotland Scotch Lamb Challenge was William T Gibb, Executive Chef from Thainstone House Hotel, with Bruce Price of St Andrews Old Course Hotel in second place and Nicola Braidwood of Murrayshall Country House Hotel in third.

The standard of entries received from both large and small establishments was extremely high and the use of Scotch lamb cuts in the recipes both innovative and exciting.

In the recipe section which follows you will find the lamb recipes from the six finalists in the 1992 competition.

The competition is now an annual event.

Why not try Scotch lamb dishes on the menu next time you visit a Taste of Scotland establishment and experience for yourself the Taste of Quality.

Picture shows in centre William T Gibb of Thainstone House Hotel – winner of the 1992
Taste of Scotland Scotch Lamb Challenge – with Bruce Price of St Andrews Old Course
Hotel (left) and Nicola Braidwood of Murrayshall Country House Hotel (right).

The Taste of Scotland
Scotch Lamb
Challenge Winner:

William T Gibb,
Executive Chef,
Thainstone House
Hotel & Country
Club,
Inverurie

Roasted Loin of Scotch Lamb
with wild mushroom mousse on a rosti potato,
rosemary sauce with flageolets, carrots and button onions

Ingredients

2 Best Ends of Lamb, c. 2½ lbs, bone in

Wild Mushroom Mousse
5 oz chicken breast
4 oz wild mushrooms
2 sprigs tarragon and basil
1 egg
5 fl oz double cream
Seasoning

Rosemary Sauce
1½ pints brown veal stock
Lamb bones
2 oz mirepoix of vegetables
Clove of garlic
2 fl oz white wine
2 fl oz Madeira wine
Sprig of rosemary
2 tablespoons double cream
1 oz butter

Accompanying Vegetables
7 oz potatoes
2 fl oz olive oil
2 oz flageolet beans
4 oz carrots
4 oz button onions
2 oz wild mushrooms
2 oz clarified butter

4 herb bouquets to garnish

(Serves four)

Method

1. Bone out best of lamb, remove all fat and sinews. Cut into 4 equal portions, seal off quickly in oil then allow to cool.

2. Finely chop lamb bones to make sauce.

3. Blend chicken breasts in food processor and pass through a fine sieve into a clean bowl over ice. Add the egg and seasoning, then gradually add the double cream with chopped tarragon, basil and diced wild mushrooms.

4. Pipe mousse on top of each portion, wrap with greased tin foil, then place in refrigerator.

5. Sweat down lamb bones, mirepoix of vegetables, deglaze with white wine and Madeira, and reduce. Add veal stock and rosemary then simmer gently for 15-20 minutes, skimming all the time. Pass through a fine muslin into a clean pan.

6. Prepare all vegetables ready for service. Blanch flageolet beans, cut carrots into 12 spheres, trim wild mushrooms, and roast button onions until golden brown.

7. Grate potatoes, sweat down with clarified butter and a little water for 4 minutes. Drain in colander then cook in 4 lightly greased rosti moulds until crisp and golden brown.

8. Roast the lamb portions at GM5/190C/375F for 6 minutes. Remove tin foil, glaze under grill until mousse is golden brown. Rest on a cooking rack before service.

9. Bring sauce to first boil and finish with cream and hard butter.
Re-heat vegetable garnish with trimmed wild mushrooms.

To serve

10. Place rosti potato in centre of each plate, crown with roasted loin of lamb. Arrange carrot spheres, wild mushrooms, button onions, flageolet beans around each portion. Finish with sauce and herb bouquet.

Loin of Scotch Lamb

surrounded by sweetbreads and parsley in puff pastry and a feuillette with leek and sautéd kidney, on an Arran Mustard and basil sauce

Second Place:

Bruce Price,
Sous Chef,
St Andrews Old
Course Hotel,
St Andrews

Ingredients

1 lb loin of lamb	1½ bunches baby carrots
4 oz lamb's sweetbreads	2 yellow courgettes
4 oz lamb's kidney	4 white turnip
1 oz Scottish dairy butter	¼ oz oyster mushrooms
4 oz puff pastry	½ bunch asparagus
1 bunch flat parsley	30 snow peas
3 eggs	12 baby corn
4 fl oz cream	4 spring onions
2 sticks leek	¼ oz carrot
¼ packet basil	¼ oz celery
½ oz lamb strips	2 tomatoes
2 fl oz sunflower oil	¼ oz onion
2 fl oz olive oil	1 litre lamb stock
2 oz potatoes	salt and pepper
3 red peppers	1 teaspoon Arran mustard
4 baby tomatoes	

(Serves four)

Method

1. The 4 portions of loin should weigh around 4 oz each. After being trimmed with all fat removed, season lamb with salt and pepper. Cook in a hot pan with sunflower oil, this should only take 3 minutes each side.

2. Prepare scrambled egg with cream and season well.

3. Sweat off finely diced shallot, add coarsely chopped parsley. Sweat off for 10-15 minutes. Steam with a little lamb stock, season with salt.

4. Blanch the sweetbreads, cool, then remove the fatty parts and fibres. Break up the sweetbreads into pieces. Place frying pan on stove, add a little oil and butter then sauté the sweetbreads. Add sweet basil. Allow to cool.

5. Roll out puff pastry thinly. Place sweetbreads, parsley, egg and red pepper, top with lamb loin and place same on top. Cover well with parsley. Refrigerate for half an hour.

6. Wash leeks well and cut to julienne. Peel and wash potatoes, cut to julienne then mix with leeks and season with salt and pepper. Dry potatoes mix, pan-fry and mix into circular shapes, lightly brown in colour.

7. Bake loin of lamb in oven for 10 minutes.

8. Trim kidney of any fat, pan-fry in olive oil for 2 minutes each side, then 4 minutes in oven. Remove from pan and keep warm – should be pink in the middle.

9. Add remainder of oil to pan, add white wine, glaze lamb stock, pass sauce through fine strainer then add Arran mustard and chopped basil. Finally whisk in butter to finish sauce.

Accompanying vegetables

10. Potatoes cocotte – to cook roast in clarified butter; oyster mushrooms – sauté in pan of butter. Blanch all vegetables (baby corn, baby carrot, baby tomato, snow peas, asparagus and white turnips) in seasoned water separately and refresh. Peel skin off all tomatoes, finish baby corn in a little touch of butter. Glaze vegetables, season to taste with salt and milled pepper. Leek rosti – keep warm in oven for 1 minute.

To serve

11. Slice lamb into 3 pieces, sit beside the leek. Warm up the kidney and sauce, layer with the leek in centre of the plate. Arrange the vegetables around the top of the plate, then pour the sauce at the bottom of the plate next to the lamb.

Third Place:

Nicola Braidwood,
Senior Chef de Partie,
Murrayshall Country
House Hotel,
Scone, nr Perth

A Buttery Puff Pastry Casket
with a rich lamb casserole enhanced with rosemary and red wine

Ingredients

Casserole

2 lb scrag, diced and fat removed*
1 lb shin meat, diced*
1 clove garlic, finely chopped
2 sprigs fresh rosemary
2 oz butter
1 onion, chopped
2 rashers streaky bacon, chopped
2-3 tablespoons flour
1 pint jellied lamb stock
1 tablespoon tomato puree
4 oz lamb's kidneys, trimmed and diced
4 oz lamb's sweetbreads, peeled

Marinade

1 clove garlic, finely chopped
½ bottle full bodied red wine
Seasoning

Vegetables

12 baby carrots
12 baby turnips
12 baby leeks
12 roast shallots
8 oz spinach, blanched
Sugar

1 lb home-made butter puff pastry, cut into four 2½ inch squares or circles.
Egg wash

*Preparation: marinate the prepared scrag and shin meat.

(Serves four)

Method

1. Drain off the marinade and reserve until later. Pat dry any excess liquid off the diced lamb.

2. Heat heavy bottomed pan or casserole dish, then add the butter. Add the lamb and fry quickly getting a golden even brownness. Add the garlic, onion and bacon and continue to brown.

3. Add the flour and cook out for a few minutes then add the tomato purée and fresh rosemary, then the reserved marinade. Simmer and reduce then add required amount of stock.

4. Leave to simmer on a very low heat half covered for 1-1½ hours. When cooked add the kidney and sweetbreads.

5. Puff pastry caskets should be brushed with egg wash and lids scored out, then baked at GM7/220C/425F for 10-15 minutes until lightly golden and well risen. Once baked the lids should be taken off and the centre of the casket scooped out.

6. Brown shallots, add a little salt, sugar and lamb stock then reduce.

7. The baby vegetables should be cooked ready to re-heat in boiling water and butter. Blanch spinach ready to sauté in butter.

To serve

8. Place the casket in the centre of the plate and fill the bottom with the sautéd spinach, then fill with the lamb casserole and place the lid on it. The vegetables and shallots to be placed around the plate in a scattered fashion.

Roast Loin of Scotch Lamb

*served with a ragout of globe artichokes and spinach layered between
crisp potato cakes, and an Arran Mustard sauce*

Runner-up:

Colin Woodward,
Demi Chef de Partie,
Westerwood Golf &
Country Club,
Cumbernauld

Ingredients

1 double best end of lamb
4 globe artichokes
1 lemon
1 lb spinach, cleaned
4 potatoes, peeled
1 oz rosemary
10 fl oz Port
2 pints jus
1 bulb garlic
4 shallots
5 fl oz cream
4 oz wild mushrooms (chanterelles)
8 oz butter
10 fl oz virgin olive oil
4 oz redcurrants
Arran mustard

(Serves four)

Method

1. Remove loins and trim, keeping trimmings and bones for sauce.

2. Marinate and leave.

3. Prepare artichokes and cook in a white stock.

4. Blanch spinach and refresh.

5. Grate potatoes for potato cakes, season and pat dry.

6. Prepare sauce by browning bones and trimmings with shallots, garlic and rosemary stalks. Deglaze, add jus and reduce to desired consistency.

7. Pan-fry potato cakes and keep warm.

8. Prepare and wash wild mushrooms.

9. Cook lamb pink and leave to rest while preparing artichokes and spinach.

10. Place potato in bottom of ring, add artichoke and spinach. Mix and put rosti on top.

To serve

11. Slice and arrange lamb.

12. Quickly sauté chanterelles. Place on top. Finish sauce and pour round.

Runner-up:

David J Hunt,
Head Chef,
Murrayshall Country
House Hotel,
Scone, nr Perth

Braised Stuffed Neck of Scotch Lamb

enhanced with red wine and Madeira, and scented with
Garden Tarragon

Ingredients

2 necks of Scotch lamb, boned
4 cloves of garlic
6 juniper berries
1 bayleaf
4-6 fresh plum tomatoes
4 oz haricot blanc beans (soaked)
2-3 pints jellied brown lamb stock
1 bunch tarragon
1 glass red wine
1 glass Madeira
6 oz mirepoix (celery, carrot, onion)
3 oz pork belly
1½-2 oz plain flour
1 tablespoon tomato puree
2 free range eggs
4 oz white breadcrumbs
2 oz lamb fat
2 oz clarified butter
2 shallots, peeled
2 oz mixed wild mushrooms
1 oz balsamic vinegar
½ oz brown sugar

Vegetables

12 baby turnips
12 baby carrots
12 shallots
12 new potatoes
12 baby leeks

(Serves four)

Method

1. Trim any excess fat off necks of lamb.

2. Sweat diced shallots, garlic, mushrooms and tarragon in butter until soft, add breadcrumbs and cook out. Cool then add egg and mix.

3. Stuff the necks, season and tie.

4. Seal necks in braising pan, remove and add half pork belly, tomato puree and three-quarters of mirepoix. Fry until caramelised and browned.

5. Add flour and cook out, then add bay leaf, tarragon, tomatoes, juniper, garlic, wines and gradually the stock.

6. Bring to the boil, add necks and cook until tender.

7. Cook haricot blanc with remainder of pork belly and mirepoix until just underdone.

8. Prepare vegetables and reserve, use any trimming for braise.

9. Remove necks when ready, pour sauce through muslin and check consistency.

10. Add some haricot blanc and chopped tarragon to sauce and reserve some for garnish.

11. Blanch vegetables and lightly caramelise with brown sugar, balsamic vinegar and butter.

To serve

12. Carve and present lamb with vegetables and finish with sauce.

Rack of Perthshire Lamb

with woodland mushrooms and goats cheese on a pear
and potato rosti with a sherry reduction

Runner-up:

Stephen Robertson,
Head Chef,
Ballathie House
Hotel,
Kinclaven, nr Perth

Ingredients

4 portions rack of lamb
6 oz woodland mushrooms
4 slices goats cheese

Potato Rosti

2 potatoes
1 pear
1 egg yolk
1 sprig of mint
2 oz butter

Sherry Reduction

1 pint lamb stock
1 measure Sherry
2 oz redcurrant jelly
2 oz butter
4 oz mushrooms
12 shallots
1 lb lamb bones
8 oz mirepoix of vegetables

Vegetables

1½ lbs baby vegetables

Seasoning

(Serves four)

Method

1. Prepare and portion lamb. Roast the bones and trimmings in the oven until brown.

2. Grate potato and pear together. Add egg yolk, butter and mint. Pan-fry with oil in a round cutter until golden brown.

3. Remove bones from oven, add to pan with lamb stock, sherry, jelly, mirepoix of vegetables, mushrooms and seasoning. Reduce down for half an hour. Pass through muslin and hold.

4. Pan-fry the lamb and cook out in the oven. Meantime sauté the woodland mushrooms and blanch vegetables. Remove lamb from oven, crown with woodland mushrooms and glaze with goats cheese.

To serve

5. Serve on top of the potato rosti with sauce around the outside with baby vegetables.

from George McKay,
Executive Chef,
Balbirnie House,
nr Glenrothes

Macallan Smoked Salmon Salad
with toasted brioche and brown butter vinaigrette

Ingredients

Allow 1½ oz of thinly sliced smoked salmon per person
Mixed lettuces – mache, frisée, bibb, spinach etc
2 toasted brioche triangles per person
red onion, finely diced
capers, chopped
parsley, chopped
creme fraiche

Brown Butter Vinaigrette

8 oz butter
2 shallots, minced
1 clove of garlic, minced
Freshly squeezed juice of ½ lemon
1 teaspoon Dijon mustard
2 measures Macallan malt whisky
2 sprigs of thyme, chopped
1 teaspoon vegetable oil

(Serves eight)

Method

1. Prepare brown butter vinaigrette by cooking butter 'a noisette'.
   Pour over shallots and garlic, and stir well to prevent scorching.

2. Add lemon juice, Dijon mustard and Macallan malt whisky.
   Slowly whip in vegetable oil. The vinaigrette should emulsify, if it does not, egg yolks may be used. Finish with thyme, salt and white pepper. Hold at room temperature.

To serve

3. Spread brioche with black pepper and creme fraiche. Arrange a few salad leaves over and top with smoked salmon slices rolled into curls. Sprinkle plate with diced onion, capers and parsley, then spoon three pools of brown butter vinaigrette around the salmon.

Salmon Alexander

from Michael Alexander, Head Chef, Morangie House Hotel, Tain

Ingredients

Sauce

4 x 8 oz salmon steaks
3 glasses white wine
2 lemons, quartered
1 bay leaf
1 oz black peppercorns
Parsley for garnish

1 lb lobster, shell split,
claws cracked, grey sac
removed
2 tablespoons flour
3 fl oz Sherry
10 fl oz single cream
½ teaspoon salt
¼ teaspoon black pepper
½ teaspoon French mustard
5 fl oz double cream
1 tablespoon lemon juice
1 teaspoon cayenne pepper

(Serves 4)

Method

1. Pre-heat oven GM4/180C/350F.
2. Poach salmon steaks in the oven in a deep tray in the white wine, lemon quarters, black peppercorns and bay leaf for 25 minutes.

Sauce

3. While salmon is cooking, remove meat and coral from the shells and claws of the lobster.
4. Chop lobster meat finely and leave aside.
5. Sauté lobster meat in butter for 2-3 minutes.
6. Remove from heat and stir in flour. Gradually add Sherry, single cream, cayenne, salt, pepper and mustard. Set aside.
7. Blend double cream and coral together with a fork then add to lobster mixture with the lemon juice.
8. Skin and bone the hot salmon and gradually heat sauce. NB do not boil sauce.
9. Pour sauce over salmon steaks, garnish with parsley and serve immediately.

from Brian Graham
Head Chef,
Gleddoch House,
Langbank

Poached Fillet of Brill
with a light orange and watercress sauce

Ingredients

4 fillets of brill
Seasoning
1½ oranges
zest of ½ orange
1 measure white wine
1 spoonful fish glace
2 shallots
2 oz butter
3 oz watercress
3 fl oz fish stock
15 fl oz double cream
5 fl oz whipped cream
2 egg yolks

(Serves four)

Method

1. Bat out fillets lightly and tressle each one.
   Season fish.

2. Melt butter and add half the shallots. Place on fish then add half the white wine and enough fish stock to just cover the fillets.

3. Bring to the boil and place in the oven GM6/200C/400F.

4. While fish is cooking, melt butter in pan, add remaining shallots, some watercress leaves, orange juice and reduce.

5. Add rest of white wine and glace to sauce, and reduce.

6. Take fish from the oven.

7. Put stock from fish on to reduce.

8. When sauce has reduced, add cream and seasoning, bring to correct consistency.

9. Place a few orange segments in sauce.

10. Remove reduced sauce from stove. Add whipped cream and egg yolks, and mix.

To serve

11. Place sauce on bottom of 4 plates, glaze under grill.

12. Place fillet of fish onto plate and garnish with fleuron, orange zest and segments, and leaf of watercress.

A Timbale of Salmon and Scallops
on a tomato and Pastis essence

from Jo Queen,
Executive Chef,
Craigendarroch Hotel
& Country Club,
Ballater

Ingredients

6 oz scallops
4 oz salmon
3 tomatoes
½ measure Pernod
2 oz spinach leaves
½ oz tarragon leaves
3 egg whites
Seasoning
1 measure Chablis
4 slices smoked salmon
Pinch of cayenne
1 clove garlic
1 pint double cream
Juice of ¼ lemon
2 oz shallots
Unsalted butter
4 pastry fleurons
Parsley

(Serves four)

Method

1. Trim and cut salmon and half the scallops into ¼ inch dice.
    Blend with shallots, cayenne, clove of garlic, egg whites, finely chopped spinach and some tarragon leaves.

2. Season then add in a touch of Pernod and lemon juice. Proceed to blend well in machine to a purée. Add some cream to give right colour and texture, then leave aside.

3. Cut rest of scallops into three and sauté in a little butter.
    Season well and remove from pan.

4. Add in Pernod and flambé, then white wine and reduce by half.
    Add tarragon leaves and double cream and leave to reduce by side of stove.

5. Blanch tomatoes and skin, de-seed and cut into fine dice.

6. Place fish mousse into 4 dariole moulds lined with smoked salmon. Place a little of the sautéd scallops and dice of tomato into centre, fill with rest of mousse and cover with grease-proof paper. Poach off in bain-marie for 12-14 minutes.

7. Add rest of diced tomatoes to sauce and check consistency. Finish with butter, napper sauce onto plate.

8. Place on poached mousse, add garnish with a sprig of tarragon and fleuron.

from Tom Brown,
Executive Chef,
Moat House
International,
Glasgow

Nage of Langoustines and Scallops
flavoured with cardamom and asparagus tips
garnished with an inkfish risotto

Ingredients

12 langoustines, cleaned and shelled
12 scallops, removed from shell
8 green cardamom pods, seeded
12 asparagus tips, cooked
8 pieces filo pastry, cut into 4 inch squares
2 pints fish stock
4 fl oz whipping cream
4 oz unsalted butter
4 oz long grain rice
2 sachets squid ink
4 oz shallots, finely diced
Chervil sprigs to garnish
Salt and pepper

(Serves four)

Method

Risotto

1. Melt some butter in a pan and gently cook off the diced shallots, add the rice and stir for a minute or two. Add 1 pint of the fish stock and squid ink and cover. Gently cook till rice is ready, season and reserve.

Filo pastry basket

2. Butter pastry squares and fold them over a dariole mould. Cook in a hot oven until crisp. Reserve.

Nage

3. Gently cook the langoustines and scallops in the fish stock.
   Remove and keep warm.

4. Add the cardamom and reduce. Pass stock through sieve, add cream and reheat. Add butter when boiled.

To serve

5. Arrange scallops and langoustines in a warm soup plate with filo basket in centre filled with risotto.

6. Heat asparagus and arrange round basket.

7. Spoon over fish stock and garnish with chervil. Serve warm with granary bread and butter.

Crofters Chicken with a Skirlie Coat

from Alan Hill,
Executive Chef,
The Gleneagles Hotel,
Auchterarder

Ingredients

4 x 4 oz chicken breasts
Salt and freshly ground pepper
3 oz Tain crowdie cream cheese
2 oz woodland mushrooms
1 fl oz honey
2 oz chicken mousse
1 oz chopped tarragon
¼ oz sage mustard
3 oz flaked toasted oatmeal flakes
2 oz breadcrumbs
2 eggs
1 oz flour
2 oz butter
2 fl oz oil

Chicken mousse
(makes c. 8 oz)

3 oz minced chicken breast
1 egg white
salt + freshly ground pepper
1 fl oz white wine
5 fl oz double cream
cayenne

(Serves four)

Method

1. Chicken Mousse:
   Place cooked chicken breast into stainless steel bowl set on a container of crushed ice. Allow mixture to cool, then beat in egg white thoroughly with a wooden spoon.

2. Once mixture is stiff, gradually add white wine and season.

3. Slowly add double cream to form the mousse. Pass through a fine sieve and check seasoning and consistency. Keep cool and use as required.

4. To complete dish:
   Place the crowdie cheese and chicken mousse into a stainless steel bowl.

5. Add the cooked woodland mushrooms along with the honey, mustard and chopped tarragon.

6. Bind well together and check the taste for seasoning.

7. Stuff the chicken breasts and cover in the skirlie coat.

8. Cook in the oil and butter until golden brown.

9. Remove, dry and allow to cool.

10. Slice to serve.

from John Winton,
Head Chef,
Fouters Bistro
Restaurant,
Ayr

Trio of Pigeon Breast
with a Port and fruit glaze

Ingredients

6 pairs of pigeon breasts, skinned
(retain carcases and legs)
4 plums
2 oz redcurrant jelly
2 tablespoons chopped carrot, celery, onion and garlic
5 fl oz Port
1 pint chicken stock
Fresh thyme and chervil
2 oz fruit vinegar
2 oz dark brown sugar
4 slices bacon

Potato Mousse

1lb grated boiled potatoes
Garlic butter

(Serves four)

Method

1. Brown pigeon carcases with chopped vegetables. Dust with flour and add chicken stock, herbs and plums (retaining one for garnish). Simmer gently until reduced by half, then add Port.

2. To cook pigeon breasts – place rashers of bacon in sauté pan and cook breasts for 3-4 minutes each side. Remove and keep warm.

3. To make potato mousse – heat garlic butter in sauté pan. Place 4 inch cutter in pan and put ¼ of potato mixture into it. Remove cutter and repeat till you have 4 in total. Cook for 3-4 minutes each side.

To serve

4. Arrange potato mousse in centre of plate.

5. Arrange 3 pigeon breasts on each mousse and cover with a little of the sauce.

6. Garnish with slices of plum warmed in a little redcurrant jelly.

Cairn O'Mhor Lamb

Ingredients

1¾ lbs loin of Scotch lamb
1 bottle Cairn O'Mhor Elderberry Wine
4 fl oz olive oil
4 fl oz red wine vinegar
Bunch of fresh mint
Seasoning
8 oz puff pastry
1 egg
8 fl oz demi-glaze (thick meat stock)
Watercress and finely chopped garden mint for garnish

(Serves four)

Method

1. Prepare the marinade of elderberry wine, olive oil, red wine vinegar, chopped mint and seasoning.

2. Place the butchered loin into a deep pan and pour the marinade over the meat. Turn and baste at regular intervals. Leave for 12 hours in a refrigerator.

3. Remove the meat from the marinade and drain.

4. Roll out pastry into a rectangle and trim edges.

5. Wrap the lamb in the pastry and trim and shape, then brush on the beaten egg.

6. Place on baking sheet and place in pre-heated oven GM6/200C/400F for 45 minutes.

7. Reduce 4 fl oz of the marinade by half and add demi-glaze. Check for taste. Sieve.

8. Carve the lamb and complement it with the sauce. Garnish with chopped mint and watercress.

. . . and one that got away from the lamb competition!

from Helen Bett, Second Chef, Newton House Hotel, nr Perth

from Graham Singer,
Chef de Partie,
Waterside Inn,
Peterhead

Medallions of Venison
served on a bed of mixed cabbage and redcurrant and Port sauce

Ingredients

12 medallions of venison cut from the loin
Salt and pepper
2 teaspoons oil
½ oz unsalted butter

Cabbage

½ oz butter
1 oz red cabbage
1 oz green cabbage
Salt and pepper
4 tablespoons red wine

Redcurrant & Port Sauce

3 fl oz Port
7 oz fresh redcurrants
11 fl oz game stock
12 flat parsley leaves to garnish

(Serves four)

Method

1. Shred cabbage finely, place in sizzling frying pan and season to taste.

2. Add red wine and continue to cook, leaving the cabbage slightly crisp.

3. Put aside 32 redcurrants and purée the rest. Pass through a fine sieve to extract the juices leaving the seeds.

4. Put the Port wine in a pan and reduce over heat until almost gone.

5. Add stock and redcurrant purée, reduce by half then pass through strainer.

6. Heat the oil in a frying pan and add the butter. When sizzling add the medallions, quickly sealing on all sides.

7. Place in a pre-heated oven GM7/220C/425F for almost 5 minutes, occasionally turning.

To serve

8. Place a small amount of the cabbage into the middle of the plate.

9. Take three pieces of venison and lay on top of cabbage.

10. Strain the sauce through a fine strainer or muslin and pour over medallions and plate.

11. Arrange 8 of the reserved redcurrants around the plate and top each medallion with a parsley leaf.

165

Braised Breast of Pheasant 'Venetian'

from Patrick McCourt,
Head Chef,
Ravenscourt House
Hotel,
Grantown-on-Spey

Ingredients

Stock

1 pint water
Pheasant carcase
2 small shallots
2 tablespoons chopped fennel
6 sprigs of fresh thyme

2 breasts of fresh pheasant
6 button mushrooms, finely chopped
2 shallots, finely chopped
1 ground bay leaf
2 sprigs of fresh thyme, chopped
2 oz cream cheese

Sauce

Pheasant stock, reduced by half
3 tablespoons tomato purée
Pinch of paprika
5 fl oz dry white wine
Seasoning

Garnish

2 crouton rounds
Peeled and chopped tomato
Chopped spring onion

(Serves two)

Method

1. Prepare the stock by bringing to the boil all the stock ingredients, then reduce to a simmer until ready to use.

2. To make the stuffing – chop the shallots and mushrooms and combine with the thyme, bay leaf and cream cheese.

3. Having removed the breast from the pheasant, gently fill it with the mixture lengthways, closing the entrance with the breast fillet and secure with 2 or 3 cocktail sticks.

4. Remove the carcase from the stock. Then add the breasts and braise in a moderate oven GM4/180C/350F for 15 minutes, remembering to turn occasionally.

5. Remove the pheasant from the stock and keep warm.

6. To the stock add 3 tablespoons of tomato purée, paprika and the wine. Bring back to boiling point, reduce the heat and simmer until the sauce is thick enough to coat the back of a spoon and has a good shine.

7. Strain the sauce through a fine sieve onto heated plates. Place the crouton in the centre. Now quickly slice the pheasant breast to reveal the stuffing and arrange around the crouton. Sprinkle with the chopped tomato and spring onions and serve at once with a green salad and simple new boiled potatoes.

from Rita Brown,
Proprietor,
Hazelton Guest House,
Crail

Chocolate, Oats and Whisky Pancakes

Ingredients

Batter

1 oz plain flour
1 oz porage oats
1 egg
1 teaspoon cocoa
5 fl oz milk
Butter for frying

Filling

6 oz plain chocolate
5 fl oz double cream
3 tablespoons whisky
2 teaspoons honey
3 tablespoons porage oats

Garnish

Single cream
Grated chocolate
Toasted oats

(Serves six)

Method

Filling

1. Mix whisky, honey and oats and leave to stand for at least a couple of hours.
2. Melt chocolate.
3. In a separate pan, heat half the cream until boiling. Slowly pour cream into chocolate stirring until smooth. Leave to cool and thicken.
4. Stir in whisky, honey and oats mixture.
5. Whip remainder of double cream and fold into chocolate, then chill mixture.

Batter

6. Combine flour, oats, cocoa and egg.
7. Gradually add milk and whisk until smooth. Leave to rest for about half an hour.
8. Fry the pancakes in the usual way, using butter to grease the pan.

To serve

9. Spoon the cold filling onto warm pancakes. Roll up and place on serving plates.
10. Drizzle single cream over, sprinkle with grated chocolate and toasted oats, then serve.

(The pancakes can easily be made in advance and warmed in the microwave before filling)

Raspberry Shortcake

from Susan Crosthwaite,
Proprietor,
Cosses,
Ballantrae

Ingredients

8 oz unsalted butter
2 tablespoons ground rice
2 oz icing sugar
10 oz plain flour

Double cream
Raspberries
Kiwi fruit

Melba sauce

9 oz sugar
7½ fl oz water
1 oz liquid glucose
1 lb raspberries
Juice of ½ lemon

(Serves twelve)

Method

1. Rub butter into sifted dry ingredients. Press ingredients together firmly then turn onto a lightly floured surface and knead lightly until smooth. (This shortbread can be made in a food processor.)

2. Roll out very thinly and cut into desired shape – e.g. circles, hearts etc – with a pastry cutter. Makes 24.

3. Place on buttered baking sheet and prick with fork.

4. Bake in pre-heated oven GM4/180C/350F for about 10 minutes until lightly baked. Remove immediately to a cooling rack. (NB shortbread can be frozen at this stage.)

Melba Sauce

5. Combine sugar, water and liquid glucose and bring to the boil.
   Allow to simmer for 3 minutes.

6. Use 5 fl oz of this syrup to 1 lb of raspberries. Put syrup into blender with raspberries and lemon juice. After blending, sieve sauce before serving.

To serve

7. Whip cream and place a generous amount on a shortcake then top with raspberries. Place another shortcake on top, a slice of kiwi fruit and a raspberry.

8. Finally pour round melba sauce and place another slice of kiwi and a raspberry at the side to garnish.

from Stewart Cameron,
Executive Chef,
The Turnberry Hotel

Poached Pear
with Eau de Vie ice-cream and butterscotch glaze

Ingredients

4 firm pears
4 small scoops Eau de Vie ice-cream
10 fl oz butterscotch sabayon
4 sprigs mint leaves

Butterscotch Sabayon

3 eggs
2 oz sugar
2 oz butterscotch sauce

(Serves four)

Method

1. Gently poach the pears in stock syrup and cool in refrigerator.

2. Carefully remove the core from the bottom of pear.

3. Make an incision 1 inch from the top of the pear straight down to the bottom. Repeat this about 6 times around the pear.

4. Place 1 scoop of ice-cream on to a chilled plate. Sit the pear on to the ice-cream and allow the pear to fan out over it.

Butterscotch sabayon

5. Whisk the egg yolks and sugar vigorously in a stainless steel bowl over a steam system until it is very white and fluffy (ribbon style).

6. Add the butterscotch sauce and whisk into mixture. Use immediately.

7. Coat 2-3 tablespoons of butterscotch sabayon over the pear.
   Glaze the sabayon with a gas burner, then lightly dust with icing sugar.

Summer Berries with a Glayva Sabayon

from Martyn Woodward,
Chef de Partie,
Golf View Hotel,
Nairn

Ingredients

4 oz redcurrants
4 oz whitecurrants
4 oz blackcurrants
4 oz raspberries
4 oz blueberries
8 oz strawberries,
halved and soaked in caster
sugar and Kirsch

Brandy snap basket
(makes 8)
3 oz butter
6 oz sugar
3 oz syrup
3 oz flour

Sabayon

6 egg yolks
1 oz caster sugar
1 fl oz Glayva

(Serves eight)

Method

1. Mix flour, butter and sugar until it makes fine breadcrumbs, then add syrup until it forms a paste.

2. Mould into 3 oz balls and bake at GM4/180C/350F for 5-10 minutes until golden brown, then remove from oven and mould into required shape.

Sabayon

3. Whisk ingredients and place in a bain marie. Whisk until it doubles its consistency and leaves a mark of the whisk through it.

To serve

4. Place a selection of berries on a plate neatly arranged, but leaving enough space for the brandy snap basket.

5. Place the sabayon between the berries and glaze until golden brown.

6. Finish with brandy snap basket of strawberries and a sprig of mint.

from Caroline Hayes,
Proprietor,
March House,
Kincraig

Raspberry and Apple Pie with Oatmeal Pastry

Ingredients

1¾ lbs Bramley cooking apples
6 oz Scottish raspberries
4 oz granulated or unrefined cane sugar

Pastry

4 oz plain flour
1 oz butter
1 oz lard
Pinch of salt
Handful of oatmeal
Egg yolk for glazing

(Serves four)

Method

Pastry

1. Rub in fat with flour. Add a little water and leave to rest in refrigerator.

Filling

2. Peel, slice and core apples. Place in saucepan and add sugar and a little water. Cover and simmer for 10 minutes.

3. Pour into pie dish and allow to cool.

4. Add raspberries.

5. Roll pastry out into oatmeal then reverse pastry over rolling pin so when you place top over pie dish the oatmeal is uppermost.

6. Glaze with yolk after decorating with excess pastry.

7. Bake in hot oven GM6/200C/400F for 15-20 minutes.

8. Serve with double cream – or ice-cream – immediately.

Yoghurt Pudding
with blackberries on a fig sauce

*from Gary Dobbie,
Head Chef,
The Moorings Hotel,
Fort William*

Ingredients

Pudding

7 oz natural yoghurt
15 fl oz double cream (52%)
1 measure Highland Park whisky
4 oz brown sugar
20 large fresh blackberries
Peppermint

Sauce

11 oz figs
2 tablespoons sultanas
2 tablespoons sugar syrup
1 tablespoon lemon juice
1 tablespoon pink peppercorns

(Serves four)

Method

Pudding

1. Add yoghurt and cream with whisky in a bowl and whisk until stiff.
2. Put 1 oz of brown sugar in each of 4 dariole moulds.
3. Line the moulds with the yoghurt mix and conceal 2 blackberries in each.
4. Fill the mould and leave to set.

Sauce

5. Peel figs and purée with sultanas.
6. Heat sugar syrup to 20C. Add lemon juice, then leave to cool.
7. Coarsely chop pink peppercorns. Mix all together then refrigerate.

To serve

8. Have a bucket of hot water ready for releasing the puddings.
9. Turn out pudding on side of the plate with the fig sauce.
10. Garnish with blackberries and a sprig of peppermint.

The 1994 Taste of Scotland Guide

is scheduled to be published in
November 1993.

To reserve a copy at the 1993 post inclusive price of £4.30, complete the coupon below and
send it with your cheque or postal order, made payable to TASTE OF SCOTLAND, to

> Taste of Scotland (Guide Sales)
> 33 Melville Street
> Edinburgh EH3 7JF

You will be placed on the priority list to receive the Guide as soon as it is published.

European and Overseas post inclusive prices are shown overleaf

- ✂

To: Taste of Scotland (Guide Sales)
    33 Melville Street
    Edinburgh EH3 7JF

Please send _____ copy/copies of
the 1994 Guide.
Cheque/Postal Order enclosed for _____

NAME: _____

ADDRESS:_____

_____

_____

_____ POST CODE _____

BLOCK CAPITALS, PLEASE

Taste of Scotland Guide 1994

European and Overseas Post Inclusive Prices

To enable us to keep prices down by avoiding excessive bank charges, the preferred methods of payment are:

Europe	£ sterling currency or Eurocheque in £ sterling to the value of £7
USA, Canada	Personal checks or bank notes in US or Can $ to the value of US $20
Note:	You may wish to enquire about local availability of the Taste of Scotland Guide with your nearest British Tourist Authority Office.

Taste of Scotland welcomes your recommendations on restaurants and hotels you have visited which you feel merit inclusion but are as yet not listed in the Taste of Scotland Guide.

KINGSMUIR HOTEL

Charming century-old country house, in leafy grounds, on quiet, south side of Peebles, yet only 5 minutes' walk through parkland to High Street. There are 10 well-appointed bedrooms, all en-suite, with TV, direct-dial phone, tea-markers and hairdrier. The very best of local produce is used in preparing the Restaurant, Bar Lunch and Bar Supper dishes. Winners of several awards for bar meals. Ideal centre for touring Edinburgh and the stately homes of the Borders.

Open all year
Personally run by Elizabeth & Norman Kerr.

Peebles, Borders
Tel 0721-720151 • Fax 0721-721795

STB *Commended*   **AA**★★

see entry page 115
see entry page 44

LOCH DUICH
HOTEL

The Loch Duich Hotel occupies the unique scenic position of being the only Hotel overlooking the famous Eilean Donan Castle.
A warm friendly Highland atmosphere is complemented by fine traditional food prepared by Chef Carol Macrae.
Proprietors: Iain Fraser & Sonia Moore

AA★   **Ardelve,**
by Kyle of Lochalsh
AA⊛   **Tel 0599-85213**
Fax 0599-85214

see entry page 43
see entry page 84

Loch Melfort Hotel

Finest location on the
West Coast of Scotland

For comfort, and that mouthwatering 'Taste of Scotland' amidst magnificent surroundings. Right beside Arduaine Gardens recently acquired by the National Trust for Scotland.

Open March 1st - January 2nd

For Brochure and Tariff including Spring and Autumn Breaks-Christmas and New Year Holidays.

Contact: **Loch Melfort Hotel**
Arduaine by Oban, Argyll PA34 4XG
Tel 08522-233 • Fax 08522-214

STB *Commended*   **AA** Inspectors Scottish Hotel of the Year   **GOOD**
AA★★★   **HOTEL**
GUIDE

MINMORE HOUSE HOTEL

Situated in 4 acres of landscaped gardens overlooking the River Livet and a short walk from the Glenlivet Distillery, Minmore House is ideal for a relaxing or active holiday. All 10 bedrooms have private bathrooms. An oak-panelled bar and sunny drawing room, both with log fires, outdoor swimming pool and tennis courts. Fishing, shooting and stalking available. Specializing in the best of local produce.
Belinda Luxmoore

Glenlivet, Ballindalloch, Banffshire AB3 9DB
Tel (Glenlivet) 08073-378 • Fax 08073-472

Taste of Scotland 'Good Hotel Guide'
Ashley Courtenay
Scottish Commended Hotels   **STB** *Commended*

Monachyle Mhor Hotel/Farmhouse

Small family run, 18th Century award winning hotel/farmhouse is set in its own 2000 acres.

All bedrooms, en-suite with the most magnificent views overlooking Lochs Voil & Doine.

The hotel is delightfully furnished with family period furniture & country fabrics.

Robert & Jean Lewis invite you to dine in our restaurant with delicious dishes including game and fresh herbs from our own estate. The farmhouse is fully licensed & non-residents are most welcome to dine with us. We serve unusual bar meals all day. Glasgow/Edinburgh 1 hour. Private fishing & stalking to guests.

Open all year.

STB *Commended*

AA ★★

Please write or telephone for bookings or further details.

Balquhidder, Lochearnhead, Perthshire FK19 8PQ
Tel 08774-622 • Fax 08774 305

see entry page 51

Scotland's Treasure Islands

Experience Orkney. A scattering of Scottish Islands with a treasure trove of history, archaeology and wildlife.

A wealth of fish, shellfish, lamb and cheese; used to create superb local dishes.

And a warm and genuine welcome in our hotels, inns, guest houses and self catering cottages.

Orkney. A holiday you'll always treasure. Phone 0856 872856 now for your free brochure or send the coupon now.

To: Tricia Scott, Orkney Tourist Board, 6 Broad Street, Kirkwall, Orkney KW15 1NX.

Name ....

Address ....

....

.... **ORKNEY**

WHAT'S IN A NAME?

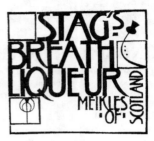

Stag's Breath is a link with The Forty-five-or '41, to be precise: 1941, when the SS Politician ran aground in a February gale off the island of Eriskay in the Outer Hebrides.

Her principal cargo was whisky - 50,000 cases, it is said: "Highland Gold and Highland Heart, Tartan Milk and Tartan Perfection, Bluebell, Northern Light... Stag's Breath."

The tale was immortalised by Sir Compton Mackenzie in Whisky Galore, from whom we learn that the last-mentioned brand was the one "particularly favoured by the inhabitants of the two Toddays in the good old days of plenty."

History does not relate what made Stag's Breath so special; however, it is safe to assume that its contemporary namesake is an altogether different 'cratur'. If whisky is ever 'mere', this is no 'mere' whisky.

It is a miraculous blend including fine Speyside whiskies and fermented heather honey-comb, which is now finding favour amongst discriminating drinkers far beyond the shores of Todday.

Send to: Taste of Scotland, 33 Melville Street, Edinburgh EH3 7JF

CAITHNESS GLASS PRESTIGE AWARD 1993

I nominate_____ (Establishment)
for a Caithness Glass Prestige Award for the following category:
(Categories)   (Please tick <u>one</u> category)

☐ Hotel of the Year   ☐ Country House Hotel of the Year

☐ Restaurant of the Year   ☐ Special Merit

Name _____

Address _____

_____

_____

Date of visit _____

Meal (if appropriate) _____

Closing date for entries: 15 September 1993

--✂

Send to: Taste of Scotland, 33 Melville Street, Edinburgh EH3 7JF

CAITHNESS GLASS PRESTIGE AWARD 1993

I nominate_____ (Establishment)
for a Caithness Glass Prestige Award for the following category:
(Categories)   (Please tick <u>one</u> category)

☐ Hotel of the Year   ☐ Country House Hotel of the Year

☐ Restaurant of the Year   ☐ Special Merit

Name _____

Address _____

_____

_____

Date of visit _____

Meal (if appropriate) _____

Closing date for entries: 15 September 1993

Comments on meals in places listed in
The Taste of Scotland Guide are welcomed.
Send to Taste of Scotland, 33 Melville Street, Edinburgh EH3 7JF

Establishment visited _____

Date _____ Meal _____

Comments _____

_____

_____

_____

_____

_____

Name _____

Address _____

_____

✂- -

Comments on meals in places listed in
The Taste of Scotland Guide are welcomed.
Send to Taste of Scotland, 33 Melville Street, Edinburgh EH3 7JF

Establishment visited _____

Date _____ Meal _____

Comments _____

_____

_____

_____

_____

_____

Name _____

Address _____

_____

Send to: Taste of Scotland, 33 Melville Street, Edinburgh EH3 7JF

CAITHNESS GLASS PRESTIGE AWARD 1993

I nominate_____ (Establishment)
for a Caithness Glass Prestige Award for the following category:
(Categories)   (Please tick one category)

☐ Hotel of the Year   ☐ Country House Hotel of the Year

☐ Restaurant of the Year   ☐ Special Merit

Name _____

Address _____

_____

_____

Date of visit _____

Meal (if appropriate) _____

Closing date for entries: 15 September 1993

- ✂

Send to: Taste of Scotland, 33 Melville Street, Edinburgh EH3 7JF

CAITHNESS GLASS PRESTIGE AWARD 1993

I nominate_____ (Establishment)
for a Caithness Glass Prestige Award for the following category:
(Categories)   (Please tick one category)

☐ Hotel of the Year   ☐ Country House Hotel of the Year

☐ Restaurant of the Year   ☐ Special Merit

Name _____

Address _____

_____

_____

Date of visit _____

Meal (if appropriate) _____

Closing date for entries: 15 September 1993

Comments on meals in places listed in
The Taste of Scotland Guide are welcomed.
Send to Taste of Scotland, 33 Melville Street, Edinburgh EH3 7JF

Establishment visited

Date   Meal

Comments

Name

Address

✂ -

Comments on meals in places listed in
The Taste of Scotland Guide are welcomed.
Send to Taste of Scotland, 33 Melville Street, Edinburgh EH3 7JF

Establishment visited

Date   Meal

Comments

Name

Address

THE SANDFORD

COUNTRY HOUSE HOTEL.

The Sandford Hotel, one of the Kingdom of Fife's most picturesque, listed, country house hotels, is renowned for its' fine Scottish and European cuisine and comfortable accommodation.

Seasonal dishes in particular, served in the oak beamed restaurant, are the hallmark of Chef, Steven Johnstone. An extensive wine list has been carefully chosen in order to complement the variety of dishes on the à la carte and table d'hôte menus.

The Sandford is located near to both St Andrews and Dundee, and provides an ideal venue for those touring, fishing, golfing or shooting in this region of Scotland.

Bar Lunch 12.00 to 2.00 pm
Bar Supper 6.00 to 8.00 pm
Dinner 7.00 to 9.00 pm
Open February to December (inclusive)
Languages: French, German, Italian

The Sandford Country House Hotel
Newton Hill, Wormit, nr Dundee, Fife DD6 8RG
Tel 0382-541802 • Fax 0382-542136

see entry page 68

TIRORAN HOUSE

A remote & enchanting Country House Hotel, beautifully situated on Loch Scridain, renowned for its good food, offers the highest standards of comfort for those seeking to explore the lovely islands of Mull, Iona & Staffa.

Private bathrooms, games room & croquet. Geophysically central for all places of interest, & set in 12 acres of lovely gardens including lawns, shrubberies & woodlands which slope down to the loch.

Own garden produce, locally caught seafood & Mull meats make dinners, which are elegantly served by candlelight, a speciality.

Resident Proprietors: Sue & Robin Blockey

ISLE OF MULL, ARGYLL

TEL 068-15232

see entry page 110

PRODUCT OF SCOTLAND

Walkers

-- ESTABLISHED 1898 --

The world's classic pure butter shortbread

Walkers Shortbread Ltd,
Aberlour-on-Spey, Scotland, AB38 9PD.
Telephone: 0340 871555 Fax: 0340 871355

WATERSIDE BAKERY

Craftsmen in Bread & Continental Confectionery.

Only 20 miles from Glasgow

Visit Strathaven's oldest family business where everything is 'Taylormade' on the premises. There is a wide variety of Scottish baking and continental confectionery. Sample our treacle crumpets with a pot of tea or a capuccino coffee with a butter croissant in our Cafe across from the bakery.

There you can enjoy a bistro-type meal starting with a delicious freshly made soup & French, Italian or Danish bread. Choose a salad from our delicatessen counter, hot vegetarian dish or spoil yourself with scrumptious cheesecake or gateau.

Planning a buffet? We can provide.

Planning a wedding or special party? You can browse through our albums & view our cake display. We will discuss your individual requirements & design a special cake just for you.

Partners: A.W.Taylor, E.M.Taylor

Strathaven • Telephone 21260

Index – 1993

** New Member

187

EDITOR
NANCY K CAMPBELL BA

PUBLISHED BY
TASTE OF SCOTLAND SCHEME LTD,
A NON-PROFIT MAKING COMPANY LIMITED BY GUARANTEE TRADING AS TASTE OF SCOTLAND

DESIGN, ILLUSTRATION & TYPESETTING
DAVID FRAME CREATIVE SERVICES
EDINBURGH

PRINTED BY
MACDONALD LINDSAY PINDAR PLC
LOANHEAD

COLOUR PHOTOGRAPHY
COURTESY OF
GEORGE YOUNG PHOTOGRAPHERS
GOUROCK

SCOTTISH BORDERS TOURIST BOARD

J D C CAMPBELL
AYR

TASTE OF SCOTLAND SCHEME LTD.
33 MELVILLE STREET
EDINBURGH
EH3 7JF
TEL: 031 220 1900
FAX: 031 220 6102

ISBN 1 871445 04 3